HOUSE & GARDEN'S

# Cook Book

Contributors:

James A. Beard

Helen Evans Brown

Eloise Davison

Ethel M. Keating

Jack King

Dione Lucas

Ruth A. Matson

Ann Roe Robbins

Dharam Jit Singh

Charlotte Turgeon

Myra Waldo

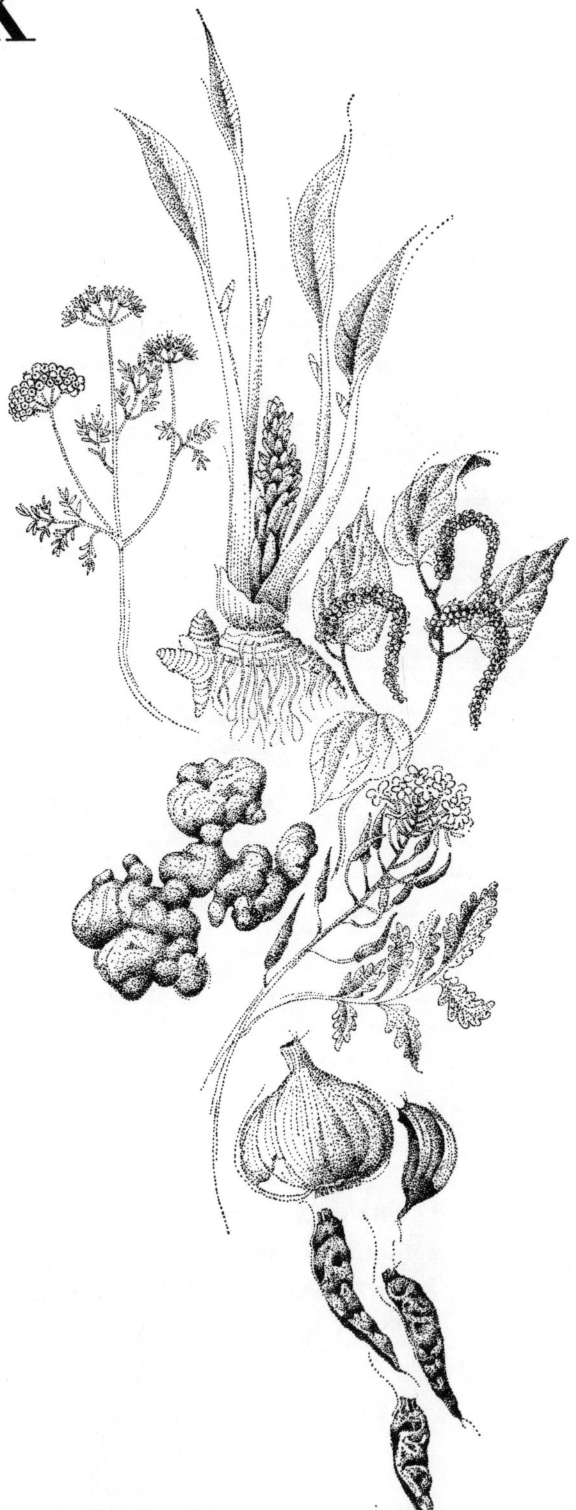

SIMON AND SCHUSTER · NEW YORK · 1958

FIRST PRINTING

*The color illustrations in this book are by:*
    RICHARD JEFFERY
    OTTO MAYA and JES BROWN
    GUY MORRISON
    JOHN STEWART

*The black-and-white illustrations are by:*
    DONALD ALMQUIST
    WILLIAM GRIGSBY
    EDWARD KASPER
    GRAMBS MILLER
    RAY PORTER
    MICHELLE STUART
    JEAN WATTS

LIBRARY OF CONGRESS CATALOG CARD NUMBER: 58-13781
MANUFACTURED IN THE UNITED STATES OF AMERICA
PRINTED AND BOUND BY RAND McNALLY & COMPANY,
CONKEY DIVISION, CHICAGO, ILL.

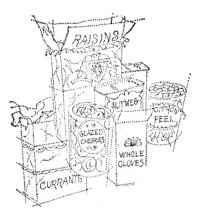

# Contents

**DICTIONARY OF COOKING TERMS**    7
    A clear and authoritative glossary of the words cooks use

**HORS D'OEUVRE**    11
    Eggs, hot and cold • Fish and shellfish for the first course • Hot and cold meat hors d'oeuvre • Quick pâté • Hors d'oeuvre salads • Asparagus vinaigrette and other vegetables • Antipasto • Melon

**SOUP**    29
    Hot soups, iced soups, jellied soups • Soups for a first course and soups that are a meal in themselves • Soups made of meat, fish, vegetables, and fruit • Thick soups and clear soups

**EGG AND CHEESE**    47
    Soft-boiled eggs and eggs mollet • Hard-boiled eggs • Scrambled eggs • Eggs en cocotte • Shirred eggs • Eggs in nests • Poached eggs • Eggs molded in timbales • Omelets • Soufflés • Four hot cheese recipes

**FISH**    65
    Basic rule for cooking fish • Fish en papillote, using aluminum foil • Broiled fish • Grilled fish • Whole stuffed pike • Sautéed fish • Oven fried fish • Poached fish • Cold fish recipes • Shrimp • Crab • Clams • Lobster • Scallops • Oysters

**BEEF**    83
    Grades and cuts of beef • Roast beef • Filet of beef • Chateaubriand • Tournedos • Beef scallops • Beef Stroganoff • Four basic ways to cook steak • Steak au poivre • Flank steak • Chinese beef rice • Boiled beef • Corned beef • Tongue • Oxtail • Tripe

**LAMB**    101
    Standard lamb cuts • Roast leg of lamb • Saddle of lamb • Crown roast • Baron of lamb • Rack of lamb • Shoulder • Chops • Lamb steaks • Breast of lamb • Moussaka • Shish kebab • Irish stew • Tongue • Liver • Kidneys

**PORK**    119
    Standard pork cuts • Roast leg of pork • Loin of pork • Pork sukiyaki • Shoulder of pork • Tenderloin • Chops • Spareribs • Pigs' feet • Sausages • Choucroute garni • Four ham recipes

**VEAL**      **137**
Standard veal cuts • Scallops • Terrine of veal • Paupiettes • Chops • Veal stews • Shoulder and breast of veal • Saddle of veal • Cold veal recipes

**POULTRY**      **155**
Roast chicken • Fried chicken • Chicken curry • Chicken breasts • Stewed fowl • Chicken paprika • Roast turkey • Roast duck • Roast goose • Squabs • Guinea fowl • Rock Cornish game fowl

**GAME**      **173**
Venison • Rabbit and hare • Wild duck • Doves • Grouse • Partridge • Pheasant • Snipe • Wild goose • Wild turkey • Quail

**BARBECUE AND ROTISSERIE**      **191**
How to barbecue steak • Kebabs • Barbecuing lamb • Ham steak • Hamburg • Sausages • Barbecuing chicken • Turkey • Duckling • Fish • Basic rotisserie suggestions • Veal • Lamb • Pork • Spareribs • Rotisserie chickens • Duck and goose

**SAUCE**      **209**
Brown stock • Meat glaze • Brown sauce • Variations on basic brown sauce • White stock • Fish stock • Bechamel sauce • Variations on white and béchamel sauces • Velouté • Horse-radish sauce • Hollandaise • Butter sauces • Mayonnaise • Dessert sauces

**PASTA AND RICE**      **227**
Spaghetti and sauces for it • Noodles • Macaroni • Lasagna • Ravioli • Gnocchi • Main course rice dishes • Risotto • Arroz con pollo • Paella

**VEGETABLE**      **245**
Asparagus • Peas • Endive • Celery • Artichokes • Fennel • Corn • Lima Beans • Green beans • Cucumbers • Eggplant • Zucchini • Acorn squash • Squash • Peppers • Spinach • Lettuce • Broccoli • Brussels sprouts • Carrots • Oyster plant • Onions • Potatoes • Beets

**SALAD**      **263**
Salads with meat • With fish • Caesar salad • Tossed green salad • Tomato salad • Cabbage and watercress • Zucchini salad • Artichoke • Potato salad • Celery root • Carrots • French beans • Egg salad • Cottage cheese • Fruit salad • Salad dressings

**DESSERT**      **281**
Apple desserts • Other fruits: strawberries, peaches, pears, pineapple, chestnuts • Crêpes and fritters • Beignets • Pies • Baked Alaska • Ice cream desserts • Cheese cake • Dessert soufflées • Dessert sauces

**CAKE, COOKIE AND BREAD**      **299**
Cakes and icings • Fruit cake • Kugelhoff • Tortes • Walnut and chocolate rolls • Small cakes • Fudge • Cookies • Coffeecake • French bread • Brioches • Croissants • Hot cross buns • Scones

**INDEX**      **317**

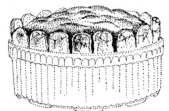

# Dictionary of Cooking Terms

**Acidulated water.** Water with lemon juice or vinegar added in ratio of 1 tablespoon to 2 or 3 cups water.

**A la king.** Food, usually chicken, prepared in a rich cream sauce.

**Al dente.** Italian term for spaghetti cooked until done but "firm to the tooth."

**Amandine.** With almonds.

**Antipasto.** Italian appetizer assortment.

**A point.** French term. Cooked just to the point of being done.

**Aspic.** A clear, savory jelly used in molds or to garnish cold dishes.

**Au beurre.** French term. Cooked in or with butter.

**Au gras.** French term. Cooked in rich meat sauce or gravy.

**Au gratin.** French term. A dish with a browned topping of grated cheese or bread crumbs or both.

**Bain Marie.** French cooking utensil. A bath of heated water in which pans are set to keep food warm without further cooking. For small amounts, a double boiler will serve.

**Bake.** To cook by dry (oven) heat.

**Barbecue.** To broil or roast on a grill or spit over charcoal. To cook with a barbecue sauce. A meal of barbecued food.

**Bard.** To cover breasts of birds with thin slices of bacon or salt pork to keep them moist without basting while roasting.

**Baste.** To drip or spoon fat, liquid or pan juices over roasting food.

**Batter.** Semi-liquid mixture that may include flour, water, milk, eggs, butter. A coating for fried food. A cake or pancake mixture.

**Beard.** To remove "beards" of mussels with a sharp knife.

**Beat.** To blend or whip with a wire whisk, rotary beater or electric mixer, using an over-and-over or circular motion.

**Beignets.** French word for deep-fried, batter-coated food. Fritters.

**Beurre manié.** French term. Flour and butter, kneaded into small balls and added to liquid mixtures as a thickening agent.

**Beurre noir.** French term. Butter heated until dark brown, used as a sauce.

**Bien fatigué.** French term. A salad of greens tossed until limp, or with a hot dressing.

**Bind.** To make a mixture hold together by adding eggs, melted butter, or other liquid.

**Bisque.** A thick cream shellfish or game soup, sometimes a puréed vegetable soup.

**Blanch.** From the French *blancher*, to whiten. Blanching has two purposes: to make skins of fruit or nuts easily removable by steeping them in boiling water for a few minutes; to reduce strong flavor or color of foods such as vegetables by immersing them briefly in water at boiling point, off the fire.

**Blaze.** To pour warmed brandy or liqueur over food and ignite.

**Blend.** To mix ingredients together until well combined and smooth.

**Boil.** To cook in liquid at boiling temperature (reached when bubbles rise to the surface and break). At sea level boiling point is 212° F; it decreases 1° for every 500 feet of altitude. At high altitudes, food takes longer to cook. Boiling point increases under pressure of steam, as in a pressure cooker.

**Bombe.** Ice cream with a flavored mousse-type center, shaped in a bombe or melon mold.

**Bone.** To remove bone from meat or fowl. A sharp-pointed boning knife is best for this.

**Bouillon.** A clear, strained soup or stock made from beef, veal or fowl cooked with vegetables, seasonings.

**Bouillon cube.** Concentrated, dehydrated form of bouillon, reconstituted by addition of hot water.

**Braise.** To brown in fat, cook gently, covered, in a little liquid in order to preserve juices. In the classic French method, the dish is lined with a layer of sliced vegetables and bacon.

**Bread.** To roll in fine bread crumbs.

**Bread crumbs.** Soft bread crumbs, made of crumbled white bread, are used in cooking, for stuffings, etc. Dry bread crumbs, used to coat foods before sautéeing or frying, are made of toasted bread or bought in cans.

**Brine.** A strong salt and water solution used for pickling.

**Brioche.** A soft French roll.

**Broil.** To cook over or under direct heat, as in barbecuing, grilling.

**Brown.** To cook in a little fat at high heat until brown, sealing juices.

**Bruise.** To crush in a mortar or a grinder.

**Brulé, Brulée.** French word meaning burnt, applied to caramelized sugar on cream dessert: *crème brulée.*

**Brush.** To spread with a light coating of beaten egg or butter.

**Canapé** A small appetizer of bread or toast topped with a savory mixture.

**Candy.** To preserve by boiling with sugar, which forms a hard coating.

**Capon.** A chicken emasculated to increase size and tenderness.

**Caramel.** Liquid burnt sugar used for coloring and flavor.

**Caramelize.** To melt sugar slowly until it turns brown and sticky.

**Chapon.** A small cube of stale French bread rubbed with garlic and tossed with the salad greens to add a hint of flavor.

**Chill.** To keep in a refrigerator until cold but not frozen

**Chop.** To cut into small pieces.

**Choux paste.** Cream-puff pastry made over heat in a saucepan.

**Clarified butter.** Melted butter, strained or skimmed if necessary to remove scum or sediment.

**Clarify.** To clear clouded liquid, such as aspic or bouillon, by first heating gently with white of egg (sometimes raw minced beef is added), then straining through a cloth.

**Coat.** To dip in flour, bread crumbs or other dry mixture before frying.

**Coat the spoon.** The stage reached in cooking when a liquid mixture is thick enough to adhere in a thin layer to the stirring spoon.

**Combine.** To mix together two or more ingredients.

7

**Compote.** Sweetened, stewed fruits.

**Consommé.** Clarified bouillon or stock.

**Core.** To remove the center of fruit or vegetables, leaving the rest intact.

**Court bouillon.** A simmered stock of white wine, water, herbs, sometimes fish bones and vegetables, used as a poaching liquid in fish cookery. Many variations.

**Cream.** To work or beat shortening or a mixture of ingredients, until consistency is soft and creamy.

**Crêpes.** Thin French pancakes.

**Crimp.** To gash around the edges with a sharp knife. Crimping prevents fat of meat curling during broiling, firms the flesh of fish.

**Crisp.** To restore texture to vegetables or salad greens by soaking in ice water. To heat bread or dry cereals in the oven until firm.

**Croissants.** Rich, flaky, crescent-shaped French rolls.

**Croquettes.** Chopped or ground cooked foods bound with egg or sauce, formed into shapes, coated and fried.

**Croûte.** French word for pastry crust in which food is baked *en croûte.*

**Croutons.** Fried or toasted bread cubes, used as a garnish.

**Crumble.** To break into small pieces with the fingers.

**Cube.** To cut into small dice.

**Cure.** To preserve meat with salt, often allied with smoking process.

**Cut.** To chop or slice.

**Cut and fold.** To blend an ingredient with a liquid mixture by first turning the spoon sideways in a cutting motion as the two are combined, then lifting the mixture from the bottom and folding it over the top until all is mixed.

**Cut in.** To amalgamate shortening with flour by working it in with a pastry blender or two knives.

**Deep fry.** Same as French fry.

**Deglaze.** To remove the dark, clinging particles from pan in which meat has browned by dissolving them with added liquid.

**Demi-glace.** Rich brown gravy reduced by rapid boiling to a sauce.

**Devil.** To prepare with hot seasoning or sauce.

**Dice.** To cut into small squares.

**Dilute.** To thin by adding liquid. To diminish strength or flavor of a liquid mixture.

**Dissolve.** To melt or liquefy.

**Dot.** To scatter small pieces of an ingredient such as butter over the surface of food, before cooking.

**Dough.** Spongy mixture of flour, liquid and other ingredients, thick enough to knead.

**Drain.** To strain liquid from solid food.

**Draw.** To remove entrails of poultry, game. To eviscerate.

**Drawn butter.** Same as clarified butter.

**Dredge.** To coat with flour or sugar.

**Dress.** To trim and clean fowl for cooking. To prepare for the table by garnishing.

**Drippings.** Fat which has become separated from meat or fowl and liquefied during cooking.

**Dumplings.** Balls of dough or finely minced fish, fowl or meat which are poached and served as garnish. Food baked or steamed in a dough crust, such as apple dumplings.

**Dust.** To sprinkle lightly with a dry ingredient such as flour, sugar.

**Duxelles.** A finely chopped mushroom garnish used in fish cookery.

**Eclair.** A choux paste confection filled with flavored cream and topped with chocolate fondant icing.

**En brochette.** French term for food broiled on a skewer.

**En papillotte.** Baked in paper. The original French method was to encase food in oiled paper wrapping but now aluminum foil is substituted.

**Essence, Extract.** A concentrated flavoring.

**Eviscerate.** Same as draw.

**Farce.** French for forcemeat.

**Fat.** Generic term for butter, margarine, lard, vegetable shortenings, also rendered drippings of meat, fowl.

**Fillet, Filet.** To remove the bone. Boneless piece of meat or fish.

**Filter.** To strain liquid through several thicknesses of cheesecloth.

**Fines herbes.** A mixture of chopped fresh or dried herbs such as chives, parsley, basil.

**Finish.** To prepare a dish for the table by garnishing.

**Flake.** To break into small pieces with a fork.

**Flambé.** French word for blaze.

**Foie gras.** Goose liver paté.

**Fold.** To lift mixture in an overlapping motion from one side of the bowl to the other.

**Fold in.** To incorporate a light mixture, such as beaten egg whites, with a heavier one without loss of air bubbles by blending it in with a spoon, using an up and over action.

**Fondant.** A slightly granulated sugar paste, kneaded until smooth.

**Fondue.** A dish of melted grated Swiss cheese, white wine.

**Forcemeat.** A seasoned stuffing. A mixture of finely minced or pounded meat, fowl, game or fish used as stuffing or cooked separately for garnish.

**Frappé.** French for frozen. A cordial served over cracked ice. Sweetened fruit juice frozen to a mush.

**Freeze.** To chill in freezing compartment until solid.

**French fry.** To cook in deep hot fat until brown and crisp.

**Fricassee.** To cook by braising. Mostly applied to chicken or veal stewed in white or brown sauce or stock.

**Fritters.** Batter-dipped, French-fried food.

**Frizzle.** To fry in hot fat until edges curl.

**Frost.** To cover with sugar icing.

**Fry.** To cook in hot fat or oil on top of the range.

**Fumet.** French term for a concentrated fish or meat stock.

**Garnish.** To decorate a dish by adding small amounts of food or herbs for color or flavor.

**Giblets.** The internal edible parts of a fowl (heart, liver, gizzard, etc.) used for stock and gravy.

**Glacé.** French word for iced, glazed or frozen foods.

**Glace de viande.** French term for concentrated meat glaze made by reducing strong brown stock to jelly-like consistency, used to flavor and color.

**Glaze.** A thin coating of syrup, gelatin or aspic. The brown particles left in a pan in which meat or poultry has roasted. To brown the sauce masking a dish in the oven or under the broiler.

**Grate.** To reduce to particles by rubbing on or grinding in a grater.

**Gravy.** Meat juices diluted with water and thickened with flour.

**Grease.** To rub the inside of a dish, mold or baking pan with fat so as to prevent food sticking to it.

**Grill.** To cook under or over direct heat. To broil.

**Grind.** To put through a food chopper. To reduce to small particles or powder in a mortar with a pestle.

**Hang.** To age game or meat by hanging in a cool unrefrigerated place.

**Hash.** A baked or sautéed dish of chopped meat or vegetables.

**Hors d'oeuvres.** French appetizer course. An assortment of small portions of meat, fish, egg, vegetables.

**Ice.** To chill in a refrigerator or over ice. A smooth mixture of frozen sweetened fruit juice. To frost.

**Icing.** Sugar frosting.

**Infusion.** Liquid drawn off tea, coffee, herbs which have steeped in boiling water.

**Julienne.** Food cut in long, thin strips.

**Knead.** To work a mixture with the hands, using a folding and pressing motion, until it is smooth and spongy.

**Lard.** To insert thin strips of salt pork or fat bacon (lardoons) into lean meat to keep it moist. A long strip of the lardoon is placed in the open end of a special larding needle. The needle point is inserted into the meat at right angles to the grain and the lardoon drawn through with a turning motion. Loose ends are cut off at the surface of the meat. Meat or poultry may also be larded by laying strips of fat on the surface (see bard).

**Leaven.** To raise by adding a lightening agent such as yeast, baking powder, eggs.

**Legumes.** Vegetables of pod family: peas, beans, lentils.

**Liaison.** French for a flour mixture, egg yolks, or cream used to thicken or bind sauces, soups, etc.

**Line.** To cover the inside of a mold or baking dish with waxed paper, crumbs, etc. before adding food to be cooked.

**Liquor.** Liquid released from shells of oysters, clams, as they open. Liquid extract from a food during cooking.

**Macedoine.** A mixture of fruits or vegetables.

**Macéré.** French word meaning steeped in wine or pickled.

**Marinade.** A seasoned liquid mixture, usually containing oil and an acid such as wine or vinegar, in which food is soaked to add extra flavor or to tenderize.

**Marinate.** To soak in a marinade or French dressing for the required time—from a few hours to several days, according to the recipe.

**Marrons glacés.** Candied chestnuts, often packed in syrup.

**Marrow.** The soft fatty substance found in the cavity of meat bones.

**Mash.** To reduce to a pulp with a fork or potato masher.

**Mask.** To cover completely with sauce, mayonnaise, gelatin, etc.

**Meat glaze.** The same as *glace de viande*. Bovril and B-V are commercial versions of this beef extract.

**Melt.** To liquefy by heat.

**Meringue.** Egg whites stiffly beaten with sugar.

**Mill.** To beat to a froth with a whisk or beater. This prevents scum forming on hot milk drinks such as chocolate, during heating.

**Mince.** To chop finely or put through a mincer or press.

**Mirepoix.** French word for a preparation of chopped vegetables, fat and seasoning put in the dish in which meat or poultry is to be braised, to add flavor.

**Mix.** To blend different ingredients by beating or stirring.

**Moisten.** To add a small amount of liquid.

**Mold.** To shape in a mold. A gelatin-stiffened mixture set in a mold.

**Mollet.** French word applied to eggs which are soft-cooked, peeled and used whole in certain dishes.

**Mortar.** A deep bowl of marble, wood, ceramic in which ingredients are crushed with a pestle.

**Mousse.** A frozen dessert of flavored gelatin and whipped cream. A molded dish of minced food and cream, stiffened with gelatin.

**Mull.** To heat an alcoholic beverage, such as ale, with sugar and spices.

**Pan broil.** To cook uncovered in a skillet with little or no fat, pouring off any fat rendered from food.

**Pan fry.** To cook in a skillet in a small amount of fat.

**Parboil.** To boil until partially cooked. Cooking is usually then completed by some other process.

**Pare.** To remove the skin of fruit or vegetables with a knife or parer.

**Parfait.** A frozen sweetened cream and egg dessert. Ice cream, fruit and whipped cream dessert served in a tall glass.

**Pass through.** To rub food through a sieve.

**Pasta.** Italian cereal products: macaroni, spaghetti, noodles, etc.

**Paste.** A mixture of flour and water. A food made smooth by evaporating and grinding, as almond paste.

**Pastry.** A stiff dough of flour, water, fat, etc. used for pie crust, patty shells. Pastry can be various kinds, i.e.: short pastry, pie pastry, puff pastry, choux pastry.

**Paté.** Seasoned liver paste.

**Peel.** To remove outer peel, skin, or shell with the fingers or a knife.

**Pickle.** To preserve in brine or vinegar.

**Pinch.** An amount less than 1/8 teaspoon. As much as can be taken up between the thumb and index finger.

**Pipe.** To decorate with a mixture forced through the nozzle of a pastry tube.

**Pit.** To remove kernel of fruit.

**Plump.** To soak in water until soft and swollen, as dried fruit.

**Poach.** To simmer in liquid just below boiling point; 205-210° F.

**Potato starch.** Flour made from potatoes which can be used as a thickening agent in place of flour.

**Pot roast.** To cook a meat roast slowly in a covered pan on top of the range with a little liquid.

**Pound.** To beat or grind with a heavy implement such as a meat mallet or a pestle.

**Preheat.** To heat oven to selected temperature before using.

**Prick.** To pierce the surface with a fork or point of knife.

**Purée.** To force through a sieve or food mill or reduce to pulp in a blender.

**Quenelles.** Forcemeat dumplings, poached and often used as garnish.

**Ragoût.** A rich brown stew.

**Ramekin.** A small individual baking dish.

**Rechauffé.** French for reheated.

**Reduce.** To cook until mixture becomes diminished in quantity and concentrated. Liquid mixtures are rapidly boiled until reduced to desired consistency.

**Render.** To free animal fat from connective tissue by heating it until liquid fat can be strained off.

**Rice.** To force food, such as boiled potatoes, through a fine sieve or ricer to give a light, fluffy consistency.

**9**

**Roast.** To cook uncovered in an oven, or in hot embers, ashes, etc.

**Roe.** Fish eggs.

**Roll out.** To spread thin with a rolling pin.

**Roll up.** To fold over and over, jelly-roll fashion.

**Roux.** A mixture of butter and flour cooked to a smooth paste in a saucepan and used as a thickening agent. A white roux is cooked for just long enough to take away the raw taste of the flour, a brown roux until the mixture turns a light brown.

**Sauté.** To brown quickly in a little oil or butter on top of the range.

**Scald.** To pour boiling water over food. To heat liquid, such as milk, until almost boiling—the point when tiny bubbles start to form around the edge.

**Scallop.** To bake in a cream sauce, topped with crumbs.

**Score.** To make gashes in the surface. Fat around meat is scored to prevent its curling.

**Scrape.** To remove the outer skin of vegetables by scraping with the blade of a paring knife.

**Sear.** To brown the surface of meat at a high temperature, either in the oven or in a little fat on top of the range.

**Season.** To add salt and pepper, or other seasonings, to food.

**Seed.** To remove seeds from vegetables such as tomatoes, cucumbers.

**Shallot.** A small brown onion with a strong but mellow flavor.

**Sherbet.** Fruit ice to which white of egg or milk is added.

**Shirr.** To cook whole eggs with cream or crumbs in a dish.

**Shortening.** Cooking fat.

**Shred.** To slice in small strips.

**Sieve.** To put or rub through a strainer or sieve.

**Sift.** To separate coarse from fine particles in dry ingredients by shaking through a sieve.

**Simmer.** To cook in liquid below boiling point, about 185°F. The liquid should do no more than move gently with bubbles forming below the surface.

**Singe.** To burn off the down or hairs from plucked game or poultry with a flame, taking care not to char the skin.

**Skewer.** A long wood or metal pin used to hold fowl or meat in position for cooking. To pierce with or thread on a skewer.

**Skim.** To remove fat or other floating matter from surface of liquid with a spoon or skimmer.

**Slivered.** Cut into tiny shreds.

**Soak.** To leave food in a large amount of liquid until it is thoroughly wet.

**Soufflé.** A baked or chilled main dish or dessert made light and fluffy by the incorporation of stiffly beaten egg whites (if baked) or whipped cream (if chilled).

**Spice.** To add seasonings or condiments to give flavor.

**Spit.** To impale on a spit for barbecuing or roasting.

**Steam.** To cook food in steam or over boiling water. Steam may be applied directly to the food, as in a perforated steamer or a pressure cooker, or to the utensil containing the food, as in a double boiler.

**Steep.** To stand food in water below boiling point in order to extract flavor or color.

**Sterilize.** To kill bacteria by steam, dry heat or boiling water at high temperatures.

**Stew.** To cook in liquid to cover at simmering temperature.

**Stir.** To blend without beating by mixing with a spoon in a circular motion.

**Stock.** The liquid strained from cooked meat, fish, vegetables, etc.

**Strain.** To remove liquid from solid food. To puree by putting through a strainer.

**Stud.** To force flavoring or garnish into the surface of food, as a ham is studded with cloves.

**Stuff.** To fill with forcemeat or other desired mixture.

**Stuffing.** A seasoned filling.

**Suet.** The hard, fatty tissue surrounding the kidneys of animals, often rendered to liquid fat.

**Swirl.** To rotate liquid in a pan to loosen clinging particles of cooked food.

**Tenderize.** To break down tough connective tissue in meat either by marinating, pounding with a meat mallet or sprinkling with a commercial meat tenderizer.

**Thicken.** To add flour, cornstarch, egg yolk or other thickening agent to a liquid mixture.

**Thin.** To dilute a mixture.

**Toast.** To brown bread by direct heat or in an oven.

**Toss.** To mix with light strokes, lifting with a fork and spoon. To flip in the air.

**Trim.** To cut away unwanted or unsightly parts of food before or after cooking. To shape.

**Truss.** To tie wings and legs of a bird to the body by means of skewers and string so that it keeps its shape during cooking.

**Try out.** The same as to render.

**Turn.** To flip over or reverse food during cooking process. To trim vegetables into small shapes for garnish.

**Water jacket.** Shallow pan of hot water in which a mold or dish of food is set to bake.

**Whip.** To beat rapidly with a whisk, beater or mixer in order to incorporate air in foods such as eggs, cream, jelly, producing expansion.

**Work.** To knead or mix slowly.

**Zest.** Oily, colored exterior skin of citrus fruit, used for flavor.

# HORS D'OEUVRE

# Hors d'oeuvre

With the increasing emphasis on lighter menus and easy serving in today's entertaining, the hors d'oeuvre now is coming into its own as an indispensable part of modern meals. Brillat-Savarin, incomparable connoisseur in the art of gourmandise, believed the discovery of a new dish was of more benefit to humanity than the discovery of a new star. From this viewpoint, the hors d'oeuvre course, a comparative newcomer to the culinary scene, can be considered the gastronomic equivalent of a whole galaxy. Although the Romans had their *gustus* or appetizer course in such foods as oysters, eggs, radishes, mushrooms and pickles, it is generally accepted that hors d'oeuvre as we know them derived from the *zakouski* of 19th century Russia, an assortment of cold and hot appetizers which were an introduction to meals, especially to dinner. Caviar, smoked and pickled fish, salads and vegetables *vinaigrette*, cold meats, galantines of chicken and goose and little *piroshki* (pies with savory fillings) were washed down with vodka. As dinner guests were often three hours late, due to the climate, road conditions and the Slavic spirit, the *zakouski* table, set up in a room adjoining the dining salon, helped the punctual to stave off hunger, while away the time and temper their tippling. This *buffet Russe*, close cousin to the Swedish smörgåsbord, was adopted by enterprising French restaurateurs and designated hors d'oeuvre (outside the work)—an indication that it was to be regarded as a stimulating and slightly frivolous adjunct to the menu. The now-classic French *hors d'oeuvre variés* (some components of which are shown on the cover), which resemble a succulent still life, show a true appreciation of the art of preparing food to beguile the eye and provoke the appetite. At first, and inevitably, controversy arose as to the proper place and purpose of the hors d'oeuvre. To purists like Escoffier, soup alone was the correct gastronomic beginning to dinner, hors d'oeuvre to luncheon, as a replacement for soup (the only exceptions he allowed were caviar and that sublime delicacy, the oyster, prized equally by Julius Caesar, the Walrus and the Carpenter). Modern American usage often applies the term hors d'oeuvre to the canapé or bite-size cocktail accessory eaten with the fingers. The exponents of *haute cuisine* frown on this and consider the hors d'oeuvre to be a complete course eaten with knife and fork at the beginning of a meal. The hostess looks on the hors d'oeuvre as one of the simplest ways to give meals a decorative touch and provide a varied and balanced menu. For instance, if the main course is to be substantial or bland, the hors d'oeuvre can be crisp and tart. Vegetable or salad hors d'oeuvre complement a meal rich in protein or carbohydrates. There is only one basic rule: an hors d'oeuvre must be delicate and stimulating to the palate, never heavy or surfeiting. Apart from this, the range is limitless. Hors d'oeuvre may be cold or hot, simple or rich, served in individual dishes, on platters or from a chafing dish. Hot hors d'oeuvre (once known, according to Larousse, as quick or little entrées) may be prepared in a suave sauce or served in miniature brioche, pastry cases, *petit choux* or *bouchées* (these French patty shells can be ordered from the baker at a day's notice). Cold hors d'oeuvre, which can be molded in aspic or arranged in colorful designs on dishes or a platter, actually help to make the table decorative when the guests sit down—a point which many hostesses count on when planning parties.

## Sicilian Eggs

*6 ¼" slices raw salami*
*1 large clove garlic*
*6 tablespoons olive oil*
*6 ½" slices Italian bread*
*6 eggs*
*1 cup canned tomato sauce*
*Grated Parmesan cheese*

Trim the hard outside crust and casing from the salami. (If the salami is small in diameter, buy 3 slices per person but have it cut thinner.) Slice the garlic and fry it gently in 4 tablespoons of oil for 3 minutes. Remove garlic. Fry the bread in the oil until golden brown on both sides. Place bread in individual earthenware dishes and keep warm in 250° oven. Fry the salami in the remaining oil, allowing 1½ minutes to each side—just long enough to warm the slices. Place the salami on the fried bread. In the same pan fry the eggs, using more oil if necessary. Heat the tomato sauce.

Place the eggs on the salami. Cover with 2 tablespoonfuls of hot tomato sauce. Sprinkle with grated cheese and put under the broiler for a few moments. Serves 6.

## Egg Fantasies

*6 hard-cooked eggs*
*¼ pound tongue (boiled or canned)*
*1 pint chicken broth*
*1 tablespoon gelatin*
*1 tablespoon water*
*3 drops yellow coloring*
*¼ teaspoon meat extract*
*Mayonnaise*
*Dry mustard*
*Water cress*

Peel the eggs and cut the tongue into thin slices using a very sharp knife. The strips should be about 1½" wide. Heat the chicken broth and add the gelatin softened in water, the yellow coloring, and the meat extract. Be sure that the broth has enough salt. Pour the broth in six individual oval or round molds or in large muffin pans and chill in the refrigerator until a ¼" shell has formed on the sides and bottom of the molds. Pour off and reserve the rest, and put the molds in a bowl of warm water to keep the aspic liquid. Line the sides (not the bottom) with the tongue strips and put in each a whole egg. Cover with the rest of the aspic and leave in the refrigerator for several hours. To serve, unmold on individual plates. Serve with a bowl of mayonnaise seasoned with dry mustard and garnish with water cress. Serves 6.

## Eggs In Fancy Dress

*6 eggs*
*1 can madrilène*
*1 lemon*
*1 tablespoon gelatin*
*½ cup water*

6 sprigs parsley
1 ripe avocado
Mayonnaise
Garlic salt
Lemon juice
Salt and black pepper
⅛ teaspoon cayenne
1 can crab meat
Lettuce
1 can pitted black olives
Italian bread sticks

Cook eggs for 4 minutes and plunge them in very cold water to cool. Heat the madrilène and add the juice of ½ lemon and the gelatin dissolved in water. Stir until the gelatin has dissolved. Dip the parsley in boiling water for 10 seconds and place in cold water. When the madrilène is partially cooled place a little in each of six chilled glass dessert cups. Rotate the cups so the aspic will coat the sides. Place a sprig of parsley in each cup and let the liquid chill until set. Peel the eggs, place them in the cups and fill each cup almost to the top with remaining madrilène. Chill 2-3 hours.

Blend or mash the avocado pulp with mayonnaise and seasonings. Be sure that the dressing is highly seasoned. Pick over crab meat. To serve, dip the molds into very hot water for half a second and unmold onto a lettuce-lined platter. Surround with avocado mixture. Cover with crab meat and dot with black olives. Serve very cold with Italian bread sticks. Serves 6.

## Coquilles Saint Jacques

½ pint scallops
½ cup dry white wine
½ teaspoon mixed dried herbs
½ teaspoon salt
2 teaspoons grated onion
¼ pound mushrooms
6 tablespoons butter
¼ lemon

½ cup light cream
3 tablespoons flour
Lemon juice
Fine bread crumbs
⅓ cup grated Gruyère cheese

Put the scallops in a saucepan with the wine, herbs, salt, onion and just enough water to cover. Bring to a boil. Cover and simmer 5 minutes. Set aside. Wash and trim the mushrooms. Put in a small saucepan with 1 tablespoon of butter, the juice of ¼ lemon and enough water to come half way up the mushrooms. Bring to a boil. Cover and cook gently for 10 minutes. Strain both the scallop and the mushroom broth into a 2-cup measure. There should be about 1½ cups liquid. Fill to 2-cup line with light cream. Melt 3 tablespoons butter. Blend in the flour. Add half the liquid and stir until smooth. Add the remaining liquid and stir until smooth. Simmer. Coarsely chop the scallops and the mushrooms. Add these to the sauce. Season with salt, pepper and lemon juice. Fill scallop shells or ramekins with the mixture. When cool, cover with fine bread crumbs, tossed with 2 tablespoons of melted butter and mixed with the grated cheese. Heat 15 minutes in 350° oven, browning under the broiler for the last few moments. Serves 6.

## Hot Shrimp Ramekins

1½ pounds raw shrimp
½ cup dry white wine
1 cup water
½ bay leaf
Pinch of thyme
¾ teaspoon salt
Melted butter
Garlic salt
Grated Parmesan cheese
Chopped parsley

Put the shrimp in a pan with wine, water, bay leaf, thyme and salt and bring to a slow boil. Cover and simmer 10 minutes. Remove and drain. Shell and de-vein the shrimp. Place the shrimp in individual ramekins. Pour a generous amount of hot melted butter over each serving. Sprinkle with garlic salt and Parmesan cheese and place in a 425° oven until the butter sizzles— about 3-4 minutes. Sprinkle with chopped parsley and serve immediately. Serves 6.

## Sardine Appetizers

2 cans boneless, skinless sardines
6 slices white bread
½ teaspoon dry mustard
2 egg yolks
1 cup light cream
½ teaspoon salt
⅛ teaspoon pepper
2 tablespoons butter
Juice of ¼ lemon
2 tablespoons chopped parsley

Open the cans and keep sardines at room temperature for at least an hour before serving. Trim the bread and toast on one side. Combine mustard, egg yolks, cream, salt and pepper in the top of a double boiler and stir over boiling water until slightly thickened. Remove from heat and add butter and lemon juice. Keep warm. Place the sardines with a little of their oil on untoasted side of bread slices on a cookie sheet. Before serving, slip under the broiler. When sardines are hot, place on a platter. Spoon sauce over each appetizer and sprinkle with parsley. Serves 6.

## Chafing Dish Normandy Shrimp

2 pounds fresh shrimp
1 pint clam broth
1 cup dry white wine
½ cup water
1 tablespoon chopped onion
¼ bay leaf
Pinch of powdered thyme
½ teaspoon salt
1 pound mushrooms
Juice of ½ lemon
Salt and pepper
3 tablespoons butter
3 tablespoons flour
4-5 drops red coloring
½ teaspoon meat extract
1 cup heavy cream
¼ cup brandy
Buttered toast
Chopped parsley

Bring the shrimp slowly to a boil with the combined clam broth, wine, water, onion, bay leaf, thyme and salt. Simmer 10 minutes and let cool in the broth. Wash, trim and slice the mushrooms. Put in a saucepan with enough water to come half way up the mushrooms, the juice of ¼ lemon, salt and pepper, and cook for 10 minutes. Strain the mushroom broth and shrimp broth into the same container.

Melt the butter and blend in the flour. Add 1 cup of mixed broths and stir until smooth over moderate flame. Add 1 more cup and stir until it boils. Reduce heat and simmer. Meanwhile shell and de-vein the shrimp. Season the sauce with remaining lemon juice, salt and pepper. Add the coloring and meat extract. Add the mushrooms and shrimp and simmer 10 minutes more. To serve, reheat the mixture in a chafing dish. Add the cream and brandy but do not boil. Serve on toast, sprinkled with chopped parsley. Serves 6.

## Lobster Gratinée

1 pound frozen lobster tails
1 can frozen lobster bisque
Juice of ¼ lemon
½ pint light cream
⅓ cup grated Gruyère
Chopped parsley

Thaw the tails so that they will be at room temperature for cooking. Combine the thawed bisque with lemon juice, cream and salt and pepper, if necessary. Place the tails in individual baking dishes, preferably oval in shape. Cover with the seasoned sauce and bake 30 minutes at 275°. Five minutes before serving, sprinkle with cheese and brown under the broiler. Garnish with chopped parsley. Serves 6.

## Parisian Oyster Patty Shells

*6 patty shells*
*1 pint shucked oysters*
*⅓ cup dry white wine*
*¼ pound mushrooms*
*Lemon juice*
*4 tablespoons butter*
*2 tablespoons flour*
*1 cup boiling water*
*3 egg yolks*
*3 tablespoons cold water*
*¼ pound butter, melted*
*Salt, pepper, cayenne*
*1 tablespoon brandy*

Patty shells may be ordered from the baker a day in advance. Simmer the oysters in their own liquor and the wine until the edges curl. Set aside. Clean, trim and slice the mushrooms. Cook 10 minutes in covered saucepan with 1 teaspoon lemon juice and 2 tablespoons butter. Set aside. The sauce is a kind of mock hollandaise. Heat remaining 2 tablespoons butter and blend in the flour. Add the boiling water and stir until smooth. Set aside. Over direct heat or in the top of a double boiler beat the egg yolks and cold water with a wire whisk until they have the consistency of mayonnaise. An electric beater will shorten this process considerably. Remove the eggs from the stove and add the melted butter, the flour mixture and enough seasonings

and lemon juice to flavor well. To serve, heat the patty shells in the oven for a few moments. Cut the drained oysters in quarters and add them and the drained mushrooms to the sauce. Just before serving, add the brandy and fill the shells. Serve on a heated platter or on individual plates. Serves 6.

## Bivalves on the Half Shell

*6-9 oysters, cherrystone clams or tiny*
*    mussels per person*
*1 cup catsup*
*1 tablespoon horse-radish*
*1 tablespoon Worcestershire sauce*
*2 quarts chopped ice*
*Dark bread*
*Unsalted butter*
*Lemon wedges*

Have the bivalves delivered, opened, as near serving time as possible. Mix and chill the catsup, horse-radish and Worcestershire for sauce. To serve, put a small cocktail glass in the center of a soup plate for the sauce. Surround the glass with the chopped ice and place the bivalves on their lower shells on the ice. Serve with dark, buttered bread and lemon wedges.

## Shrimp and Caviar Tartlets

*6 tartlets*
*1 large jar red caviar*
*½ lemon*
*Black pepper*
*1 small can cleaned shrimp*
*½ cup mayonnaise*
*½ teaspoon tomato paste*
*2 hard-cooked eggs*
*1 tablespoon chopped parsley*

Make the tartlets according to recipe for Chicken Liver Tartlets and let them cool. Rinse the excess salt from the caviar by placing it in a strainer and letting cold water run through it. Season with a little lemon juice and black pepper. Chill while preparing the rest of the appetizer. Crush the shrimp with the back of a fork, and mix thoroughly with the combined mayonnaise and tomato paste. Quarter the eggs lengthwise and crush two quarters into the shrimp mixture. Season with salt, pepper and lemon juice. To serve, spread a thick layer of caviar in each tartlet. Cover with a layer of the shrimp mayonnaise and garnish with an egg quarter and parsley. Serves 6.

## Spanish Fish Bowl

*4-6 chicken lobsters or crayfish*
*4-6 crabs*
*2 pounds cooked shrimp*
*1 dozen mussels or cherrystone clams*

Buy the freshest shell fish possible. Boil lobsters and crabs in salted water but do not overcook. Clams are served raw but the mussels should be cooked in very little water and allowed to cool in the juice. They are served in the shell. Chill all the shell fish thoroughly. Remove the claws and the tails from the lobsters. Cut the tails into three pieces and crack the claws. Wipe the crabs if necessary. Put a layer of chopped ice in the bottom of a large bowl or platter. Prop the lobster bodies in the center and then surround with the rest of the shell fish, using the mussels or clams for the outer edge. Serve with dry sherry or dry white wine. Provide finger bowls and extra large napkins. Serves 6.

## Smoked Oyster Salad Baskets

*6 pastry shells*
*1 can smoked oysters*
*1 small package cream cheese*
*1 large clove garlic, minced*
*1 tablespoon soy sauce*
*3 tablespoons chopped parsley*
*Mayonnaise*
*Water cress or parsley*

Make the shells according to directions under Chicken Salad Baskets and let them cool. Chop the smoked oysters rather coarsely. Combine the cream cheese, garlic, soy sauce and chopped parsley until thoroughly blended. Add the oysters and enough mayonnaise to give the mixture a soft, but not a runny consistency. To serve, put a few sprigs of water cress or parsley in each pastry shell and fill with the smoked oyster salad. Serves 6.

## Caviar Toast

2 large jars red caviar
Juice of ½ lemon
2 teaspoons chopped scallions
Black pepper
4 hard-cooked eggs
2 tablespoons chopped parsley
6 slices white bread
Unsalted butter curls

Place the caviar in a strainer and rinse it under the cold water faucet. Put in a bowl and season with lemon juice, chopped scallions and black pepper. Chill well. Separate the egg whites from the yolks. Chop the whites and cover to keep from discoloring. Sieve the egg yolks. Trim the bread and cut diagonally. Toast bread. To serve, place a little mound of cold caviar on small individual plates. Surround with chopped egg white and sprinkle first with the sieved egg yolk and then with chopped parsley. Flank with toast slices, dotted with butter curls. Put a breakfast or butter knife on each plate. Serves 6.

## Tuna Sardine Salad

4 cold boiled potatoes
1 large can tuna steaks
1 large can boneless, skinless sardines
3 hard-cooked eggs
1 clove garlic, minced
1 cup mayonnaise
1 tablespoon chopped pickles
3 green olives
3 black olives
1½ cups shredded carrots
Parsley

Dice the potatoes. Cut the tuna into rectangular strips as near the size of the sardines as possible. Split the sardines lengthwise. Halve the eggs and crush the egg yolks. Combine the garlic with 1 cup of mayonnaise. Mix all but 2 tablespoonfuls of the mayonnaise into the potatoes, season well with salt and pepper. On a platter, form the mixture into a long mound with a narrow top and sloping sides. Alternate sardine halves and tuna fish sticks around the sides. Add the rest of the mayonnaise to the egg yolks and the pickles, season and stuff the egg whites. Place them on the top alternately with a green and a black olive. Chill in the refrigerator. Surround the salad with a ring of grated carrot and garnish each end with bouquets of parsley. Serves 6.

## Bouchées Grenelle

1 package frozen sweetbreads
⅔ cup dry white wine
½ teaspoon dried mixed herbs
1 can frozen shrimp soup
1 teaspoon tomato paste
6 eggs
6 patty shells
1 tablespoon chopped parsley

Place the sweetbreads, wine, herbs and a pinch of salt in a saucepan. Barely cover with water and bring gradually to a boil. Cover and simmer 10 minutes. Remove the sweetbreads and strain the broth into a large measuring cup. Remove the filaments from the sweetbreads. Combine 1 cup of the broth with the shrimp soup and the tomato paste in the top of a double boiler, stirring until blended. Break the eggs into small buttered muffin tins or custard cups; 15 minutes before serving bake the eggs in a 400° oven. Heat the patty shells for a few minutes in the oven while the eggs are baking. Reheat the sweetbreads in the remaining broth. Place the shells on a platter. Put a warm sweetbread in each one, top with a baked egg and cover with the shrimp sauce. Garnish with chopped parsley. Serves 6.

## Hot Tongue Appetizers

*½ pound thinly sliced beef tongue*
*⅓ cup seedless white raisins*
*⅓ cup Madeira or port*
*4 tablespoons butter*
*2 tablespoons chopped onion*
*3 tablespoons flour*
*1½ cups consommé*
*½ teaspoon sharp mustard*
*1 tablespoon tomato paste*
*Salt and pepper*
*Chopped parsley*

Soak raisins in wine, using a non-metal cup. Heat the butter and sauté the onion, letting the butter brown. Sprinkle with flour, let it brown, then add the consommé mixed with mustard and tomato paste. Add water if sauce is too thick. Season with salt and pepper. Place a thin layer of sauce in the bottom of individual baking dishes. Cover with tongue slices. Add the raisins and wine to the rest of the sauce and spoon over the tongue. Heat in a 300° oven for 20 minutes before serving. Garnish with chopped parsley. Serves 6.

## Ham Croutons

*¾ pound boiled ham, sliced paper thin*
*6 slices white bread*
*1 jar shrimp paste*
*1 bunch small seedless white grapes*
*4 tablespoons butter*
*2 teaspoons chopped onion*
*2 tablespoons flour*
*1½ cups chicken broth (fresh or canned)*
*½ teaspoon mixed dried herbs*
*⅓ cup Madeira*
*Salt and pepper*
*Lemon juice*

Trim the bread and toast it lightly. Spread with shrimp paste and place on cooky sheet. Stem the grapes and chill them. Heat the butter and sauté the onion without letting it brown. When onion is soft, add the flour and blend in well. Add half the chicken broth and stir until smooth. Add the rest. When it boils, add the dried herbs, Madeira, salt and pepper. Reduce the heat and simmer 10 minutes. Taste for seasoning, adding a little lemon juice. If the sauce is thick, add a little more broth. To serve, reheat the toast in the oven. Put several wafers of ham on each slice of toast. Cover with piping hot sauce and garnish with icy-cold grapes. Serves 6.

## Avignon Rolls

*Pancake batter*
*3 tablespoons butter*
*3 tablespoons flour*
*1 cup chicken stock*
*1 cup rich milk*
*Salt and pepper*
*½ teaspoon Worcestershire Sauce*
*1 teaspoon dry mustard*
*1 large can sliced mushrooms*
*1 cup diced ham*
*2 tablespoons brandy*
*2 tablespoons chopped parsley*
*4 tablespoons grated sharp Cheddar*

Make a thin pancake batter from your favorite recipe or follow directions on box of prepared pancake mix. Let it stand while making the filling. Melt the butter and blend in the flour. Stir in the stock and when smooth, add the milk. Stir until the sauce thickens. Season with salt, pepper, Worcestershire sauce and dry mustard. Simmer for 10 minutes. Remove from the stove and measure out ½ cup. Add the mushrooms, ham and brandy to the remaining sauce. Let this cool. Make the pancakes, about 5″ in diameter (allow 3 for each serving). Spread a tablespoonful of ham-

mushroom mixture in the center of each thin pancake, leaving a margin around the edge. Roll and place seam side down in a buttered baking dish. Mix the rest of the sauce with the parsley, spread it over the rolled pancakes and bake in a 325° oven for 30 minutes. During the last five minutes, sprinkle with grated cheese and brown under the broiler. Serves 6.

## Quick Pâté

*1 pound liverwurst or goose liver*
*½ pound sweet butter*
*½ cup heavy cream*
*¼ teaspoon nutmeg*
*⅛ teaspoon white pepper*
*½ cup port*
*1 small can chopped truffles and/or*
*3 cooked chicken livers, chopped*
*⅓ cup chopped pistachio nuts*
*1 can jellied consommé*
*Water cress, jellied aspic, truffles,*
  *for garnish*

Place the first eight ingredients in a mixing bowl, with ⅓ of the consommé. Beat

5 minutes with an electric beater. Melt the remaining consommé and pour into shallow pan to set. Place the pâté in a buttered mold and let stand in a cool place. To serve, unmold the pâté onto a small platter and decorate with rounds of jellied aspic, water cress and bits of truffle. Serves 6.

## Chicken Liver Appetizers

*6 chicken livers*
*3 tablespoons butter*
*½ teaspoon powdered oregano*
*2 tablespoons brandy*
*3 cups seasoned tomato juice*
*2 scant tablespoons gelatin*
*¼ cup water*
*Salt and fresh ground black pepper*
*3 tablespoons minced celery*
*½ cup mayonnaise*
*1 tablespoon soy sauce*
*Pumpernickel*

Sauté livers in butter allowing 2-3 minutes for each side, depending on size. Sprinkle with oregano. Add the brandy. When it has heated for a moment, ignite and stir the livers gently while the flame burns. Remove from the stove and cool. Heat the tomato juice, soften the gelatin in the water and add. When the gelatin is dissolved, fill custard cups or individual molds half full with the juice mixture. Chill in the refrigerator until firm. Keep the rest of the juice at room temperature. Chop the livers very coarsely and season with salt and plenty of black pepper. Scoop a small hole in the set aspic and fill with the chopped livers. Fill the cups ¾ full with the liquid aspic and place ½ tablespoon of minced celery at the top. Chill in the refrigerator. To serve, unmold appetizers onto individual plates. Garnish with mayonnaise flavored with soy sauce and serve with buttered pumpernickel bread. Serves 6.

## Chicken Liver Tartlets with Port

*6 tartlets*
*4 tablespoons butter*
*2 teaspoons chopped onion*
*12 chicken livers*
*⅓ cup port*
*1 teaspoon flour*
*Salt, pepper*
*½ teaspoon lemon juice*
*Parsley*

To make tartlets, follow the recipe on a package of pastry mix, substituting rich milk for the water. Roll out ⅛″ thick and cut in 4″ circles. Line tartlet pans or drape the pastry circles on the back of large muffin pans. Prick well. Bake 10 minutes at 450°. Heat 2 tablespoons butter and sauté the chopped onion until tender. Remove from the butter with a slotted spoon and put in the livers. Cook them 1½ minutes on each side. Heat the port, add to the livers and simmer 10 minutes. Remove the livers with a slotted spoon and put in a double boiler to keep warm or to be reheated later. Cream remaining butter and flour and form into little balls. Drop them into the sauce one at a time stirring after each addition. Season with salt, pepper and lemon juice. Cut the chicken livers into three pieces and put in the warm tart shells. Spoon the hot sauce into the tarts. Garnish with parsley. Serves 6.

## Chicken Breasts in Aspic

*3 large chicken breasts*
*1 quart chicken broth*
*2 cups mixed cooked vegetables,*
  *canned or frozen*
*2 cold boiled potatoes, diced*
*1 clove garlic, minced*
*1 tablespoon wine vinegar*
*3 tablespoons olive oil*
*Salt and pepper*
*2 tablespoons gelatin*
*¼ cup cold water*
*3 tablespoons butter*
*3 tablespoons flour*
*½ cup cream*
*Yellow coloring*
*½ teaspoon meat extract*
*Mayonnaise*

Place the chicken in a deep frying pan with a quart of well seasoned, clear chicken broth (canned or home-made). Cover and cook gently for 40 minutes. Meanwhile combine the mixed vegetables with the potatoes, garlic, vinegar and oil and season with salt and pepper. Remove the chicken from the broth and cool. Chill 15 minutes in refrigerator and then cut each breast in two. Meanwhile, skim any fat from the broth and strain through a linen towel into a bowl. Add the gelatin, softened in the cold water, and stir until dissolved. In a small saucepan, heat the butter and blend in the flour. Measure out 1½ cups of the broth. Add half of this to the mixture, stirring until smooth. Add the remaining half and the cream and simmer without letting it boil for 10 minutes. Season with salt and pepper. Cool. Place in the refrigerator for a few minutes but do not let it set. Arrange chicken breasts on a grill over a platter. Spoon the cooled sauce over the chicken breasts, covering each piece twice. Make a flower or a leaf pattern on each breast, using cooked egg whites and yolks, or tarragon leaves, or cherry tomatoes and truffles. Put platter in the refrigerator to chill. Lightly color remaining broth (which has been kept at room temperature) with the yellow coloring and meat extract and chill in the refrigerator for a few moments until it becomes syrupy. Remove chicken breasts from the refrigerator and spoon this colored aspic over them, taking care not to disturb the design. Return the chicken breasts to the refrigerator once more and after a few moments give them one more coating of aspic. Chill remaining aspic. Bind the vegetable salad with a little mayonnaise and taste for seasoning. To serve, form flat mounds of vegetable salad (the same size and shape as the chicken breasts) on individual salad plates. Place a breast on each mound. Stir up the remaining aspic with a fork or a wire whisk and arrange it around each mound. If the chicken breasts have not been decorated, garnish them with crisp lettuce and tiny yellow or red cherry tomatoes. Serves 6.

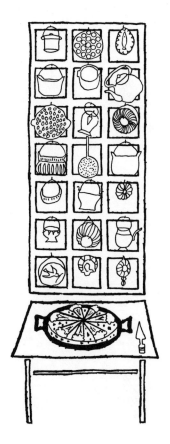

## Chicken Salad Baskets

*1 cup boiling water*
*½ teaspoon salt*
*¼ pound butter*
*1 cup sifted flour*
*4 eggs*
*1½ cups diced chicken*
*½ cup shredded almonds*
*Lemon juice*
*Salt and pepper*
*Mayonnaise*

Bring the water, salt and butter to a boil. Remove from stove and put the flour into the pan all at once. Stir hard with a wooden spoon and put back over a gentle heat to dry the pastry until none of it sticks to the side. Add the eggs one by one, beating very hard after each addition. Remove from the stove and continue beating for several minutes. Using two tablespoons, drop the mixture onto a buttered and floured baking sheet. (This will make more than the 6 pastry shells you will need—it will make 10-12—but they keep for several days.) Bake 15 minutes at 450°. Reduce heat to 350° and bake 15-20 minutes longer. Cool before filling. Combine chicken, almonds, lemon juice, salt and pepper and mayonnaise. Cut the tops off the shells. Line with a lettuce leaf and fill with the chicken salad mixture. Serves 6.

## French Cucumber Salad

*4-6 medium cucumbers*
*Salt*
*¼ cup tarragon vinegar*
*¼ teaspoon sugar*
*⅛ teaspoon white pepper*
*⅛ teaspoon paprika*
*½ cup salad or peanut oil*
*1 tablespoon chopped fresh tarragon*
*1 tablespoon chopped parsley*

23

Peel the cucumbers and split them lengthwise. Scoop out the seeds with a teaspoon. Slice the cucumbers, place them in a non-metal bowl and sprinkle them very generously with salt. Chill for several hours in the refrigerator. Combine the remaining ingredients, except the chopped herbs, for the dressing. To serve, drain off *all* the liquid from the cucumbers. Arrange them on individual salad plates. Spoon the well mixed dressing over the cucumbers and garnish with the chopped herbs. Serves 6-8.

## French Tomato Salad

6-8 *firm ripe tomatoes*
1/3 *cup red wine vinegar*
3/4 *teaspoon salt*
1/8 *teaspoon black pepper*
1/3 *cup olive oil*
1/3 *cup peanut or salad oil*
2 *tablespoons chopped parsley*
1 *tablespoon chopped scallion or shallots*

Dip the tomatoes in boiling water for two seconds and peel off the skins. Chill in refrigerator. Combine vinegar, seasoning and oils for the dressing. To serve, slice the tomatoes and put 8-10 slices on individual salad plates. Spoon well mixed dressing

over them (about two tablespoons per serving). Sprinkle with chopped parsley and scallion. Serves 6.

## Tomato Cups

6 *firm ripe tomatoes*
2 *potatoes*
2 *tablespoons tarragon vinegar*
2 *tablespoons scraped onion*
*Salt and pepper*
7 *pitted black olives*
1 *small cucumber, diced*
*Mayonnaise*

Dip the tomatoes in boiling water and slip off the skins. Cut off the top third. Hollow out the interior of the tomatoes leaving a 1/2″ thick cup. Turn the tomatoes upside down on a plate to drain and chill in the refrigerator. Peel and dice the potatoes and boil in salted water for 10 minutes. Drain and season immediately with vinegar, onion, salt and pepper. Cool. Chop four olives coarsely. Add olives, cucumber, and enough mayonnaise to bind to the potatoes. To serve, fill the tomatoes with the potato salad. Cover the potatoes with mayonnaise and garnish with half a black olive. Serves 6.

## Artichoke Roses

*6 large artichokes*
*1½ teaspoons salt*
*¼ teaspoon fresh black pepper*
*½ teaspoon prepared mustard*
*1 large clove garlic, minced*
*3 tablespoons chopped parsley*
*⅓ cup red wine vinegar*
*⅔ cup olive oil*

Cut off the top quarter of the artichokes with a sharp knife. Remove the hard woody leaves at the base and pare the bottom evenly. Boil 20 minutes in salted water. Drain and cool upside down in a colander. When cool, twist out the spiny choke and place artichokes on individual plates. Flatten down the outside leaves all around and turn back the rest to make the artichokes look like full blown roses. Combine the remaining ingredients for the sauce. Chill and stir well. Serve sauce separately. Serves 6.

## Artichokes Bigote

*6 artichokes*
*6 slices boiled ham, ¼″ thick*
*3 tablespoons butter*
*1 pint sour cream*
*Mace*

Boil the artichokes in salted water for 20 minutes or until the outer leaves pull off easily. Drain upside down in a colander until cool enough to handle. Remove the chokes and the outer leaves down to the point where the leaves are pale green and completely edible. Keep warm in a strainer suspended over hot water (if the artichokes are prepared in advance they can be reheated by plunging them in boiling water for 1 minute). Sauté the ham slices in the butter over a moderate flame, allowing 3 minutes for each side. Meanwhile warm the sour cream in the top of a double boiler. Place the ham slices on a heated platter,

cover each one with an artichoke, rounded side up. Cover with the cream and dust with mace. Serves 6.

## Cold Asparagus Vinaigrette

*2 pounds asparagus*
*⅓ cup red wine vinegar*
*½ teaspoon sharp mustard*
*1 clove garlic, minced*
*¾ teaspoon salt*
*⅛ teaspoon pepper*
*⅔ cup olive oil*
*1 small can red pimento*
*3 tablespoons chopped parsley*

Wash and trim the asparagus. Place on a trivet in boiling salted water in a deep frying pan (or stand upright in bottom of a double boiler with top section inverted as a cover). Boil 10-12 minutes. Drain thoroughly and chill in the refrigerator. Combine the remaining ingredients (except the pimento and parsley) for the dressing. Chill. Cut the pimentos into thin strips. Arrange the cold asparagus on individual plates. Garnish each serving with three strips of pimento and ½ tablespoon parsley. Spoon a little of the well mixed dressing on each portion of asparagus and serve the rest in a separate bowl. Serves 6.

*VARIATION*

Serve cold cooked leeks in the same way.

## Hot Asparagus Appetizer

*2 pounds asparagus*
*2 tablespoons tarragon vinegar*
*4 tablespoons water*
*½ teaspoon salt*
*⅛ teaspoon white pepper*
*4 egg yolks*
*½ pound butter*
*6 pieces white bread*
*Cayenne*

Wash the asparagus and trim off the inedible part. Place on a trivet that will fit into a deep frying pan (or stand upright in a double boiler). Boil in salted water for 10-12 minutes just before serving. Lift the trivet out with two forks and place over a pan to drain. Asparagus must be well drained but transferring it to a colander often breaks the stalks, so the trivet method is better. Combine the vinegar, water, salt, pepper and egg yolks in the top of a double boiler. Stir over simmering water until the mixture thickens, using a wire whisk. Add the butter in three stages. Cover and keep over hot water until serving time. Trim and toast the bread. To serve, place the toast on heated salad plates. Cover with asparagus and spoon sauce over each portion. Sprinkle with cayenne. Serve immediately. Serves 6.

### Anchovy and Pepper Antipasto

2 red peppers
1 green pepper
1/3 cup olive oil
1 tablespoon wine vinegar
1 teaspoon capers
Salt and black pepper
18 anchovy filets
1 loaf Italian bread
1 white onion

With a fork, hold the peppers over a hot flame, turning until toasted on all sides. Place in a dish of cold water and immediately peel off the skins. Split the peppers, remove the seeds and cut peppers in thin strips. Place in a flat dish and marinate for 2 to 3 hours in a mixture of the oil, vinegar and capers, seasoned with a little salt and plenty of black pepper. To serve, arrange alternating strips of red and green pepper and anchovy filets on half-inch slice; of day-old Italian bread. Spoon the vinaigrette marinade over the appetizers and cover

with paper-thin slices of raw onion—2 to 3 to a serving. Serves 6.

### Mushrooms in Sour Cream

1 1/2 pounds mushrooms
4 tablespoons butter
Salt and pepper
1/2 teaspoon oregano
1/8 teaspoon nutmeg
Juice of 1/4 lemon
8 slices French bread
1 pint sour cream

This is a good appetizer to prepare in a chafing dish. Wash, trim and slice the mushrooms lengthwise, cap and stem together. Saute in butter over moderate flame and cook in a covered pan for 10 minutes. Remove from the stove and season with salt, pepper, oregano, nutmeg and lemon juice. Toast French bread. Reheat the mushrooms in a chafing dish and add the sour cream, stirring while it heats. Do not bring quite to the boiling point or the cream will separate. Serve on toasted bread. Serves 8.

### Savory Turkey Mushroom Caps

24 medium size mushroom caps
5 tablespoons butter
1 small can (4 ounces) smoked turkey
2 teaspoons poultry dressing
2 tablespoons chopped onion
Salt and black pepper
1/2 cup sour cream
3 tablespoons cognac
6 rounds stale white bread
Parsley

Trim, stem and wash the mushrooms. Scoop out the gills with a spoon to make room for the stuffing. Melt 3 tablespoons of butter in a frying pan and sauté the caps lightly on each side. Remove to a roasting pan or cooky sheet. Chop the gills, half the stems and the smoked turkey. Add the poultry dressing. Add 2 more tablespoons of butter to the frying pan and sauté the onion for 3 minutes over a moderate flame. Add the turkey mixture, stir well and continue cooking for 7 minutes. Season with salt and pepper. Remove from the stove and cool 5 minutes before adding the cream and cognac. Stuff mushroom caps with the mixture. Add more butter to the frying pan, if necessary, and fry the bread. Place the bread on another cooky sheet. Heat the mushroom caps in a 275° oven 30 minutes before serving. Reheat the fried bread during the final 10 minutes. To serve, place the bread on a heated platter and cover each slice with 4 stuffed mushrooms. Garnish with sprigs of fresh parsley. Serves 6.

### Mushrooms Cambon

*1 pound mushrooms*
*2 tablespoons butter*
*Juice of ½ lemon*
*1 chicken bouillon cube*
*3 tablespoons butter*
*3 tablespoons flour*
*2 tablespoons brandy*
*6 eggs*

Wash and trim the mushrooms and slice them very thin. Place them in a saucepan with 2 tablespoons butter, lemon juice and water to half cover mushrooms. Cook gently for 10 minutes with cover on. Strain the broth into a measuring cup. Add enough hot water to make 2 cups and dissolve the bouillon cube in the broth. Place the mushrooms in a double boiler. Heat the 3 tablespoons butter and blend in the flour. Stir in half the broth and blend. When the sauce

is smooth, add the rest of the liquid. Simmer 10 minutes. Taste for seasoning and add the brandy. Pour this mixture over the mushrooms. To serve, arrange the mushrooms on a deep platter. Garnish with the shelled eggs which have been cooked 4 minutes. Serves 6.

## Russian Salad in Scallop Shells

*3 cups mixed cooked vegetables (fresh, frozen or canned)*
*2 tablespoons red wine vinegar*
*½ teaspoon scraped onion*
*1 teaspoon salt*
*⅛ teaspoon white pepper*
*Pinch of monosodium glutamate (Ac'cent or MSG)*
*⅓ cup salad oil*
*1 tablespoon gelatin*
*2 tablespoons water*
*1 cup mayonnaise*
*1 can anchovies*
*Capers*
*Parsley*

Put the vegetables in a bowl and season with the vinegar, onion, salt, pepper and monosodium glutamate. Mix well, then add the oil. Let stand at least 1 hour. Drain and place in scallop shells or individual shallow dishes. Chill 30 minutes. Meanwhile, soften the gelatin in water and melt in double boiler. Mix with half the mayonnaise and keep over warm water until ready to use. Split the anchovies in two lengthwise. To serve, frost the surface of the vegetable salad with a layer of unstiffened mayonnaise. Make a lattice of anchovies on the surface of each salad and alternate capers with sprigs of parsley in the openings. Force the stiff mayonnaise through a small pastry tube around the edge of each shell for a decorative border. Serves 6.

## Vodka Melon Coupe

*3 small ripe cantaloupes*
*1 lime*
*1 small honeydew melon*
*3 tablespoons vodka*
*⅓ cup sugar*
*Mint leaves*

Halve and seed the cantaloupes. Rub the insides with the cut side of a lime. Sprinkle very lightly with sugar and place in the refrigerator. Split and seed the honeydew melon and cut into small balls with a vegetable cutter. Mix with the juice of the lime, vodka and ⅓ cup sugar. Cover and chill. To serve, fill the cantaloupe cavities with the honeydew balls and divide the syrup from them among the six melon halves. Garnish with a sprig of mint. Serves 6.

# SOUP

# Soup

Soup, now too often regarded as a dispensable first course, was a robust meal in itself to our ancestors. Those early soups were melanges of meat and vegetables served forth in their own broth or "brewis." They were divided into two categories: thin (soople meat) and thick (spoon meat). A character in *The Comedy of Errors* remarks, "Expect spoon meat." For centuries the big simmering household soup pot (for which the French *pot-au-feu* is named) sustained and comforted the peasants of Europe. During the eight lean years that Pierre Larousse, famous French lexicographer, labored on his works, he existed, it is said, solely on onion soup, cooked in secret at two in the morning. Not only authors but armies were invigorated by soup. A soup kitchen was the quickest and cheapest way to feed an army in the field, especially when the field supplied the ingredients. The Black Prince's army defeated the French at Crécy after being heartened by a golden soup made from the famous

Crécy carrots. Wine soup helped Joan of Arc raise the siege of Orleans. An old American Civil War song has the refrain, "Hayfoot, strawfoot, bellyful of bean soup." Kings, too, were apt to play favorites in the matter of soup. King James IV, a leek-loving Scot, rallied his guests with the words, "My lords and lieges, let us all to dinner, for the cock-a-leekie is a-cooling." When Louis XV returned to his lodge after a long day's hunting, soup-hungry, to find the larder bare except for onions, butter and champagne, onion soup was born.

Every country has cherished a soup specialty. The Germans and Scandinavians feature fruit soups, the Greeks a soup sharply fragrant with lemon. Armenians add chicken and rice, and the Turks curry and leeks. (Leeks, one of the most honored of pot herbs, have lent their unique flavor to the roughest peasant soup and to velvety Vichysoisse, originated by Louis Diat at the old New York Ritz.) American chowders, a happy blend of the fruits of the sea and land of this continent, were borrowed from the Indians by the Pilgrim fathers.

Soup has the great culinary grace of being adaptable to all tastes and pockets. It can be simple, exotic, economical, extravagant (a French chef, Soyen, once invented a soup that cost $525 to make). The 18th century housewife could find a recipe for a hop-top soup or a vine-bud potage. We can choose a birds' nest soup, actually made from the gelatinous binding of sea birds' nests, or kangaroo-tail soup which, like mock turtle, never knew its namesake.

As usual, it was the French who nurtured and perfected the art of soup making (a chef estimated that 10,000 soups originated in Paris kitchens alone). One of the first French cook books was a 1456 treatise on soup, and Voltaire found "the best written book is a recipe for potage." Alexandre Dumas, *père*, crowned his literary career with a *Grand Dictionary of Cooking,* his 500th book, in which he includes a recipe for *potage aux choux* calling for a cabbage "stuffed with the remains of game and finely sliced ham, boiled in yesterday's bouillon." During the last century, soups lost much of their substance. They were refined and elaborated until they could be supped or sipped without quenching the appetite. Yet even today, what will revive the faint and famished like a tureen of honest soup—minestrone, oyster stew, onion soup? And when Esau sold his birthright for a mess of red Egyptian lentil potage we know how great the temptation must have been.

## Potato and Water Cress Soup

### (Potage Cressonnière)

*2 tablespoons chicken fat or butter*
*4 large potatoes*
*2 medium size onions*
*2 cups water*
*Salt, black pepper*
*2 bunches water cress*
*1 cup milk*
*¾ cup light cream*
*1½ cups light croutons*

Dissolve the fat in a deep heavy kettle. Add the potatoes and onions skinned and finely sliced. Add the water, salt and pepper; cover the pan and cook very slowly until the vegetables are quite mushy. Add the stalks and leaves of the water cress, reserving some of the best leaves; cover and cook another minute. Rub through a fine strainer, add the milk, the reserved water cress leaves and the cream. Add more seasoning if necessary. Reheat, do not boil; serve with the croutons. Serves 4.

## Cream of Tomato and Potato Soup

### (Potage Crème Aurore)

*4 tablespoons chicken fat*
*4 medium size potatoes*
*3 small onions*
*2 cloves garlic*
*1 cup water*
*Salt, cracked black pepper*
*1 cup milk*
*1 lb. ripe tomatoes*
*2 tablespoons tomato paste*
*2 level tablespoons flour*
*1½ cups chicken stock*
*¼ teaspoon dried sage*
*¾ cup light cream*
*Chopped parsley*
*4 tablespoons whipped cream*

Melt 2 tablespoons of the chicken fat in a deep heavy kettle. Finely slice the peeled potatoes, two onions and one clove of garlic. Add to the pan with the water, season with salt and pepper, cover, and cook slowly until the vegetables are mushy. Rub through a fine strainer and add the milk. In another pan melt the remaining chicken fat, add all but one of the tomatoes, sliced with the skins on, the remaining onion, sliced, and clove of garlic. Add salt, pepper, and cook briskly for five minutes. Stir in the tomato paste and the flour and pour on the chicken stock. Add the sage and stir over the fire until it comes to a boil. Rub through a fine strainer and combine with the potato soup. Mix in the light cream and garnish with the chopped parsley and the reserved tomato, skinned, seeded and shredded. Serve topped with a tablespoon of whipped cream for each person. Serves 4.

*Note:* The cream of tomato and cream of potato soups can be served separately, if desired.

## Potage Gentilhomme

*2 tablespoons chicken or bacon fat*
*5 potatoes*
*1 large onion*
*Salt, black pepper*
*3 cups water*
*2 carrots*
*2 leeks*
*1 small head Boston lettuce*
*¼ cup butter*
*2 egg yolks*
*¼ cup chopped fresh chervil*

Heat the fat in a pan; cut the peeled potatoes into eighths, add the finely chopped onion, a little salt and pepper and stir well over high heat for two or three minutes. Add half the water, cover the pan and cook very slowly until the vegetables are mushy. Rub through a fine strainer, add the remaining water and if too thick, a little more water. Add the following garnish: slice the outer, red part of the carrots to the size of fine matchsticks, slice the white part of the leeks similarly and cut the lettuce into shreds. Heat the butter in a sauté pan, and when it has just melted, but is not too hot, add the vegetables with a little salt and pepper. Cover and cook very slowly until quite soft. Add to the soup. Put in a soup tureen the egg yolks diluted with two or three tablespoons water; pour the soup on slowly, stirring all the time, and garnish with the chopped chervil. Serves 4.

## Cream of Carrot Soup
### (Potage Crécy)

*4 large carrots*
*4 small potatoes*
*1 onion*
*1½ cups water*
*2 tablespoons butter*
*Salt, black pepper*
*1 clove garlic*
*1½ cups boiled milk*
*1 egg yolk*
*1 cup light cream*
*2 tablespoons chopped chives*
*1 teaspoon chopped parsley*
*1½ cups croutons*

Peel the carrots, onion, and potatoes; cut them into slices; put into a heavy pan with the water, butter and seasoning. Cover and cook until the vegetables are all very soft. Rub through a very fine strainer and add the boiled milk. Mix the egg yolk well into the cream and pour the hot carrot soup onto it. Sprinkle with the chopped chives and parsley and serve the croutons separately. Serves 4.

## Cream of Cauliflower Soup
### (Crème DuBarry)

*1 large head cauliflower*
*2 tablespoons lemon juice*
*6 tablespoons butter*
*4 tablespoons flour*
*Salt, cayenne pepper*
*4 cups light chicken stock*
*½ cup boiled milk*
*½ cup cooked tapioca*
*2 egg yolks*
*½ cup light cream*
*1 tablespoon chopped chives*
*1 cup croutons*

Remove about ½ cup of cauliflowerets from the head. Blanch them for 8 to 10 minutes in boiling salted water with 2 teaspoons of the lemon juice. Drain and set aside. Slice the rest of the cauliflower and blanch for 15 minutes with the rest of the lemon juice in boiling salted water. Melt the butter in a heavy pan, stir in the flour off the fire and season with salt and pepper. Pour on the stock and stir over the fire until it comes to a boil. Drain the cauliflower and add to this mixture. Continue cooking slowly until the cauliflower is very soft and skim when necessary. Rub through a very fine strainer, return to the pan, add the boiled milk, reheat, add the tapioca, the egg yolks mixed into the cream, the chives, and lastly, the cauliflowerets. Serve croutons separately. Serves 4.

33

### Cream of Pea Soup

#### (Potage St. Germain)

*1 pound dried peas*
*6 cups water*
*2 onions*
*2 cloves*
*1 large carrot*
*½ cup butter*
*1 ham bone*
*3 or 4 leek greens, cut in pieces*
*Salt, freshly cracked pepper*
*Sugar*
*½ cup fresh cooked or canned peas*
*4 ounces boiled ham, cut in fine shreds*
*½ cup boiled milk*
*1 cup small fried croutons for garnish*

Soak the dried peas overnight in plenty of water. Drain. Wash thoroughly. Put in a pan with just enough of the 6 cups water to cover. Bring to a boil, skim, add the onions studded with the cloves, the carrot, thinly sliced and sautéed in 2 teaspoons butter, and the ham bone. Add the leek greens and allow to cook very slowly for 1½ hours. Rub through a very fine strainer and dilute with a little of the water (the soup should be rather on the thick side). Season with salt and pepper and add a little sugar to remove the bitter taste of the onion. Beat in, bit by bit, the remaining butter. Add the ½ cup peas, the ham and the boiled milk. Serve garnished with the croutons. Serves 4.

### Cream of Pea and Vermicelli Soup

#### (Potage Longchamps)

*1 lb. dried peas*
*6 cups water*
*2 onions*
*6 cloves*
*1 large carrot*
*½ cup butter*
*1 ham bone*
*3 or 4 leek greens, cut in pieces*
*Salt, freshly cracked pepper, sugar*
*2 ounces boiled vermicelli*
*½ cup fresh peas (or canned)*
*4 ounces boiled ham, cut in fine shreds*
*½ cup light cream*
*½ cup finely shredded sorrel*
*1 tablespoon finely chopped chervil*
*1 cup small fried croutons*

Soak the dried peas overnight in plenty of water. Drain. Wash thoroughly. Put in a pan with just enough of the 6 cups water to cover. Bring to a boil, skim, add the peeled onions studded with the cloves, the carrot, cut into thin slices and sautéed in 2 teaspoons of butter, and the ham bone. Add the green part of the leeks, allow to cook very slowly for 1½ hours. Rub through a very fine strainer and dilute with a little of the water (it should be rather on the thick side). Season and add a little sugar to remove the bitterness of the onion. Beat in, bit by bit, the rest of the butter. Add the boiled vermicelli, the peas, the ham, the sorrel slowly cooked in butter, and the light cream. Sprinkle the chopped chervil on the top. Serve garnished with the croutons. Serves 4.

### Cream of Chestnut Soup

*2 lbs. chestnuts*
*6 tablespoons butter*
*1 small celery stalk, sliced*
*1 small onion, sliced*
*1 small carrot, sliced*
*Salt and black pepper*
*4 cups strong chicken stock*
*1 egg yolk*
*2 tablespoons dry sherry*
*1 cup light cream*
*4 marrons glacés or 1½ ounces marrons glacés pieces*
*1 tablespoon chives, finely chopped*
*1 cup whipped cream*

Cover the chestnuts with water and bring them slowly to a boil. Simmer for a few minutes, drain and carefully remove both the outer and inner skins (canned, cooked chestnuts may be substituted). Melt 4 tablespoons butter in a deep heavy pan, add celery, onion, carrot, season with salt and pepper and cook slowly for 2 to 3 minutes. Add the skinned chestnuts. Pour over the chicken stock, bring to a boil and simmer until the chestnuts are quite soft. Rub all through a fine strainer, return to pan. Add rest of butter bit by bit. Beat the egg yolk well with the sherry; mix in the light cream. Pour the soup onto this mixture. Add the marrons glacés, in small pieces, and the chives. Season well, pour into individual earthenware bowls. Top each with a tablespoon of whipped cream and brown under the broiler. Serves 4.

## Chicken Soup, Fromage

*1 cup chopped onion*
*2 tablespoons minced ham*
*3 tablespoons butter*
*2 ounces freshly grated Parmesan cheese*
*1 herb bouquet (parsley, rosemary, small piece bay leaf, 1 blade mace)*
*3 egg yolks*
*1 cup heavy cream*
*4 cups rich chicken stock*

*1 ounce grated Gruyère*
*Paprika*

Cook onion and ham in butter until onion is wilted. Add chicken stock and herb bouquet. Simmer for 20 minutes and remove herb bouquet. Mix together egg yolks, cream, Parmesan and Gruyère cheeses. Mix a cup of the hot stock into this, then stir in the remaining soup. Heat, correct seasoning, strain, and serve garnished with paprika. Serves 6-8.

## Lobster Bisque

*5 cups fish stock*
*¾ stick butter*
*4 tablespoons flour*
*2 teaspoons tomato paste*
*Salt, cayenne pepper*
*1 small boiled lobster*
*¾ stick sweet butter*
*2 teaspoons fresh chopped parsley*
*6 thin slices bread, cut into croutons*

To make fish stock put 3 or 4 sole bones, a cod's head, 1 sliced onion, 1 sliced carrot, 1 sliced stalk of celery, 1 sprig of fresh dill, 4 peppercorns, 1 small bay leaf, ½ cup dry white wine, 6 cups water and 2 teaspoons salt in a pot and bring slowly to a boil. Simmer slowly for ¾ hour. Strain, and reserve 5 cups stock.

Melt ¾ stick butter in a pan. Stir in, off the fire, the flour, tomato paste and seasonings. Pour on the fish stock and stir over the fire until it comes to a boil. Simmer 10 minutes. Meanwhile, shell the lobster, reserve the meat and crush the shells in a mortar with a pestle. Mix in the ¾ stick sweet butter. Crush mixture again. Rub through a fine strainer. Add this lobster butter, bit by bit, to the soup. Garnish with the cooled, diced lobster meat and the parsley. Crisp croutons in oven until golden brown and serve separately. Serves 4.

## Shrimp Bisque

2 carrots (1 sliced)
1 onion, sliced
2 turnips
6 tablespoons chicken fat
Salt, black pepper
1½ lbs. raw shrimp
¼ cup cognac
½ cup white wine
3 cups fish stock
6 tablespoons rice flour
A few drops cochineal
¾ cup butter
2 cups light cream
Cayenne and paprika
1 tablespoon cognac
1½ cups small croutons

### To make fish stock:

Put 4 sole bones or 4 flounder bones in a pan with 5 cups water, bring slowly to a boil, skim well. Add sliced carrot, onion, 1 bay leaf, 1 sliced stalk celery, 1 sprig parsley, 4 peppercorns, ¼ cup white wine. Reduce to 3 cups. Strain and set aside.

Dice the other vegetables. Heat 1 tablespoon fat in a large heavy pan, add the vegetables with a little salt and pepper, cover and cook very slowly until just soft. Add the raw shrimp in their shells and sauté a few moments. Pour the cognac over and flame and then add the white wine. Add salt and pepper, and cook 8 to 10 minutes. Remove the shrimp and set aside to cool. Add the fish stock to the vegetables and rub through a fine strainer. Melt the rest of the chicken fat in a pan, stir in the rice flour off the fire, pour on the fish stock and stir over the fire until it comes to a boil. Color with the cochineal and allow to simmer gently for 10 minutes. Shell the shrimp and crush the shells in a large wooden bowl with a pestle. Add the butter and continue crushing until well mixed. Color with a little cochineal and rub through a very fine

strainer. Add this butter bit by bit to the soup, beating well with a whisk. Add the light cream; season well with a little cayenne and paprika mixed; cut the shrimp into very thin slices; add to the soup and just before serving, stir in 1 tablespoon cognac. Garnish with the croutons. Serves 4.

## New England Clam Chowder

1 large white onion
2 large cloves garlic
3 ounces very hard butter
2 dozen chowder clams, steamed
2 cups clam juice
Salt, cracked black pepper
6 ounces salt pork
2 Idaho potatoes
2 cups light cream
1 tablespoon chopped parsley
1 tablespoon chopped chives
Coarsely cracked black and white
    peppercorns
Rock salt
3 small French rolls

Finely chop or grate the onion; crush the garlic to a smooth paste with very little salt; melt 1 tablespoon of butter in a pan, add the onion and garlic and cook very slowly for 4 minutes. Put the clams through a fine meat chopper (or use canned minced clams), add another tablespoon of butter, moisten with 4 tablespoons of clam juice, season with salt and black pepper, add to onion and garlic, cover and cook very slowly for 10 to 15 minutes. Cut the salt pork into very small dice and fry in a large heavy pan until nearly crisp. Skin and dice the

potatoes, put into boiling water for 2 minutes, drain and add to the salt pork. Pour on the remaining clam juice, bring slowly to a boil and simmer gently until the potatoes are soft. Remove from the heat and mix in the clams. Carefully add the cream and stir over the fire until hot, do not boil. Cut the remaining butter into thin slices, float it on top of the soup, sprinkle well with chopped chives and parsley, the crushed black and white peppercorns and a little rock salt. Cut the rolls into very thin slices lengthwise and toast quickly. Serve separately in a napkin to keep them hot. Serves 4.

## Mussel Soup

1 quart large mussels
Dry mustard
Bones of 2 flounders
1 small carrot, sliced
1 small onion, sliced
1 small celery stalk, sliced
Bouquet of fresh herbs
2 teaspoons salt
8 mixed black and white peppercorns
½ cup very dry white wine
5 cups water
3 tablespoons butter
2 tablespoons rice flour or 3 tablespoons flour
¼ teaspoon cayenne pepper
2 tablespoons finely chopped parsley
1 cup light cream
1½ cups small croutons

Soak the mussels in well salted water with dry mustard added (about 2 tablespoons mustard to 2 quarts water.) Leave for about 1 hour, then scrub thoroughly with a small brush and rinse in cold water. Place mussels in a deep heavy pan with the flounder bones, sliced vegetables, herb bouquet, 1 teaspoon salt and the peppercorns. Pour over the wine and water. Cover the pan and bring slowly to a boil. Reduce heat and

simmer for 2 minutes. Strain. Remove mussels from their shells, take off the small beards around the sides of the mussels and set cleaned mussels aside to keep warm. Melt the butter in a deep 2-quart saucepan, stir in the rice flour or flour and add 1 teaspoon salt and the cayenne pepper. Slowly and carefully stir in the mussel stock and stir mixture over the fire until it comes to a boil. Reduce heat and simmer for 5 to 10 minutes. Add the mussels, chopped parsley and cream (for a richer soup, mix the cream with one or two well beaten egg yolks and stir into the soup before adding the mussels and parsley). Do not let the soup boil, but serve quickly with separate dishes of croutons. Serves 4.

## Oyster Stew

2 dozen shelled large oysters
½ cup water
1 small piece celery with leaf, finely chopped
3 ounces sweet butter
2 small shallots, finely chopped
1 small onion, finely chopped
3 large cloves garlic, finely chopped
Salt and freshly cracked black pepper
3 cups light cream
6 juniper berries, crushed
1 cup whipped cream
Small, crisp crackers

Carefully remove any pieces of shell from the oysters, place in a thin saucepan, pour over the water, add celery leaves and ½ teaspoon salt. Bring slowly to a boil. Remove from fire, leave oysters in the liquor while the rest of stew is being prepared. Melt 1 ounce of the butter in a deep heavy pan, add the shallots, onion, garlic and celery stalk, season with salt and pepper and cook very slowly for 4 to 5 minutes, stirring frequently. Pour on the light cream which has been brought to a boil with the juniper berries, ½ teaspoon salt and ½ tea-

37

spoon pepper, and then strained. Add the drained oysters with ¼ cup of their cooking liquor. Just before serving, add the whipped cream and the remaining butter, well chilled and cut into small cubes, so that the butter is not quite melted when the soup is served. Serve with small crackers. Serves 4.

## Russian Fish Soup

½ pound salmon or tuna,
   cooked until firm and chilled
4 tablespoons lemon juice
2 cups cooked rice
4 tablespoons leeks, chopped
½ clove garlic, chopped
6 tablespoons chopped parsley
   stalks or root
1½ pounds unfilleted flounder or sea-bass
6 tablespoons dry white wine
2 quarts water
¾ teaspoon black pepper
1 teaspoon salt
¼ pound fresh boiled shrimp

Cut chilled salmon or tuna into pieces about 1″ long, ½″ broad and ¼″ thick. Dip in lemon juice and cover with cooked rice. Press firmly to embed rice. Reserve for the moment.

Butter the bottom of a heavy cast iron casserole. Put in chopped leeks, chopped garlic, and parsley stalks or root. Lay unfilleted fish upon this. Add juice of ½ lemon. Place on fire, and cover tightly. Cook over medium heat, shaking the casserole a few times. After 7 minutes add white wine. Cook uncovered for ¼ hour on very low heat. Then add 2 quarts water. Boil once, clear any scum, season and cook very gently for 25 minutes.

Strain soup, add pieces of fish and cut-up shrimp. Cook for 10 minutes. Place in a tureen tuna or salmon and 2 tablespoons rice for each serving. Pour soup over them. Serves 6-8.

## Onion Soup au Gratin

4 tablespoons butter
2 tablespoons vegetable oil
6 medium size onions, finely sliced
Salt and pepper
1 teaspoon flour
½ teaspoon French mustard
½ cup dry white wine
2½ cups stock or water
4 tablespoons grated American cheese
4 tablespoons grated Parmesan cheese
French bread

Melt butter and heat the oil in a casserole. Add the onions, salt, pepper. Sauté slowly over a low fire until onions are a very dark brown—20 to 30 minutes. Add flour and mustard and stir until smooth. Continue stirring while adding the wine and stock, and bring slowly to a boil. Draw aside and leave to simmer for 15 minutes. Put thick slices of toasted French bread into an earthenware casserole or soup bowl. Add soup. Sprinkle the top with grated American cheese and brown quickly under the broiler. Sprinkle sliced French bread with oil and the Parmesan. Brown in the oven and serve separately. Serves 4.

## Consommé

3 lbs. side round of beef
2 large veal knuckle bones
10 cups cold water
1 tablespoon rock salt
8 black peppercorns
4 leeks, sliced
4 large carrots, sliced
6 young turnips, sliced
1 bouquet of herbs (chervil, parsley, thyme,
    bay leaf, celery, and Italian parsley)
1 large onion, stuck with 4 cloves
1 large Bermuda onion
2 tablespoons tomato paste
1 ripe tomato, sliced
3 egg whites
½ cup dry sherry

Whenever you are boiling beef for a meal, take the opportunity to make a batch of stock or cleared consommé. The ingredients add extra flavor to the meat. Stock or consommé can be kept for a week in the refrigerator or, frozen, for many months.

Place the meat and bones in a heavy casserole or earthenware marmite with the water. Bring to a boil very slowly. Skim off fat carefully. Add salt, peppercorns, sliced leeks, carrots and turnips, the herb bouquet and the onion stuck with the cloves. Add the Bermuda onion, which has been cut into thick slices, and browned in a heavy pan with a little skimmed beef fat until almost black. Skim again and reboil. Lower the heat and simmer very gently, covered, for 3 hours. Remove excess fat. Strain and reserve the beef for other uses. Allow the strained stock to get quite cold. Remove all fat. Put into a pan with the tomato paste, tomato and the stiffly beaten egg whites. Beat over a slow fire until the mixture comes to a boil. Draw aside and allow to stand for 15 minutes. Soak a fine cloth in cold water and wring out. Line a strainer with the cloth and carefully pour the soup through this. Return to the pan.

Add the dry sherry. Reheat; add a little more sherry if desired. Serves 4.

## Clear Borsch

3 lbs. side round beef
2 large veal knuckles
12 cups cold water
1 tablespoon rock salt
8 black peppercorns
2 leeks
2 carrots
2 turnips
1 stalk celery
1 medium onion stuck with 2 cloves
1 large Bermuda onion
Bouquet of herbs (celery, Italian parsley,
    thyme)
2 bunches raw beets
3 tablespoons tomato paste
1 cup red wine
3 egg whites
1 cup heavy sour cream
1 clove garlic, finely chopped with a
    little salt
1 teaspoon grated lemon rind
½ teaspoon coarsely cracked pepper

Place the meat and the bones in a heavy casserole or earthenware marmite, and cover with the water. Bring to a boil very slowly. Skim carefully. Add salt, peppercorns, and the thickly sliced leeks, carrots, turnips and celery. Add the onion stuck with cloves; add the Bermuda onion, thickly sliced, and browned in a heavy pan until almost black. Reboil and skim again carefully. Lower the heat, add the herb bouquet and simmer very gently for 3 hours with the cover on. Remove excess fat and strain, reserving the meat to be used as boiled beef. Allow the stock to get quite cold, and remove all the fat. Skin the beets and put through a coarse grater. Add them to the stock with the tomato paste, red wine, and stiffly beaten egg whites. Beat over a

slow fire until the soup comes to a boil. Draw aside and allow to stand for 15 minutes. Soak a fine cloth in cold water and wring out. Line a strainer with the cloth and carefully pour the soup through it. Return the soup to the pan and reheat. Mix the sour cream, garlic, lemon rind and pepper together and serve separately for a garnish. Serves 4.

## Vegetable Borsch

1 Bermuda onion
2 large carrots
2 large turnips
1 large parsnip
1 large piece of celery
2 bunches of beets
Bouquet fresh dill
4 tablespoons chicken fat
2 cloves garlic
Salt, freshly cracked black pepper
2 tablespoons tomato paste
4 large ripe tomatoes, skinned and sliced
12 cups water
1 green cabbage, finely shredded
Sugar
1 cup raw fresh beet juice
Chopped fresh dill

### Garnish

2 cups heavy sour cream
1 clove garlic
1 teaspoon salt
½ teaspoon freshly cracked black pepper
1 teaspoon grated lemon rind
¼ teaspoon sugar

Shred the onion, carrots, turnips, parsnip, celery, beets and dill bouquet. Put in a heavy pan with the chicken fat, crushed garlic, salt and black pepper. Cover the pan and cook very slowly for 5-10 minutes, without browning, stirring frequently. Add the tomato paste, the skinned and sliced tomatoes, and, little by little, the water. When the vegetables are half cooked, add the shredded cabbage. Add a little sugar, salt and pepper to taste. Simmer all this together until the vegetables are just soft, without being mushy. Then add the raw beet juice (to make this, grate raw beets, put into a cloth and squeeze to get the juice). Sprinkle with chopped fresh dill and serve with 2 cups sour cream mixed with 1 clove crushed garlic, 1 teaspoon salt, ½ teaspoon fresh ground pepper, 1 teaspoon grated lemon rind and ¼ teaspoon sugar as a garnish. Serves 4-6.

## Cabbage Soup

1 large green cabbage
6 ounces salt pork
3 onions, peeled
2 cloves garlic, crushed
5 cups beef stock
4 cloves
1 teaspoon caraway seeds
Salt, black pepper
2 large potatoes, peeled and diced
3 frankfurters or small garlic sausages
1 tablespoon honey
French bread, sliced and toasted
4 tablespoons frozen butter

Put the cabbage in boiling water, off the fire, and leave for 10 minutes. Drain and cut into eighths. Remove all the hard part. Dice the pork and sauté in a heated, heavy pan for 5 or 6 minutes. Dice two onions and sauté them in the pan for a few minutes. Add the cabbage and the garlic. Pour over the stock, bring to a boil and add the remaining onion, stuck with the cloves. Add the caraway seeds, salt and pepper. Cover and cook very gently until the vegetables are nearly cooked, then add the diced raw potatoes, the frankfurters, blanched and sliced, and the honey. Pour into an earthenware tureen or casserole. Cook for ¾ hour in a slow oven. To serve, put 2 or 3 slices of French bread in a soup plate, ladle the soup over and top each with 1 tablespoon frozen butter. Serves 4.

## Lentil Soup

2 cups dried lentils
3 quarts strong beef stock
1 ham knuckle
¼ lb. piece of salt pork
4 small potatoes, diced
½ cup celery, diced
2 teaspoons flour
½ cup sour cream
Salt, black pepper
A little nutmeg
1 small garlic sausage
4 tablespoons sweet butter

Wash and drain the lentils well. Put them in a bowl, with water to cover and let them soak for 2 hours. Drain. Cover again with cold water and bring slowly to a boil. Boil for 10 minutes, then drain. Pour on the beef stock; add the ham knuckle and salt pork. Bring to a boil and simmer slowly for 2½ to 3 hours. Rub through a strainer. Twenty minutes before serving, add the potatoes and celery. Mix the flour into the sour cream and moisten it with a little of the soup. Stir carefully into the soup and simmer until the potatoes are just soft. Season well with salt, pepper and nutmeg. Cover the garlic sausage with water,

simmer for 10 minutes, drain and slice. Place a few slices in each serving plate or bowl. Pour the lentil soup over and serve, topped with a pat of butter. Serves 4.

## Pot-au-Feu

3 lbs. side round beef
2 large veal knuckle bones
10 cups cold water
1 tablespoon rock salt
8 black peppercorns
4 leeks
4 large carrots
6 young turnips
1 large onion, stuck with 4 cloves
1 large Bermuda onion
1 bouquet of herbs (chervil, parsley, thyme, bay leaf, celery and Italian parsley)
Garnishing vegetables: small onions, small potatoes, turnips, leeks, carrots, spring cabbage

Put the meat and the bones in a heavy casserole or earthenware marmite and cover with the water. Bring to a boil very slowly. Skim carefully. Add salt, peppercorns and the thickly sliced leeks, carrots and turnips. Add the onion stuck with cloves and the Bermuda onion which has been thickly sliced and browned in a heavy pan with a little beef fat until almost black. Reskim and reboil. Lower the heat, add the herb bouquet and simmer very gently, covered, for 3 hours. Remove excess fat and strain. Garnishing vegetables, such as onions, carrots, turnips, leeks, quarters of spring cabbage, small potatoes, may be cooked in the following manner: Reheat the stock and remove any excess fat. Add the small onions, and the carrots and turnips cut into large olive shapes. Simmer gently until half cooked. Add the leeks, a quartered spring cabbage and the small peeled potatoes. Add the beef and continue cooking until the beef is heated through and the vegetables are just soft. Slice as much beef as needed. Arrange slices overlapping on a serving dish surrounded by the vegetables. Serve the soup in a sauceboat with a ladle. Serves 6.

## Minestrone

2 tablespoons butter
2 tablespoons olive oil
½ cup diced raw ham
6 ounces finely diced salt pork
1 cup onion, finely diced
1 cup carrot, finely diced
½ cup finely diced celery
2 cloves garlic, diced
1 cup shelled peas
¼ small shredded green cabbage
1 tablespoon tomato paste
2 quarts boiling water
Salt, freshly cracked black pepper
½ cup small elbow macaroni
3 tomatoes, skinned, seeded and diced
2 ounces spinach leaves
1 tablespoon chopped parsley
1½ cups Parmesan or Romano cheese

Heat the butter and oil in a deep heavy pan. Add the diced ham and pork with all the fat removed and cook over low heat for 5 to 6 minutes. Add the diced onion, carrot, celery and garlic. Cook slowly, covered, for 10 minutes. Add peas and cabbage and stir in the tomato paste. Pour on water and bring to a boil. Season with salt and pepper, add macaroni and simmer very slowly until all ingredients are tender. Add tomatoes and heat through. Cut spinach leaves into coarse shreds and add to the soup at the last minute, with the chopped parsley, so they are just wilted but not cooked. Serve in a large soup tureen accompanied by a big bowl of grated cheese. Serves 4-6.

*Note:* Minestrone requires one pasta, one starch vegetable and one leaf vegetable.

You may substitute rice for macaroni, beans for peas if you wish.

## Green Potage

¼ cup sliced scallions
⅓ cup butter
2 cups diced raw potatoes
1 teaspoon salt
2 cups chicken broth
½ bunch water cress
1 cup spinach leaves, lightly packed
2 cups lettuce, torn into small pieces
Chopped chives or
Sour cream and paprika

Cook scallions in butter for about 5 minutes over moderate heat, stirring frequently. Add potatoes, salt, and chicken broth. Bring to boil and cook, covered, for 10 minutes. Add the water cress in coarse pieces, spinach leaves, and the torn up lettuce. Continue cooking until potatoes are tender, about 5 minutes longer. Strain off about 1 cup of broth. Place vegetables and remaining broth in blender. Cover container and turn on blender. Blend until smooth, add remaining broth and reheat. Serve garnished with chopped chives, or sour cream sprinkled with paprika. Serves 4.

## Helvetia Soup

1 cup chopped onion
⅓ cup butter
6 cups finely diced dry bread
6 cups rich chicken stock
2 egg yolks
1 cup cream
1½ cups grated Swiss cheese
Salt, white pepper
Grated nutmeg

Cook the onion in butter until lightly colored. Add diced bread and allow to brown, then pour in chicken stock. Simmer 8 or 10 minutes, and mix in an electric blender

or force through a sieve. Combine the egg yolks, cream and cheese and add. Season to taste with salt, pepper and nutmeg, and heat gently before serving. (This soup may be thinned with chicken stock or milk, if desired.) Serves 8-10.

## Vichyssoise

4 large potatoes, peeled and sliced
6 small white leeks, peeled and sliced
4 stalks celery, sliced
1 onion, peeled and sliced
1 cup water
Salt, cayenne pepper
1½ cups strong chicken stock
2 cups light cream
2 tablespoons finely chopped fresh chives
        or
2 tablespoons finely shredded cooked
    carrots and 2 tablespoons red caviar

Put the potatoes, leeks, celery, and onion into a pan with the water, salt and pepper. Cover and cook very slowly until quite soft. Stir in the stock and add a little extra seasoning. Stir over the fire until it comes to a boil, rub first through a coarse strainer and then through a very fine strainer. Chill until ice cold in the refrigerator, add the cream and garnish with either the chives or the carrots and caviar. Serve in individual bowls surrounded by crushed ice. Serves 4.

## Iced Cucumber and Mint Soup

4 cucumbers
1 small bunch scallions
3 cups water
Salt, pepper, cayenne pepper
6 tablespoons flour
3 tablespoons chopped fresh mint
1½ cups light cream

Peel the cucumbers. Reserve half a cucumber. Thinly slice the rest. Finely slice the scallions and put them into a pan with the sliced cucumbers and water to cover. Season with salt and pepper and cook very slowly until quite soft. Blend the flour with a little water, add to the cucumbers and scallions and stir in the rest of the water. Season with a little more salt and cayenne pepper and stir over the fire until the mixture comes to a boil. Rub through a very fine strainer. Put in a cold pan or bowl; add the mint; stir over a bowl of crushed ice until very cold. Stir in the cream and garnish with the reserved cucumber which has been blanched, shredded and well drained. Serve in small bowls placed in crushed ice. Garnish with a little more freshly chopped mint just before serving. Serves 4.

## Iced Broccoli Soup

4 tablespoons vegetable oil
½ cup finely chopped onion
½ cup finely chopped celery
Salt, black cracked pepper
4 tablespoons flour
1 bunch broccoli
3 cups chicken stock
2 cups light cream
1 tablespoon finely chopped chives
1 teaspoon finely chopped fresh rosemary
    or ½ teaspoon crushed dried rosemary

Gently heat the oil; add the onion and celery and cook slowly for 2 or 3 minutes.

43

Season with salt and pepper. Stir in the flour off the fire. Cut the broccoli into pieces, put into boiling water, off the fire, for 10 minutes. Drain and cook until tender in the chicken stock. Add this to the onion-celery mixture and bring to a boil. Rub through a fine strainer, cool in the refrigerator. Add the light cream and serve garnished with chives and rosemary. Serves 4.

## Iced Pea and Curry Soup

### (Potage Singhalese)

*2 cups shelled peas*
*1 cup water*
*2 tablespoons rice flour*
*2 cups beef stock*
*Salt, cayenne pepper*
*½ cup finely chopped onion*
*¼ cup finely chopped carrot*
*¼ cup finely chopped celery*
*1 tablespoon Indian curry powder*
*1 cup light cream*
*1 cup heavy cream*
*¼ cup finely chopped green pepper*
*¼ cup finely chopped red pepper*

Put the peas in a pan with the water; season and cook slowly until just soft, being careful not to allow them to lose their fresh green color. Mix the rice flour with a little beef stock, add to the peas, season with salt and cayenne. Add remaining stock, onion, carrot, celery and stir over the fire until the mixture comes to a boil. Simmer gently until the vegetables are very soft. Rub through a very fine strainer. Put the curry powder in a mortar with a few drops of light cream, salt and pepper, and grind with the pestle until very smooth. Add this to the soup and chill until ice cold in the refrigerator. Mix in the remaining light cream, whip the heavy cream and blend in. Garnish with the finely chopped red and green pepper. Serve in metal bowls surrounded by crushed ice. Serves 4.

## Greek Lemon Soup

### (Soupe Agholemono)

*⅓ cup rice*
*6 cups chicken stock*
*4 egg yolks*
*Grated rind and juice of two lemons*
*1 cup sour cream*
*Salt, cayenne pepper*
*1 cup light cream*
*1 cup whipped cream*
*Paprika*

Wash the rice in a little water to remove all excess starch and drain thoroughly. Add the rice slowly to the chicken stock and cook for 30 minutes until the rice is very soft. Rub through a fine strainer. Beat the egg yolks thoroughly with the grated rind of one lemon. Slowly add the juice of two lemons. Mix in the sour cream and slowly pour on the hot soup, making sure the liquid does not curdle. Season and stir over a slow fire until the soup coats the back of a wooden spoon. Chill thoroughly. Stir in the light cream. Serve in individual bowls surrounded by crushed ice. Put a tablespoon of whipped cream on the top of each and garnish with the remaining lemon rind and a little paprika. Serves 4.

## Iced Tomato and Mint Soup

*2 tablespoons vegetable oil*
*1 onion, finely chopped*
*1 clove garlic, finely chopped*
*1 small bunch scallions, chopped*

*Salt, freshly cracked black pepper*
*6 large ripe tomatoes,*
  *sliced with skins on*
*1 tablespoon tomato paste*
*5 level tablespoons flour*
*3 cups chicken stock*
*1 cup light cream*
*2 small skinned tomatoes*
*2 tablespoons fresh chopped mint*

Heat the vegetable oil a little in a heavy pan. Add the chopped onion and garlic and cook for a few minutes. Add the chopped scallions. Add salt, pepper and the six sliced tomatoes. Cover and cook slowly for seven or eight minutes. Remove from heat and stir in the tomato paste and the flour. Pour on the chicken stock and stir over the fire until it comes to a boil. Simmer for 10 minutes. Rub through a fine strainer. Simmer for three minutes. Add 1 tablespoon chopped mint. Chill until very cold in the refrigerator. (The soup will keep in the refrigerator for several days in this state.) Just before serving, stir in the light cream and the skinned tomatoes, seeded and cut into fine shreds, and the remaining chopped mint. Serve the soup in bowls, surrounded by crushed ice. Serves 4.

## Iced Garlic Soup
### (Tourain à l'Ail)

*12 small cloves garlic*
*1 teaspoon salt*
*1 tablespoon butter*
*2 tablespoons olive oil*
*4 cups strong chicken stock.*
*Salt, cayenne pepper*
*3 egg yolks*
*1 cup heavy cream*
*Grated nutmeg*
*2 teaspoons finely chopped chives*

Peel the garlic and chop very fine with the salt. Heat the butter and oil in the bottom of a heavy soup pan. Add garlic and

cook slowly until a golden brown, but not too brown. Pour on the chicken stock. Add salt and pepper to taste. Bring slowly to a boil and simmer for 30 to 40 minutes. Strain through fine cheese cloth onto the well beaten egg yolks. Stir over a slow fire until the soup thickens but does not boil. Chill. Stir in the cream. Serve in small bowls surrounded by crushed ice. Sprinkle the top with nutmeg and chopped chives. Serve Melba toast separately. Serves 4-6.

## Gazpacho
### (Iced Vegetable Soup)

*2 green peppers*
*1 red pepper*
*1 Bermuda onion*
*2 small carrots*
*1 small stalk celery*
*1 cucumber*
*1 large brine-pickled cucumber*
*1 teaspoon salt, ½ teaspoon black pepper*
*¼ teaspoon cinnamon*
*2 teaspoons sugar*
*2 small cloves garlic*
*¼ cup olive oil*
*4 tomatoes, skinned, seeded and quartered*
*1 teaspoon tomato paste*
*½ teaspoon meat glaze*
*24 ice cubes*
*1 cup rough red wine*
*1 cup coarse bread crumbs*
*2 tablespoons chopped parsley*
*10 radishes*
*1 cup grated Parmesan cheese*

Prepare and cut into small even dice one green pepper, the red pepper, onion, carrots, celery, cucumber and pickled cucumber. Place vegetables in the bottom of a deep, earthenware crock and sprinkle with the salt, pepper, cinnamon and sugar. Finely chop the garlic and heat gently in half the olive oil for a few minutes. Pour over the vegetables, cover the crock and marinate overnight. Rub the tomatoes through a fine strainer and mix the puréed pulp with the tomato paste and meat glaze Pour this over the ice cubes with the red wine and let stand in refrigerator until the ice has melted. Add to the marinated vegetables. Serve in small glass bowls surrounded by cracked ice. Serve separately side dishes of bread crumbs, fried until golden brown with the remaining oil and mixed with the parsley; thinly sliced radishes sprinkled with a little salt and sugar and mixed with the remaining green pepper, finely diced; and grated cheese. This soup is better if allowed to stand 36 hours before serving. Serves 4.

## Minted Jellied Boysenberry Soup

*1 quart boysenberries*
*¼ cup brown sugar*
*1 quart sauterne*
*Salt*
*1" stick cinnamon*
*3 whole cloves*
*4 fresh mint leaves, chopped*
*1 envelope gelatin*
*⅓ cup cold water*
*Whole mint leaves*

Wash the boysenberries and pick them over well. Drain, and crush lightly with a potato masher. Stir in the brown sugar and sauterne. Carefully bring to a boil. Season with salt, cinnamon, cloves and coarsely chopped mint leaves. Bring slowly to a boil, remove and strain. Dissolve gelatin in cold water. Stir the soup into the gelatin. Chill until barely set. Serve in clear crystal glasses and garnish each with a mint leaf. Serves 4.

## Jellied Tomato Soup

*2 cups tomato juice*
*1 onion, chopped*
*¼ cup chopped celery*
*½ teaspoon celery seed*
*1 cup canned consommé*
*1 bay leaf*
*1 tablespoon gelatin*
*¼ cup cold water*
*1 tablespoon lemon juice*
*⅛ teaspoon Tabasco sauce*

Combine the tomato juice, onion, celery, celery seed, consommé and bay leaf in a saucepan. Bring to a boil and cook over low heat 10 minutes. Strain. Soften the gelatin in the water; add hot tomato mixture, stirring until dissolved. Add lemon juice and Tabasco. Mix. Chill until firm. Serves 4.

## Cream of Sorrel Soup

*1 pound sorrel (sour grass)*
*6 cups chicken stock (fresh or canned)*
*2 teaspoons salt*
*Dash of nutmeg*
*2 egg yolks*
*2 cups light cream*

Wash the sorrel thoroughly in several changes of water. Cut off the stems. Break the leaves into thirds. Combine the sorrel, stock, salt and nutmeg in a saucepan. Bring to a boil and cook over low heat for 30 minutes. Force through a sieve or purée in an electric blender. Beat the egg yolks and cream together. Gradually add the sorrel purée, mixing steadily to prevent curdling. Serve very cold with a dab of whipped cream, if desired. Serves 8.
*Note:* To make larger amounts for freezing, prepare just the sorrel mixture. The day before it is to be served, heat and combine with the eggs and cream. Chill again.

EGG and CHEESE

# Egg and Cheese

The ubiquitous egg is a cook's best friend. There is the egg that binds, the egg that enriches, the egg that gives substance to a sauce and the egg that gives a soufflé its splendor. Apart from the egg's protean ability to combine with other foods it is—dressed in different ways—a meal in itself, as nutritious as a steak and at a fraction of the cost. For centuries, the creators of truly great dishes have devoted a large measure of their inventiveness and artistry to the ennoblement of the egg's unique flavor and consistency. But it takes an uncommon cook to do justice to the common egg. There are few abominations to equal an egg scrambled or fried to tough tastelessness. *Chefs de cuisine* of eminence have long considered the egg a worthy companion to the most sophisticated foods, fit to crown with a Madeira sauce, to be poached in Burgundy, to recline on a purée of chestnuts or to be covered with foie gras.

Another humble food capable of being served in the most exotic and exciting variety is cheese, amongst whose historic and fictional admirers was Zoroaster, the Persian mystic of 600 B.C. He lived on nothing but cheese for thirty years in the belief that it would ward off old age. The Greeks trained their Olympic athletes on cheese, averring it had been invented by the son of Apollo and so had divine powers. Actually, the origin of cheese was more mundane than miraculous.

Wherever there were milk-giving animals (sheep, cows, goats, camels, even yaks, reindeer and water buffaloes) tame enough to submit to man's pilferage, there was some form of cheese, the by-product of curdled milk. More esoteric cheeses were the result of accident or experiment. Roquefort cheese, made from ewe's milk by the monks of Conques as early as 1070, is said to have been the inspired blunder of a shepherd boy who left his cheese sandwich in a cool, humid limestone cave and found it, months later, green with mold and ripely flavored. Camembert was the invention of Madame Harel, a

48

Normandy innkeeper. It earned her a kiss from Napoleon and a statue in her native town. Cheese-making once flourished in the dairies and kitchens of Europe and America, but now it is big business all over the world. The bewildering array of contemporary cheeses (there are over 500) and the ways in which they may be eaten, cooked and uncooked, often daunts the novice.

Cheeses can be divided into six main categories: hard; semi-soft smooth; semi-soft crumbly; firm; soft and ripened; fresh and soft. Hard cheeses such as Parmesan are mostly grated for cooking. Semi-soft smooth cheeses—Port du Salut, Taleggio, Münster—are eaten with fruit at the end of a meal, or with beer as a snack. Crumbly cheeses, the blue-veined Roquefort, for example, are fine eating and give a tang to salad dressings and canapé spreads. Firm cheeses with a definite but not overriding flavor—Swiss, Cheddar—are the heart of cheese soufflés and entrées, as well as good to eat alone. The soft, ripened cheeses—Brie, Liederkranz, Camembert—are the strongest. Soft, fresh cheeses—cottage cheese, ricotta, cream cheese, mozzarella—have a short life and a creamy blandness that blends smoothly with cooked desserts and entrées. All cheeses to be eaten in their natural state (except cream and cottage) taste best when they have been allowed to stand at room temperature for two or three hours. No one need be a stranger to the delights of cheese. There is one to suit every palate and preference. Like the robust character in *The Merry Wives of Windsor*, we can enjoy the delightful prospect of the perfect end to dinner: "There's pippins and cheese to come."

49

## Boiled Eggs

There are several methods for the seemingly simple matter of boiling an egg. When saving time is no consideration, and tender, delicate eggs are needed, the following method is excellent:

Boil one quart of water. Plunge in six very fresh eggs and leave for five to eight minutes without boiling. The eggs will lower the temperature of the water and bring it to about 180 degrees, that is 30 degrees lower than the boiling point. The white will then be of a creamy consistency, more apt to blend with the yolk and much easier to digest. Another method of boiling eggs is to put them in a sufficient quantity of water to cover and bring the water to a boil. The eggs are then ready to serve.

## Eggs Mollet

Eggs mollet should be properly classified as soft-boiled eggs. In preparing them, it is again absolutely necessary that the eggs be fresh. Plunge them into boiling water, draw the pan aside, and leave for eight minutes without boiling. Plunge into ice water for two minutes, after which the shell may be easily removed without damaging or breaking the egg inside. Put the egg back in water or broth until ready to serve or until added to other ingredients in a recipe.

## Brandade d'Oeufs Mollet

*6 eggs mollet*
*1 lb. fresh cod*
*1½ cups olive oil*
*4 large cloves garlic, crushed*
*¾ cup boiled milk*
*Salt, freshly cracked pepper*
*½ cup clarified butter*
*1 tbsp. freshly chopped chives*
*6 tbsp. whipped cream*
*6 slices white bread*

Season the cod with salt and pepper and steam between two plates for about 30 minutes or until quite cooked. Then skin. bone and flake roughly with a fork. Put in a heavy pan with ¼ cup olive oil and the crushed cloves of garlic. Stir briskly with a spoon until well crushed and smooth, adding the rest of the oil slowly, tablespoon by tablespoon. After having added 6 tbsp. of oil, add 3 tbsp. of boiled milk. Continue adding oil and milk until the fish is the consistency of light mashed potato. Then correct the seasoning, being a little heavy handed on the pepper. Arrange down the center of a hot, flat serving dish in the form of a bed. Make six indentations in the center. Put a teaspoon of clarified butter and one egg mollet in each indentation. Mix the chives and the rest of the clarified butter and coat the eggs with this mixture. Put 1 tbsp. of whipped cream on top of each egg and place under a very hot broiler just to scorch the cream. Then remove the crusts from the slices of bread and cut in half diagonally. Fry in the rest of the olive oil until golden brown on each side. Surround dish with fried bread.

## Oeufs Mollet en Surprise

*6 eggs mollet*
*6 tbsp. salt butter*
*3 tbsp. flour*
*¾ cup milk*
*1 tsp. French mustard*
*Salt, cayenne pepper*

¾ *cup grated Gruyère cheese*
½ *cup grated Parmesan cheese*
*4 eggs, separated*
¼ *cup buttered bread crumbs*
*3 oz. firm white mushrooms*
*Few drops lemon juice*
*6 slices ham*
*2 tsp. freshly chopped parsley*
*2 tsp. freshly chopped dill*
*6 tbsp. sour cream*
*1 egg white*

Melt half the butter. Stir in the flour, off the fire. Pour on the milk and stir over the fire until it thickens. Then stir in French mustard, salt, pepper, Gruyère cheese, half the Parmesan cheese and the egg yolks. Beat well together. Fold in the stiffly beaten egg whites. Butter a shallow ovenproof glass baking dish, dust with a few buttered bread crumbs and a little Parmesan cheese. Half fill with the soufflé mixture. Make six indentations with the back of a wet spoon. Slice the white mushrooms and sauté them briskly in half the remaining butter with salt, pepper and lemon juice. Divide them and put equal amounts in each indentation. Wrap the eggs mollet in thin slices of ham and place them on top of the mushrooms. Mix the herbs with the sour cream; season, and put a spoonful on top of each egg wrapped in ham. Cover with the rest of the soufflé mixture, sprinkle the top with the rest of the buttered bread crumbs and Parmesan cheese and sprinkle the top with the rest of the butter, melted. Bake briskly in a 375° oven for 15 minutes. Remove from the oven and serve at once.

## Hard-boiled Eggs

In order that eggs should be properly hard boiled, they should be put into boiling water and allowed to remain there for ten minutes only and then cooled off right away in cold water. If cooked longer than ten minutes, the yolk acquires a greenish tinge on the outside and the white will expel a very unpleasant odor. Very few people are aware that eggs which are cooked and cooled off and then found to be not sufficiently done cannot be cooked any more if put back into boiling water. Hard-boiled eggs can be kept a long time in a cool place if they remain in their shell, but if shelled they should be rubbed with a weak solution of lemon juice and water and used as soon as possible.

## Mixed Hard-boiled Egg Salad

*6 hard-boiled eggs*
½ *lb. sweet butter*
*6 oz. cream cheese*
*2 tbsp. tomato paste*
*Salt, cayenne pepper*
*1 cup white tuna fish*
*1 cup diced cooked green beans*
*1 cup diced cooked carrots*
*1 cup diced skinned cucumber*
*1 cup diced skinned and pitted tomato*
*4 cups boiled rice*
½ *cup vegetable oil*
*2 tbsp. tarragon vinegar*
*2 tsp. salt*
½ *tsp. lemon juice*
*1 whole beaten egg*
*1 bunch watercress*
*3 small gherkins*
*A little pimiento*

Shell the eggs, cut in half lengthwise. Carefully remove the yolks and place the whites in a bowl of cold, clear water. Rub the egg yolks through a strainer. Beat the sweet butter until light and fluffy. Add the egg yolks and continue beating for a few moments. Divide the mixture in half and add to one half the beaten cream cheese and the tomato paste. Season with salt and pepper and set aside. Rub the tuna fish through a strainer and mix with the other half of the egg mixture. Season and set aside. Mix all the diced vegetables lightly and carefully with the rice. Put into a screw-top jar the oil, vinegar, salt, pepper, lemon juice and beaten egg. Shake well and mix into the rice. Arrange in a large salad bowl and make a hole in the center. Fill the hole with the watercress. Place around the edge the drained hard-boiled egg whites and fill them alternately with the tuna fish mixture and the cream cheese mixture, using for one a pastry bag with a large plain tube and for the other a pastry bag with a rose tube. Decorate the tops with the sliced gherkins and pimientos and serve.

## Oeufs à la Tripe

6 hard-boiled eggs
4 large Bermuda onions
4 oz. butter
¼ cup olive oil
3 tbsp. chopped fresh parsley
4 tbsp. flour
1 cup milk
½ cup grated Gruyère cheese
2 tsp. dry mustard
¼ cup light cream
Salt, cayenne pepper

Skin the onions; cut in half and then in thin slivers. Plunge them into boiling water for a minute or two. Drain well. Sauté them in olive oil and half the butter until soft but not brown. Shell the eggs, remove the egg yolks and put them through a coarse strainer. Cut the egg white into thin slices and mix with the strained hard-boiled egg yolks. Grease a shallow baking dish. Put a layer of onions, a layer of egg, a sprinkling of parsley, then another layer of onions, egg, parsley, until the dish is full. Pour over the following sauce. Melt 4 tablespoons of butter in a pan. Stir in the flour off the fire. Season with salt, pepper and mustard. Pour on the milk and stir over the fire until the

mixture comes to a boil. Then add the grated cheese and, bit by bit, the rest of the butter. Add the cream and simmer 5 minutes. When the egg dish has been well coated with this sauce, sprinkle with a little more butter and brown quickly under the broiler just before serving.

## Oeufs Carême

6 hard-boiled eggs
6 cooked artichoke bottoms
3 truffles
¼ lb. of foie gras
¼ lb. firm white mushrooms
¼ lb. butter
2 tsp. lemon juice
Salt, freshly cracked pepper
1 tsp. freshly chopped tarragon

Shell the hard-boiled eggs and cut each one into 6 even wedges. Cut the artichoke bottoms into 6 slices. Dice the truffles. Allow the foie gras to get well chilled, then cut into thick dice. Slice the mushrooms thickly and sauté briskly in the butter, lemon juice and seasonings. Carefully mix all these ingredients together and arrange in the bottom of an au gratin dish. Cover with a piece of greased waxed paper and keep warm.

### Bercy Sauce

2 tbsp. salt butter
2 tbsp. finely chopped shallots
1 cup dry white wine
¾ cup strong chicken stock
1 tsp. finely chopped tarragon
1 tsp. finely chopped parsley
3 level tbsp. flour mixed into
4 tbsp. sweet butter
Salt, freshly cracked pepper

Melt the salt butter. Add the finely chopped shallots and cook very slowly until soft but not brown. Pour on the dry white wine and chicken stock and add the herbs. Season with salt and pepper and stir over a slow fire until the mixture comes to a boil. Stir in the combined flour and butter bit by bit. Reboil. Simmer 10 minutes. Remove waxed paper from the egg dish, pour the sauce over and serve at once.

## Oeufs Durs Boulangère

(Hot French sandwich to serve 3 people)

*6 hard-boiled eggs*
*6 small French rolls*
*½ cup diced boiled tongue*
*½ cup diced smoked ham*
*2 tsps. chopped garlic*
*2 tbsp. chopped fresh chives*
*½ cup drawn butter*
*2 tbsp. chopped fresh parsley*
*½ cup sour cream*
*1 tbsp. French mustard*
*Salt, freshly cracked pepper*
*A little hot olive oil*

Cut a thin slice off each end of the rolls and very carefully remove all the white part. Pour a little melted butter through each roll. Shell the hard-boiled eggs and chop them up coarsely. Mix with the ham and tongue. Add the chopped garlic to the rest of the hot butter, stir for a few moments. Then add parsley, chives, sour cream, French mustard, salt and freshly cracked pepper. Mix this into the chopped hard-boiled egg mixture and stuff each roll well with this filling. Brush all over the outside of the rolls with hot olive oil. Roll up in sheets of aluminum foil and bake 10 minutes in a 350° oven. Serve piping hot individually wrapped in a starched napkin.

## Scrambled Eggs

For a dish of scrambled eggs to be at its best, it should be served immediately after leaving the hands of the cook, as in that form eggs tend to deteriorate rapidly in taste and quality.

Some cooks use cream or cream sauce to keep scrambled eggs in condition for a reasonable period of time. I do not recommend the use of sauce unless it is absolutely necessary; cream or water is much more satisfactory. The most important point is never, on any account, to overcook the eggs. This general recipe will give satisfaction if the directions are strictly followed.

Butter a sauté pan liberally. Put into it six well beaten eggs. Season with salt and pepper and put on the fire. Keep stirring constantly with a whisk or a wooden spoon until the eggs become cream-like in consistency. Then add two more ounces of good sweet butter and if the eggs can't be served immediately, add heavy cream, approximately 1 tablespoon to every two eggs, or 1 teaspoonful of cold water for each egg before cooking.

## Scrambled Eggs August

*6 eggs, scrambled*
*4 cups cooked peas*
*2 cups sliced mushrooms, sautéed in butter,*
*  lemon juice, seasonings*
*1 cup finely shredded smoked beef*
*½ cup melted butter*
*Salt, pepper*
*Finely chopped hard boiled egg yolk*
*Finely chopped fresh parsley*
*Large croutons of fried bread*

Lightly mix the peas, mushrooms and beef together with the melted butter and seasonings. Half fill one side of a shallow, hot *au gratin* dish with this mixture. Fill the other side with the scrambled eggs. Sprinkle the top of the scrambled eggs with the parsley and the top of the pea mixture with the hard-boiled egg yolk. Surround with the croutons of fried bread and serve.

## Scrambled Eggs Turbigo

6 eggs, scrambled
6 small brioches
2 ounces salt butter
6 lamb kidneys
A little chopped garlic
6 mushroom caps
1 tsp. tomato paste
¼ cup chopped shallots
1 cup red wine
½ cup beef stock
2 tsp. potato flour
1 tsp. meat glaze
Salt, pepper
A little freshly chopped parsley

Carefully remove the caps of the brioches and take out all the soft part. Pour a teaspoon of melted butter in the bottom of each and wrap them individually in aluminum foil. Heat for 5 minutes in a 350° oven. Skin the kidneys; split down the middle and remove white core. Brown them very quickly in hot butter with the garlic and shallots. Remove the kidneys and brown the mushrooms quickly in the same butter. Remove mushrooms and stir into the same pan tomato paste, meat glaze, potato flour. Pour on the red wine and the stock and stir over the fire until it comes to a boil. Simmer 5 minutes. Remove brioches from oven and take them out of foil. Fill them with the scrambled eggs. Place on top of each a mushroom cap. Place on top of each mushroom cap a kidney. Cover with the tops of the brioches. Arrange on a hot serving dish. Just before serving pour over the sauce, sprinkle with parsley and serve.

## Scrambled Eggs Française

6 eggs, scrambled
6 large artichoke bottoms
½ cup chicken stock
½ cup sautéed mushrooms
2 shredded truffles
½ cup grated Gruyère cheese
4 tbsp. melted butter
¼ cup grated Parmesan cheese

### Brown Sauce

2 tbsp. butter
1 tsp. potato flour
2 tbsp. meat glaze
1 tsp. tomato paste
½ cup red wine

½ *cup chicken stock*
*A little pepper*

Heat the artichoke bottoms in the chicken stock; drain and arrange them down a long flat serving dish. Mix mushrooms, truffles, Gruyère cheese and butter with scrambled eggs. Fill artichoke bottoms with this mixture; sprinkle tops with Parmesan cheese. Pour over each a little melted butter and brown quickly under the broiler. Pour around the dish the following brown sauce. Melt butter, stir in potato flour, meat glaze, tomato paste. Pour on wine and stock and stir over fire until it comes to a boil. Season with pepper, simmer five minutes before pouring around the dish.

## Eggs en Cocotte

Eggs *en cocotte* are prepared in much the same way as eggs cooked in timbales with the exception that the eggs are not turned out. The cocottes should be made of fine porcelain or earthenware, preferably with little handles attached, and set in a water bath for cooking. Cooking time is from 6 to 10 minutes, according to the heat and preparation. If the cocottes are lined with force-meat, the cooking time should be lengthened accordingly to allow for this.

## Eggs Cocotte Lorraine

*6 fresh eggs*
*3 slices bacon*
*3 thin slices Gruyère cheese, halved*
*1 cup heavy cream*
*Salt, freshly cracked pepper*

Cut the bacon into very thin dice and fry lightly until crisp. Drain. Divide bacon and put in bottom of 6 little cocottes. Then line each dish with a thin slice of Gruyère. Put a spoonful of heavy cream on top of the Gruyere and break a fresh egg on top of the cream. Pour another spoonful of cream on top of the egg and season with salt and freshly cracked black pepper. Bake in a 350° oven for 6 minutes or until just set.

## Eggs Cocotte Sagan

*6 fresh eggs*
*2 pairs of calves' brains*
*A little chicken stock*
*½ cup heavy cream*
*2 oz. butter, melted*
*¼ cup grated Parmesan cheese*
*Salt, black pepper*

Simmer the calves' brains in a little chicken stock for 10 minutes. Drain and chill. Cut in squares and mix with half the cream and half the melted butter. Season with salt and pepper and half fill 6 cocottes with this mixture. Break a fresh egg on the top of each. Season with salt and freshly cracked pepper. Pour over each the rest of the cream. Sprinkle with grated Parmesan cheese, a little melted butter, and bake 6 minutes in a 350° oven.

## Shirred Eggs

Shirred eggs are cooked and served in small china dishes especially made for the purpose. Butter the dish lightly and break into it either three or four eggs. Pour a little hot melted butter over the yolks and cook in a slow oven for a few moments until the yolks look as though they are covered with a veil. The seasoning, if no sauce accompanies the eggs, should be left to the eater, as salt and pepper would destroy their beauty.

## Shirred Eggs Bretonne

*6 fresh eggs*
*2 cups baby white onions*
*2 oz. butter*
*1 cup sliced sautéed mushrooms*
*½ cup heavy cream*
*Salt, freshly cracked pepper*

Blanch the baby white onions which should be very small, about the size of a large pea. Drain them and sauté in the butter with salt and pepper until soft and a little brown. Mix the sautéed mushrooms with the onions and cover the bottom of a large shirred egg dish. Make 6 hollows in the mixture and break an egg in each. Pour over the cream and cook 8 minutes in a 300° oven. Remove and season at the table.

## Shirred Eggs à la Greque

6 fresh eggs
Rind of large orange
3 oz. butter
1 clove garlic, finely chopped
1 large blanched potato
2 medium-sized onions
1 green pepper
1 red pepper
1 very small eggplant
2 tbsp. olive oil
4 firm white mushrooms
2 large, skinned tomatoes
Salt, pepper

Cut orange rind into fine shreds. Melt half the butter and add the orange rind with the finely chopped garlic. Cook slowly 2 minutes. Add blanched potato cut into dice. Cook another 3 minutes. Add the onions cut into large dice. Cook another 2 minutes. Add the green and red peppers cut into large dice and cook another 2 minutes. Add the eggplant, salted, diced and sautéed in the oil. Then add the mushrooms, sliced

and sautéed in the remaining butter. Lastly, add the diced, skinned tomatoes. Season this mixture with salt and pepper and arrange on the bottom of a large shirred egg dish. Make 6 indentations and place an egg in each. Bake 6 minutes in a 350° oven and serve them at once.

## Shirred Eggs Bock

6 shirred eggs
1 oz. butter
1 chopped clove garlic
2 tbsp. finely chopped shallots
6 small, skinned tomatoes
6 slices broiled bacon
Salt, freshly cracked black pepper

Heat butter in a pan. Add garlic and chopped shallots and cook briskly 2 minutes. Cut the tomatoes in thick slices, add and season with salt and pepper, cook briskly for 3 minutes. Cover the eggs with this mixture and garnish the top with the broiled slices of bacon.

## Eggs in Nests

2 eggs
½ teaspoon salt
⅛ teaspoon pepper
⅛ teaspoon paprika
1 teaspoon chopped parsley

Carefully separate the eggs. Beat the whites until stiff and pile into a buttered baking dish. Make two depressions in the egg white and carefully slide one yolk into each. Sprinkle with the salt, pepper and paprika.

Bake 10 minutes in a preheated 350° oven, or until yolks are set and whites delicately browned. Sprinkle with the parsley.

## Eggs Florentine

Put cooked spinach in the bottom of a baking dish and make little hollows in it. Slip raw eggs into hollows, cover with sauce Mornay (see recipe under Sauces), sprinkle with cheese, and bake until the eggs are set.

## Poached Eggs

Poached eggs are merely eggs cooked in water without the shell. The most important requisite is that the egg be fresh. A stale egg will never poach well. There are two methods of poaching eggs. The first method is to fill a deep pan three-quarters full of water and add a teaspoon of salt and a tablespoon of tarragon vinegar for each quart of water. Turn down the heat and allow to simmer gently. Stir with a spoon to make a whirlpool, slide in the shelled egg. Simmer for 3½ minutes, remove at once and put into a bowl of warm or cold clear water with a little lemon juice, depending on whether you plan to use the eggs hot or cold. The second method is to stand the lightly greased poaching bowl in a pan of shallow hot water. Break the eggs into each mold and simmer gently for 3½ minutes. The first method is the best as the yolks should be surrounded by the whites.

## Oeufs Pochés à l'Estragon

*6 poached eggs, cold*
*6 cups clear chicken stock*
*½ cup dry sherry*
*2 tbsp. brandy*
*2 tbsp. tomato paste*
*6 tbsp. plain gelatin*
*3 beaten egg whites*
*¼ cup fresh tarragon leaves*

Rinse out a ring mold in cold water and set in refrigerator to chill. Put the stock, sherry, brandy, tomato paste, gelatin and egg whites into a pan. Beat over the fire until the mixture comes to a boil, draw aside and leave for 15 minutes. Pour through a damp cloth. Half fill the ring mold with this aspic when on the point of setting. Decorate the top of the aspic with the tarragon leaves and arrange the cold, dry poached eggs on the top, evenly spaced. Cover with more of the aspic and put to set in the refrigerator. Take also 6 baby timbale molds and half fill them with aspic on the point of setting. Put several tarragon leaves on top of the aspic and fill up the little molds with the rest of the aspic. Put to set in the refrigerator. Turn out the large mold in the center of a flat silver dish. Turn out the little molds and arrange around the edge of the dish. Serve very cold.

## Oeufs Pochés Georgette

*6 poached eggs*
*6 small baked potatoes*
*2 cups whipped potatoes*
*A little beaten egg*
*Lump of butter*
*Salt, cayenne pepper*
*1 cup sliced cooked shrimps*
*1 tbsp. finely chopped parsley*
*4 oz. butter*
*4 tbsp. flour*
*1 cup milk*
*3 tbsp. light cream*
*1 cup grated Parmesan cheese*

Carefully cut the tops off the small baked potatoes. Remove all the potato without breaking the skin. Rub the potato through a strainer and mix it with the whipped potato. Mix in a little beaten egg, a lump of butter, salt and cayenne pepper. Put mixture into a large pastry bag with a large rose tube. Pipe six small rosettes, evenly spaced, on the bottom of a flat serving dish. Anchor a potato skin on the top of each rosette. Mix the chopped parsley with the sliced cooked shrimps. Melt half the butter in a pan; stir in the flour, off the fire; season with salt, pepper, and pour on the milk. Stir over the fire until mixture comes to a boil. Then add the grated cheese and the cream. Simmer slowly 5 minutes. Put a spoonful of the shrimp and sauce mixture

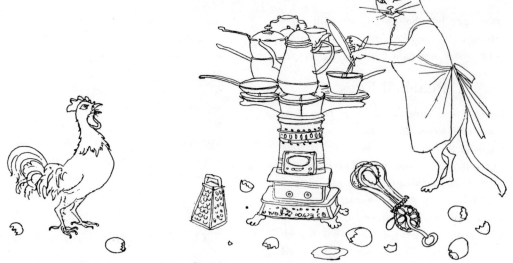

in the bottom of each potato skin; place a poached egg on top; cover the poached egg with a little more sauce. Top with potato cap and cover the cap completely with the mashed potato forced through the rose tube of the pastry bag. Sprinkle a little beaten egg over the top and brown quickly under the broiler before serving.

## Macédoine d'Oeufs Pochés Mayonnaise

*6 poached eggs, cold*
*1 cup diced cooked green beans*
*1 cup small cooked lima beans*
*1 cup diced cooked carrots*
*1 cup cooked peas*
*1 cup diced cooked turnips*
*1 cup diced raw cucumber*
*1 cup diced, skinned and seeded tomatoes*
*Squeeze of lemon juice*
*Salt, freshly cracked pepper*
*3 egg yolks*
*1 tsp. French mustard*
*Salt, cayenne pepper*
*2 tbsp. tarragon vinegar*
*2 cups vegetable oil*
*½ cup light cream*
*A few sprigs fresh watercress*

Mix all the vegetables together lightly with two forks. Season with salt, pepper and lemon juice. Arrange them on the bottom of a shallow, ovenproof dish. Carefully place the drained cold poached eggs on top. Pour over the following mayonnaise sauce. Put the egg yolks in a bowl with salt, cayenne pepper and mustard. Beat until light and very fluffy. Mix in vinegar and slowly add, drop by drop, the oil. Lastly, add the ½ cup light cream and, if necessary, a little more. The sauce should be a thick, pourable consistency. Pour it over the eggs and garnish the top of each with watercress.

## Eggs Molded in Timbales

The term *timbale* in cookery is properly applied to anything having the shape of a small goblet. However, today many molds of different shapes are termed timbales. Eggs molded in timbales require the same treatment as eggs in cocottes or eggs in cases with one difference: they are not served in the molds but are turned out upon the dish or plate in the form of the mold. Eggs prepared in this manner should always be cooked in a water bath. The greased, filled molds are set in a pan and hot water added until it reaches halfway up the side of the mold. The eggs are then poached in the oven until they are done.

## Oeufs en Timbale Cardinal

*6 fresh eggs*
*½ cup lobster coral*
*2 oz. butter*
*2 tbsp. flour*
*½ cup light cream*
*1 chopped truffle*
*½ cup heavy cream*
*4 tbsp. brandy*
*½ cup chopped lobster meat*

Thoroughly grease 6 small timbale molds. Line them with the lobster coral, finely chopped. Break an egg into each; season with salt and pepper and place them in a water bath. Cover the tops with well greased waxed paper and cook 6 minutes in a 350° oven. Melt half the butter in a pan and stir in the flour off the fire. Add the light cream and stir over the fire until it comes to a boil. Then add the truffle, heavy cream, brandy, and lobster meat. Add, bit by bit, the rest of the butter and simmer gently for 2 or 3 minutes. Pour this sauce on the bottom of a hot shallow dish for serving. Remove the timbales from the oven, turn them out and place down the center of the dish.

# Omelets

There are three most important rules to be followed in the preparation of an omelet. *First*, the omelet pan should be kept extremely clean and never used for any other purpose whatsoever. When not in use, it should always be left a little greasy with butter, wrapped up in aluminum foil and kept in a cool place. Water or any other liquid should never touch the pan. In the rare and unhappy event that it has to be cleaned, heat the pan gently first and then rub it out with plain steel wool. Use a clean rag and vegetable oil to wipe off any steel wool that may be left there. *Second*, the eggs should be well beaten with one teaspoon of

ice water and ¼ teaspoon of salt added for each egg. After beating, the eggs should be strained. This is the only way to remove the little white spots which can otherwise only be eliminated by over-beating. *Third*, the pan must always be heated before any butter is put in and the omelet cooked over a brisk fire. A fork is the very best implement for making an omelet.

To make an omelet for two, break four large eggs in a bowl. Beat with 4 teaspoons of water and a little salt. No pepper should be added until after the omelet is made. Then strain the eggs into another bowl. Heat the omelet pan. When it is hot enough to make the butter sizzle without browning, put in a lump of butter about the size of a pigeon's egg and almost at once add the strained egg mixture. Stir with a fork, shaking briskly with your left hand the whole time until the eggs are nearly set. Spread out the mixture so that no holes are left on the bottom of the pan. Then tip up the omelet, fold it over with the edge of the fork and turn it swiftly out onto a hot flat serving dish. The best way is to grasp the handle of the pan with the left hand, hold the dish near the end of the pan and tip the two together. The whole thing should take not more than two minutes, and great care should be taken not to overcook the omelet. The egg mixture should be stirred so quickly that it never touches the bottom of the pan without being moved. This will ensure a perfect omelet.

## Mushroom Omelet

The following omelet recipes serve 2.
*4 beaten egg omelet mixture*
*½ lb. firm white mushrooms*
*2½ oz. salt butter*
*1 tsp. lemon juice*
*Salt, black pepper*
Melt the 2½ oz. of butter in a shallow heavy pan and when almost on the point of brown-

ing, add the sliced mushrooms with salt, pepper and lemon juice. Sauté briskly 3 minutes. Add this to the egg mixture and make omelet in the ordinary way.

## Watercress and Sour Cream Omelet

*4 beaten-egg omelet mixture*
*1 cup large watercress leaves*
*1 cup sour cream*
*Salt, pepper*

Mix the watercress leaves with the egg mixture. Make the omelet in the ordinary way and turn out on a hot flat serving dish. Pour over the sour cream and garnish with a sprig of fresh watercress.

## Ham and Chicken Liver Omelet

*4 beaten-egg omelet mixture*
*4 chicken livers*
*1 oz. salt butter*
*½ tsp. meat glaze*
*½ tsp. potato flour*
*2 tbsp. brandy*
*¼ cup stock*
*1 cup finely shredded boiled ham*
*1 tsp. freshly chopped parsley*
*Salt, pepper*

Brown the chicken livers quickly in the hot butter. Remove, slice, set aside. Stir into the pan the meat glaze, potato flour, brandy and stock and seasonings. Bring to a boil. Replace the sliced chicken livers. Mix the shredded ham into the egg mixture and make the omelet in the ordinary way. Before serving, stuff with chicken liver mixture. Turn out on a serving dish.

## Chestnut and Chocolate Omelet

*4 beaten-egg omelet mixture*
*4 oz. dark sweet chocolate*
*1 cup sliced glacéed chestnuts*
*Confectioner's sugar*
*½ cup rum*

Dissolve the chocolate in a heavy pan over a very slow fire. Add the chestnuts, roughly cut up, and a little of the chestnut syrup. Make up the omelet in the ordinary way, stuff with the chestnuts and chocolate. Turn out, dust with confectioners' sugar, crisscross top with red-hot skewers and pour flaming rum over before serving.

## Soufflés

The thing to remember about soufflés is to follow meticulously the instructions in any good recipe, and, of course, pray. It is extremely important that the egg whites should be shiny and not "dead" in appearance before they are folded very gently into the mixture.

## Cheese Soufflé

*1 cup milk*
*Small bay leaf*
*1 shallot, sliced*
*Small clove garlic*
*Small piece celery*
*1 teaspoon salt*
*6 mixed peppercorns*
*3 tablespoons butter*
*3 tablespoons flour*
*⅛ teaspoon (scant) cayenne pepper*
*1 teaspoon English dry mustard*
*½ teaspoon French mustard*
*¼ cup Camembert cheese, strained*
*¼ cup freshly grated Gruyère cheese*
*¼ cup grated Parmesan cheese*
*5 egg yolks*
*Few bread crumbs*
*7 egg whites*
*Little paprika*

Put milk, bay leaf, shallot, garlic, celery, salt and peppercorns in a pan. Stir over

slow fire till mixture comes to a boil. Cover, allow to steep for 5 minutes. Melt butter in small heavy pan. Stir in flour off fire. Add cayenne pepper, mustards, and strain on milk. Stir over fire till it comes to a boil. Add Camembert and Gruyère cheeses and ½ the Parmesan cheese. Mix well. Beat egg yolks until light and fluffy and mix into sauce. Butter an 8″ soufflé dish and dust with a few bread crumbs and a little Parmesan cheese. Put egg whites into metal bowl and beat by hand with wire whisk until very stiff. Add cheese sauce. Fold gently but not too thoroughly so that a little of the egg white still shows. Fill soufflé dish, leaving ¼″ rim at top. Sprinkle top with rest of Parmesan cheese and bread crumbs. Stand in shallow pan of water. Bake in preheated 375° oven for 45 or 50 minutes or until just firm to the touch. Do not open door until soufflé has been in oven for at least 25 minutes. Remove and sprinkle with a little paprika, and serve at once. Serves 4.

## Kipper Soufflé

*1 pair kippers*
*2 sliced, skinned tomatoes*
*Oil*
*1 large onion, chopped, or*
  *1 teaspoon chopped garlic*
*2 tablespoons fat (bacon, chicken*
  *or goose)*
*3 tablespoons flour*
*Salt, cayenne pepper*
*¾ cup milk*
*3 or 4 egg yolks*
*½ teaspoon dry mustard*
*1 tablespoon grated Parmesan cheese*
*4 or 5 egg whites, beaten stiff*
*¼ cup crisp shreds of bacon*

Simmer kippers in water for 5 minutes. Remove bones, flake with fork and mix gently into tomatoes, which have been cooked in a little hot oil with chopped onion or garlic. Set aside. Melt fat in a pan and stir in flour, salt and cayenne pepper. Pour on milk and stir over fire until mixture thickens, but do not boil. Remove and mix in egg yolks, mustard and cheese. Lastly, gently fold in stiffly beaten egg whites and kipper mixture. Grease an 8″ soufflé dish, tie a band of waxed paper on outside several inches higher than dish. Pour in mixture and bake for 30 minutes in 350° oven. Remove paper; sprinkle top with bacon; serve at once. Serves 4-6.

## Chicken Soufflé

*1 cup cooked white meat of chicken, ground*
*3 tablespoons butter*
*3 tablespoons flour*
*¾ cup milk*
*¼ cup brandy or sherry*
*Salt, white pepper*
*Pinch of dry mustard*
*4 egg yolks*
*6 egg whites, beaten stiff*

Carefully remove all skin, bone and gristle from chicken. Put it through fine blade of meat grinder twice, giving a total of 1 cup. Melt butter in a saucepan. Blend in flour off fire. Add milk and stir over fire until mixture comes to a boil. Remove and add brandy or sherry. Season with salt, white pepper and a pinch of dry mustard. Beat in egg yolks, one at a time. Add chicken. Fold the beaten egg whites into chicken mixture.

Butter an 8″ soufflé dish and tie a band of buttered wax paper around the outside. Fill with soufflé mixture. Bake for 40 to 50 minutes in preheated 350° oven until top is lightly browned and soufflé feels a little firm to the touch. Do not open the door until the soufflé has cooked at least 40 minutes or it may fall. Remove, carefully take off wax paper and serve immediately. Serves 4-6.

## Onion Soufflé

*3 level tablespoons butter*
*3 level tablespoons flour*
*Salt, cayenne pepper*
*¼ teaspoon dry mustard*
*¾ cup milk*
*¼ cup grated Parmesan cheese*
*4 egg yolks*
*3 white onions, sliced and browned*
*2 tablespoons sherry*
*5 egg whites, beaten stiff*
*Paprika*

Melt butter in a pan. Stir in flour off fire. Season with salt, cayenne pepper and mustard. Pour on milk and stir over fire until it thickens; it must not boil. Add grated cheese, egg yolks, onion and sherry. Fold in egg whites. Grease an 8″ soufflé dish and tie oiled paper around outside. Fill with mixture and bake at 350° for ½ hour or until firm to the touch. Remove. Sprinkle with a little cheese, and paprika. Carefully remove paper and serve. Serves 4-6.

## Mushroom Soufflé

*2 level tablespoons fat (chicken, bacon)*
*3 tablespoons flour*
*½ teaspoon salt, pinch of cayenne pepper*
*¾ cup milk*
*½ cup sliced sautéed mushrooms*
*3 or 4 egg yolks*
*2 tablespoons grated Parmesan cheese*
*5 egg whites, beaten stiff*

Melt fat, remove from fire, and stir in flour, salt, and cayenne pepper. When well blended, pour on milk and stir over fire until mixture thickens. Then add mushrooms, mix in egg yolks and grated cheese. Fold in egg whites. Grease an 8″ soufflé dish and tie wax paper on outside. Pour in mixture and bake for 30 minutes at 400°. Serves 6 as first course, 4 as main course.

## Curried Shrimp Soufflé

*2 tablespoons olive oil*
*1½ cups beaten yogurt*
*2 teaspoons dark brown sugar*
*¼ cup grated fresh coconut*
*¼ cup grated toasted coconut*

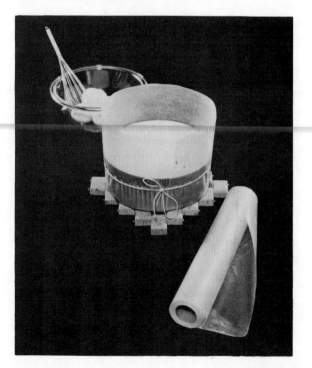

2 tablespoons butter
2 medium size onions, chopped
1 clove garlic, chopped
2 teaspoons curry powder
2 tablespoons glacé ginger, chopped fine
3 tablespoons flour
2 tablespoons milk
4 egg yolks
¾ cup cooked, puréed peas
1 cup shelled, cooked, chopped shrimp
6 egg whites
Salt
Cayenne pepper
Little chopped parsley

Brush an 8″ soufflé dish with a little of the olive oil and set aside in a warm place.

Put beaten yogurt, brown sugar and coconut into a bowl. Stir well and set aside for at least an hour. Melt rest of oil and butter in a heavy pan. Add chopped onion and garlic and cook slowly for two or three minutes. Stir in curry powder and cook slowly for another three minutes. Then add chopped ginger, carefully stir in yogurt mixture and cook over a gentle flame for about ten minutes. Mix flour and milk to a smooth paste and slowly add this to yogurt mixture. Continue cooking for another five minutes, stirring constantly. Beat egg yolks in a bowl until light. Mix them into curry sauce and stir in pea purée and chopped shrimps. Mix well. Put egg whites in a metal bowl with salt and cayenne pepper and beat until stiff with wire whisk. Fold carefully into shrimp mixture and pour into soufflé dish. Bake in a pre-heated 375° oven for 40 to 45 minutes. Remove and sprinkle top with chopped parsley. Serve at once. Serves 4-6.

## Chilis Rellenos Con Queso

½ lb. Monterey Jack cheese
2 cans peeled green chili peppers
4 eggs, separated
½ teaspoon salt
¼ cup flour
Fat for frying
Mexican sauce

These chili peppers stuffed with cheese, and fried in a light and delicate batter may be served with or without sauce. Where chili peppers, even canned ones, are not available, canned pimientos may be used; the flavor will be milder.

Wrap domino-size pieces of Jack cheese in strips of canned peeled green chilis or pimientos. Separate eggs, beat the yolks with the salt. Mix in the flour, then fold in stiffly beaten egg whites. Heat 2″ of lard or oil in a skillet. Dip the chili-wrapped cheese in the batter and take up in a large spoon. Slip into the hot fat, turn immediately, then fry until brown. Turn and brown other side. Serve with Mexican sauce. If pimiento is used, add a teaspoon·of chili powder to the batter. Serves 8.

### Mexican Sauce

1 finely minced clove garlic
1 tablespoon oil
1 cup tomato purée
1 cup bouillon or chicken stock
¾ teaspoon salt
½ teaspoon oregano
Tabasco

For a quick Mexican sauce, cook garlic in oil, add tomato purée, bouillon, salt, oregano and as much Tabasco as your palate tolerates. Heat all together. Makes 2 cups.

An easy adaptation of this recipe is to make sandwiches of sliced Jack cheese and peeled green chilis, dipping them in a mixture of 3 (for 6 slices of bread) slightly beaten eggs, 1 cup of milk, and ½ teaspoon of salt, and browning them on both sides in a little butter or shortening.

## Cheese-Olive Tart

10" pastry shell, unbaked
8 slices bacon
1 cup ripe olives
1 cup shredded Swiss cheese
4 eggs
2 cups cream
1 teaspoon salt
Dash Tabasco

Line a 10" pie pan with pastry and flute the edges. Brush with slightly beaten egg white, and chill while preparing the filling. Cook the bacon crisp, then break in large pieces and combine with the ripe olives, stoned and cut up (or green olives, if you like them better), and the Swiss cheese. Mix together the slightly beaten eggs, cream, salt and Tabasco. Arrange bacon mixture in the pie shell, pour on the egg mixture, and bake at 425° for 12 minutes. Reduce heat to 300° and bake another 40 minutes, until knife inserted near the center comes out clean. This serves 6 or 8.

## Swiss Cheese Fondue

1 garlic clove
12 ounces Swiss cheese
2 tablespoons flour
1 teaspoon salt
Freshly ground black pepper
1½ cups white wine
2 ounces kirsch, cognac or light rum
1 loaf French bread

Rub a 2½-quart earthenware casserole with a cut clove of garlic. Coarsely grate Swiss cheese and mix it with the flour, salt and pepper. Heat the wine in the casserole over very low heat, preferably at the table. When the wine is hot but not boiling, add the cheese, a little at a time, adding more as it melts. Keep stirring over *low* heat and when all is softly bubbling, add the kirsch, cognac, or light rum. Cut a loaf of crusty French bread into cubes so that each piece has a bit of crust. Spear pieces of bread on forks and dunk them in the dish, giving the fondue a stir. The fondue should be kept warm, but not hot. If it becomes too thick, add more wine, heated. Serves 3 or 4 as main dish, 12 as appetizer.

## Welsh Rabbit

½ lb. Cheddar cheese
1 tablespoon butter
3 tablespoons ale
Mustard or cayenne
Toast

There are innumerable recipes for Welsh rabbit, but the classic one is the simplest. Cut cheese in small pieces. Put in the top of a chafing dish with butter and ale. Add a little mustard or cayenne and cook slowly until the cheese is melted into a smooth cream. Keep stirring. Serve over toast. Some cooks recommend adding 2 beaten eggs to the rabbit. Serves 2 or 3.

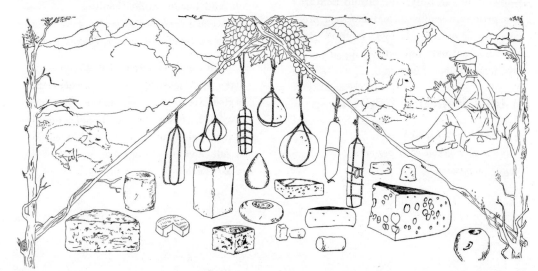

# FISH

# Fish

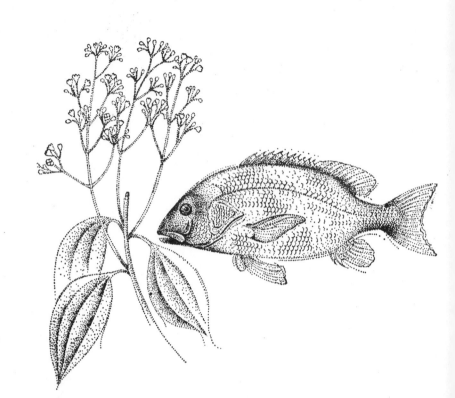

To millions of Americans, perhaps even to *most* Americans, fish is a food that is dipped in flour or cornmeal and fried until it is dry and hard. A typically American way to eat fish is to douse it with catsup, a practice we can explain only by theorizing that people have found out that catsup has a distinct flavor while overcooked fish does not. Many Americans eat fish without the slightest notion of what fish they are eating.

The culinary maltreatment of fish seems strange in view of its abundance. There are literally hundreds of varieties of edible fish in our coastal waters, rivers and lakes. Fresh, frozen, smoked and canned fish is available in our markets the year round. The mystery remains: why isn't more fish cooked better?

Every spring, fresh-water fishermen check their gear and depart on weekend excursions to lakes and mountain streams. What will happen to all the pike, rainbow trout and small-mouthed bass they proudly bring home? Some will be eaten by dutiful families, anxious not to hurt father's feelings. Some will be given away to the family next door. But many, far too many, simply will be thrown away.

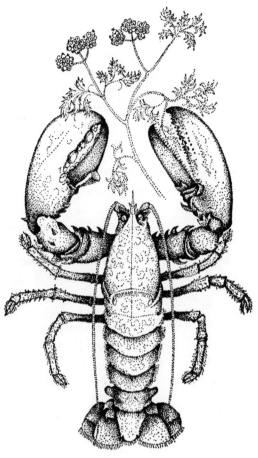

We suspect widespread waste of fish will cease in this country only when housewives become aware how simple it is to cook. In general, fish is so tender and bland that complicated preparations are not needed. Nearly every variety that can be bought or caught can be made into delicious dishes. We have encountered only a few sorts of fish that are best left in the water.

All fish—fresh water, salt water, shellfish—is delicate fare. The cardinal rule is never, *never*, overcook it. Cook it quickly, gently, just to the point of doneness—not a minute more. Doneness means the flesh is flaky and still moist. Fish does not call for strong condiments. Use delicate sauces that enhance it, rather than overwhelm it. When calculating servings, allow ⅓ to ½ lb. edible fish (minus bones, tail and head) per person or about 1 lb. whole fish.

Fish properly cooked, still moist and tender, combines well with crisp accompaniments: fried potatoes or heater potato chips; slices of cucumber, firm and bitey; French fried parsley; corn bread squares, toasted tortillas or toasted French bread. The touch of perfection is to serve fish accompanied by a bottle of chilled white wine, always dry, never sweet. Among many good selections are France's great white Burgundies, including Chablis and Pouilly Fuissé; the charming wines of the Loire district, such as Muscadet and Sancerre; the drier Alsatian and German wines; dry California whites, such as Riesling and Pinot Blanc.

Here are fish recipes to help you get the best from this delectable food—interesting ways to prepare small whole fish or fillets of fish; unusual ways to use shrimp, one of the great favorites, and other shellfish; and ways to simplify your cooking problems and cleaning problems by using foil.

## Fillets of Shad en Papillote

This popular French method of preparing fish is the best way to preserve all the flavor and juices during cooking. It used to be a complicated process that involved cutting parchment, oiling it and folding it into cases. Now with aluminum cooking foil we can accomplish the same job with no trouble. Allow one good sized fillet for each serving. For each fillet, tear off a piece of aluminum foil large enough to wrap it completely. Brush one side of the foil with melted butter or olive oil and place the fillet in the center. Season the fish with salt, freshly ground black pepper, and a squeeze or two of lemon juice if you like. Dot it with butter. Bring the foil up over the top of the fish fillet and double-fold the edges to form a tight package. Close the ends of the foil by folding them over and turning them up so the juices will not run out.

Heat the oven to 425 degrees. Arrange the packages of fillets in a row on a baking sheet and cook them for 18 minutes. Then open one package and test the fish with a fork or toothpick. If the fish flakes easily, it is done. If not, return it to the oven and cook for a few more minutes.

Serve the fillet in its foil package so that none of the juices are lost in transferring it to the plate.

### VARIATIONS

● Prepare the fillets of shad as above, but to each fillet add 1 teaspoon of grated raw onion and 1 tablespoon of finely chopped parsley.
● Prepare the fillets of shad as above, but to each fillet add 1 tablespoon of cream and a little grated Parmesan cheese.
● Prepare the fillets of shad as above, but add 1 or 2 teaspoons of duxelles to each.

### DUXELLES

To prepare duxelles (a concentrated mushroom paste with many uses in cooking), chop one medium onion very fine and chop one-half pound of fresh mushrooms, caps and stems. Press the chopped mushrooms in a folded napkin or towel to remove all excess moisture. Melt 6 tablespoons of butter in a skillet and add the onion. Cook this gently over a very low flame until just transparent. Then add the mushrooms and let the mixture cook slowly until it is reduced to a paste. Add 1 teaspoon of chopped parsley, salt and freshly ground pepper to taste. Continue cooking until there is little or no moisture left. This paste may be stored in a jar in the refrigerator where it will keep for weeks. It is a delicious addition to various fish dishes.

## Other Fillets en Papillote

Fillets of any other white-meated fish, such as cod, haddock, ocean perch, and sole, may be cooked in the same manner as fillets of shad.

## Frozen Fillets en Papillote

Thaw frozen fillets at room temperature or thaw on the shelf in the refrigerator until they can be separated easily. Do not let them become mushy. Cook according to any of the recipes above.

## Trout en Papillote

This calls for small trout, not over 12 inches. Allow 1 or 2 per serving, depending on the size of the fish. If you catch the trout yourself, here is the way to clean it. With a sharp knife slit the belly of the fish from the vent near the tail to the head and then remove the intestines. Wash the fish

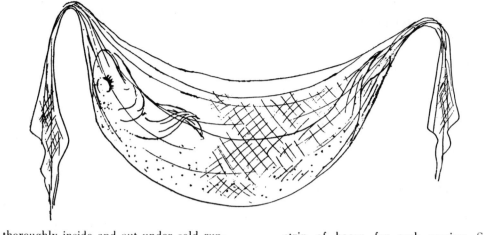

thoroughly inside and out under cold running water. Small trout are usually served whole with head and tail intact. It this disturbs you too much, you may cut them off, but you will have a tastier dish if you don't.

For each trout, take a piece of foil large enough to wrap it completely. Brush one side of the foil with melted butter or oil and place the fish in the center. Season the inside of the fish with salt and pepper and tuck in 1 or 2 sprigs of parsley. Brush the top of the fish with butter, season with salt and pepper and top with a slice of lemon. Bring the foil up over the fish, overlap about 2 inches and fold. Then fold up the ends to hold in the juices.

Heat the oven to 400 degrees. Arrange the packages of trout on a baking sheet and bake for 10 minutes. Then open the foil at the top and turn it back slightly. Continue cooking until the fish flakes easily when tested with a fork or toothpick. This will take only a few minutes; so watch it closely.

*VARIATIONS*

● For each trout chop 2 mushrooms and sauté them lightly in butter. Prepare the trout as above. Top with mushrooms and a teaspoon of chopped chives.

● Prepare the trout as above, and top with 1 teaspoon of grated onion, 2 tablespoons of tomato paste and a pinch of dried basil. While the trout are baking, fry a strip of bacon for each serving. Serve topped with crumbled bacon bits.

## Stuffed Striped Bass en Papillote

This recipe is suitable for any 3 to 5 pound fish to be cooked whole. When you buy the fish, have it cleaned and prepared for stuffing at the fish market. If you clean it yourself, here is the method. Place the fish on a table, holding it by the tail with one hand, and with a sharp knife scrape toward the head removing all the scales. It is easier to do this if the fish is wet. Next, slit the belly from the vent near the tail to the head and remove the intestines. Remove the fins by cutting around them and then pulling them out. Do not try to cut them off with shears, for this does not remove the tiny bones at the base of the fins. Cut into the backbone on both sides at the base of the head, and then place the fish so that the head is hanging over the edge of the table. It can then be easily snapped off. Cut off the tail. Finally, wash the fish thoroughly under cold running water. For the stuffing you will need:

*2 slices of salt pork*
*4 tablespoons of butter*
*½ cup of finely chopped onion*
*¼ cup of finely chopped celery*
*¼ cup of finely chopped green pepper*
*1 cup of fine crumbs*

*1 teaspoon of thyme*
*¼ cup of chopped toasted almonds*

Melt the butter in a skillet and add chopped salt pork. After it has cooked and browned, add the onion, celery and green pepper and cook until they are just soft. Then combine this mixture with all the rest of the ingredients. Stuff the fish; fasten with skewers or tie with string.

Take a piece of aluminum foil large enough to hold the fish and brush it with melted butter on one side. Place the stuffed fish in the center and arrange 2 or 3 strips of bacon over the top of the fish. Sprinkle with freshly ground black pepper. Bring the foil up over the fish, overlap it and then fold. Close the ends of the foil and fold these upward to hold the juices. Arrange the packaged fish on a baking sheet.

Heat the oven to 400 degrees and bake the fish for 30 minutes. Then open the foil and fold it back at the top. Continue baking for about 10 to 15 minutes, or until the fish flakes easily when tested with a fork. Baste once with the juices in the foil package.

Transfer the fish in its foil wrapping to a hot serving platter.

## Shad Roe en Papillote

Shad roe is a great delicacy if properly prepared. There is nothing worse, however, if it is overcooked and dry. Cooking en papillote seems to bring out its best qualities. Shad roe is generally sold in pairs. Allow 1 or a whole pair per serving, depending on the size.

Take a piece of foil for each roe and brush it with melted butter on one side. Place the roe in the center, season it with salt and freshly ground pepper, and add liberal dabs of butter. Top with a generous amount of finely chopped parsley and fold the foil up over the roe, closing it tightly. Fold up the ends of the foil.

Heat the oven to 400 degrees and bake the roe for 20 minutes.

### VARIATIONS

● Substitute a partially cooked strip of bacon for the butter on top of the roe.
● Add a good tablespoon of chopped chives to the roe.
● Add a teaspoon or more of duxelles according to taste (see duxelles recipe under Fillets of Shad en Papillote).

## Broiled Fillets of Fish

Select any fresh or frozen fish fillets—cod, haddock, ocean perch, flounder, sole, sea bass, or red snapper—and allow one good sized fillet for each serving. If you are using frozen fillets, let them thaw until you are able to separate them easily. Do not let them get mushy.

Most fish fillets need no turning during the broiling, and cook best in the broiler pan or on a shallow baking sheet. Line the pan with foil, and you will have little trouble cleaning it. Brush the foil with melted butter and arrange the fillets on it. Dot them

liberally with butter and season to taste with salt, pepper and a little lemon juice, if you wish. If you like a really brown finish on your broiled fish, sprinkle the fillets very, very lightly with flour.

Heat the broiler for 10 minutes and then place the fish about 2 inches from the flame. They will be done in about 8 minutes, but test them with a fork or toothpick. Baste once or twice during the broiling with melted butter.

Serve the fish from the broiler pan, or slip them—foil and all—onto a hot platter.

*VARIATIONS*

● Baste the fillets with a dry white wine and add a good sprinkling of chopped parsley 2 minutes before they are done.
● For each fillet, sauté 2 chopped mushrooms in butter. When the fillets are half cooked, top each one with the sautéed mushrooms and a teaspoon of chopped chives. Baste with a mixture of dry white wine and butter.
● Heat a package of Maxim's frozen Sauce Armoricaine or Sauce Ile de France (available in most fine food stores) and serve the sauce separately.

## Broiled Fillet of Sole with Shrimp Sauce

For four fillets buy 8 large shrimp or 16 small shrimp. Into a pan pour enough dry white wine and water—half and half—to cover the shrimp and add 1 teaspoon of salt, 1 teaspoon of dried tarragon, 3 or 4 peppercorns and a large slice of lemon. Bring this to a boil and add the unshelled shrimp. Cook them for 3 to 5 minutes, depending on their size. Remove the shrimp with a slotted spoon and let the liquid continue cooking. Shell the shrimp and return the shells to the bouillon. Let this all cook

at a rolling boil until the liquid has been reduced to about ½ cup. Strain. In a skillet melt 1 tablespoon of butter and blend in 1 tablespoon of flour. Slowly add the strained fish broth and cook until thickened. Beat 1 egg yolk with ½ cup of cream and blend this into the thickened sauce. Cook until just heated through and thick; do not boil. Chop the shrimp; add to sauce.

Broil the fillets according to previous directions, and when they are done, spread the sauce over them; sprinkle it lightly with grated Parmesan cheese and return to the broiler just long enough to melt the cheese and glaze the sauce.

*VARIATIONS*

● Use half the amount of shrimp and add ⅓ cup of crab meat to the sauce.
● Instead of making the fish bouillon, use ½ cup of clam liquor to make the sauce and add minced clams.

## Fillet of Sole Florentine

*1 cup chopped mushrooms*
*¼ cup minced onion*
*¼ cup butter*
*6 fillets sole*
*2 bunches spinach, cooked*
*2 cups sauce Mornay*
*¼ cup grated Parmesan cheese*

Cook the mushrooms and onion in the butter until wilted. Spread on the fillets and fold them over. Arrange on a bed of cooked, chopped and seasoned spinach and mask with the sauce Mornay (see recipe under Sauces). Sprinkle with cheese and bake at 350° for 25 minutes. Serves 6.

## Broiled Whole Fish

Small fish may be broiled whole without splitting. If the head and tail are left on the fish will be juicier. Clean the fish (see instructions for trout and striped bass) and dust with flour. Line the broiler pan with foil to catch the juices and grease the rack well with butter or oil. Rub the fish thoroughly with butter and season.

Heat the broiler for 10 minutes; place the fish on the rack about 3 inches from the flame. Broil for 5 minutes on the first side and then turn, brushing with more butter. (Very thin fish, such as flounder, will not need to be turned.) Cook for 5 more minutes and test for doneness with a fork or toothpick. Be sure to get the skin very crisp. If necessary, move the fish closer to the flame for the last minute of broiling.

Serve with lemon wedges and melted butter with chopped parsley.

## Broiled Fish Steaks

Fish steaks may be cooked in the same way as fillets. If they are very thick and meaty, they will need to be turned once during the broiling. Cook them for 5 minutes before turning, and be sure to brush them well with melted butter on the second side. Cook for another 5 minutes and then test for doneness with a fork. Baste often to prevent dryness.

## Grilled Fish with Herbs

Select a whole fish—striped bass or salmon trout would be a good choice—and clean it according to directions for striped bass, or have your fish dealer clean it for you. Split it open for broiling, and arrange it on a well greased broiler rack, skin side down. If you prefer, arrange it on foil in the broiling pan. Sprinkle it lightly with flour, dot with plenty of butter and season to taste.

Heat the broiler for 10 minutes and place the fish 3 inches from the flame. Baste several times during the cooking with melted butter. Split whole fish will cook without turning in about 10 minutes, but the length of time depends on the thickness. Test for doneness.

When the fish is done, put a good layer of dried parsley and dried fennel or thyme on a flameproof platter. Place the broiled fish on top of this and top it with more dried herbs. Pour 2 ounces of warm cognac over the fish and ignite it. Bring the flaming platter to the table.

## Whole Stuffed Pike

*1 pike, about 2½ pounds*
*Brandy*
*1½ pounds salmon, cut from tail or*
  *1 pound center cut salmon*
*2 egg whites*
    *1½ cups light cream*
    *2 teaspoons salt*
    *A little cayenne pepper*
    *2 ounces butter*
    *Hollandaise Sauce*

Remove scales from fish with a scaler, working from the tail toward the head, and remove the fins. Cut fish down the back (not the belly), bone it and remove the inedible parts. Wash in cold water. Dry on paper towels. Spread it out on a board and brush inside with brandy.

Skin and bone the salmon and put through a fine meat chopper. Put in an electric mixer with the egg whites, beat well and slowly add the cream and salt. Beat until very thick, then add the pepper. Stuff pike with this salmon mousse, reshape fish and arrange on a greased baking dish. Make a few scores on top with a knife. Melt the butter, add 2 tablespoons brandy and pour over the fish. Bake in a 375° oven for 25 minutes. Prepare garnishes. Just before serving, pour Hollandaise Sauce over fish and brown for a minute or two under the broiler. Serves 4 as main course.

## Sautéed Whole Fish

The classic French cooking method, sauté meunière, is excellent for small whole fish, such as trout, smelt, butterfish, porgies and dabs.

Clean the fish according to instructions for trout and striped bass. You may leave the heads and tails on or remove them, as you wish. Wash fish well and dip in milk and then in flour. In a large skillet heat butter and good olive oil, half and half. The oil is very important, for it prevents the butter from scorching and giving the fish a burned flavor. You will need plenty of butter and oil—at least a tablespoon for each fish. When it is bubbling and hot, place the fish in the skillet and sauté them until they are nicely browned on one side. Turn them carefully, season to taste with salt and pepper and finish cooking the other side. Test for doneness with a fork or toothpick to see if it flakes easily. Add more butter

and oil after turning the fish if it is necessary.

When the fish are done, remove to a hot platter, add butter to the pan to melt, toss in a handful of chopped parsley and pour this over the fish.

## Oven Fried Fish

For four servings, select 4 small whole fish or 4 fillets. If you are using whole fish, clean them as for striped bass; remove heads and tails.

Melt ½ cup of butter and pour half of it over the bottom of a baking dish lined with foil. Heat the oven to 500 degrees and then heat the baking dish for 3 minutes before you place the fish in it. Meanwhile beat 1 egg yolk with ⅓ cup of cream or rich milk, and salt and pepper to taste. Dip each fish or fillet in the egg and milk and then roll it in fine dry bread crumbs. When the fish are all coated and the baking dish is hot, arrange the fish in the dish, pour the rest of the melted butter over them and bake for 10 minutes, or until they flake easily when tested with a work. Serve with lemon wedges and tartar sauce.

## Sea Bass Niçoise

Select a small sea bass—one small enough to be sautéed whole. Proceed as for sautéed whole fish and add one thinly sliced onion to the skillet while the fish is cooking. Meanwhile, peel, seed and chop a medium sized tomato. When the fish is done, remove it to a hot platter and add the tomato to the onion in the skillet. Cook this rapidly until it is thoroughly soft and add ½ cup of dry white wine and a generous number of tiny pitted black olives. Heat through and blend with the pan juices and pour over the fish. Garnish with anchovy fillets.

## Poached Fillets of Fish

In a shallow pan put just enough water and dry white wine—half and half—to cover the fish fillets. Add salt to taste, 2 or 3 peppercorns, 1 bay leaf, 1 onion and 1 teaspoon or thyme. Bring this liquid to a boil and cook for 10 or 15 minutes to mellow the flavors. Add the fish fillets, and a little more wine, if the liquid has boiled down too much. Poach the fish gently—do not boil it—in this stock (called court bouillon) until it is barely done. This takes only a few minutes. Test with a fork or toothpick. When the fillets flake easily, remove them to a hot platter and keep them warm in a low oven.

Reduce the liquid over a brisk flame until it is a rich broth. For 4 fillets, you will need about ¾ cup of broth. In the upper part of a double boiler, melt 4 tablespoons of butter. Blend in 3 tablespoons of flour and gradually add the fish stock, stirring constantly to keep the mixture smooth. Add ¾ cup of milk and cream mixed and continue stirring until the sauce is smooth and thickened. Season to taste with salt and freshly ground black pepper. Spread this sauce over the fillets; dust with buttered crumbs or grated cheese, and glaze under the broiler flame. Garnish with sliced hard cooked eggs, chopped parsley.

### *VARIATIONS*

● Substitute tomato juice for the water in the bouillon and add 1 clove of garlic, minced and sautéed in a little butter. When the fillets are done, remove them to a hot platter and reduce the liquid to 1 cup. Add 2 tablespoons of tomato purée and cook and blend this sauce until rich. Taste for seasoning. Pour over the fillets. Garnish with black olives, anchovy fillets and chopped parsley.
● When the fillets are done, remove them to a hot platter and reduce the liquid over

a brisk flame to ½ cup. Take the broth from the fire and gradually add it to two lightly beaten egg yolks. Heat 1 package of Maxim's frozen Sauce Armoricaine and slowly stir in the egg yolk and broth mixture, being careful not to let it boil. Pour this sauce over the fillets and serve garnished with chopped parsley.

## Poached Whole Fish

Use a whole striped bass, sea bass, red snapper, sea trout or any other fish of around 5 pounds, prepared for cooking as under Stuffed Bass en Papillote.

Prepare a bouillon as for poached fillets. Wrap the fish in a large piece of cheesecloth, leaving long loose ends of the cloth to use as handles, and lower it into the boiling liquid. Or place the fish on a rack and lower it into the liquid. Poach it gently—do not boil—allowing about 8 minutes per pound. Test for doneness with a fork.

Cover a hot platter with a folded linen napkin the length of the fish. Carefully unwrap the fish from the cheesecloth and place it on the napkin. Remove skin, and decorate with lemon slices.

## Cold Salmon in Jelly

Select a large center slice of salmon weighing 3 to 4 pounds. Pour enough white wine and water—half and half—into a kettle to cover the fish. Add one half lemon, 5 or 6 peppercorns, salt to taste, an onion stuck with 2 or 3 cloves, 1 teaspoon of dried thyme and several sprigs of parsley. Bring this to a boil and boil for 15 minutes. Wrap the salmon in a strip of cheesecloth, leaving long ends of the cloth to use as handles. Lower it into the water, or place it on a rack in the water. Bring the bouillon to the boil again, lower the flame and let the fish simmer. Allow about 8 to 10 minutes to the pound (the length of time will depend on the thickness of the fish) and then test for doneness near the bone.

Remove the fish to a platter and take off the skin. Continue cooking the broth at a rolling boil until it is reduced to 1 cup. Strain. Return it to the stove, add the white and the shell of one egg and beat with a rotary beater while the egg cooks in the broth for a minute or so. Remove beater and continue cooking broth for 1 more minute. Strain it through a very fine sieve or a linen napkin.

Soak ½ envelope of plain gelatin in ¼ cup of cold water and add this to the broth. Heat until the gelatin is thoroughly melted, then set the broth aside to jell. When it is partly set, but not firm, beat ½ of it into ½ cup of mayonnaise. Add 2 tablespoons of chopped parsley, 2 tablespoons of chopped chives (or little green onions) and 2 tablespoons of chopped fresh dill, if available. Chill the mayonnaise mixture until it is firm enough to hold its shape; then spread on the salmon. Cover the top of the fish with this mixture and decorate it with stuffed olives, pimiento strips, green pepper rings and parsley. Surround with stuffed hard-cooked eggs, sprigs of watercress and the rest of the jellied broth, chopped and heaped in small mounds.

You can use other fish for this recipe or substitute fish steaks or fillets.

## Coulibiac

*Brioche dough*
*3 hard-cooked eggs, chopped*
*½ pint sour cream*

*1 pound smoked salmon, thinly sliced*
*¾ pound cooked shrimp*
*Fresh chopped dill*
*Beaten egg yolk*

To make brioche dough, put 1½ cups flour in a bowl and add 3 large beaten eggs, 2 teaspoons sugar and ½ teaspoon salt. Work to a dough and beat on a board until light. Mix in 5 ounces creamed butter and 1 package yeast that has been dissolved in ¼ cup warm water. Mix in ½ cup more flour and let stand until dough rises. Place in a lightly greased and floured bowl, cover with a cloth, and allow to rise until double its bulk at room temperature. Chill overnight in the refrigerator (or for 1 hour in the deep-freeze). Remove, roll out to ½″ thickness on a floured board, brush with melted butter and sprinkle with a few browned bread crumbs.

Put a layer of finely chopped egg on top of the dough and dot with sour cream. On top of this put thin slices of salmon, thin slices of shrimp and sprinkle with dill. Dot with more sour cream and roll up like a jelly roll. Put in a well greased bread tin, cover with a cloth and put to rise in a warm place for ¼ hour. Brush with beaten egg yolk and bake in a 425° oven for 30 minutes. Remove, turn out and serve. Serves 6.

## Smoked Salmon Mousse

*1½ tablespoons gelatin*
*3 tablespoons cold water*
*2 tablespoons butter*
*2 tablespoons flour*
*½ teaspoon salt*
*1 cup light cream*
*¼ lb. cream cheese*
*¼ teaspoon freshly ground black pepper*
*3 egg yolks, beaten*
*½ lb. smoked salmon, minced*
*1 cup whipped cream*
*3 egg whites, stiffly beaten*

Soak the gelatin in the water while preparing the white sauce. Melt the butter in a saucepan; stir in the flour and salt. Gradually add the cream, stirring constantly until it reaches the boiling point. Cook over low heat for 5 minutes. Remove from heat and add gelatin, stirring until dissolved. Mash the cheese and add with the pepper. Gradually add the egg yolks, stirring constantly to prevent curdling. Cool for 15 minutes. Fold in the salmon, whipped cream and egg whites. Turn into a buttered 1½ quart casserole or soufflé dish. Chill until set, about 4 hours. Unmold, or serve directly from the dish as an appetizer or luncheon main course. Serves 4-6.

## Escabeche of Fish

This cold fish dish is a perfect choice for a luncheon on a hot summer day, for a first course at dinner or for a surprise dish at a buffet. Select 2 pounds of fish fillets or steaks. Dip them in lemon juice, dust them with flour and sauté them in butter and oil, as for sautéed fish. When they are done, remove any skin and bones and arrange them neatly in a deep dish.

Make a cold sauce by mixing ½ cup of olive oil, 3 tablespoons of wine vinegar, ¼ cup of chopped onion, ¼ cup of chopped green pepper, 1 teaspoon of dried tarragon, 2 tablespoons of finely chopped parsley and salt to taste. Pour this over the fish and let it stand in the refrigerator for 24 hours.

To serve, garnish with green olives and lemon or lime wedges.

### VARIATION

● Substitute the following sauce: Mix ½ cup of olive oil, 3 tablespoons of lemon juice, 1 tablespoon of chopped fresh dill, 2 tablespoons of chopped parsley, 1 small minced onion, 1 tablespoon of capers and salt to taste. Garnish with green olives and lemon wedges.

## Fish Loaf, Gastronome

*4 pounds salmon, white fish or shrimp*
*1 onion, chopped*
*2 egg yolks*
*2 tablespoons cracker meal*
*3½ teaspoons salt*
*½ teaspoon white pepper*
*2 tablespoons minced parsley*
*2 egg whites, stiffly beaten*
*3 onions, sliced*
*4 cups water*
*½ teaspoon freshly ground black pepper*
*1 tablespoon gelatin*

When buying fish, ask for the head and skin. Grind the fish or cleaned shrimp, then chop it together with the chopped onion, egg yolks, cracker meal, 1½ teaspoons salt, white pepper and parsley. Fold in the egg whites. Combine the fish heads, sliced onions, water, 2 teaspoons salt, and black pepper in a saucepan. Bring to a boil. Shape the fish mixture into 1 large or 2 small loaves. Place on a rack or wrap in cheesecloth and lower gently into the boiling liquid. Cover and cook over low heat for 1½ hours. Taste the stock, adding more salt and pepper if necessary. Carefully remove the loaves and place in a pan or serving dish at least 3″ deep. Soften the gelatin in ¼ cup cold water for 5 minutes. Strain the stock and add the gelatin, stirring until dissolved. Pour over the fish loaf. Chill. Slice and serve with horse radish as an appetizer. Serves 6-8.

## Shrimp Floridian en Papillote

For 4 servings, buy 2 pounds of raw shrimp. Shell and clean them. Blend ½ pound of blue cheese, Roquefort or Gorgonzola, with 1 8-ounce package of cream cheese. Add 1 tablespoon of chopped chives, 1 tablespoon of chopped parsley and 1 clove of garlic finely chopped. Thin this mixture with ¾ cup of dry white wine.

Take four large squares of cooking foil. Place ¼ of the cheese mixture in the center of each piece of foil and top with ¼ of the shrimp and a slice of lemon. Bring the edges of the foil up over the shrimp and fold them together. Fold up the ends of the foil to make a tight package. Arrange the packages on a baking sheet and bake in a 400 degree oven for 30 minutes.

## Indian Shrimp Curry (Trinidad)

*2 pounds shrimp*
*3 tablespoons lemon juice*
*3 tablespoons butter*
*3 tablespoons oil*
*2 onions, sliced*
*4 tomatoes, chopped*
*1 teaspoon each turmeric, coriander, cumin*
*½ teaspoon mustard seed*
*2 bay leaves*
*1 teaspoon black pepper*
*½ teaspoon salt*
*2 cups water*
*Pimentos*

Put the shrimp in boiling water. When just pink and no more, remove them. Cool and

shell. Wash in lemon juice. Reserve. Melt the butter and oil; fry the sliced onions, chopped tomatoes, the spices, salt and herbs, well pounded. Cover and simmer for 10 minutes over very low heat. Put in the shrimp and 2 cups water. Cover and simmer ½ hour. Serve with strips of pimento (soaked in salt and vinegar) arranged on top of shrimp. Serves 4.

## Special Broiled Shrimp (India)

*2 pounds shrimp*
*1 cup oil*
*1½ teaspoons chili powder mixed with*
  *1 tablespoon vinegar*
*¼ teaspoon black pepper*
*3 cloves garlic, minced*
*1 teaspoon salt*
*1 tablespoon basil*
*1 tablespoon chopped mint leaves*

Wash, shell and dry the shrimp. Make a marinade of the oil, spices, garlic, salt and herbs. Mix well, pour over shrimp and leave to marinate overnight or at least for 4 hours. Place the shrimp with the marinade in a broiling pan. Under a high flame, broil the shrimp for 6 to 10 minutes (depending on their size). Turn them once while broiling and serve with as much marinade as you prefer. Serves 4.

## Shrimp Ondines

*2 cans (7¾ ounces) salmon*
*4 tablespoons butter*
*1 cup whipped cream*
*2 cups cooked chopped shrimp*
*¾ cup mayonnaise*
*1 tablespoon gelatin*
*3 tablespoons cold water*
*¾ cup white wine*
*6 whole cooked shrimp*
*Chopped parsley*

You may prepare the ondines the day before they are to be served. Drain the salmon and mash very fine. Cream the butter, adding the salmon gradually. Beat until light and fluffy. Fold in the whipped cream. Use 6 shells or small individual dishes or cocottes. Line each with some of the salmon mixture, reserving enough to use as a cover. Mix the chopped shrimp and mayonnaise together. Fill the prepared dishes with the shrimp and cover with the remaining salmon mixture. Place in the freezing compartment. Soften the gelatin in the water for 5 minutes. Place over hot water until gelatin dissolves and is clear. Stir in the wine. Spoon over the top of the salmon mixture and chill until firm. Garnish with a whole shrimp and chopped parsley. Serves 6.

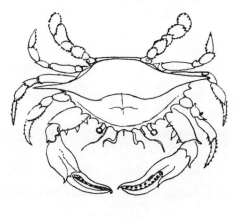

## Crab

If you are fortunate enough to have live hard shelled crabs to cook, you can enjoy them at their best. Boil them as you would lobster, by plunging them into boiling salted water, or a mild court bouillon made with half water and half white wine and seasoned with salt and peppercorns. Allow 8 minutes per pound. When the crab is cooked, remove it from the liquid and let it cool enough to handle. Break off the claws and crack them so the meat will be easy to extract. Pull off the back and remove the spongy parts underneath. Remove the apron from the underside of the body. Split crab in two.

Serve this cracked fresh crab with a rich olive oil mayonnaise flavored with a bit of dry mustard and lemon juice, or with melted butter and lemon juice. This with hot French bread, sweet butter and a bottle of dry white wine is wonderful fare. (The amount of meat in a crab varies according to its size and type. Some crabs contain very little meat; ask your fish dealer how many you will need per serving.)

## Pilaff of Crab

Sauté 6 slices of bacon in a large skillet. When they are brown and crisp, remove them and break them into bits. Add 2 medium onions, chopped, and 1 clove of garlic, minced. Cook slowly until barely colored. Add ½ pound of smoked cooked ham cut in thin strips; heat it through, and then add 1 ripe tomato, peeled, seeded and chopped. Cook this down and when it is thoroughly blended and soft, add 3 tablespoons of tomato purée and 1 pound of crab meat. Pour ⅓ cup of warm dark rum or cognac over and ignite it. When it has flamed, add 1 pint of dry white wine, 2 tablespoons of chopped parsley and a tiny pinch of sugar. Simmer for 15 minutes. Add the bacon bits, taste for seasoning and add salt, if necessary. Finally add ⅓ cup of heavy cream, and blend and heat through. Serve with fluffy rice. Serves 4.

## Crab Soufflé

*2 tablespoons vegetable oil*
*6 tablespoons water*
*4 tablespoons flour*
*2 tablespoons plain gelatin*
*Salt, cayenne pepper*
*1½ cups light cream*

*2 tablespoons sherry*
*5 eggs, separated*
*2 cups crab flakes*
*1½ cups whipped cream*
*2 hard-cooked eggs*
*2 tablespoons chopped parsley*

Heat oil and water over slow fire. Mix flour and gelatin and add to oil, off fire. Season with salt and cayenne. Mix in light cream, off fire. Stir over fire until it comes to a boil and then add sherry. Beat in egg yolks, one at a time, and add crab meat. Stir over ice until cool and fold in stiffly beaten egg whites and whipped cream.

Tie a band of oiled paper around a 6″ soufflé dish. Pour in mixture and put in refrigerator to set for about 2 hours. To serve, carefully take off paper. Sprinkle top with chopped hard-cooked egg and chopped parsley. Serve very cold. Serves 8-10.

## Clams

There are two main species of clam—the long-necked soft shell and the little-necked hard shell. It is the hard shell that is most commonly found in the markets. These recipes are for the "little neck" or "round clam" of the Atlantic coast, but can be used for any hard shell variety.

## Clam Tart

Wash enough clams to make 1 cup of minced clam meat. Remove the clams from the shells, being careful not to lose any of the clam juice. Grind the meat and measure 1 cup. Line a 9-inch pie tin with pastry made with your favorite recipe and put it in the refrigerator to chill. Sauté 4 bacon slices until crisp, drain and crumble into bits. Sauté 2 tablespoons of minced onion in the bacon fat until just soft but not brown. Drain. Remove the pie shell from the refrigerator, sprinkle the bacon on the bottom and add the sautéed onion. Over this spread the minced clams. Beat 4 eggs into the clam liquor and add enough cream to make 1½ cups of liquid. Add salt and pepper to taste and pour over the clams. Bake in a 450-degree oven for 10 minutes. Reduce the heat to 350 degrees and continue baking until the custard is done. Do not overcook. Test with a knife. When it comes out clean, the pie is done. Serves 4

## Lobster

As with crab, the best way to appreciate the full flavor of a lobster is to eat it freshly boiled. It is plunged into boiling salted water, or a simple court bouillon (see crab recipe), and cooked 5 minutes for the first pound and 3 minutes for each additional pound. (The most common error in preparing lobster is overcooking.) When it is done, remove it and place it on its back on a board or work table top. With a heavy knife and mallet, split the lobster lengthwise down the middle. Remove the stomach and intestines, but do not throw away the grayish-green liver—or tomalley. This is a delicacy. If there are reddish deposits, they are the roe, known as lobster coral—also good eating. Crack the claws, so the meat can be easily extracted. Serve hot or cold with melted butter and lemon quarters, or with a rich mayonnaise. Allow at least a 1½ pound lobster per serving.

## Lobster Curry (Singapore)

*6 tablespoons butter*
*2 onions, sliced*
*¼ teaspoon powdered cinnamon*
*¼ teaspoon powdered cloves*
*½ teaspoon cumin*
*¼ teaspoon chili powder*
*1 teaspoon coriander*
*1 tablespoon turmeric*
*2 tomatoes, sliced*
*½ teaspoon salt*
*½ teaspoon sugar*
*1 tablespoon lemon juice*
*4 cups milk*
*2 cloves garlic, finely minced*
*3-pound lobster, parboiled*
*1 cucumber*

Melt half the butter and fry sliced onions with cinnamon, cloves, cumin, chili, coriander, turmeric, and tomatoes. Mix well and add the salt, sugar, lemon juice and milk. Simmer on very low heat for 15 minutes. In another pan, melt the remaining butter and lightly fry the garlic. Add the lobster meat and coat it well with butter. Cook for 5 minutes, then add the milk and spice sauce. Cook covered till the liquid is reduced by ⅓. Slice the cucumber very thin. Add to lobster. Cook together for 10 minutes and serve hot. Serves 6.

## Lobster Rossini

*3 boiled lobsters, split*
*½ pound crab meat, flaked*
*3 tablespoons tomato paste*

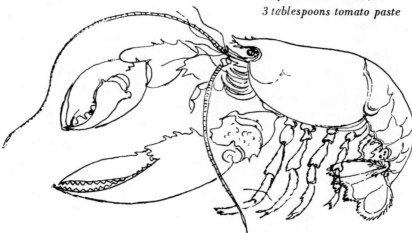

*1 cup mayonnaise*
*2 teaspoons chopped chives*
*6 anchovy fillets*
*2 pimentos, thinly sliced*

Carefully remove the tail meat from the lobsters and reserve. Crack the claws and remove the meat; dice the claw meat and combine with the crabmeat, tomato paste, ⅓ cup of the mayonnaise and chives. Stuff the shells with the mixture and cover with the meat of the lobster tails. Press down gently. Decorate the top of each with the balance of the mayonnaise, forced through a pastry tube, if desired. Arrange the anchovies and pimentos on top. Chill until ready to serve. Serves 6.

## Scallops

The delicate tiny bay scallops are so delicious by themselves and so easily overwhelmed by elaborate sauces that the best way to prepare them is a simple sauté. Wash them and dry them and sprinkle just very lightly with flour. Heat half olive oil and half butter and add the scallops, tossing them about to brown a bit. They will only need a minute or two. Season with salt and pepper while they cook and add a sprinkling of chopped parsley and a pinch or so of tarragon, if you like. At the very last minute, add a dash or two of lemon juice and a bit of dry white wine. Do not overcook the scallops. They should be tender and juicy. As with oysters, the amount per serving depends on the size of the scallops.

Larger ocean scallops take to more definite seasonings such as the following recipe with an Oriental marinade.

## Broiled Scallops Chinese

Mix equal parts of olive oil, dry sherry, soy sauce and flavor with a spoonful of grated fresh ginger and a minced clove of garlic. Soak the scallops in the marinade for 1 to 2 hours. When you are ready to cook, you may arrange the scallops on individual skewers, if you wish, or broil them on a rack. In either case, pre-heat the broiler, place the scallops about 2 inches from the flame and broil quickly, turning to brown on all sides. They should not take more than 4 or 5 minutes to cook. Baste once or twice with the marinade. Serve with fried rice.

## Oysters

The best oysters should be eaten raw—on the half shell. Serve them on a bed of ice, and no catsup, please. A squirt of lemon juice and a dash of freshly ground black pepper is all any worthwhile oyster needs. Size of serving depends, of course, on the size of the oysters. Six is the usual number, but some of the tinier varieties are so small that any hungry male could easily consume three dozen.

## Oysters Broiled with Herbs

For 12 medium-sized oysters, mix 4 ounces of sweet butter with ½ cup of chopped parsley, ¼ cup of chopped chives, ¼ cup of chopped chervil, 1 teaspoon of freshly ground black pepper and salt to taste. Top each oyster on the half shell with a goodly spoonful of the mixed herbs and butter, arrange the oysters on a flame-proof pan and run under a broiler flame for a very short time. Oysters really need to be just heated through. They are done when the edges begin to curl.

*VARIATION:* These may be heated in a 475-degree oven for 4 to 5 minutes.

## Oyster Soufflé

*1½ dozen oysters, with ½ cup liquor*
*4 tablespoons butter*
*4 tablespoons flour*
*Salt, cayenne pepper*
*¾ cup milk*
*1 teaspoon chopped fresh thyme*
*    or ¼ teaspoon dried thyme*
*1 tablespoon chopped fresh parsley*
*½ teaspoon sautéed garlic,*
*    chopped fine*
*½ cup chopped sautéed shallots*
*4 egg yolks*
*2 tablespoons sour cream*
*6 egg whites*
*Grated Parmesan-cheese*
*Bread crumbs*

Melt butter in pan. Stir in flour off fire. Season with salt and cayenne pepper. Mix in ½ cup of oyster liquor and the milk. Stir over fire till it comes to a boil. Add herbs, garlic and shallots. Beat in egg yolks, add sour cream, mix in oysters. Carefully fold in stiffly beaten egg whites. Tie a band of oiled waxed paper around an 8″ soufflé dish. Fill with mixture. Sprinkle top with a few bread crumbs and a little grated cheese. Bake in a 375° oven for 45 minutes or until just firm to the touch. Serve at once. Serves 4-6.

## Minced Oysters (Cambodia)

*24 oysters*
*3 tablespoons butter or oil*
*½ tablespoon chopped parsley*
*1 cup mushrooms, thinly sliced*
*1 cup milk*
*1 cup buttermilk*
*¾ teaspoon cumin seed*
*2 crushed red chili peppers*
*2 egg yolks*
*½ cup cream*
*¼ teaspoon salt*

Poach the oysters in water and their own liquor. Drain and mince them. Melt the butter or oil and add the chopped parsley. Fry for ½ minute and add the mushrooms. Then add the combined milk and buttermilk, ⅔ cup at a time, boiling away the liquid after each addition. Add the cumin and 2 tablespoons water in which the crushed peppers have been soaked; discard peppers. Beat the egg yolks with the cream. Add with oysters and salt to mushroom mixture. Cover and draw aside from fire for 3 minutes before serving. Serves 4.

# BEEF

# Beef

Among the honored names in the annals of good eating is that of Edward Heardson, the beloved "Chef Ned" of the renowned Beefsteak Society of London, which was founded in 1735 and dedicated to the enjoyment of that most royal of meats, rare beef. When Chef Ned lay dying, so the story goes, he asked that he might breathe his last in the society's dining room. His wish was granted, and here are lines commemorating the event:

"We who partook of all his fleshly toils,
  Received his bastings, too, and shared his broils,
  Now in our turn a mouthful carve and trim
  And dress at Phoebus' fire our steak for him.
  His fondest hopes, betrayed with many a tear,
  Were that his life's last spark might glimmer here,
  And the last words that choked his parting sigh,
  'Oh, at your feet, dear masters, let me die!' "

Chef Ned's devotion to his task and to the hungry members of the Beefsteak Society is expressive of a British trait now centuries old: the British dearly love beef. The 17th century poet Richard Leveridge went so far as to attribute British courage and statesmanship to the "mighty roast beef of Old England." Today British beef, especially Scottish, is still the best in Europe.

But the finest, juiciest, tenderest beef in the world now

comes from the plains and western ranges of the United States, and even a beef-loving Englishman will concede it, knowing that American fondness for beef is simply one of the Anglo-Saxon traditions transplanted in the New World. And we have gone one step beyond praising the "good red meat" itself; we have woven the production of beef into our culture. The Western cowboy (or cowpuncher or cowhand) is an American folklore hero. We sing his songs, idealize him in story and celebrate his prowess in rodeos. In real life he may be neither so gaudily attired nor so quick on the draw as the Western movie suggests, but he well deserves our acclaim, for he was a participant in the opening of the West and its frontier cattle wars, and he still is an indispensable cog in the fascinating process that converts a Texas steer into a "New York cut" on your plate at dinnertime.

When shopping for beef, it is an advantage to have basic knowledge of the grades of beef and of the ideal treatment of the various cuts. Beef graded prime by the standards of the U. S. Department of Agriculture is the very best quality. It is good from tail to snout, and in many localities it is not easy to find; most of the nation's prime beef goes to fine restaurants in big cities. Yet there is a chance your butcher may be able to supply you with it, and if this is so, you are lucky indeed—but you will pay for your elegant taste. Prime beef is cherry red with creamy marblings of fat that give tenderness to the meat as it cooks. This top grade is invariably well-aged, often covered outside with mold and even pungent to the nostrils. Don't let the mold distress you; the butcher will cut it off.

Choice beef is fine meat, one grade below prime. When choice beef is properly aged, only the person with a trained palate can distinguish it from prime. Choice beef is plentiful and almost as costly as prime. Beef graded good is just that. It is not quite as tender as the two top grades, but filets of good and the next grade, commercial, can be excellent buys. Other cuts of these grades will require long cooking or tenderizing.

To clear up one point that mystifies people: a steer is also an ox, particularly if the steer is full grown or used as a draft animal. Ox is the old Anglo-Saxon term; it is still used in designating such cuts as oxtail. Beef is from the Latin and a more elegant term. Like our ancestors, we are great beef eaters. It is estimated we consume around 83.5 pounds a head each year, proof that this meatiest of meats is as popular a part of the menu now as it was in the days of the stalwart Elizabethans.

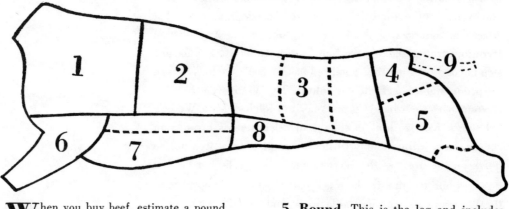

When you buy beef, estimate a pound of meat per person, taking fat and bone into consideration.

**1. Chuck, Shoulder and Arm.** These are less tender cuts to be used for long cooking. Try them for Swiss steaks, stews, carbonnades, *oiseaux sans têtes*, braised beef, pot roasts.

**2. Ribs.** One of the best cuts. Use as roast or steaks. The first five ribs make the choicest roast. They should be cut short and well tied. Use the rib ends (short ribs) that the butcher cuts off the roast for braising. A two-rib roast may be roasted on the spit with bone left in.

**3. Loin.** This portion of the animal furnishes steaks: sirloin, porterhouse, club or strip steak (the boneless sirloin). Pan-broil, broil or sauté. The English roast beef is generally a large sirloin roasted in the oven just to the rare stage.

**4. Rump or Hip.** Excellent steaks.

**5. Round.** This is the leg and includes top and bottom round. Top is considered a little finer. Use these cuts for braising, for Swiss steak, for the best stews, and for fine lean ground beef.

**6. Shank.** This cut from either the shoulder or the leg has a great deal of muscle. Use it for soups and stews.

**7. Plate, Brisket, Short Ribs.** These have fine flavor. Use them for braising or boiling. Plate or brisket make delicious *pot au feu*. They are also excellent when corned.

**8. Flank.** This is used for London Broil. It is a thin oval-shaped piece with definite coarse grain. Broil or sauté very quickly—it should be red rare in the center—and carve into paper thin slices, cutting them on the diagonal.

**9. Tail.** This gives wonderful flavor to soups and stews. It can also be used by itself as braised oxtail.

## Roast Ribs of Beef

A standing rib roast of beef has a great deal of bone. We always allow at least 1 pound per serving.

There are two schools of thought on roasting beef. Some prefer the searing method; others insist slow cooking is better. We admit that slow roasting at one steady temperature is easier and more economical because there is less shrinkage and the meat needs no attention. However, the finished roast lacks a rich glazed exterior. We like our roast beef crunchy and brown on the outside and juicy and red in the center. To get this result we use the searing method. It takes more trouble—it has to be watched and basted—but is well worth the effort.

Rub the roast well with salt and with very coarsely ground black pepper (use a coffee grinder to get the pepper really coarse or substitute the cracked pepper now sold by some spice firms). Insert a meat thermometer in the thickest part of the roast, making certain that it does not touch the bone. Put the roast in a baking pan and place a small piece of beef suet in the bottom of the pan. Roast in a 450° oven, basting every 10 minutes while cooking at high heat. Some people advise turning the heat down after 20 minutes, but we have kept large beef roasts at high heat for as much as an hour before reducing the temperature. Use your own judgment; turn the heat down to 325° after the meat has achieved a good brown glaze on the outside. Continue basting and cooking until the meat thermometer registers close to 120°. This is for very rare roast beef. If you prefer it less rare, let meat cook until thermometer reaches desired mark. Remove the meat from the oven and let it stand for 15 minutes before carving. It will continue to cook with its own heat and the juices will settle.

## Small Two-Rib Roast

A small roast of two ribs will serve two persons amply. Have the butcher trim it and tie it firmly. This can be roasted quickly in the oven, of course, but we prefer to do these smaller cuts on a rotisserie. Spit the meat diagonally, balancing it carefully so that the spit will not wobble as it revolves. Cook at high heat for about 1 hour for rare beef or insert a thermometer and cook until it registers 120° or desired mark. Carve this small rib roast as you would a steak; that is, slice it down from top to bottom, rather that in toward the bone.

## Prime Rib Burgundy

*8-pound prime rib roast, short ribs removed*
*1 teaspoon powdered cardamom*
*1 tablespoon soy sauce*
*½ cup Burgundy*

Secure roast on spit, then spread with cardamom and soy sauce. Roast about 2½ hours, or until meat thermometer registers "rare." Baste frequently with Burgundy. Serves 6-8.

## Filet de Boeuf

A filet of beef, perfectly cooked, is one of the most elegant of party dishes. It is expensive, but there is no waste—no bone, no gristle, no fat—and it cooks quickly. A filet weighs from 4 to 8 pounds. Allow about 1 pound per serving.

Since the fat has been trimmed from the filet, some recipes will call for barding. To bard a whole filet, do not cover the entire piece of meat with fat but use a strip 1½″ wide and wrap it around the filet the long way, tying it securely. Insert a meat thermometer in the thickest part of the meat and roast in a 450° oven for 30 to 40 minutes, or until the thermometer registers 120° for a very rare filet. If you prefer it a little less rare, roast to 125°; 135° for medium. Season the filet with salt and pepper as it cooks and baste often with the pan juices. If you cook it without barding, baste with melted butter and beef fat.

Roast filet may be served in any of the following ways:

### Sauce Bearnaise
Chop 3 shallots or small green onions very fine. Add 1 teaspoon of chopped parsley and 2 teaspoons of chopped fresh tarragon (or 1 teaspoon of dried tarragon). Cook these in ½ cup of wine vinegar until they are almost reduced to a glaze. Strain. In the upper part of a double boiler put 4 egg yolks. Place over hot, not boiling, water and

whisk with a wire whisk. Add the strained liquid a little at a time, whisking constantly. Be careful not to let the water boil. Continue cooking and whisking until the mixture thickens. Add, one at a time, 8 tablespoons softened butter, beating each in thoroughly. Season to taste with salt and a tiny bit of cayenne pepper and add fresh chopped parsley and tarragon if you like.

### Quick Sauce Bordelaise

This is a short cut version of the famous French sauce that is very satisfactory. Chop 2 small white onions very fine and slice 4 or 5 mushrooms. Sauté gently in butter until they are soft and lightly browned. Add 1½ cups of dry white wine and 1½ cups of stock, broth or bouillon. Simmer until reduced to about 2 cups of liquid. Season to taste with salt and freshly ground black pepper and stir in 1 tablespoon of tomato purée or paste. Thicken the sauce with small balls of butter and flour kneaded together.

## Filet of Beef with Red Wine

Select a whole filet and do not have it barded. Rub it well with butter, salt, rosemary, coarsely ground black pepper and finely chopped parsley. Roast in the oven (see Filet de Boeuf) basting frequently with red wine. Serve with braised onions and Sauce Bordelaise.

## Strasbourg Beef Fillet

*Larded 3-pound fillet of beef*
*14 chicken livers*
*4 tablespoons butter*
*2 onions, chopped*
*2 teaspoons salt*
*¾ teaspoon pepper*
*¼ teaspoon thyme*
*1 bay leaf*

*2 cups Madeira or port wine*
*1 tablespoon gelatin*
*3 tablespoons water*
*1 cup hot beef consommé (fresh or canned)*
*1 cup port wine*

Prepare the fillet the day before you plan to serve it. Have the butcher make a hollow in the center of the larded 3-pound fillet, 1″ in diameter down the entire length. (You can keep the removed piece for broiling or sautéeing.)

Cut the chicken livers in half and press into the hollow of the beef, packing them tightly together. Stuff pieces of aluminum foil into the ends. Melt the butter in a Dutch oven or heavy saucepan. Place the fillet in it and brown on all sides. Add the onions and continue browning. Add the salt, pepper, thyme, bay leaf and wine. Cover and cook over low heat for 1½ hours. Remove fillet and strain the gravy. Chill overnight. Soften the gelatin in the water for 5 minutes. Add the consommé and stir until dissolved. Add the port and reserved gravy, mixing well. Chill until it begins to thicken and set. Place the fillet on a long serving dish and slice it ½″ thick, but do not separate the slices. Spoon the gelatin mixture over it to coat it well. Chill until set. If there is any gelatin left over, chop it and use as a garnish. Serves 6-8.

## Chateaubriand à la Jackson

*1 whole beef tenderloin (4-6 pounds)*
*1 cup Chablis*
*¼ pound butter*
*½ cup cognac*
*¼ teaspoon thyme*
*½ bay leaf*
*1 onion, sliced paper-thin*
*1 pound fresh mushrooms, sliced thin*

Marinate tenderloin overnight in the Chablis. Melt butter in saucepan, add cognac and seasonings and stir well. Add onion slices and simmer until mixture cooks down to half volume. Add mushrooms and cook until tender, about 4 minutes. Remove meat from marinade, and cut a pocket in tenderloin. Stuff with onion-mushroom mix-

## Tournedos Bayard

Tournedos are thick slices of filet (1½″-2″), surrounded with barding fat. Allow 1 tournedos per serving.

Sauté 4 tournedos in 6 tablespoons of butter, beef fat, or butter and beef fat mixed. Sear them quickly to a nice brown on both sides, then lower the heat and cook until hot through but still juicy and rare in the center. Season with salt and pepper.

Arrange the tournedos on a hot platter or hot plates and top each one with an artichoke heart heated in butter and garnished with a slice of foie gras or homemade liver pâté.

To the pan in which the tournedos were cooked, add ¼ cup of port, 2 tablespoons of butter and 2 tablespoons of heavy consommé, beef extract or *glace de viande.* Heat together and pour over the tournedos. Serve with Pommes Vapeur (steamed potatoes or boiled potatoes steamed until dry and fluffy). Serves 4.

## Beef Scallops with Cognac

Buy 1½ pounds of beef filet or sirloin and have the butcher cut the meat into small flat scallops as if he were preparing veal scallopine. Flour the scallops lightly and sauté them quickly in hot beef fat (about 3 tablespoons of rendered beef suet is needed to cook 1½ pounds of scallops). These thin beef slices will only take a minute or two to cook; to brown nicely allow about ½ minute for each side.

Remove the scallops to a hot platter and keep them hot. Pour off the fat from the pan and add 1 teaspoon of salt, 1 table-

spoon of Worcestershire sauce, 1 tablespoon of tomato purée and ½ cup of chopped parsley. Blend and heat thoroughly and add 2 ounces of cognac. Pour this sauce over the meat and serve with steamed rice and buttered leeks. Serves 4.

## Beef Collops Flambés

*2 pounds top sirloin, cut into 2″ cubes*
*2 onions, sliced paper thin*
*1 cup red wine*
*2 tablespoons tarragon vinegar*
*½ cup olive oil*
*2 teaspoons salt*
*½ teaspoon pepper*
*¼ teaspoon marjoram, rosemary*
  *or oregano*
*Whole mushroom crowns*
*Green pepper slices*
*Small whole tomatoes*
*½ cup brandy*

Marinate the meat overnight in the onion-wine-vinegar-oil-herb-salt-pepper mixture. When ready to roast, alternate pieces of meat on spit with mushroom crowns, green pepper slices and tomatoes. Roast about 15 minutes, basting frequently. When ready

to serve, warm brandy, ignite, pour over meat, and serve flambé. Serves 4.

## VARIATIONS

● 2″ cubes of beef, rolled in bacon, and alternated on spit with tomato slices and canned onions. Roast about 15 minutes, basting with sherry and Worcestershire sauce.

● 2″ cubes of beef, marinated in soy sauce, alternated on spit with chicken livers. Roast for 15 minutes, basting with the marinade to which a little vermouth is added.

## Beef Stroganoff

1½ pounds tender beef filet or sirloin, cut
  in thin strips
5 tablespoons butter
2 tablespoons olive oil
2 chopped green onions
¼ cup white wine
Dash of Worcestershire sauce
1½ cups sour cream
Salt, freshly ground black pepper
Chopped parsley

Melt 4 tablespoons butter in a skillet or chafing dish and add 1 tablespoon oil to keep the butter from burning. Sauté beef strips in the hot fat very quickly, browning on both sides. It should take only a minute or so to cook. Remove meat to a hot platter and add remaining butter and oil. Add green onions and let them cook down for a minute. Add wine, Worcestershire sauce and sour cream. Be sure the heat is low. The sour cream must not boil or it will curdle. Stir sauce until well blended and heated through and season to taste with salt and pepper. Pour sauce over beef slices and top with chopped parsley. Serve with rice. Serves 4. This dish should be cooked quickly just before it is eaten. It may be cooked right at the table, in a chafing dish.

## Steak

There are four basic ways to cook steak. Your choice of method should be governed by the cut you are using and the thickness of the meat.

**Broiled in the oven.** Steaks for broiling should be thick—at least 1″ and if possible 2-2½″ or even 3″ thick. Good cuts are sirloin, porterhouse, thick T-bones, thick rib steaks, rump steaks.

If you have an oven thermometer, put it in the broiler and heat to 350°. Otherwise, get the broiler good and hot and then reduce the flame or heating unit a bit. You should cook the steak with heat that is better than medium, but not roaring high. Grease the hot rack with a little fat cut from the edge of the meat and arrange the steak on it. Place it about 3″ from the heating unit. Cook a 1½″-2″ steak 4 to 5 minutes before turning. Then cook for another 5 minutes. This should give you a rare steak, but make sure by testing with a tiny cut near the bone. The outside of the meat should be crusty brown. If it isn't, raise the heat a little during the last minute.

If you like your steak less rare, cook it for 6 to 8 minutes on the first side and finish cooking the other side until it is done to your satisfaction.

Very thick steaks (3″) should be seared thoroughly on each side very quickly before cooking through. Simply sear the first side with a high heat, then turn and sear the other side. Then lower the heat and cook for several minutes on each side until done to your satisfaction.

Season the steak toward the end of the broiling with salt and pepper.

**Charcoal Broiled Steak.** As with oven broiling, larger thicker steaks are the best choice for this cooking method. Be sure you start your fire well in advance and have a

good bed of ashy coals. Arrange the coals over an area slightly larger than the shape of your steak. Grease the rack and place the steak about 4″ to 5″ from the hot coals. For rare meat, cook a 2″ steak for 5 to 6 minutes on each side. Move the firebox up to char the outside of the meat during the last minute of cooking. Season to taste with salt and pepper.

**Pan Broiled.** This method is especially good for large steaks about 1½″ thick. You will need a very heavy skillet: stainless steel or cast aluminum is best. Be sure to trim all excess fat from the steak to prevent unnecessary smoking.

Put the skillet over the heat and get it almost red hot. Then add a thin layer of salt all over the bottom of the pan. Let the salt heat thoroughly and place the steak on top, searing it quickly. Turn and sear the other side. Lower the heat and cook for about 5 minutes on each side. This should give you a rare steak, but test for doneness by cutting into the flesh near the bone. If you do not like very rare steak, allow more minutes of cooking on each side—about 8-10 minutes per side will give you medium rare.

Season with pepper (no salt needed, of course).

**Sautéed.** This method is popular in France and Italy and some of the most famous recipes—Steak au Poivre, for example—call for it. It is the best method for small steaks, thin steaks, and those with little or no fat. Tiny club steaks, minute steaks and filet mignon are all good choices.

You can sauté steak in butter but it tends to burn over very high heat. It is wiser to use beef fat or oil, or part butter and part beef fat or oil. Heat a good heavy skillet and add enough fat to make a very thin film over the bottom. When the grease is piping hot add the steak and sear it quickly. Lower the heat and finish cooking on the bottom. A very thin steak, say ½″, will only take a minute per side. Allow 2-3 minutes per side for a 1″-thick steak, and 4 to 5 minutes for a 1½″-thick steak. When the first side is cooked, turn the meat and turn up the flame to sear the second side. Then finish cooking over a lowered flame. If the steak is fairly thick—1 to 1½″—sear it on both sides before lowering the flame to cook through. Do not try to sauté steaks over 1½″ thick. Season with salt and pepper.

### Suggestions for Serving Steak

Here are some good ways to serve steak cooked in any of the ways listed above. The following sauces and seasonings add interesting flavors and give more variety.

**Parisienne.** Add finely chopped parsley to creamed sweet butter and heap it on hot steak. This is usually served with crisp French fried potatoes.

**Herbed.** Add tarragon and chopped cress to the butter and serve in the same way.

**Provençal.** Pound or grind anchovies and mix with sweet butter to spread on the steak.

**Olive Butter.** This is another favorite from the south of France. Chop green olives

91

very fine and blend them with butter to spread on steaks.

**Mustard Sauce.** Melt ¼ pound of butter in a saucepan and add ¼ cup of chopped green onions, 2 tablespoons of prepared mustard, ¼ cup of chopped parsley and ½ teaspoon of tarragon. Pour over steak.

**Onions.** Steak smothered in onions is an old-fashioned favorite. Cover the steak with a thick layer of onion rings sautéed in butter until golden and tender. Allow 1 tablespoon of butter to each onion and cook them gently, covering the pan during the last few minutes to steam the onions tender. You can also use French fried onion rings, really crisp and crunchy.

**Mushroomed Steak.** For 4 servings, sauté the caps from 2 pounds of mushrooms in 6 tablespoons of butter and 6 tablespoons of olive oil. Add a chopped garlic clove and cook gently until thoroughly tender. Then add a good handful of chopped parsley (Italian variety, if possible) and season to taste with salt and pepper. Some people like to cook the mushrooms down until they are almost black and then add a dash of Worcestershire sauce to them. Or you may flavor them with a dash or two of sherry or Madeira. Pour over hot steak.

## Steak au Poivre

Use small 12-ounce minute steaks for this popular French steak dish. Allow 1 to a serving. Sauté them in beef fat or half butter and half beef fat.

A supply of freshly crushed peppercorns soaked in cognac makes a more tasty steak au poivre. Crush the peppercorns with a rolling pin until they are coarsely cracked, heap them into a jar and cover with cognac. Put a lid on the jar and set it aside, so that you have cognac-pepper ready whenever you cook a steak. Failing this,

use plain crushed peppercorns. Press the pepper into the steak on both sides with the heel of your hand, and use plenty of pepper.

Heat the fat in the skillet, allowing about 1 tablespoon of fat for each steak. If you are cooking several steaks, you will need at least two skillets. When the fat is piping hot, put in the steaks and sear them quickly on the bottom. Lower the heat a bit and cook for about 2 minutes; then turn the steaks and repeat on the other side. Remove to hot plates and season with salt.

Rinse the skillets with cognac, allowing about ¼ cup for each pan. Pour this over the steaks and serve with watercress and grilled tomatoes.

*VARIATIONS*

1. After adding the cognac to the pan, add ½ cup of heavy cream and heat through. Pour this sauce over the steaks.
2. After adding the cognac to the pan, add ¼ cup of bouillon and 1 cup of sour cream. Blend thoroughly and heat through but do not boil. Pour over the steaks.

## Flank Steak (London Broil)

Flank steak, cooked just to the rare stage and carved in thin slices on the diagonal, is excellent eating. Have the butcher trim the steak well. Broil it quickly, allowing 3 to 4 minutes to a side, until it is nicely charred on the outside and still juicy red in the middle. Season to taste with salt and pepper and cut it on the diagonal, holding the knife so that it slopes from left to right.

*VARIATIONS*

**Oriental.** Marinate the steak in ½ cup of sherry, ½ cup of soy sauce, 2 chopped cloves of garlic and ¼ cup of chopped fresh ginger or 1 teaspoon of ground ginger. Soak it for several hours, turning frequently. Broil and carve as above.

**Chili-Oriental.** Add 1 tablespoon of chili powder to the Oriental Marinade.

## Chinese Beef Rice

*4 cups cooked rice*
*2 tablespoons oil or melted lard*
*¾ cup lean beef (tenderloin or top round)*
*1 tablespoon soy sauce*
*½ cup green pepper, chopped*
*½ onion, thinly sliced*
*1½ cups Chinese cabbage, shredded*
*½ teaspoon salt*

Boil rice, drain and keep warm. In skillet melt 1 tablespoon oil or lard and add rice. Stir gently but well for 3 minutes over brisk fire. Remove from fire and reserve.

In another skillet warm remaining oil or lard, and add beef cut in slivers and mixed with soy sauce. Cook and stir until beef loses raw look. Then add green pepper, onion and Chinese cabbage. Cook and stir for not more than 3 minutes over medium fire. Add salt at last moment. Serve on rice. Serves 4.

## Roulades of Beef

*12 3″ x 5″ pieces round steak, about ¼″-½″*
  *thick*
*1 cup mashed potatoes*
*¼ cup chopped smoked ham*
*½ cup chopped sautéed mushrooms*
*1 cup finely chopped hard-cooked egg*
*¼ cup chopped parsley*
*Salt, pepper*
*Flour*
*Butter*
*½ cup sherry*
*½ cup bouillon*
*1 pint sour cream*
*Chopped parsley for garnish*

Pound the meat pieces very flat or ask the butcher to do this for you when he cuts them. Mix the potatoes, ham, mushrooms, egg, and parsley together and season to taste with salt and pepper. Put a heaping spoonful of this stuffing on each beef piece, roll it up and tie it securely. Roll the pieces in flour and sear them on all sides in butter. Add the sherry and bouillon, cover the pan and simmer gently for 2 hours. Remove the meat to a hot platter and skim the fat from the juices in the pan. Add the sour cream, stirring it in to blend thoroughly, but do not let it come to a boil or it will curdle. Heat through and pour over the roulades. Garnish with chopped parsley and serve with braised cabbage. Serves 6.

### VARIATIONS

1. Stuff the roulades with chopped anchovies, green onions and ripe olives. Brown the rolls in olive oil, add two minced cloves of garlic and tomato sauce and bouillon for the liquid. Instead of sour cream, add more tomato sauce to make the broth.
2. Stuff the beef rolls with strips of dill pickle and seasoned bread crumbs. Add a touch of dill to the liquid and use sour cream to make the sauce.

## Braised Beef with Olives

4-pound piece shin, bottom round or chuck
4 tablespoons chopped suet
¼ pound salt pork
2 pounds veal knuckle
1 piece marrow bone
2 tablespoons cognac
¼ cup white wine
2 leeks, sliced
1 stalk celery, sliced
1 sprig parsley, minced
1 teaspoon thyme
1 bay leaf
1 tablespoon tomato paste
1½ cups hot consommé
1½ cups small green olives, sliced

Have the butcher tie the piece of beef firmly so that it will hold its shape. Chop the suet coarsely and cut the salt pork into cubes. Try out the beef suet and to the fat from the suet add the veal knuckle, marrow bone, salt pork cubes and the beef. Turn the heat down and cook this gently for 20 minutes, turning occasionally. Add the cognac, white wine, leeks, celery, parsley, thyme and bay leaf and cover the pot. Cook very gently for 3 hours, turning the meat from time to time. Uncover the pot and cook for 15 minutes or until the liquid is completely evaporated. Pour off any fat, and add the tomato paste, hot consommé and sliced olives. Cook for 10 minutes, or until well blended and heated through.

Serve the meat and sauce with steamed potatoes and an endive salad. Serves 4-6.

## Pot Roast Niçoise

4-5 pound piece top round or rump
2 cloves garlic, slivered
Salt, pepper, rosemary
Flour
6 tablespoons olive oil
2 cups red wine
2 mashed cloves garlic
1 large onion stuck with cloves
1 bay leaf
1 teaspoon rosemary
1¼ cups tomato purée
½ cup cognac
1 cup black olives, sliced
Chopped parsley

If you buy well aged prime or choice grade of beef, there is no need to have it larded. Otherwise, ask the butcher to lard the piece in several places with pork fat. Make 8 to 10 slashes in the flesh and insert garlic slivers. Rub the roast well with salt, pepper and rosemary and dredge it with flour. Heat oil in a deep kettle and brown the meat on all sides. Add the wine, the mashed garlic, the onion, bay leaf, 1 teaspoon rosemary and 1 cup tomato purée. Cover the pan and simmer gently for 4 hours, basting the meat frequently with the juices in the kettle. Remove the roast to a hot platter, skim the fat from the liquid and taste for seasoning. Add ¼ cup tomato purée, the cognac, black olives and cook for 4-5 minutes, or until thoroughly blended and hot through. Sprinkle the sauce with chopped parsley and serve with the pot roast. Serves 4-6. Good accompaniments are polenta and sautéed eggplant. To make polenta, mix 1½ cups of cornmeal with 3 cups of boiling salted water very slowly. Stir the cornmeal in a bit at a time to be sure the mixture is smooth. Pour it into a mold or a colander lined with thick cloth and steam over hot water for three hours, or until very firm. Serve in slices with plenty of butter, salt and freshly ground black pepper.

## Boeuf à la Mode

5-6 pound piece top round steak
4 tablespoons butter or pork fat
Salt pork slices
1 calf's foot
2 onions stuck with cloves

*3 carrots, sliced*
*2 leeks, sliced*
*1 small turnip, sliced*
*1 bay leaf*
*1 teaspoon thyme*
*Handful of parsley*
*Salt, pepper*
*1 bottle red wine*
*¼ cup cognac*

Have the butcher lard the steak for you in about six places. If you have a larding needle and can do this job yourself, soak larding pork in cognac for a day before putting it in the beef. Brown the piece of round steak in butter or pork fat or a mixture of both. In a large heavy kettle with a tight lid place a layer of salt pork. Put the round steak on top and add the calf's foot, onions, carrots, leeks, turnip, bay leaf, thyme, parsley and salt and pepper to taste. Pour red wine over and add enough water to cover. Put a lid on the kettle, bring the liquid to a boil, lower the heat and simmer for 4 or 5 hours. The liquid must be kept just below the boiling point. If you can cook this in a very slow oven it is easier to regulate the temperature.

Remove the meat and blaze it with the cognac. Skim the fat from the pan juices and serve juices with the meat. Accompany with boiled potatoes and braised onions. Serves 4-6.

**To serve cold:** In a large mold place a bed of thin carrot slices, sliced stuffed olives, capers and sliced pickles. Cover this with a thin layer of aspic. Trim the meat and cut into slices—not too thin—and arrange these in a neat layer in the mold. Skim the excess fat from the liquid and reduce it a little over high heat. For each 2 cups of liquid, dissolve 1 envelope of unflavored gelatin in ¼ cup of water. Stir this into the hot liquid until melted. Cool and pour over the meat in the mold. Chill thoroughly and unmold on a platter. Serve with Mustard Sauce. You can make individual molds if you choose.

Serve with potato salad and thinly sliced tomatoes dressed with oil and vinegar.

### Mustard Sauce

First prepare a rich cream sauce as follows: melt 4 tablespoons of butter in a saucepan and blend in 4 tablespoons of flour. Slowly add 1 cup of milk mixed with 1 cup of cream, stirring constantly. Continue stirring and cooking until the mixture is smooth and thick. Season to taste with salt and pepper. Add 2 tablespoons of prepared French mustard and 2 teaspoons of dry mustard. Blend thoroughly.

## Steak and Kidney Pie

*2 pounds top round steak*
*3 veal kidneys*
*Flour*
*6 tablespoons butter or oil*
*2 medium onions, sliced very thin*
*½ pound sliced mushrooms*
*1 teaspoon salt*
*1 teaspoon freshly ground pepper*
*1 teaspoon crushed rosemary leaves*
*1 tablespoon tomato paste*
*2 ounces cognac*
*1 cup red wine*
*Puff paste*

Cut the round steak into 2″ cubes. Trim the fat from the kidneys and cut them into small cubes. Dredge the steak and kidneys in the flour and sear them quickly in the hot butter or oil. Add onions to the hot fat and let them cook until just soft. In a deep baking dish arrange the meat, onions and sliced mushrooms. Mix the salt, pepper, rosemary, tomato paste, cognac and wine together and pour over the meat. Cover the dish and bake in a 350° oven for 3 hours, adding more wine if the liquid gets too low.

While the meat is cooking, prepare a puff paste: Knead and cream ½ pound of sweet butter with your hands until it is soft and smooth. Place it in a napkin or clean cloth and squeeze out any excess moisture. Then form it into a rectangle about ½″ thick and chill. Sift 2 cups of flour with ½ teaspoon of salt into a mound on a work table or board. Pour ¾ cup of ice water into the center of the flour, a bit at a time, working it in with your fingers as you go. Add the water very slowly; you may not need all of it. The dough is finished when it forms a soft ball about the same consistency as the creamed butter.

Place the dough on a floured board and roll it out into a rectangle ½″ thick. Place the chilled butter rectangle on top, and fold a flap of the dough over the butter from the left to the center. Then fold the dough at the right over the butter. Press the edges together and chill for 20 minutes. With a floured rolling pin roll the dough out into another rectangle ½″ thick, being careful not to break the dough covering. The butter should not ooze out. Fold the dough over again as you did before. Roll again and fold again. Chill for 20 minutes.

Repeat the rolling and folding twice more, chill again for 20 minutes and then roll and fold two more times. Chill for 15 minutes and then roll the dough into a circle 2″ larger than the top of the baking dish

containing the meat. Place the dough on a cookie or baking sheet and bake at 450° for 10 minutes. Reduce the heat to 350° and finish baking until puffed and brown.

Remove the cover from the meat dish and slip the puff paste on top. Serve at once. Serves 4.

## Boeuf à la Bourguignonne

*3-4 pounds lean beef (chuck or top round)*
*cut into 1½″ to 2″ cubes*
*4 large slices salt pork, cut into small*
*cubes*
*Flour*
*1 teaspoon salt*
*1 teaspoon freshly ground black pepper*
*1 leek, well washed*
*Sprig of thyme*
*2-3 sprigs parsley*
*2 cloves garlic*
*Red wine*
*½ pound mushrooms*
*4 tablespoons butter*

Put the cubes of salt pork in a large heavy skillet that has a tight cover or a Dutch oven. Try out pork over a low flame. Meanwhile, roll the beef cubes in flour. Add to the pan and brown on all sides. Add a little butter or bacon fat if necessary. When cubes are browned, add salt, pepper, leek, thyme, parsley and garlic. Cover with red wine, bring just to a boil and lower flame to simmer. Cover the pan tightly and let the beef cook gently until thoroughly tender. Remove beef from pan and strain sauce. Meanwhile, sauté the mushrooms in the butter until lightly browned. Add to the beef and strained sauce. Thicken the sauce if you wish with small balls of butter and flour kneaded together. Taste for seasoning. Serves 6.

Serve with boiled potatoes, lavishly buttered, and tiny white onions glazed in butter and sugar. (To prepare glazed onions, peel 18-24 small onions and steam gently in butter, turning frequently. When browned, sprinkle 1 teaspoon sugar evenly over top of onions. Cover pan and shake vigorously for a minute or two until onions are glazed. Uncover and season to taste.)

## Carbonnade Flamande

*3-4 pounds lean beef (chuck or round)*
*cut into cubes*
*5 tablespoons butter*
*2 pounds onions, sliced*
*Flour*
*4-6 tablespoons beef fat, butter or butter*
*and oil*
*1 teaspoon salt*
*1 teaspoon freshly ground black pepper*
*2 cloves garlic*
*1 pint beer*

Melt butter in a large Dutch oven or large heavy skillet and sauté the onions until soft and just lightly browned. Roll beef cubes in flour and brown them in the beef fat, butter or butter and oil. Add browned meat to

onions with salt, pepper and garlic and enough beer to cover. Cover pan with tightly fitting lid and simmer gently until meat is thoroughly tender. If you prefer a thicker sauce, add small balls of flour and butter kneaded together and stir in until sauce is smooth and thickened. Serves 6. Serve with boiled or baked potatoes and plenty of beer to drink.

## Sauerbraten

*4-pound piece of beef (round, chuck or*
*rump)*
*1½ cups red wine vinegar*
*½ cup dry red wine*
*2 onions, sliced*
*2 carrots, sliced*
*1 bay leaf*
*3 allspice berries*
*3 cloves*
*1 tablespoon peppercorns*
*1 tablespoon salt*
*8 tablespoons butter*
*1 tablespoon oil*
*5 tablespoons flour*
*1 tablespoon sugar*
*⅔ cup gingersnaps, crumbled*

Ask the butcher to tie the meat so that it will hold its shape. Make a marinade of the mixed vinegar, wine, onions, carrots, bay leaf, allspice, cloves, peppercorns and salt. Put the beef in a deep bowl and pour the marinade over it. Cover and leave in the refrigerator to soak for 3 days, turning the meat occasionally during this time.

When the beef is well soaked, remove from the marinade and wipe dry. Melt 4 tablespoons of butter with the oil in a heavy Dutch oven. Brown the beef on all sides in the hot fat and sprinkle it lightly with flour as you turn it. Heat the marinade and pour over the browned beef. Cover the kettle, lower the heat and simmer gently until the beef is thoroughly tender, about 3 hours.

When the meat is done, pour off the sauce and set the kettle on one side to keep the meat warm. Skim fat from sauce and strain it. In a heavy skillet, melt 4 tablespoons butter and blend in 4 tablespoons flour and the sugar. Cook gently until flour and sugar are slightly browned. Add the strained sauce slowly, stirring it until it is smooth and thickened. Add the gingersnaps to the sauce. Pour over the meat, cover and cook gently for ½ hour. The traditional accompaniment for sauerbraten is dumplings, but I prefer noodles. Serves 4.

## Braised Brisket with Sauerkraut

*3-4 pounds sauerkraut*
*2 coarsely chopped garlic cloves*
*1½ teaspoons cracked pepper*
*1 bottle white wine (riesling or traminer)*
*4-pound piece brisket*
*1 garlic clove, slivered*
*Flour*
*Beef fat*
*Salt*

In a large Dutch oven or heavy kettle combine the sauerkraut, garlic cloves, cracked pepper and wine, reserving one cup. Cover and simmer for 3 hours.

Slash the piece of brisket in several places and insert slivers of garlic. Dredge the meat in flour and brown on all sides in hot beef fat. Season to taste with salt, add ½ cup of white wine and cook, covered, over a very low flame for 30 minutes. Turn the meat several times as it cooks. Then put the beef on top of the sauerkraut, add the juices from the pan in which the beef has cooked and the remaining ½ cup of white wine. Cover and simmer for 2 hours or until the meat is thoroughly tender. Serves 6-8.

Serve with plain boiled potatoes dressed with butter and chopped parsley.

## Corned Beef

This homely fare is really a delicate dish, delicious hot, cold or in hash. We prefer the corned brisket or boneless rump. If you buy brisket, be sure it is not too fat. In New York and in some other areas there is a special pickled corned beef, well seasoned with bay leaf, mustard seed and thyme. This, if you can find it, is especially good. Buy 1 pound of corned beef per serving, to allow for fat and shrinkage.

Put the piece of beef in a large kettle with cold water to cover and bring to a boil. Lower the heat and simmer for 10 minutes; then pour off the water. Add 1 onion stuck with cloves, a bay leaf, 2 cloves of garlic, a sprig of parsley and a stalk of celery. Cover with fresh cold water and bring to a boil again. Put a lid on the kettle, lower the heat and simmer until the corned beef is tender. This will take about 3 or 4 hours.

Serve the meat cut in very thin slices with potatoes boiled in their jackets and a selection of mustards. Steamed buttered cabbage, turnips, carrots and onions are all excellent accompaniments.

## Cold Corned Beef

Cook corned beef according to directions above. Remove it from the hot liquid and put it in a large flat bowl that has been rubbed with a cut clove of garlic. Weight the meat down thoroughly. You can do this by placing a large plate on top of it and heaping the plate with heavy canned goods; or put a brick or your electric iron on top of the plate. Weighting the meat as it cools makes it firmer and easier to cut in slices.

When the corned beef is cold, remove the weights and slice the meat very thin. Serve with mustards, horse-radish and potato salad garnished with onion rings.

## Braised Short Ribs of Beef

*4 pounds lean, meaty short ribs*
*Flour*
*Salt, pepper*
*4 tablespoons beef fat or butter*
*2 bay leaves*
*2 cloves garlic*
*1 onion stuck with cloves*
*1 teaspoon rosemary*
*3 carrots*
*1 turnip*
*1 cup red wine*

Dredge the ribs with seasoned flour and brown them in the hot fat. Add the bay leaves, garlic, onion, rosemary, carrots, turnip and enough water to cover. Bring to a boil quickly and then lower the heat, cover the pan and simmer gently for 1 hour. Add the red wine and continue cooking for another hour or until the ribs are thoroughly tender and permeated with the various flavors. Serves 4. You may add potatoes to the pot during the last hour, if you like, or serve the braised ribs with buttered noodles.

## Beef Tongue, Alsatian

Buy a fresh beef tongue and soak it in acidulated water (1 tablespoon of vinegar to 1 quart of water) for 2 hours. Remove, trim and place in a large kettle. Cover the tongue with fresh cold water and add 2 leeks, 2 carrots, 2 turnips, a sprig of parsley, 2 onions stuck with cloves, and salt and

pepper. Bring this to a boil, lower the heat and cover the pan. Simmer gently for 3 hours or until the tongue is tender. Remove and skin and return to liquid to keep hot.

Serve bowls of the broth and put the sliced meat and vegetables on a platter to be served together. Serves 6. Good accompaniments are horse-radish, horse-radish mustard, or horse-radish, prepared mustard and sour cream blended together. Braised Brussels sprouts or spinach dressed with oil and garlic go well with this boiled tongue.

## Oxtail Ragoût

Buy 2 or 3 oxtails and ask the butcher to disjoint them. This does mean *disjoint*—cut through at the joints—not simply hack into pieces. Also buy 1 calf's foot.

Place the oxtails in flat baking dish, season them to taste with salt and pepper and sprinkle very lightly with flour. Roast in a 450° oven for 30 minutes, shaking the pan from time to time and basting the meat with juices in the pan.

Remove the meat from the oven, pour off the fat and blaze the oxtails with 2 ounces of cognac. Transfer the pieces of oxtail to a deep casserole and add 2 carrots, cut in pieces, an onion stuck with cloves, 1 teaspoon of thyme, a sprig of parsley and a bay leaf. Cover with water or broth and cook in a 350° oven for 3 hours. Reduce the heat to 250° and cook for 3 hours. Serve in deep bowls, giving each person plenty of the rich broth. Serves 4-6. With it serve boiled potatoes and braised cabbage sprinkled with poppy seeds.

Oxtail ragoût is even better if made the day before. Let it cool, skim off the fat and reheat before serving.

*VARIATION*

Substitute red wine and water for the plain water or broth in the recipe.

## Tripe with Red Wine

This hearty dish can be made well ahead of time. It will keep for several days in the refrigerator and is good reheated.

Buy 3 pounds of tripe cut into small strips, 2 calf's feet split in two or a large veal knuckle, and ¼ pound of beef suet. Chop the suet and slice 3 or 4 medium onions. In a large casserole make a layer of the chopped suet; add the tripe, the sliced onions, the calf's feet or veal knuckle, 1 bay leaf, 1 teaspoon of thyme, 1 tablespoon of salt, 1 tablespoon of freshly ground pepper, 4 ounces of cognac and enough red wine to cover. Put a lid on the casserole and seal it tightly with a flour and water paste. Bake in a 350° oven for 3 hours. Reduce the heat to 250° and bake for 5 more hours. Remove the casserole from the oven and let it cool. Skim off the fat and reheat. Serve very hot with boiled potatoes or rice. Serves 4-6.

## Beef Kidney Stew

Buy 1 beef kidney. Trim off the fat and gristle and remove the membrane. In a bowl put 2 cups of water and 2 tablespoons of vinegar. Soak the kidney in this for 2 hours.

Remove the kidney from the water and cut it into thin slices. Dredge these in flour seasoned with salt and pepper. Heat 2 tablespoons of butter with 1 tablespoon of olive oil and sear the kidney slices quickly, browning them on both sides. Add 1 finely chopped onion and cook for 2 or 3 minutes. Sprinkle with a pinch of thyme and 1 tablespoon of chopped parsley and add 1 cup of red wine. Cover and simmer gently for 15 or 20 minutes, or until the kidney slices are tender.

Serve with boiled potatoes. Serves 4.

## Beef Liver Julienne in Cream

Cut 1 pound beef liver into thin strips and roll each strip in flour seasoned with salt, pepper and paprika. In a heavy skillet heat 2 tablespoons of butter with 2 tablespoons of olive oil and brown the liver strips quickly on all sides. Add 2 finely chopped green onions and a handful of chopped parsley and pour over all ½ cup of dry vermouth. Cover and let the liver simmer very gently until tender. Remove the hot liver to a platter and add 1 cup of sour or heavy sweet cream to the pan. Stir this into the juices, being careful not to let it boil or the cream will curdle. When it is hot through pour it over the liver strips. Serve with boiled rice. Serves 4.

# LAMB

# Lamb

You may have noticed that the familiar Anglo-American institution known as the "steak and chop house" offers a fair selection of steaks but that often you must run your finger some distance down the *à la carte* side of the menu before you come upon lamb chops. We are a nation of beef eaters; and we like pig. Lamb is a poor third in our country, and we think this is so mainly because many restaurateurs and housewives do not quite understand how to buy, cook or serve it. We seldom eat lamb at its best. Frequently we eat it at its worst.

Now, the fact is that young lamb can be tenderer and tastier than any other meat. In Brittany lamb is called *présalé* because the animals eat from the salty meadows around the sea and the channel. As a result, the meat has a fine, delicate flavor. This region has produced some of the classic recipes for roast lamb. Lamb is enormously popular in the Old World. It is the featured dish of the Paschal or Easter feast in Italy. It is the basic ingredient of the multitudinous *shish kebabs* of the Near East. And who has not heard of the wonderful British invention called the double lamb chop?

If in your lifetime you have not tasted lamb that rivaled the best beef in flavor and texture, then probably you have eaten lamb that was too mature. Or you have eaten lamb that was too well done. Or you have eaten lamb served on a cold plate. This seemingly minor point is a culinary crime; when lamb is served on a cold plate, the lukewarm fat congeals and the meat becomes unappetizing, both to look at and to eat.

At its best, lamb is young. We like to cook it only until the meat is pinkish inside and serve it rare and juicy, on piping hot plates. This, however, is a matter of personal preference.

Buy U. S. Prime or Choice grade. Good lamb has medium red flesh and creamy fat with a slightly pink cast. If the bones

have pink streaks, the lamb is young. Pure white bones mean the animal is too mature, and that consequently the meat will have a strong flavor even though it may still be tender. Mature, well aged mutton is excellent fare, but that is another dish. What you should avoid is the in-between lamb—too old to be delicate, too young to be aged as good hearty mutton.

*Agneau de lait,* the tiny baby lamb, is a choice dish in France, Spain, Italy and other Mediterranean countries, where it is often roasted whole. Baby lamb is hard to find in this country. In New York and other large cities the place to shop for it is a Greek or Armenian market. We have included several recipes for this baby lamb just on the chance it may be available in your area. Unlike the larger lamb, these tiny morsels should be served well done.

Lamb, properly cooked, is a dish to inspire poets. John Gay spoke in these rhapsodic terms of dining on lamb: "On the table spread the cloth, Let the knives be sharp and clean, Pickles get and salad both, Let the meat be fresh and clean. With small beer, good ale and wine, Oh, ye Gods! How I shall dine!"

## STANDARD LAMB CUTS

1. leg
2. loin
3. ribs
4. breast
5. shank
6. shoulder
7. neck

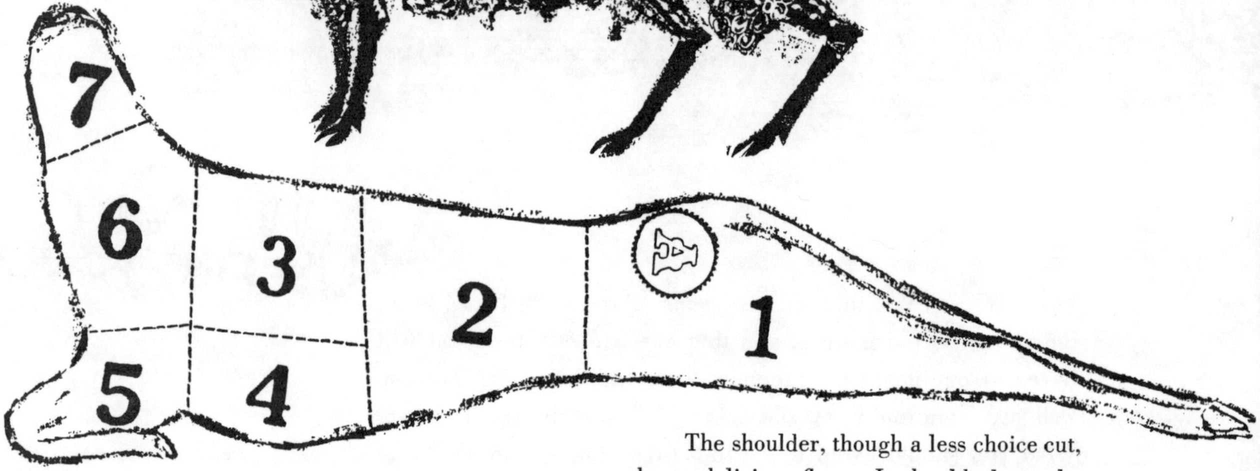

As you can see on the accompanying chart, almost all the lamb is edible. The most popular roast is the leg. If the two legs are left joined and part of the saddle included in the cut, it is called a baron of lamb. This makes a spectacular dish, ideal for a big outdoor grill with a revolving spit, and a fine selection for a dinner party.

The whole saddle, which includes the two loins, the tenderloins and part of the ribs, is another impressive party roast. Small racks of lamb ribs make tasty dinners for a small group and can be cooked very quickly in a hot oven.

The shoulder, though a less choice cut, has a delicious flavor. It should always be boned and rolled for roasting. The various types of lamb chops (described under lamb chop recipes) are excellent for quick broiling.

Lamb shanks, notable for chewy, moist meat, have an ardent following. They are one of my favorites and certainly a most inexpensive treat. The humblest cut of lamb is the breast, but if it is not too fatty, it can be a delectable crisp dish, as tasty as any spareribs. Breast and neck (another inexpensive cut) are frequently used for stew.

The kidneys, liver and tongue of lamb, often ignored, are delicately flavored and make fine eating.

## Roast Leg of Lamb (Gigot)

If a whole leg is too big a roast for your needs, have part of it cut into steaks to use later. Allow at least ½ pound per person; to be on the safe side, we usually order almost a pound per person. For example, we buy a 6-pound leg to serve 8 people. If lamb is left over, it need not be a problem. There are delicious ways to use it listed under recipes for Moussaka.

A French leg of lamb is cut whole with the shank bone intact. Some butchers split the shank, so that the leg will fit more easily into a roasting pan. Others remove the bone entirely and turn the flesh under to make a more compact piece of meat. We prefer to have the shank bone left on, for the rather gristly meat around it cooks to a crisp chewy stage and is fine to nibble.

To roast, rub the leg well with salt and freshly ground pepper and place it on a rack in a roasting pan. Insert a meat thermometer in the fleshiest part of the leg. Roast in a 325° oven without basting until the internal temperature registers 140° for rare —about 150° for medium rare and 160° for well done meat. The average cooking time for a rare leg of lamb is 1 to 1¼ hours, for medium 1½ to 2 hours and for well done 2½ hours.

*VARIATIONS*

**With garlic.** Peel and cut two or three cloves of garlic into slivers. Make deep incisions in the flesh of the leg and insert the slivers of garlic. Salt and pepper well and proceed as above.

**With rosemary.** Insert garlic slivers as above and rub rosemary leaves well into the meat. Season with salt and pepper and follow directions for roasting.

**With tarragon.** Omit the garlic. Rub the leg well with tarragon leaves and insert some of the leaves in small incisions in the roast. Season with salt and pepper and roast as above. Baste with melted butter and white wine mixed and flavored with tarragon leaves.

Be certain that you have hot, hot plates and platter! There is nothing less appetizing than lamb fat congealed on a lukewarm plate—and this it will do unless your plates are really hot.

Potatoes roasted in the pan with the meat are delicious with any of the lamb roasts. Small new potatoes whole, or Idaho or California potatoes peeled and cut into serving size pieces may be roasted for the last hour of cooking time. Turn the potatoes once or twice during the cooking. Salt and pepper them while they roast.

If you are serving wine with the roast —and custom and propriety certainly sanction the accompaniment—please refrain from the early American custom of currant jelly or, what is even worse, mint jelly. In fact, while I am on the subject of mint, let me urge you to forget all about the sauce made with vinegar and sugar and mint for lamb. Lamb can stand on its own.

Peas are traditionally served with lamb, but braised celery, braised endive, string beans sautéed in butter or string beans with crisp bacon and almonds and a touch of onion are vegetables which go excellently with lamb and are a most welcome change.

## Gigot Bretonne

Insert garlic cloves into the flesh of a leg of lamb and roast it in the usual manner, basting it occasionally with a little consommé or veal broth. You should have about 1 cup liquid in the pan when the gigot is cooked. It should be cooked rare or at the most, medium rare.

In the meantime cook 1 pound of white pea beans (to serve 6 persons) which have been soaked overnight. Or use the processed beans which require no soaking. Flavor the beans with salt and pepper and a clove of garlic and add ¼ cup of tomato purée.

When the roast is done, remove it to a hot platter. Drain the beans, add 2 tablespoons butter and the pan juices from the roast and blend well. Sprinkle liberally with chopped parsley and serve at once with the lamb. With this serve a bottle of a good rosé—either an Almadén from California or a Tavel—and some leaf spinach. Finish with a fine Camembert or a Brie and you have a superb meal.

## Gigot Bouquetière

This version of lamb needs a large baking dish about 2½" to 3" deep in which a rack for the meat will fit. In the baking dish arrange about 18 small new potatoes, 18 small white peeled onions, 2 cloves garlic, peeled and chopped, 8 small carrots peeled and left whole, 8 tiny turnips peeled and left whole and about ¼ cup of chopped parsley. Salt and pepper the vegetables to taste and add 2 cups of consommé. Place the rack in the pan and on top put a leg of young lamb. Season it with salt and pepper and insert a meat thermometer. Roast at 325° until the internal temperature of the lamb reaches 145° or 150°. If you wish, you may add peas and string beans to the vegetable mixture, or you may serve them separately.

## Lamb with a Spoon

This is a dish for those who like well done meat.

Have the butcher bone and tie a leg of lamb. Take the bones too and also buy a veal knuckle and a pound of neck of veal. Put the leg into a large bowl or dish. Add ½ cup of olive oil, ½ cup of cognac, 3 carrots finely chopped, 3 onions finely chopped, 2 stalks of celery finely cut, 3 cloves of gar-

lic finely chopped, a good handful of parsley and 1 teaspoon each of salt and freshly ground pepper. Let the leg stand in the mixture for at least 12 hours, turning it frequently to be sure it is evenly bathed.

In the meantime, brown the lamb bones and the veal with a little butter in a 400° oven. Remove them from the oven, cover with water and season with salt and pepper. Continue cooking on top of the stove for 3 hours.

Remove the leg from the marinade and strain the liquid. Add the vegetables to the broth made from the bones and veal. Wipe the lamb dry and brown it on all sides in 4 tablespoons butter. Add 2 carrots and 2 medium onions cut in quarters and brown them slightly. Add 1 cup of white wine and let it cook down for a few moments. Add the lamb, the vegetables and wine to the broth on the stove and also add 1 large clove crushed garlic, a sprig of thyme, a stalk of celery and a handful of parsley. Bring all to a boil on top of the stove. Cover and place in a 350° oven for 4-5 hours. Baste with the juices in the pan several times. When liquid is cooked down and the vegetables blended almost to a paste, remove the nearly disintegrated lamb to a hot platter. Garnish with rice and braised celery. Strain the sauce or blend it in an electric blender to mix all the vegetable flavors. Serve separately.

## Helen and Philip Brown's Picnic Gigot

Have a leg of lamb boned but not tied. Rub it well with garlic, oil, salt, pepper and rosemary.

Build a good charcoal fire and let it burn down to a glow of snowy coals. When the temperature of the surface of the fire is about 325° to 350°, start the leg broiling. It should be spread out well on the grill and turned often, so that it gets a beautiful brown crust on the outside but remains delicately pink on the inside (one of the basket-type grills is ideal for this).

Serve this broiled lamb with crusty bread toasted over the coals, a big bowl of string beans vinaigrette, sliced raw onions, a good wine, and some cheese, fruit and more wine for a finale. This makes an outdoor meal you will long remember.

## Cold Leg of Lamb

Roast a leg according to any of the above recipes and let it cool but do not chill. When we plan to serve a cold leg of lamb for dinner, we roast it in the late morning and let it cool off gently at room temperature without putting it into the refrigerator.

Slice it paper thin and trim off all the fat. Serve with a sharp mustard-flavored mayonnaise, cold rice with finely chopped pimentos, peppers and onion and a simple vinaigrette sauce. Peas *à la bonne femme* and grilled mushrooms are good hot dishes to serve with cold lamb.

## Roast Saddle of Lamb

The saddle is the whole loin with some of the bones removed and the flank ends rolled and trimmed. The whole piece should be thoroughly tied. Sometimes it is stuffed with kidneys before tying. This luxurious roast is a perfect choice for a formal party.

Roast it as you would a leg, at 325° without basting, until the internal temperature reaches about 150°-155°.

A saddle of lamb is carved differently from other roasts. It should be sliced in long strips parallel to the spinal column. It is incorrect to carve it down between the bones. To reach the tenderloin, the roast will have to be turned over and cut into through the protective section of the flank.

Serve saddle of lamb with a *sauce poivrade*, puréed chestnuts or a purée of peas.

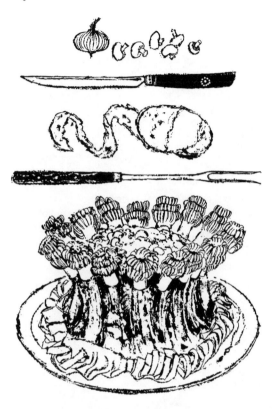

## Crown Roast of Lamb

Many people like the crown because it makes a beautiful display at table. It is made from the rib sections of two loins sewn together in a crown shape, and is usually served with puréed peas or chestnuts or sautéed mushrooms heaped in the center.

When you prepare the roast for the oven, slip a cube of salt pork over the tip of each bone to protect it from charring. Season the meat and roast at 325° for about 1 to 1¼ hours. It should be rare, not well done. Arrange it on a hot platter, remove the pieces of salt pork, and replace them with paper frills. Fill the center with the vegetable of your choice and garnish the platter with mushroom caps.

107

## Baron of Lamb

This dish is as noble as its name. Few ovens today can hold a baron of lamb, but there are many charcoal spits that will accommodate one easily. If you have the wide 30" oven you can cook it indoors. The younger the lamb the better. It will not take up as much room. The baron includes the two legs with a bit of the saddle. Roast it as you would the leg or shoulder at 325° until the internal temperature is 145°-155°. This will take about 18-20 minutes per pound. Bring it to the table on a huge platter or board; carve down from the rump in long slices.

## Roast Rack of Lamb

A small rack of lamb ribs makes an ideal roast for two or three persons. It cooks very quickly and is a most pleasant sight.

Rub the rack with butter and with garlic, rosemary or tarragon. Season with salt and pepper and roast at 400° very quickly, basting every few minutes to give it a nice

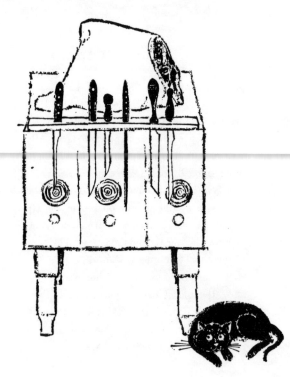

color. Serve the rack with braised new potatoes and the edible pod Chinese peas cooked quickly in a little water and then sautéed with mushrooms.

## Roast Shoulder

There are many people who feel that a boned and rolled shoulder is even more flavorful than the leg. It is a versatile cut that can be prepared in many different ways.

Follow any of the rules for roasting a leg of lamb. It is important to watch the temperature carefully in roasting a boned shoulder, for meat without bone cooks more slowly.

## Shoulder of Lamb à la Crème

Rub a boned and rolled shoulder of lamb well with salt, pepper and tarragon. Roast it at 325°, basting occasionally with a little white wine and tarragon blended together. When the lamb has been cooked to your favorite state, remove it to a very hot platter and let it stand for a few minutes. Skim the excess fat from the juices in the pan and add 1 cup of heavy cream. Blend this well with pan juices. Let the mixture cook and reduce for a minute. Serve with the meat and potatoes Anna and braised lettuce.

## Braised Shoulder of Lamb, Provençale

Make small incisions in a boned and rolled shoulder of lamb and insert slivers of garlic. You will need about 2 cloves. Rub the outside of the shoulder with olive oil and salt and pepper and sear it in a very hot oven (500°) for 20 minutes. Then add to the pan 1 clove garlic, finely cut, 2 cups of diced eggplant, 2 medium onions thinly sliced and 2 cups of tomato pulp (peeled, seeded and chopped tomato). You may use a tomato purée if you like. Also add 1 cup of red or rosé wine. Roast at 325°, basting thoroughly every 20 minutes. A few minutes before the roast is done, add 1 cup of ripe olives and let them blend well with the sauce. Remove the roast to a hot platter and surround with the sauce. Sprinkle lavishly with chopped parsley and serve with a rice pilau and an endive salad. Crisp rolls or bread will be needed to mop up all the delicious juices.

## Rotisserie Shoulder of Lamb

This is an ideal cut for the electric rotisserie or for the rotisseries built into some of the new ovens.

If you like garlic with lamb, and most people do, make several incisions in the flesh and insert slivers of garlic. Rub the meat well with salt and freshly ground pepper and a bit of rosemary if you wish. Run the meat thermometer into the flesh. Spit the roast carefully so that it balances well and roast it till the internal temperature on the meat thermometer registers 145° for rare, or 155° for medium rare.

## Braised Shoulder of Lamb

Buy a shoulder of lamb that is not too fatty and rub it with salt and pepper and a little butter. Place it in a large oval casserole or gratin dish and brown it in a very hot oven (500°) for 20 minutes. Insert a meat thermometer in the flesh. Arrange around the lamb 12-14 small new potatoes, peeled or not, as you wish, and 12-14 small white onions which have been browned in a little butter and caramelized with a pinch of powdered sugar. Pour melted butter over the potatoes and onions. Also add a sprig

of parsley, a bay leaf and a bit of thyme to the pan. Roast at 350° until the potatoes are cooked through and the meat has reached an internal temperature of 145°-155° or 160°, according to the state of doneness you prefer. Baste several times with the pan juices during cooking.

## Braised Shoulder of Lamb Bonne Femme

Have the butcher bone the shoulder but not tie it. Prepare the following stuffing: Mix 2 cups finely grated bread crumbs, ½ cup chopped parsley, ½ cup finely chopped onion sautéed in 6 tablespoons butter, and 2 tablespoons softened butter. Season with salt, pepper and a little rosemary. Stuff the shoulder with this mixture and tie it well.

Place it in a large casserole and roast at 325° for 1 hour. Meanwhile cook 1 pint of white beans until almost done. After the lamb has cooked 1 hour, add the beans, 1½ cups finely diced carrots, 1 cup finely chopped onion which has been lightly sautéed in butter and 2 cloves garlic. Continue roasting until beans are tender and meat is done. Serve from the casserole.

## Lamb Chops

These are the various types of lamb chops:

**1. Loin Chops.** The best, to my mind, are loin chops. They are always expensive, but if you are planning to serve them don't stint. There is nothing more disappointing than a thin chop. Have them cut thick—1½″-2″ —and have the excess fat trimmed off. If you wish, have a kidney rolled into the chop. We prefer to serve the kidneys separately because sometimes the chops cook a little more slowly and the kidneys become overcooked and hard.

**2. English Chops.** These are large double chops cut across the saddle, and they include two loins and two tenderloins. These are best when cut 1½"-2" thick.

**3. Rib Chops.** These chops are delicious and dainty after they have been trimmed. They should be cut as thick as 1½"-2".

**4. French Chops.** This is the name for rib chops very carefully trimmed with all the meat scraped off the bone at the end. Paper frills are then put on the rib bones for a glamorous effect. These chops are exceedingly popular for luncheon parties but one gives merely a few mouthfuls. You will need two or three chops per serving.

**5. Shoulder Chops.** Chops from the shoulder are not as well formed but have good flavor. There is sometimes a good deal of bone in them, so, though they are cheaper, in the long run they may not be an economy.

## Broiled Lamb Chops

We feel that broiled chops are by far the best. They should be nicely browned on both sides with the fat crispened a bit and the meat should be pleasantly pink or deep pink in the center. Certainly nothing, with the possible exception of a beef steak, suffers so much from overcooking as a fine lamb chop.

Start the chops at medium heat, brown on one side and then turn to brown on the other. Be sure the fat is cooked crisp. A 1½" chop will take around 8 minutes for rare, 14 for medium rare and 18 for medium. Bring up the heat at the last minute if you like a brown crust. Season to taste.

## Helen Brown's Herb Stuffed Lamb Chops

Make a pocket in a thick lamb chop by slitting the meat in the thickest part. Cream butter with finely chopped garlic and parsley, salt and pepper, and stuff the chops with this mixture. Secure them with toothpicks. Broil the chops in the usual way and serve them with additional herb butter.

*VARIATIONS*

1. Cream butter and tarragon, fresh ground pepper and salt and stuff the chops. Use plenty of tarragon; the flavor is excellent with lamb. Proceed as above. Serve with more tarragon butter.
2. Do the same thing with rosemary butter.

## English Lamb Chops

These chops should be thick and should be broiled slowly and carefully. We like to serve broiled lamb kidneys, a strip of bacon and one or two broiled mushroom caps with them. This plate with a good baked potato, stuffed or plain, and a really good cole slaw makes a perfect dinner for autumn or winter. A nice claret or a California Cabernet makes it a festive occasion.

## Pan Broiled Lamb Chops

Lamb chops can be good when they are pan broiled (or sautéed) if it is done properly. Get the pan quite hot and rub it with just a little of the fat from the chops. Cook the chops, turning them often during the cooking process. Then turn them on edge so the fat cooks for a few minutes to give it a brown crispness. Salt and pepper at the last minute. If you like garlic, toss a chopped clove into the pan while the chops are sautéing.

## Baby Lamb Chops

These tiny chops, which are so popular in Italy and Spain, are cut from a very young lamb and cut very thin. In this case, the lamb is much better when crisp and cooked through. Broil over charcoal until well done and very brown. Serve about five or six of these tiny chops per person.

## Broiled Lamb Steaks

Lamb steaks may be cut from the leg or from the rolled, boned shoulder. Both have fine flavor.

Broil the steaks over charcoal or in the broiler to the state you prefer. Salt and pepper to taste and serve with English mustard or with *sauce diable* (see recipe under Deviled Turkey in the Poultry Cook Book, December 1956).

## Lamb Steaks Oriental

Marinate the steaks as you do breast of lamb Oriental. Then broil as above. These are outstandingly good.

### Barbecued Lamb Steaks

Broil the steaks until almost done. Then spread them with French mustard and a bit of honey, and sprinkle with a little tarragon. Return to the fire to glaze and finish cooking. These are delicious eaten with some roasted corn on the cob and sliced ripe tomatoes sprinkled with chopped dill or fresh basil and dressed with oil and a tiny bit of vinegar. Crusty bread and cheese, juicy pears or apples and a bottle of a good California claret make this a fine meal.

## Braised Lamb Shanks with Lentils

Nearly every country has its own version of this dish. This is the way we like to prepare it but other versions are good, too.

Allow one lamb shank for each person. This recipe is for six shanks. Trim the meat of any excess fat. Dust the shanks lightly with flour and rub with salt and pepper. Sear them well in 4 tablespoons of butter mixed with 2 tablespoons of oil. When they are nicely browned, add 2 cloves of garlic, finely chopped, 1 bay leaf, 1 teaspoon of oregano or tarragon and 1 cup of consommé or broth. Cover and simmer for 1 hour.

In the meantime prepare 2 cups of lentils according to the directions on the package. There are quick-cooking lentils available that need only about 30 minutes cooking. Flavor them with an onion stuck with cloves and a bay leaf. Be careful not to let them get overdone or they will be mushy.

When the lentils are cooked, drain and mix them with ¼ cup of finely chopped parsley, ¼ cup of chopped green onions or scallions and salt and pepper to taste. Arrange them in a large baking dish and top them with the lamb shanks. Pour the pan juices over all and add a little of the broth

from the lentils, if necessary. Bake, covered, for 25 minutes at 350°. Remove the cover, and continue baking at 350° for another 20-30 minutes or until the lamb shanks are tender and the lentils nicely blended with the flavorings.

## Barbecued Breast of Lamb

This is done over charcoal just as you do spareribs. Allow about 1 pound of lamb breast per person. Rub with salt and pepper and garlic. Arrange on the spit and cook over charcoal or simply broil on the charcoal grill. (Spitting is by far the better method.) Grill or roast for about an hour or even more. The lamb should be very brown and crisp and well done all through. Serve with a tomato and onion salad and broiled or sautéed green peppers.

## Marinated Breast of Lamb

Buy a pound of lamb breast per person. Marinate for 12 hours or more in the following red wine marinade: 2 cups of red wine, 2 onions thinly sliced, a bay leaf, 2 cloves of garlic, 1 teaspoon of oregano, salt, pepper and plenty of parsley. Either spit the breasts and charcoal roast them as above or roast them in a 325° oven on a rack, basting them occasionally with the marinade. Serve with rice and string beans vinaigrette.

## Breast of Lamb Diable

For 4 persons buy 4 pounds of lamb breast. Place the meat in a deep pot with 1 onion stuck with 2 cloves, a bay leaf, 1 clove of garlic, some parsley, a stalk of celery and a carrot. Cover with cold water and bring to a boil. Then lower the heat and simmer until the lamb is tender. This takes about an hour. Remove the breasts to a flat plate or

platter and pull out the little rib bones. Cover with another plate and weight it down while cooling to give firm consistency.

Here are three ways to finish this dish:

**1. The French way.** Brush sections of the cold cooked lamb with French mustard, salt and pepper and then roll them in bread crumbs. Grill over charcoal or broil in the oven, basting with butter to keep the crumbs from burning. Turn several times to heat and brown evenly. Serve with a *sauce diable*. This is an excellent outdoor dish.

**2. The English way.** Dip pieces of cold cooked lamb breast in beaten egg and then in crumbs. Sauté in butter until crisp and brown on all sides. Serve with a *sauce diable* or a *sauce soubise:* a cream sauce mixed with some finely chopped onions that have been steamed in butter; a little grated Gruyère cheese may also be added if you wish.

**3. The Italian way.** Cut the cold, cooked lamb into sections. Dip each in egg, lightly beaten, and then in crumbs. Sauté in olive oil with a little garlic added. Serve with a rich tomato sauce and buttered noodles.

## Breast of Lamb Oriental

Choose breasts of young lamb and allow 1 pound per person. Marinate the breasts in white wine or sherry seasoned with finely chopped garlic, soy sauce and fresh ginger. Turn the meat several times during the marinating to make sure that it has evenly bathed.

Remove from the marinade and broil over charcoal or in the broiler of your stove until nicely browned and crisp. This should take about 45 minutes under a low flame.

Serve with buttered rice and a salad of Chinese cabbage and tomatoes.

## Moussaka I

Peel 1 large or 2 medium eggplants (you will need a little over a pound). Cut in rather thin slices and soak in salted water for a half hour. Dry the slices, dredge them in flour and brown quickly in olive oil.

Chop 1 large onion rather coarsely and sauté it in 5 tablespoons of butter. When it is just tender add ½ cup bouillon and keep very hot.

Blend together 1 cup of tomato juice and 1 can of tomato purée.

Grind enough leftover lamb to make 2 cups—or brown 1 pound ground lamb in 4 tablespoons butter. Season the lamb with salt, pepper and paprika and add the onion and bouillon mixture to it.

In a deep casserole or baking dish make a layer of eggplant then a layer of meat and then the tomato mixture and continue making layers until all ingredients are used up. Dot with butter and bake at 350° for approximately 1 hour or until the liquid is absorbed. The top should be crisp and the interior rather creamy. Serves 4.

## Moussaka II

Peel 1 large or 2 medium eggplants carefully, taking the skin off in large pieces and saving them. Cut 10 slices from the eggplants and chop the rest of the vegetable. You will need about 1 pound of chopped eggplant. Brown it quickly in oil and sauté the 10 slices in oil as well.

Then sauté 1 large onion, finely chopped, in 4 tablespoons of butter. Chop or grind 2 pounds of leftover lamb and chop a half pound of mushrooms.

Blend all these ingredients except the eggplant slices with 4 or 5 tablespoons of bread crumbs, 1 garlic clove, finely chopped, 2 tablespoons of chopped parsley, 3 eggs, slightly beaten, a dash of nutmeg, and salt and pepper to taste. Finally add ¾ cup of tomato purée.

Oil a round deep mold, such as a charlotte mold, or an ovenproof glass casserole and line it with the skin of the eggplant, purple side down. Put in a layer of the mixed meat and eggplant and then a layer of eggplant slices, then the meat mixture and continue the layers until the casserole or mold is filled. Cover the top with more eggplant skin and stand the casserole or mold in a pan of hot water. Bake in a 350° oven for an hour or an hour and a quarter. Let the mold stand outside of the hot water for a few minutes and then unmold on a

large hot platter. Decorate with chopped parsley and serve with a tomato sauce, if you wish, and a rice pilaff. Serves 4.

## Persian Kebabs

These are unusually delicious. Combine 2 pounds of ground lamb with ½ cup of pine nuts, ½ cup of chopped parsley, 1 teaspoon of salt, 1 teaspoon of freshly ground black pepper, 2 finely chopped cloves of garlic and 1 egg. Blend well, adding a spoonful or two of olive oil as you do. Mold this mixture around skewers, brush well with oil and broil in the broiling oven or over charcoal till nicely browned and fairly well done. Serve on rice flavored with bay leaves and a chunk of butter. Serves 4.

## Shish Kebab I

Cut 3 pounds of lamb into 1½″ cubes. The leg or the shoulder is the best cut for kebabs. Mix 1 pint of red wine, ½ cup of olive oil, 1 large onion sliced, 2 crushed cloves garlic and 1 teaspoon of thyme or oregano. Marinate the meat cubes in this mixture for 1-4 hours, the longer the better.

Arrange the lamb on skewers, with thin slices of green pepper or onion between the cubes. Brush with oil and broil over coals or in the broiling oven till nicely browned on all sides—but do not overcook them. Salt and pepper to taste at the last and serve with broiled or sautéed eggplant slices, broiled tomatoes and green pepper slices.

Note: We find that it is much better to cook and serve the vegetables separately, rather than to try to arrange all the vegetables on the skewers with the meat. (Alternatively, you may broil them in one of the adjustable double racks used for hamburg-

ers or steak.) If they are cooked together, the meat is overcooked before the vegetables are done. Serves 4-6.

## Shish Kebab II

Marinate 2-3 pounds of cubed lamb in olive oil, lemon juice, chopped garlic and quantities of chopped parsley. Skewer and broil as above. These have a most distinctive flavor. Sometimes we alternate the meat cubes with large stuffed green olives for a pleasant contrast in texture and flavor.

Serve with zucchini sautéed with garlic in olive oil. Cook this delicate squash just long enough to be lightly colored but do not let it get soft. It should be crisp to the teeth. Have some good crisp bread on which to slide the bits of meat from the skewers, and some excellent red wine—it need not be an expensive one. This is a delectable *al fresco* meal. Serves 4-6.

## Shashlik

Marinate 3 pounds of cubed leg or shoulder of lamb for 36 hours (in the refrigerator) in 1 cup of olive oil mixed with 4 good sized onions, finely chopped, 1 teaspoon of salt and 1½ teaspoons of black pepper, freshly ground. When you are ready to cook, arrange the meat on skewers and broil until nicely browned on all sides. Serve with a rice pilaff, broiled tomatoes and scallions. Serves 4-6.

We suggest a green vegetable to follow this: green beans with bacon or peas à la bonne femme.

## Navarin of Lamb with Spring Vegetables

This classic ragoût is one of the great stews of the world. It takes a little trouble to prepare, but the result is worth the effort.

For 4 persons cut 2 generous pounds of shoulder of lamb into even pieces.

Sear the pieces of lamb thoroughly in 6 tablespoons of butter or fat. Season with salt and pepper and sprinkle with a little granulated sugar so that the meat will caramelize and gain additional color. When the lamb is well browned, pour off three-quarters of the fat in the pan and sprinkle the meat with 2 tablespoons of flour. Shake the pan and toss the meat around to give the flour a chance to brown a little. Add ½ cup of tomato purée, 1 or 2 cloves garlic, slightly crushed, and a *bouquet garni* of thyme, parsley and a bay leaf. Cover with hot water and let come to a boil. Cook for a while on top of the stove, removing any scum that may form on top of the stew. Then cover the pan and place it in a moderate oven (350°) for 1 hour.

At the end of the hour, remove the pieces of meat and return the pan to the top of the stove. Boil the sauce to reduce it, then strain. Return the meat to the pan and add 12 small new potatoes, 12 small white onions that have been browned in butter and a sprinkling of sugar, 12 baby carrots browned in butter and sugar, 12 tiny new turnips and about 1 cup of green peas. Pour the sauce over this, cover the pan again and return it to the oven. Continue cooking for another 45 minutes to 1 hour.

Serve it from the casserole or arrange the meat on a platter and surround it with the vegetables. Pour the sauce over the top.

## Blanquette d'Agneau

This is a slightly different version of the usual blanquette, and one we like.

Cut 3 pounds of boneless shoulder of lamb into small cubes about 1¼″ square. Brown them very lightly in 4 tablespoons butter. Then salt and pepper to taste, lower the heat and simmer for about 20 minutes, tossing the meat from time to time to cook it evenly. Sauté 18 small white onions in butter and add ½ pound of mushroom caps. Add the lamb to the onion and mushroom mixture and rinse the pan in which the lamb was cooking with ½ cup Madeira or sherry. Pour over meat and vegetables. Gradually beat in another ½ cup cream and add this sauce to the meat mixture. Cover and simmer over a low flame for 30-35 minutes. Serve with a rice pilaff. Serves 4.

## Oriental Ragout of Lamb

Cut 2½ pounds of lamb shoulder into even pieces. Brown the meat in 5 tablespoons of butter. When it begins to brown lightly add 1¼ cups of finely chopped onions and let

them blend and brown with the meat. Dust with 2 tablespoons flour and turn the meat well so that the flour browns slightly. Salt and pepper to taste and add 1½-2 cups of strained canned tomatoes. Be sure you remove all the seeds. Or use 1½ pounds of fresh tomatoes, peeled, seeded and chopped. Add 1 cup of water or bouillon, 1 crushed clove of garlic, a tiny pinch of saffron, a sprig of parsley, a bay leaf and ½ teaspoon of thyme. Cover the pan and simmer for an hour. Uncover and add 1½ cups of washed raw rice and a little more water or bouillon. Re-cover, and put in the oven. Bake at 350° for about 35 minutes or until the rice is cooked. Serves 4-6.

With this ragoût we like an endive and spinach salad with a little chopped beet added to a simple French dressing. For dessert, fresh fruit.

## Irish Stew

In spite of its name, this dish is always referred to in French books as an example of English cookery.

Cut 3 pounds of shoulder and breast of lamb into uniform size pieces. In a casserole, arrange a layer of meat, then a layer of potatoes cut in rather thick slices, then a layer of sliced onions, another layer of meat, and so on until you have used up all the lamb. Add a good sized sprig of parsley, a teaspoon of thyme, a stalk of celery, a bay leaf, and salt and pepper to taste. Cover the meat well with water and bring to a boil. Then put a lid on the casserole and place it in a moderate oven for 1½ hours. This with well buttered noodles. Serves 2.

## Lambs' Tongues Poulette

You will need about 2 or 3 tongues per person. Cover the tongues with water and add 1 onion stuck with 2 cloves, 1 bay leaf, 1 teaspoon salt, 1 teaspoon freshly ground black pepper, 1 carrot and 1 stalk of celery. Bring to a boil, then lower the heat and simmer until the tongues are tender when tested with a fork. Remove the cooked tongues and when they are cool enough to handle, skin and trim them carefully. Return them to the broth for several minutes to reheat while you go about preparing the following *sauce poulette*. In a saucepan blend 3 tablespoons butter and 3 tablespoons of flour. When they have cooked for a few minutes, add salt and pepper to taste and 1½ cups of the broth in which the tongues cooked. Stir and cook until smooth and thick and then add the juice of a lemon. Beat 2 egg yolks lightly and blend with a few spoonfuls of the sauce. Stir this into the sauce thoroughly and reheat but do not allow it to boil. Taste for flavoring. You may find that you prefer a little more lemon in the sauce.

## Lambs' Tongues Vinaigrette

Prepare lambs' tongues as above and serve them hot with a vinaigrette sauce or a *sauce gribiche*. This is a simple vinaigrette to which you have added chopped parsley, chives, or green onions, chopped hard-cooked eggs, a little dill pickle and a dash of tarragon. It is delicious with this particular dish. With this have plain boiled

potatoes and a garnish of hard-cooked eggs. We like a watercress salad with no dressing. The dressing with the meat is enough.

## Pickled Lambs' Tongues

Buy 5 pounds of lambs' tongues and prepare as above. When they are cool, peel them, split them and arrange in a large jar. Add 3 bay leaves, 2 onions sliced very thin, 1 tablespoon of tarragon, 3 cloves of garlic, a small piece of cinnamon bark and 2 or 3 cloves. Heat 1½ pints of wine vinegar with 1 cup of white wine and ¼ cup olive oil until just at the boiling point. Do not let it boil. Pour this over the tongues and let them cool; then cover them and put them in the refrigerator to chill. They will keep for a week or more and improve with age as they mellow and are permeated with the flavors in the sauce. Serve these with green salad, potato salad or rice salad.

## Lamb's Liver Julienne

Cut 1 pound of lamb's liver into thin slices and then cut these into fine strips about ⅜″ wide. Shake them in a paper bag with 3 tablespoons of flour and 1 teaspoon each of salt and freshly ground black pepper. Shake well to coat each strip.

Heat 4 tablespoons butter with a spoonful of oil and sauté ½ cup of finely chopped green onions or scallions in the fat for 1 minute. Add the liver strips and shake them in the pan to brown them on all sides. Cook them very quickly—about 2 minutes is enough. Remove the liver to a hot platter or serving dish and rinse the pan with ½ cup of white wine or dry vermouth. To the juices add 1 cup of sour cream and 3 tablespoons of chopped parsley. Stir until the cream is just heated through but do not boil. Pour the sauce over the liver and serve with well buttered noodles. Serves 2.

## Lamb Kidneys and Bacon En Brochette

Allow 3-5 kidneys for each serving and use the same number of slices of bacon. Precook the bacon for 4-5 minutes until done but not crisp.

Clean the kidneys, remove the outside film and split them. Stuff them with herb butter: for 4 persons you will want ¼ pound butter with ½ cup each of chopped parsley and scallions and 2 teaspoons of lemon juice. Blend these thoroughly. Wrap each stuffed kidney with a piece of bacon and arrange them on skewers. Broil under or over a low fire so that the bacon becomes crisp and the kidneys are cooked to the proper state for you.

## Lamb Kidneys Saute

Clean and split 12 lamb kidneys. Dust them very lightly with flour and sprinkle with salt and pepper. Sauté them in 4 tablespoons butter heated with 3 tablespoons olive or peanut oil. Turn kidneys and shake the pan so that they will cook evenly. When the kidneys are nicely browned on the outside but still pink inside, transfer them to a very hot platter or serving dish. Add ½ cup of dry vermouth to the pan and swirl it around to collect all the brown crust. Season the pan juices with 1 teaspoon of dry mustard, 1 teaspoon of freshly ground black pepper, 2 tablespoons of freshly grated onion and salt to taste. Cook for 2 minutes and add 1 cup of sour cream. Blend well until it is heated through but not boiling. Pour over the kidneys and sprinkle liberally with chopped parsley. Serve with rice pilaff. Serves 3-4.

# PORK

# Pork

Distinguished writers have always been willing to devote their talents to extolling food. But surely no morsel, however delicate or tasty, ever won more praise than Charles Lamb heaped on pork in his *Dissertation Upon Roast Pig*. Consider this mouth watering endorsement: "There is no flavor comparable, I will contend, to that of the crisp, tawny, well-watched, not over-roasted *crackling*, as it is well called—the very teeth are invited to their share of the pleasure at this banquet in overcoming the coy, brittle resistance—with the adhesive oleaginous —O call it not fat—but an indefinable sweetness growing up to it—the tender blossoming of fat—fat cropped in the bud—taken in the shoot—the lean, no lean but a kind of animal manna . . ."

Our own praise of pig begins with the thought that of all domesticated creatures that provide food for man, the pig is most plainly intended to be eaten. The very shape of a plump porker seems to proclaim: "Eat me! That's what I'm for." And it is no exaggeration that almost all of the pig can be served up in appetizing fashion. Pork has been a favorite dish in China for thousands of years. It's the *pièce de résistance* of all native celebrations in the islands of the Pacific. It's considered a banquet dish by African savages. To the Irish peasants the pig was not only a staple of the daily diet but also "the gintleman that pays the rint." Both the Romans and the Saxons were great pork eaters. The Roman women were adept at sausage-making and bacon was a popular food until the rising tide of luxury living relegated bacon to the soldiers and plebes while the richer citizens feasted on more costly and esoteric foods. Pork vied with beef as the favored meat of old England (both could be bought in the days of Henry VIII for a halfpenny a pound). An extract from the Journal of Elizabeth Woodward, later Queen to Edward IV, records, "10 May 1451 . . . Seven o'clock. Supper at the table. . . . The goose pie too much baked and the loin of pork almost roasted to rags."

One good reason for mankind's love of pork is its gastronomic versatility. You seldom tire of pork because it comes in so many guises, all delicious. First there's Charles Lamb's crisp crackling, an almost compulsive food; crisp barbecued spare-ribs that demand to be gnawed to the succulent end; sausages in endless array—some bland and others highly seasoned—

from Italy, France, Germany, Spain and Poland; homely scrapple from Pennsylvania; old-fashioned smoked bacon giving off a pungent smell as it sizzles in the pan; all manner of smoked, cured and aged hams; pork liver made into delicious pâtés as frothy as a mousse; and, of course, all the fine fresh cuts.

Pork must be well done. It sometimes harbors trichinae, microscopic worms which deal unkindly with humans. To be sure of killing any trichinae that may be present in fresh pork, cook until it reaches an internal temperature of at least 155° or allow 25-30 minutes per pound. Some people go overboard and cook pork until it is overdone and flavorless. This is not necessary.

Someone once started the theory that pork was not a good dish for summer eating. Properly cooked, this meat can be delicate and tasty and a cold roast crown of pork or fresh ham, thinly sliced, is delicious on a hot day. Indeed, pork properly cooked is delicious anytime and fully deserves the accolade of the ancient Greek physician Galen "the most nutritious of all meats."

## STANDARD PORK CUTS

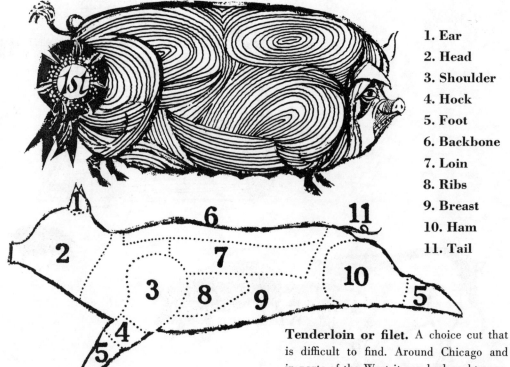

1. Ear
2. Head
3. Shoulder
4. Hock
5. Foot
6. Backbone
7. Loin
8. Ribs
9. Breast
10. Ham
11. Tail

**Fresh hams.** Try to get these from a butcher who will leave the skin on. This makes "crackling." Fresh hams (legs) should be roasted. For spitting, they should be boned, rolled and tied. Italian butchers bone them, stuff them with herbs and then tie them. Delectable! If a whole leg is too large, you can generally buy a half.

**Loin.** You may buy the complete loin (the loin and rib in one piece), the loin end or the rib end. These cuts are for roasting or braising. Chops come from this section also. Loin chops containing a small piece of the tenderloin are first choice. Rib chops are excellent but not as meaty. They should be cut quite thick to prevent drying out during the cooking. Chops for stuffing must be cut doubly thick with a pocket slashed in each.

**Tenderloin or filet.** A choice cut that is difficult to find. Around Chicago and in parts of the West it can be bought regularly. In other areas, you may have to make special arrangements with your butcher.

**Shoulder.** If you plan to roast the shoulder, ask the butcher to leave the skin on. You'll have crackling again! If you plan to braise or boil it, have this cut boned and rolled for easier carving. Meat from the shoulder makes good ragouts, sausages or ground pork meat.

**Breast.** A fatty cut that is often smoked.

**Rib cage:** This section, trimmed from the siding, is the part that furnishes spareribs.

**Fat portions of the belly.** These cuts become larding pork or corned pork.

**Backbone.** Bony as the name implies, but flavorful. Often cooked with beans or with sauerkraut.

**Feet and hocks.** Tasty bits when wrapped in muslin, boiled with seasonings and then grilled. They are also a standard ingredient in many of the classic sauerkraut dishes, and in certain types of pot-au-feu so popular throughout the rural sections of Europe.

**Tails.** These are a much neglected delicacy. They are especially delicious plain boiled and may be treated in the same manner as feet or ears.

**Head.** The basis of Head Cheese, a popular cold cut.

**Ears.** Boiled and then sautéed these morsels come close to being as elegant as any silk purse.

**Smoked pork.** Hams, loins, shoulders, side meat, jowls and sausage are all smoked and form a special category of meat.

**Charcuterie.** Sausages and other specialties made of pork meat are endless. Each area has its own selection.

When buying pork, estimate 1 pound per serving for cuts including the bone. One half pound of boneless cuts, such as tenderloin, will serve one person.

## Fresh Ham or Leg

Fresh ham or the leg of pig is delicate of texture and not too fat. This cut ranges from 8-20 pounds. The larger, more mature hams are better.

We much prefer leg of pork with the skin left on. This gives you the crisp crackling that is one of the tastiest of tidbits. It is not easy to find an unskinned fresh ham. You may have to order it in advance.

## Roast Leg of Pork

Buy a leg with skin if possible. Score the skin in squares or diamonds, cutting well into the fat. Rub with salt, freshly ground black pepper and a little fennel or thyme. We like just a hint of garlic added to this, although it is considered rather unorthodox.

Put it on a rack in a roasting pan and cook for 30-35 minutes per pound in a 325° oven, basting occasionally with some of the fat in the pan to crisp the crackling thoroughly. If you have a meat thermometer, insert it in the flesh, being careful not to let it touch the bone. Pork must reach an internal temperature of at least 150° and is even better if roasted to 170°-175°. Remove the cooked roast from the oven and keep it in a warm place for 20 minutes before carving. This allows the juices to settle.

## Roast Leg of Pork Jardinière

Choose a rather small leg and score the skin as above. Stud the skin in several places with slivers of garlic. Place the roast on a rack in a fairly deep pan in a 325° oven, allowing 30-35 minutes a pound cooking time. Baste every 20 minutes with warm white wine.

Roast small potatoes in the pan during the last hour; or heat frozen rissolé potatoes in a buttered pan in the oven for 35 minutes.

Heat a large deep platter and place the roast and the potatoes on it. Skim the excess fat from the pan and add enough white wine to make 1 cup of liquid. Combine with 1 cup sour cream, salt and pepper to taste. Blend well and heat through but do not let it boil or the cream will curdle. I like a great deal of freshly ground pepper.

Surround the roast and potatoes with tiny French peas cooked with butter, tiny white onions braised in butter and tiny sautéed mushroom caps. Serve with the sauce and sautéed apple slices.

## Loin of Pork

This is the simplest of the pork roasts. It can be a tiny roast just right for two or a whole loin with filet for a large party. When you buy a loin roast ask to have the chine bone cut away so that the carver will be able to cut straight through the roast and give everyone delicious small chops.

The best part is the loin end with the filet; yet the smaller rib end is a delicate morsel and made into a crown roast is a most glamorous dish.

## Roast Loin of Pork

For 6 persons buy a 5-6 pound loin roast. Have the butcher saw through the chine bone and trim the roast well. Rub the outside with salt, pepper and a little thyme. Roast at 325°, allowing about 30 minutes per pound cooking time. If you use a meat thermometer, it should register about 175° when the roast is done. Basting is not necessary unless you are serving a special sauce made with the pan juices.

Serve roast loin with potatoes cooked in the pan during the last hour and with sautéed apple slices.

### VARIATIONS

**Gascogne.** Stud the loin of pork with garlic cloves cut in strips, using about 5 cloves for a 5-pound roast. Rub the outside of the meat with coarse salt, freshly ground pepper and a little thyme. Roast at 325°, basting occasionally with red wine. Remove to a hot platter, anoint with 4 ounces warm cognac and blaze. Skim the excess fat from the pan and pour the pan juices over the roast. Serve with mashed potatoes.

**Rosemary Roast Loin.** Rub a 4-pound loin with garlic, salt and rosemary, pressing the leaves well into the meat. Place in a pan and put a few leaves of rosemary in the pan. Roast as for basic loin roast. When the meat is cooked, remove it to a hot platter. Skim the excess fat from the pan juices. Add ¼ cup white wine, ½ cup heavy cream, and a good sprinkling of salt and a heavy grinding of black pepper. Cook and blend for a few minutes and pour over the pork roast. Serve with potatoes roasted in the pan and spinach dressed with olive oil and lemon juice.

**Loin of Pork with Prunes.** Make two long incisions in the fleshiest part of the loin, cutting almost to the bone. Fill the incisions with pitted dried prunes that have been soaked in port or sherry for twelve hours, making two rows of prunes slightly overlapping. Press the meat together and tie the roast firmly with butcher's twine. Rub lightly with salt. Roast in a 325° oven according to directions above, basting occasionally with the wine in which you soaked the prunes. When the loin is done, remove it and let it stand on a hot platter for 15 minutes before carving. Remove the twine before serving. Buttered noodles and a cole slaw with a dressing of half mayonnaise and half sour cream flavored slightly with dill make this an outstanding dinner.

This dish is excellent cold. Serve with

a hot mustard sauce and a dilled potato salad, made with plenty of chopped parsley and onion.

## French Loin of Pork

Roast the loin according to previous directions. When the meat is about two thirds done, pour off all the fat and surround the roast with finely sliced, peeled apples, dotted with butter and sprinkled with a very little sugar. Continue roasting, basting the apples with pan juices from time to time. Remove the cooked roast to a hot platter and let it rest for 15-20 minutes in a warm spot. Add 1 cup heavy cream to the apples in the roasting pan and return it to the oven for 15 minutes to heat the cream and blend it well with the pan juices. Serve the pork with this sauce and mashed potatoes beaten with plenty of butter.

## Pot-Roasted Loin

Buy a 3½-4 pound loin roast. It is easier to prepare this dish if you have the loin boned and tied though it can be cooked with the bone left in.

Try out a little pork fat in a Dutch oven or heavy kettle and sear the loin in the fat, browning it on all sides. Add 3 small carrots cut in quarters, 3 cloves garlic, 4 small onions peeled and sliced, 1 teaspoon salt, 1 teaspoon thyme and dash of freshly ground black pepper. Cover the kettle and simmer the roast, allowing 35 minutes per pound. Remove the roast and add 1 cup broth (or 1 cup of hot water in which you have dissolved a bouillon cube) to the pan juices and blend and heat thoroughly. Put the sauce through a food mill or mix it in an electric blender until the vegetables are blended with the liquid. Taste for seasoning. Garnish the roast with small tomatoes baked with a topping of chopped parsley and crumbs. Serve with the sauce and steamed rice liberally buttered.

## Pork Sukiyaki

This dish takes only a short time to prepare and may be cooked at the table in an electric skillet or a chafing dish. The most important thing is to be sure that the raw vegetables are beautifully arranged on a large platter when they are brought in and placed beside the skillet, for part of the enjoyment of sukiyaki is in the fresh crisp appearance of the food before it is cooked. For 4 servings, buy 1 pound loin of pork, have it boned and sliced paper thin. For vegetables use 8 tiny young green onions, ½ lb. mushrooms, firm and snowy white, ½ lb. tender leaves of spinach, 4 inside tender stalks of celery, ½ bunch crisp fresh watercress, 1 small can bamboo shoots, 12 water chestnuts and 1 small can bean sprouts. If there is an Oriental market in your area, buy long rice (this is called rice noodles) and bean curd.

Wash the fresh vegetables. Cut the onions, mushrooms, and celery into uniform slices and arrange neatly on a large platter. Arrange the spinach and watercress in neat bunches. Open cans of water chestnuts, bamboo shoots and bean sprouts and arrange these on the platter. Add the strips of pork and bean curd. Soak long rice in hot water.

Place the platter beside the skillet with pitchers of meat stock and soy sauce.

Heat the skillet thoroughly and grease it lightly with pork fat. Add the sliced onions and let them wilt slightly. Push these to one side and add the thinly sliced pork. Cook the meat for several minutes, turning it to cook on both sides. Then add the vegetables that take the longest cooking: mushrooms and celery. As the vegetables cook, push them to one side and add the water chestnuts and bamboo shoots. Pour a little stock and soy sauce over the ingredients in the skillet from time to time to keep them from sticking. They should just steam.

Finally add the bean sprouts, the spinach and watercress and let these just wilt a bit. Top with the bean curd and the soaked long rice and heat through.

Be careful not to overcook any of the vegetables. One of the special qualities of Oriental cookery is the crispness of the cooked food.

Serve with bowls of hot steaming rice and soy sauce and separate bowl of raw beaten egg into which sukiyaki is dipped.

## Crown Roast of Pork

A crown of pork is made by tying one or two loins into a circle. Your butcher will prepare this for you, sewing up the crown so that it holds its shape. Top each bone with a cube of salt pork to prevent charring. Season the meat with salt, pepper and garlic and sprinkle it with a touch of rosemary and crumbled bay leaf. Cook the crown on a rack in a roasting pan, basting it often with pan juices. Follow directions for roast loin. When the meat is done, remove it to a hot platter and take the fat pork off the bones. Fill center with any of the following:

> Sauerkraut cooked in white wine.
> Mashed potatoes dressed with a great deal of parsley and butter.
> Sautéed mushroom caps.
> Buttered noodles.
> Rice mixed with peas and parsley.
> Sautéed apple slices, crisp and brown.

The crown roast is carved simply. Merely cut into individual chops and serve one or two to a person.

## Shoulder

The shoulder is a toothsome morsel for braising and may also be cooked in any of the ways suggested for fresh ham. If you roast a shoulder, it should be boned and tied to make carving simpler. Ask the butcher to leave the crackling on the meat; roast pork skin is too good to miss.

If you plan to braise the shoulder, ask the butcher to skin, bone and roll it, and take the skin home with you. Try it out in a slow oven until crisp and crunchy and you will have wonderful crackling for snacks with cocktails.

## Braised Shoulder with Beans

Soak 1 pound white pea beans for several hours. Drain them, cover with fresh water and add 1 bay leaf, an onion stuck with 2 cloves, and salt. Cook gently until tender.

Have a shoulder of pork skinned, boned and tied. Brown it quickly in a small amount of pork fat. Add 1 cup bouillon, 3 finely chopped cloves garlic and a touch rosemary. Cover the pan and simmer for 30 minutes. Add the beans and a little of the bean broth and simmer until the pork is tender and the beans have blended thoroughly with the meat, about 1 hour. Add 1 tablespoon tomato purée, an ample amount of finely chopped parsley and 1 finely chopped fresh garlic clove.

Serve with puréed spinach dressed with oil and lemon juice.

## Braised Shoulder with Cabbage

Buy a shoulder of pork and have it skinned, boned and rolled. Brown it quickly in a small amount of pork fat and season to taste with salt and pepper. Add 1 cup white wine, cover and simmer for 2-3 hours, or until the meat is tender. Add a little more wine if the liquid cooks down too much.

Meanwhile, shred a large, firm head of cabbage and blanch it quickly in boiling, salted water. Drain. Melt 6 tablespoons bacon fat in a large skillet. Add the cabbage and braise it over a brisk flame until it is just colored. Add 1 cup white wine, 1 teaspoon salt, 1 teaspoon freshly ground black pepper and cover the pan. Simmer gently for 1 hour, stirring occasionally.

Serve the pork with the cabbage, boiled potatoes, a choice of brisk mustards and a Waldorf salad.

## Carbonnades

Ask the butcher to cut 3 pounds shoulder of pork into cubes about 2″ square. Flour these lightly and brown them in pork fat. Salt and pepper to taste.

Slice 3 pounds onions and brown them lightly in 6 tablespoons butter. Drain and mix with the pork cubes. Add 1 bay leaf, ½ teaspoon thyme and 1 pint beer. Cover the pan and simmer for 1½-2 hours. If you like a thicker sauce, add a little *beurre manié* (flour and butter kneaded together) and stir it into the juices until thickened and smooth.

Serve with boiled potatoes and a celery salad dressed with a mustard-flavored vinaigrette sauce.

## Sweet and Pungent Pork

*Peanut oil*
*1 egg, well beaten*
*1 pound lean pork shoulder cut in ½″ cubes*
*Flour*
*1 teaspoon monosodium glutamate*
*½ teaspoon salt*
*½ cup chicken broth*
*1 cup canned or frozen pineapple chunks*
*2 tablespoons chopped onion*
*1 green pepper cut in ¼″ inch dice*
*2 teaspoons cornstarch*
*2 teaspoons Chinese soy sauce*
*¼ cup brown sugar*
*½ cup pineapple juice*
*1 tablespoon tomato sauce or catsup*

Heat peanut oil in a large skillet about 1″ deep until about 365° or 370°.

Beat the egg well and coat the pieces of pork with the egg and then roll in flour mixed with monosodium glutamate and salt.

Brown pork pieces very quickly, reduce the heat to 325° and let the pieces cook through—about 7 minutes or more. Remove the pieces of pork to absorbent paper and remove all fat except for 2 tablespoons.

Add to this the chicken broth, pineapple, onion, green pepper. Cook this mixture for five minutes, add the cooked pork, mix well and simmer for 10 minutes.

Bind the mixture with the cornstarch mixed with soy sauce, brown sugar, pineapple juice and tomato sauce.

Cook, stirring well, until the mixture is thickened lightly and smooth. Serve with steamed rice. Serves 4.

## Tenderloin

Pork tenderloins are delicate in flavor and, as their name implies, tender. Unfortunately, they are hard to come by in most areas. Those who live in the Midwest will have the best luck. Small tenderloins will serve one person. Larger ones may be cut in half to serve two. Allow about 6 to 8 ounces per serving.

## Broiled Tenderloin

Allow one small tenderloin per person. Rub them well with thyme or oregano and freshly ground black pepper. Brush with melted butter and broil over medium heat until the tenderloins are thoroughly cooked and nicely browned on both sides. Brush with melted butter or pork fat several times during the cooking. Salt to taste and serve with crisp sautéed potatoes and unsweetened apple sauce.

## Sautéed Tenderloins with Cream

Soak four pork tenderloins for 2 hours in enough heavy cream to cover them. Drain and reserve the cream. Melt 6 tablespoons butter in a skillet. Roll the meat lightly in flour and brown quickly on both sides in the butter. Salt and pepper to taste, add ¼ cup warmed cognac and blaze. Add 1 teaspoon tarragon and cover the pan. Simmer gently for 25 minutes, or until the pork is cooked through. Remove the tenderloins to a hot platter. Add 2 ounces cognac to the pan and swirl it around. Add the cream in which the meat was soaked and enough to make 1½ cups. Heat thoroughly and add *beurre manié* (small balls of butter and flour kneaded together). Continue cooking and stirring until the sauce is lightly thickened. Pour this over the tenderloins and sprinkle liberally with chopped parsley.

Serve with lemon wedges, tiny new, or frozen rissolé, potatoes browned in butter. Braised celery gives flavor contrast.

## Tenderloin Orientale

Marinate 4 tenderloins in equal parts soy sauce and sherry flavored with 3 finely chopped cloves garlic and 4 tablespoons chopped fresh or preserved ginger. Soak the meat for 3 hours. Broil or roast the tenderloins, brushing them as they cook with a mixture of Grand Marnier and hot mustard blended to a paste. Brush them with this about every 15 minutes. Serve with fried rice and crisp raw vegetables.

## Fried Rice

Sauté 4 cups cooked rice in 3 tablespoons oil for a few minutes. Add ¼ cup each chopped green onions, shredded ham or pork and sliced cooked mushrooms. Cook for 3 minutes. Beat 2 eggs thoroughly with 2 tablespoons soy sauce and stir into the rice. Cook until the eggs are set. Garnish with chopped green onions, chopped parsley and fresh coriander, if available.

Boned and tied loin of pork can be substituted for the tenderloins.

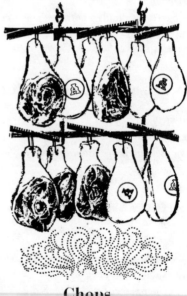

## Chops

The loin and the ribs make the best chops, and of these, loin chops with the bit of tenderloin included are the choicest. I like them cut on the thick side for sautéeing and thinner if they are to be grilled. As a matter of fact I find that grilled pork chops tend to be hard and tough. A sautéed chop is much more succulent and delicious.

One good-sized chop or two smaller ones will make an excellent serving.

## Grilled Chops

If you insist on grilling these chops, cook them slowly under or over a medium flame so that they are thoroughly cooked through. If you are grilling over charcoal, bring up the heat at the last to char the outside slightly. Salt and pepper the chops to taste and serve with a mustard or Diable sauce.

## Sautéed Chops

Melt a small amount of butter or—better still—pork fat in a heavy skillet. Sauté the chops gently, covering them for a brief period if you wish. When they are browned and thoroughly done but not dry, salt and pepper them well and serve with puréed potatoes and buttered beets sprinkled with parsley.

## Chops Milanaise

Dip the chops in flour, then in beaten eggs and then roll them in crumbs mixed with grated Parmesan cheese. Brown the crumbed chops very quickly in butter or pork fat and when they are beautifully brown, reduce the heat, cover the pan and cook gently for a few minutes. Remove the cover and continue cooking until the chops are thoroughly done. Season to taste and serve with a bowl of lemon wedges. Buttered noodles and a fine tossed salad are excellent with these chops.

## Chops Niçoise

Brown the chops lightly on each side in pork fat or a bit of olive oil. For 6 chops add 4 ripe tomatoes, peeled, seeded, and chopped very fine; 3 finely chopped cloves garlic; 1 medium green pepper finely chopped and 1 teaspoon basil. Cover the pan and simmer for 25 minutes, turning the chops once during the cooking. Add ½ cup black olives and continue cooking for 10 minutes more over a very low flame.

Serve these delectable chops with rice mixed with a great deal of chopped parsley.

## Chops Charcutière

This is a classic way of serving pork chops in France. Sauté 8 chops in pork fat. When they are browned and have simmered for a few minutes add 2 large onions, finely chopped. Cover the pan and let the onions cook down with the meat. Uncover and salt and pepper to taste. When the chops are done remove them to a hot platter. Add 1½ cups bouillon (or boiling water and a bouillon cube) to the pan and bring it to a boil. Add ½ cup tomato purée, 1 teaspoon dry mustard and ½ teaspoon freshly ground black pepper. Thicken the sauce lightly with *beurre manié* (butter and flour kneaded together into small balls). Just before serving add 2 tablespoons or more of finely chopped sour gherkins and sprinkle with chopped parsley. Arrange the chops around a mound of creamy mashed potatoes and serve the sauce separately.

## Baked Chilied Chops

Marinate 6 chops in a mixture of ½ cup white wine, 3 tablespoons chili powder, 1 cup tomato purée, the juice of a lemon, 3 finely chopped cloves garlic, 1 teaspoon oregano, 1 teaspoon chopped fresh coriander (if not available, use 1 teaspoon coriander seeds). Let the chops soak for 2-3 hours turning them once or twice. Bake the chops in the marinade for approximately 1 hour in a 350° oven, turning them once during the cooking. Add more liquid if the meat gets too dry.

## Chops Baked in Milk or Cream

Salt and pepper 4 thick chops and rub them well with thyme or oregano. Arrange them in a baking dish and cover with milk or light cream. Bake at 350° until the chops are tender. Sprinkle liberally with chopped parsley and serve with baked potatoes and sautéed zucchini.

## Stuffed Chops

For this recipe you need very thick chops with deep slits for the stuffing. One chop per serving is ample. The following suggested stuffings are enough for 6 chops:

1. 1½ pounds chopped mushrooms sautéed slowly in 6 tablespoons butter until cooked down, and thickened with a little flour. Stuff the chops with these sautéed mushrooms and season with salt and freshly ground pepper.

2. 2½ cups finely chopped onion, ½ cup crumbs, ¼ cup chopped parsley, 1 teaspoon tarragon, salt and pepper to taste. Blend with ¼ cup melted butter and 1 egg. Stuff chops with this mixture.

3. ½ cup ground pork and ½ cup ground onion sautéed in 4 tablespoons butter and mixed with ½ cup crumbs and 1 teaspoon oregano. Salt, pepper to taste.

4. 4 garlic cloves finely chopped, ½ cup chopped parsley, ½ cup crumbs, ½ teaspoon basil and ¼ cup melted butter. Salt and pepper to taste.

5. Thin slices of prosciutto alternated with slices of onion.

After stuffing, sear the chops in pork fat. Add 1 cup liquid (wine, bouillon or tomato purée) to the pan and cover. Simmer for 1 hour over a feeble flame. Test for tenderness. Or bake the chops in a buttered casserole at 350° for 1 hour with a little liquid (wine, bouillon, tomato purée) in the bottom of the casserole. Add more liquid if the meat begins to dry out.

## Stuffed Chops Flambé

Buy 4 chops about 3" thick and have the butcher cut a pocket in each one. Fill the pockets with the following stuffing: chop 1 small onion very fine and combine it with 2 finely chopped cloves garlic, 1 cup bread crumbs heated with 6 tablespoons butter, 1 teaspoon tarragon, ¼ cup finely chopped cooked tongue, ½ cup pine nuts, 2 ounces cognac, ½ teaspoon salt and ½ teaspoon pepper. Fasten the chops securely with small skewers. Brown them well in butter or pork fat and when they are nicely colored on both sides add ¼ cup white wine and salt and pepper to taste. Cover the pan and simmer until the meat is tender. This will take 45 minutes to 1 hour. Uncover the pan and blaze the chops with ¼ cup warmed cognac. Remove the chops to a hot platter and add 1 cup heavy cream to the pan juices and blend thoroughly. If you wish a thicker sauce add balls of *beurre manié* (butter and flour kneaded together) and stir until smooth. Correct the seasoning and sprinkle with chopped parsley.

Serve the chops with this sauce, potatoes Anna (see recipe in H&G's Vegetable Cook Book, August '56), crisply sautéed apple slices and a good cole slaw.

## Chops with Sauerkraut and Beer

Cook 3 pounds of sauerkraut in beer for 3 hours.

Brown 6 thick chops in butter or pork fat on both sides. Salt and pepper to taste. Place a layer of the cooked sauerkraut in the bottom of a large casserole. Sprinkle liberally with freshly ground black pepper and add 3 finely chopped cloves of garlic. Arrange the pork chops on the bed of sauerkraut and cover with a layer of grated raw apple. Top the apple with another layer of sauerkraut and then a layer of grated raw potato. Add a final layer of sauerkraut and pour in enough beer to reach the top of the casserole. Cover and bake at 375° for 45

minutes. Uncover and continue baking at 350° for 15 to 20 minutes.

Serve with plain boiled potatoes (the grated potato in the casserole is for thickening), a good mustard, pickles and beer.

## Spareribs

These popular tidbits make gnawing a joy. Long slabs of the ribs are best and if you can roast or grill them over charcoal you will find that the smoky flavor adds immeasurably to the rich taste of the pork.

## Roasted Spareribs

Allow 1 pound of spareribs per person. Salt and pepper them to taste and place them on rack in roasting pan, or weave on spit for roasting in a rotisserie or over coals.

If you roast them in the oven, cook them at 350° for about 1 hour, turning frequently. If spitted, roast in a rotisserie or over charcoal at medium heat for about 1 hour. When crisp and well done, serve these spareribs with mashed potatoes and a selection of mustards.

*VARIATIONS*

1. Brush the spareribs with soy sauce before cooking and several times as they roast. Omit the salt but pepper them. Serve with fried potatoes and watercress.

2. Glazed: Rub the ribs with garlic and chopped fresh or preserved ginger and brush them with soy sauce. Let them stand for 2 hours and brush them with soy sauce again. Roast as above, and just before they finish cooking, brush them well with honey. Continue roasting until glazed. Serve with lemon wedges.

3. Line a roasting pan with thin slices of salt pork or bacon. Add a layer of sauerkraut, a layer of sliced onions, another layer of sauerkraut and top with grated apple, freshly ground black pepper and two or three sides of spareribs. Roast in a 350° oven as above.

## Favorite Spareribs

Chop 4 cloves garlic very fine and mix with the juice of 4 lemons, ¼ cup soy sauce, ½ cup honey, 2 teaspoons basil, 1½ teaspoons freshly ground black pepper and ¼ cup chopped parsley. Put two sides of spareribs in this mixture and let them stand for 2 hours, turning them frequently. Wind the ribs on spits or put them on a rack in a roasting pan. Grill over medium heat or cook in a 350° oven for about 1 hour. Brush occasionally with a mixture of honey and lemon juice. The ribs should be nicely glazed when done.

Serve with fried rice and broiled onion slices or thinly sliced beefsteak tomatoes and thinly sliced onion with basil dressing.

## Jellied Pigs' Feet

Buy 6 or 8 good size pigs' feet and wash them well. Put them, unwrapped, in a kettle with 2 bay leaves, 1 teaspoon salt, 6 peppercorns, 1 teaspoon tarragon, 2 onions stuck with 2 cloves each, 2 cloves garlic and 2 cups white wine plus enough water to cover the pigs' feet. Bring this to a boil and skim the scum from the surface. Cover the kettle and simmer gently for about 5 hours or until the pigs' feet are so well done that they almost fall apart. Remove them from the broth and set aside to cool. Clarify the broth with an egg white and shell and strain it through a linen napkin.

When the pigs' feet are cool enough to handle, take the meat from the bones and arrange it in a mold. Top the meat with a few sliced sour pickles, a few pistachio nuts and some diced cooked tongue, if you like. Cover with the broth and then with a layer of foil. Put a plate on top and heap it with heavy objects to weight the meat down. Canned goods make excellent weights. Let the meat cool.

This can be sliced and served as hors d'oeuvre or as a main luncheon course.

## Pork Hocks with Sauerkraut

Buy 2 pig hocks and wash them well. Put them in a kettle with 1 pound sauerkraut and add white wine or beer to cover. Season with a generous sprinkling of freshly ground black pepper and chopped garlic. Bring to a boil, lower the heat and simmer gently for about 5 hours. Add more wine or beer if the liquid gets too low.

Serve with boiled potatoes and a selection of mustards.

## Sausages

There are so many different kinds of sausages available in our markets that it seems a pity to buy only the heavily saged products put up by the big packers. In some areas of the country you can find excellent local brands of sausage.

Look also for the wonderful Italian sausages. They are large, coarse in texture and come both sweet and hot. The sweet are usually seasoned with fennel or basil and garlic; the hot, as the name implies, are fiery with pepper. Spanish markets carry similar sausages called *chorizo*; these, too, come sweet or hot. Another Italian sausage—very large—that is delicious is the *cotechino*. Try this boiled and served with boiled white beans dressed with butter, garlic and tomato sauce. Or slice it and use it in a cassoulet. Then there is the Italian *zamponi*—a pig's foot stuffed with sausage meat, salted and dried.

Polish *kolbasa* is excellent cooked with beans or sauerkraut or simply steamed and served with polenta (see recipe in H&G's Beef Cook Book, Sept. '57). Chinese markets carry tasty small sausages, coarse in texture; and in some cities French butchers make their native versions.

## Grilled Sausages

To cook sausages—regular or Italian—place them in a skillet and cover with water or white wine. Bring to a boil, lower the heat and simmer gently for 5 to 20 minutes, depending on size. If you use water, pour it all off and let the sausages brown slowly in the pan, turning them to color on all sides.

If you use wine, pour off half, and let the sausages cook down in the rest of the wine and brown on all sides.

Serve sausages with any of the following:

1. Creamy mashed potatoes and sautéed apple slices or rings. This, of course, is the classic combination.

2. Kidney beans cooked with red wine and onion. Use 2 cans of beans for 4 persons. Drain the beans and combine them

with 1 medium onion, well chopped, and 1 cup red wine. Simmer for 30 minutes. Dress well with chopped parsley and a nice chunk of butter and arrange sausages around it.

3. Boiled potatoes, plenty of butter and mustard sauce.

4. Red cabbage. Shred 1 head of red cabbage and blanch for 10 minutes in boiling water. Drain. Melt 6 tablespoons goose fat or pork fat in a large skillet and add the cabbage. Sauté until the cabbage is thoroughly cooked. Add 1 finely chopped clove garlic, 3 tablespoons brown sugar, salt to taste and 1 cup red wine. Let the mixture cook down over a low flame for 20 minutes. Add 1 tablespoon wine vinegar and taste for seasoning. Arrange in a mound on a hot platter and surround with sausages and plain boiled potatoes.

5. Pancakes. Roll sausages in well buttered pancakes and arrange in a baking dish. Heat in a 450° oven for 5 minutes and serve with plenty of butter and sautéed apple slices or rings. An excellent breakfast dish.

6. Corn. Heat 5 tablespoons olive oil in a skillet and sauté 2 finely chopped cloves garlic until lightly colored. Add 1 can whole kernel corn, blend well and heat through. Add 1 tablespoon Italian tomato paste, ¼ cup grated Parmesan cheese and 2 tablespoons sesame seeds. Cook for 4 minutes. Heap on a hot platter and surround with sausages.

## Choucroute Garni

A fine choucroute is definitely a classic dish. This recipe will serve 6 to 8 people with some left over for the next day when it will be even better.

Line a large, heavy kettle with strips of salt pork and add about 5-6 pounds of fresh sauerkraut, a tablespoon freshly ground or cracked black pepper, the same amount of chopped garlic and about 2 pounds additional salt pork. Cover with white wine, add a few juniper berries and bring to a boil. Put a lid on the kettle and simmer for 6-8 hours. One hour before the sauerkraut is done add another piece of

salt pork, well washed. After half an hour, add 2 large garlic sausages, and 15 minutes later 12 good frankfurters. Cut some freshly boiled or baked ham into thin slices and keep warm. Let the choucroute cook 15 more minutes.

Heap the sauerkraut in the center of a large platter. Slice the garlic sausages and place them on one side. Put the frankfurters on another, slices of salt pork at both ends and slices of ham on top. Surround the meat with whole boiled potatoes and serve with a variety of mustards and a white Alsatian wine or a good beer.

## VARIATIONS

Cook pigs' feet with the sauerkraut for 4 hours. Add the sausage as above, but omit the ham.

Cook smoked or fresh pork loin with the sauerkraut during the last 2 hours. Add the sausages but omit the ham.

Add 12-18 pigs' tails to cook with the sauerkraut during the last 3 hours. Add the sausages but omit the ham.

## Liver Pâté

Buy 2½ pounds pork liver and 3½ pounds fresh pork with a good deal of fat. Grind both very fine and mix together thoroughly. Add 2 finely chopped medium onions, 3 chopped cloves garlic, 1 teaspoon thyme, 1½ tablespoons salt, 2 teaspoons freshly ground black pepper, ½ cup cognac, 4 eggs, beaten in one at a time and ½ cup flour. Blend thoroughly, using an electric mixer if possible.

Line individual casseroles with thin slices of pork siding and fill with the mixture. Top with sliced pork siding and then cover the casseroles with lids or foil. The pâtés must be sealed in tightly. Place the casseroles in a pan of boiling water and bake in a 350° oven for 2 hours. Remove

from the oven and cool for 15 minutes. Then take off the lids, cover the pâtés with foil and weight them down while they cool thoroughly.

## Steamed pork and ham
### (Jing Gee Yuke Beang)

*1 pound ground lean pork*
*1 pound ground ham—Virginia or hickory*
  *smoked ham is best*
*1 tablespoon soy sauce*
*1 teaspoon cornstarch*
*5 green onions, finely cut*
*5-6 thinly sliced water chestnuts*
*2 tablespoons peanut oil*

Blend all the ingredients together well and pack into a mold or metal bowl. Place on a trivet in a deep saucepan with a tight fitting cover. Place water about 1″ deep in the pan and steam the mixture for 1 hour and 15 minutes or until the pork is thoroughly cooked. Serve with white steamed rice and garnish with thinly cut strips of Chinese parsley if available or with shredded green onions and thin strips of ham. Serves 4.

This is a recipe from John Kan's restaurant in San Francisco.

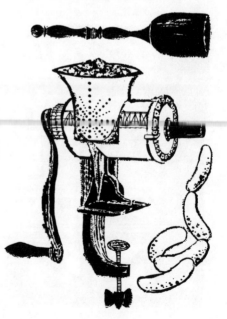

## Ham en Croûte

*12-pound ham*
*2 quarts beer*
*18 peppercorns, bruised*
*4 cloves, bruised*
*¾ cup red burgundy*
*½ cup brandy, flamed*
*3 tablespoons honey*
*6 cups flour*
*½ teaspoon powdered juniper berries*
*4 teaspoons double-acting baking powder*
*½ teaspoon powdered sage*
*1 teaspoon dry mustard*
*2 teaspoons salt*
*1 cup firm lard*
*1½ cups iced milk*
*1 beaten egg*

If the ham is the Virginia or smoked type, scrub it well and soak in cold water for 36 hours, changing the water every 6-8 hours. Drain, put in a deep pot and cover with boiling beer. Add peppercorns and cloves. Bring to a boil again, reduce heat and simmer gently 1½ hours, replenishing beer if necessary to keep ham covered. Drain and dry thoroughly with paper towels. Carefully remove rind and all but about a ¼″ coating of fat. Place in a deep roasting pan and pour over the burgundy and flaming brandy. Roast in a 350° oven for 2½-3 hours, basting frequently.

Lay the ham on a wooden board and carefully carve in thin slices. Replace slices and reshape ham. Mix 3 tablespoons of wine from the roasting pan with the honey and brush all over the ham. Set in the refrigerator for 10 minutes to firm so it holds together.

Meanwhile make dough for the crust. Sift the flour with the other dry ingredients. Rub in the lard until the mixture resembles coarse corn meal. Add the milk. Turn the dough out onto a pastry board and knead for a minute or two until it is quite smooth on top. Roll out to ¼″ thickness and cover the chilled ham completely with it, folding it over and encasing the ham. Trim off edges and make leaves, flowers, geometric shapes or any decorative designs with the discarded dough to embellish the top of the crust. Brush crust with beaten egg. Bake in a 450° oven for 10 minutes, then reduce heat to 350° and bake, brushing the crust twice with cold milk, for 15 minutes. Serve hot or cold with applesauce, chilled cranberry sauce, horse-radish sauce or black raspberry jelly.

## Glazed Ham

*1 tenderized ham, about 10 pounds*
*1 pound ground pork*
*1 onion, grated*
*½ cup fresh bread crumbs*
*1 egg*
*½ cup tomato juice*
*¾ teaspoon salt*
*½ teaspoon pepper*
*1 teaspoon powdered ginger*
*½ cup currants*
*4 cups apricot jam*

Prepare the ham the day before it is required. Have the butcher remove the bones from the ham and skewer the shank end, but leave opening at other end for stuffing. Mix together the pork, onion, bread crumbs, egg, tomato juice, salt, pepper, ginger and currants. Fill the ham with this stuffing and fasten the opening. Wrap the ham in aluminum foil and place in a roasting pan. Add 4 cups boiling water. Cover the pan and roast in a 350° oven (allowing 25 minutes a pound) until ham is tender. Trim the skin and remove excess fat. Cool slightly. Heat the jam and force it through a sieve. Place the ham (foil removed) in the roasting pan and brush half of the jam over the surface. Bake at 400° for 10 minutes. Brush with the remaining jam and bake 10 minutes longer. Chill overnight. Serves 12-16.

135

## Ham Mousse

4 tablespoons butter
⅓ cup flour
3 cups milk
2 tablespoons gelatin
¼ cup cold water
1 cup soft bread crumbs
½ cup light cream
2 pounds cooked ham, ground 3 times
4 tablespoons catchup
¾ teaspoon freshly ground black pepper
1 cup whipped cream

Prepare the mousse the day before it is required. Melt the butter in a saucepan; stir in the flour and then the milk. Cook over low heat, stirring constantly until mixture reaches the boiling point. Continue to cook over low heat for 5 minutes. Soften the gelatin in the water for 5 minutes; then add to the hot sauce, stirring until dissolved. Soak the bread crumbs in the cream. Combine the cream sauce, bread crumbs, ham, catchup, and pepper. Mix well; taste for seasoning. Let cool for 20 minutes. Fold in the whipped cream. Grease a 2-3 quart mold with a little salad oil. Pack the mixture into it. Cover and chill overnight. Unmold carefully before serving and garnish the platter with crisp fresh vegetables. Serve with the following sauce: 1 cup sour cream, mixed with 1 cup applesauce and 6 tablespoons prepared horse radish. Serves 6-8.

## Ham in Cider

2 tablespoons gelatin
¼ cup water
4 cups cider
1 cup currants
¼ cup brown sugar
1 teaspoon powdered ginger
1 tablespoon lemon juice
2 cups diced cooked ham

Soften the gelatin in the water for 5 minutes. Combine the cider, currants, brown sugar and ginger in a saucepan. Bring to a boil. Add the gelatin and lemon juice, stirring until dissolved. Set aside until it begins to thicken. Add the ham and pour into a lightly oiled 2-quart mold. Chill until firm. Carefully unmold onto a platter. Serve with cucumber salad and decorate with watercress. Serves 6-8.

# VEAL

# Veal

Veal, that most delicate of meats, has never had the full co-operation in these United States that it deserves. Too often, alas, the "breaded veal cutlet" appears on the menus of restaurants where gastronomy has never been heard or even thought of. This culinary error has poisoned the thinking of millions who might otherwise have been interested in knowing more about veal.

It has remained for the Italian and French restaurants to show us the joys of eating veal. Delicate little *scaloppine* cooked in butter and oil and served with a hint of wine or other seasonings; the tenderness of a creamy *blanquette de veau* accompanied by tiny white onions and mushrooms (try a cold *blanquette* sometime); the lustiness of *ossi bucchi* with the rich marrow oozing from the bones, the tomato-flavored sauce with saffron rice—all these delicacies have proved to me that veal is food to cherish. It can be as delicate as chicken and as flavorful as good cooking can make it. Veal is a great companion of garlic, tarragon, basil, wine and vermouth, and made for butter, cream and olive oil.

Food experts claim that the best veal in the world is found in Italy and France—especially France. The great chefs and restaurateurs of that food-conscious nation have always demanded the freshest milk-fed veal, slaughtered at a tender age. The flesh is pale, almost white, faintly tinged with pink and finely textured. The fat, especially around the kidneys, is thick, firm and white. Unfortunately, most of the veal sold in American butcher shops is really baby beef with flesh almost the color of beef. When veal is not slaughtered young enough, it is tough, stringy and flavorless. A regular supply of good veal is hard to find but if you live in an area that boasts an Italian market, buy veal there. Italians know good veal.

Because it is a delicate, young meat, veal takes careful cooking. Don't stew or braise it until all the juices run out and the texture turns coarse. It must be well done, true, but *à point*—tender yet firm.

Like chicken, veal is just as wonderful cold as hot. It's a fine choice for summer luncheons as well as for elegant winter meals.

## STANDARD VEAL CUTS

1. Shoulder
2. Shank, breast
3. Ribs
4. Loin
5. Rump and Leg

**Shoulder of veal.** Boned and rolled shoulder of veal may be roasted or braised. Shoulder steaks (blade bone or arm bone) may be prepared according to recipes for veal chops (they are less expensive than chops). Shoulder meat may be used in stews, in veal sauté or blanquette of veal.

**Veal shank, breast.** Shank can be braised or used in stews. This is the cut you use for ossi bucchi. Breast of veal can be stuffed and braised in one piece; or used for stews, veal sauté, etc.

**Ribs and loin of veal.** Saddle of veal (both loins with the tenderloin included) is roasted. Rack of veal (from loin or from ribs) is roasted. Chops (from loin or rib section) can be prepared in many ways.

**Rump and leg of veal.** A cut from the rump or leg may be roasted or braised. Some recipes call for a boned and rolled roast from the leg. Scallops (escalopes, scaloppini) are generally cut from the leg. These tidbits are sautéed or sometimes gently braised. Make paupiettes of veal (veal rolls) with thin slices of meat cut from the leg. Paupiettes are braised in liquid.

## Veal Scallops

Scallops (also called escalopes de veau or scaloppini of veal) are small slices of veal usually cut from the leg and pounded to paper thinness. The pounding tenderizes the meat and makes it possible to cook the scallops quickly. If your butcher is not co-operative about pounding scallops, you may use a meat pounder—good Italian or French models are available—and do it yourself.

3 thin scallops are enough for the average serving. A plate heaped high with these tender morsels, some of which are apt to be left uneaten, is a shameful waste.

Scallops should be floured, or dipped in batter, or in beaten eggs and crumbs. Cook them quickly in butter blended with a little olive oil. The oil prevents the fat from burning or discoloring. Brown the meat on both sides and cook until just tender—about 5 to 8 minutes depending on the thickness and tenderness of the veal. When browned, add seasonings. Some recipes call for rinsing the pan with wine or spirits to make a sauce for the meat.

Remember—the important point in cooking scallops is speed. Do not let them cook on and on, stewing or simmering. They are done the minute they are cooked through and tender. Serve immediately.

Scallops may be prepared at the table

in an electric skillet or chafing dish.

These tidbits are often served with rice, noodles or potatoes, sometimes with only a green vegetable or salad.

The following recipes are based on 1½ pounds of very thin scallops—enough for 4 to 6 persons, depending on appetites.

## Scallops alla Jerez

Dip scallops in flour, then in milk and again in flour. Sauté them quickly, turning once or twice to brown them evenly. When they are done, sprinkle with salt and pepper and remove them to a hot platter. Add ½ cup of cream sherry or oloroso to the pan and swirl it around to rinse the pan thoroughly. Pour this over the scallops and sprinkle with chopped parsley.

### VARIATIONS

Add ⅔ cup of cream sherry or oloroso to the pan after the scallops have browned and let the meat cook in the wine very rapidly for about 3 minutes. Turn the scallops once during this process to bathe them well. Remove the scallops to a hot platter, pour the sauce over them and sprinkle with chopped parsley.

**Au porto.** Prepare as above but substitute tawny port for the sherry.

**Alla Marsala.** Prepare the scallops as above but substitute Marsala for the sherry.

**Au cognac.** Prepare the scallops as above but substitute cognac for the wine. If you wish, you may blaze the cognac just before pouring the sauce over the meat.

## Scallops with Cream

Dip the scallops in flour and sauté them in butter until lightly browned. Salt and pepper to taste and add ⅔ cup of heavy cream.

Let this cook down until it is well blended with the pan juices. Remove the scallops to a hot platter. Add a little more heavy cream to the pan, stir it around and heat it thoroughly. Pour the sauce over the scallops.

## Scallops Amandine

Dip the scallops in flour, then in milk and again in flour. Sauté them in butter and oil until delicately browned on both sides. Add ½ cup of slivered almonds that have been sautéed in 4 tablespoons of butter until golden and crisp. Toss the almonds and scallops together. Season to taste and remove to a hot platter. Spoon the oil and butter over them, and add a touch of chopped parsley.

### VARIATION

Add ¼ cup of white wine to the pan when the scallops are removed. Rinse pan with the wine and pour juices over meat.

## Scallops Piquant

Mix together 1 cup of toasted bread crumbs, 1 tablespoon of finely chopped garlic, 2 tablespoons of chopped parsley, 1 teaspoon of dry mustard, ¼ cup of grated Parmesan cheese and a dash of cayenne pepper. Dip scallops in flour, then in white wine and finally press them into the crumb mixture. Sauté them in butter and oil, turning each one carefully with a spatula. When the scallops are browned and tender, remove them to a hot platter. Add ½ cup of white wine, a dash of Worcestershire sauce and a dash of Tabasco sauce to the pan. Cook and blend for 1 minute and pour over scallops.

## Scallops Paprika

Dip the scallops in a mixture of ¼ cup of flour and ¼ cup of paprika, then dip them

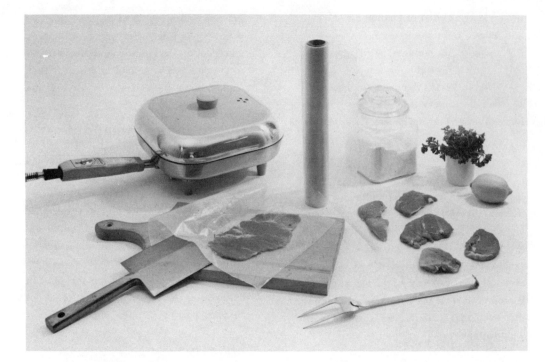

in milk and finally in the flour and paprika again. Proceed as for Scallops with Cream, adding dash of paprika with the cream.

## Saltimbocca No. I

Pound scallops to a round shape and trim each one to about 2-2½" diameter. Cut a piece of prosciutto to match each scallop and fasten the two together with a sprig of rosemary or sage. If sprigs of these herbs are not available, place leaves of the herbs between slices of prosciutto and veal and then fasten the slices together with toothpicks. Sauté these little "sandwiches" quickly until the veal is tender. Salt and pepper to taste and remove to a hot platter. Rinse the pan with a little Marsala or cognac and pour the juices over the saltimbocca. Garnish with chopped parsley.

## Saltimbocca No. II

Allow 2 scallops per serving. Spread each one with a little soft, fresh ricotta (Italian cheese), then add 1 slice of mozzarella cheese, 1 thin slice of prosciutto and a leaf of sage. Top with another scallop of veal—making a sandwich—and fasten the edges together by sealing them with a mallet or meat pounder. Dust lightly with flour and sauté in 6 or 7 tablespoons of olive oil. Turn these sandwiches carefully with a spatula and fork. When nicely browned and tender, season to taste with salt and pepper and add ¼ cup of dry vermouth. Remove the scallops to a hot platter, add another ¼ cup of dry vermouth to the pan and let it cook down for 1 minute. Pour the juices over the meat.

## Scallops Fines Herbes

Dip the scallops in flour and sauté them in butter and oil until delicately browned on both sides. Add 2 tablespoons of finely chopped chives, 2 tablespoons of finely chopped parsley, 1 teaspoon of dried tarragon or 1 tablespoon of finely chopped fresh tarragon. Blend in ⅔ cup of white wine and cook for 2 minutes at high heat. Season to taste with salt and pepper and remove the scallops to a hot platter. Pour on pan juices.

## Scallops Smitaine

Dip the scallops in flour, then in milk and again in flour. Sauté them quickly in butter and oil until nicely browned and season to taste with salt and pepper. Remove the scallops to a hot platter. Add 1 tablespoon of finely chopped shallots or green onions to the pan and let them cook very quickly. Add 2 tablespoons of tomato purée and season to taste. Blend in ⅔ cup of sour cream and let the cream just heat through. Do not let it boil or it will curdle. Spoon the mixture over the scallops.

## Scallops Niçoise

Dip the scallops in flour, then in beaten egg and finally in flour seasoned with 1 teaspoon of salt, 1 tablespoon of chopped parsley, 2 tablespoons of grated Parmesan cheese and 2 finely chopped garlic cloves. Sauté 1 tablespoon of finely chopped onion and 1 tablespoon of finely chopped green pepper in enough olive oil to cover the bottom of the skillet. Cook for 3-4 minutes. Add the scallops and sauté them very quickly until nicely browned. Add 1 teaspoon of dried basil or 1½ tablespoons of finely chopped fresh basil, ⅔ cup of tomato sauce and ½ cup pitted black olives. Cook mixture with the meat for 3 or 4 minutes. Remove the scallops to a hot platter, pour the sauce over them and sprinkle with chopped parsley. Serve with sautéed eggplant slices.

## Wiener Schnitzel

There are two versions of this famous dish. In one the veal is sautéed in butter until beautifully browned. In the other it is deep fat fried. We are not sure which is the authentic method, but we prefer the first.

Pound the scallops rather flat and a little larger than usual. Allow 2 per serving. Dip them in seasoned flour, then in beaten eggs and finally in crumbs. Sauté in butter or deep fry at 370°. When nicely browned and done, remove to a hot platter. Garnish each scallop with anchovy butter on a lemon slice, a green olive and an anchovy filet. Surround with small mounds of chopped hard-cooked egg, tiny mounds of capers and sprinkle with chopped parsley.

*VARIATION*

Serve each person one large scallop topped with a fried egg, a filet of anchovy and a slice of lemon.

## Terrine of Veal

This delicious terrine is served cold, cut into very thin slices. It is an excellent choice to have with cocktails, or for a cold buffet or picnic.

Buy 2 pounds of veal scallops and have them pounded very thin. Also buy 2 pounds of cooked ham or Canadian bacon, sliced very thin. Chop 12 to 15 young green onions (scallions) and enough parsley to make ½ to ¾ cup. Line a mold or bread tin with strips of bacon and put a layer of veal scallops on the bottom. Sprinkle the meat with some of the chopped onion and parsley, add a touch of thyme, a bit of crumbled bay leaf and a good grind of black pepper. Top with a layer of the sliced cooked ham or Canadian bacon. Then add another layer of veal and sprinkle it with the seasonings; then a layer of the ham. Repeat these layers until the mold is full and the meat used. Top with more strips of bacon and add about ½ cup of white wine to the pan. Cover and bake in a 300° oven for 2 hours, or until the meat is thoroughly cooked and the flavors well blended.

Remove the pan from the oven and take

143

off the cover. Weight down the terrine while it cools. To do this, cover with layers of heavy foil, place a plate on top and heap heavy weights on this. For weights, use canned goods or an electric iron or a brick. Any heavy object will do. When the terrine reaches room temperature, put it—weights and all—in the refrigerator to chill. The juices will form a rich jelly around the meat. When cold, remove the weights and the plate or foil and turn the meat with the jellied juices out onto a decorative platter or plate. Cut into thin slices and serve a bit of the jelly with each slice.

## Paupiettes de Veau

These delicate morsels are thin, thin slices from the leg, stuffed and rolled and then braised in some flavorful liquid. The pan juices form the sauce for the dish. Paupiettes are tastier if they are wrapped (barded) in thin slices of salt pork or bacon and then tied. The fat should be removed during the last few minutes of cooking and the rolls glazed with the pan juices.

Have the butcher prepare slices that measure about 2½" wide by 4" long after they have been pounded very thin. Allow 2 rolls per serving. Try to form neat slender paupiettes. Fat stuffy ones are unattractive.

## Paupiettes Ali-Bab

For 6 servings, order 12 thin slices of veal and 12 thin slices of pork fat.

Prepare a stuffing by mixing 1 cup of chopped cooked chicken, 1 small onion, chopped, ½ cup of fine bread crumbs, ¼ cup of chopped parsley, 1 teaspoon of tarragon, 1 teaspoon of salt, ½ teaspoon of freshly ground black pepper and 2 eggs. Mix thoroughly into a paste. Spread each slice of veal with some of this mixture; roll and then wrap in a slice of pork fat. Tie securely at each end.

In a large skillet melt 4 tablespoons of butter and heat thoroughly but do not let it discolor. Add the veal rolls and sauté them gently for 10 minutes, turning them several times to brown on all sides. Add ½ cup of broth and ½ cup of Madeira. When the liquid begins to bubble, lower the heat and cover the pan. Simmer gently for about 25 minutes or until the meat is tender. Remove the pork fat and string and let the rolls glaze lightly in the sauce. Remove to a hot platter.

Add ¼ cup of Madeira to the pan juices and heat and blend. If you like a slightly thickened sauce, add *beurre manié* (soft butter and flour kneaded together into small balls). Sprinkle the *beurre manié* over the sauce and stir it in, cooking and stirring until thickened. Taste for seasoning and pour over the paupiettes.

## Paupiettes, Italian No. I

On each veal slice place a thin slice of prosciutto and then spread this with ricotta and sprinkle with a touch of oregano and some freshly ground black pepper. Roll and fasten as above.

Sauté gently in olive oil for 10 minutes and then add ½ cup of red wine, ½ cup of tomato purée and salt and pepper to taste. Cover and simmer until done. Serve on a bed of cooked green noodles dressed with butter and grated Parmesan cheese.

## Paupiettes, Italian No. II

Prepare the veal rolls with prosciutto as above and then brown gently in olive oil to which you have added 2 thinly sliced onions. Add 1 cup of tomato paste and ½ cup of broth, cover and simmer until the meat is tender. Remove the rolls and arrange them on a bed of cooked chopped spinach in a buttered baking dish. Add a touch of basil and ¼ cup of chopped parsley to the pan juices, blend well and pour over the rolls. Cover with thin slices of mozzarella cheese and heat in the oven until the cheese is melted. Sprinkle with grated Parmesan cheese and serve with polenta.

## Paupiettes with Cream

Prepare the veal rolls with the following stuffing: sauté ½ cup of finely chopped onion and ½ cup of finely chopped mushrooms in 6 tablespoons of butter until soft and lightly colored. Mix with 1 cup of buttered crumbs, 1 teaspoon of thyme and salt and pepper to taste. Spread on veal and roll and tie. Sauté the rolls gently in 6 tablespoons of butter. When they are delicately brown, add ½ cup of broth, cover the pan and simmer until the meat is tender. Remove the rolls to a hot platter. Blend 3 tablespoons of flour with the pan juices and cook for several minutes. Gradually stir in 1½ cups of hot cream and continue stirring and cooking until the sauce is well blended and slightly thickened. Season to taste.

Pour the sauce over the veal and serve with buttered noodles.

## Paupiettes Paprika

Prepare the rolls as for Paupiettes with Cream. When the meat is rolled and tied, sauté 1 medium onion, finely chopped, in butter and when it is golden brown add the veal rolls and continue cooking until the veal is delicately colored. Add ¼ cup of paprika, ½ cup of tomato purée and ¼ cup of broth. Cover and simmer gently until the meat is tender. Remove the veal rolls and arrange them on a bed of buttered noodles on a large platter. Add 1½ cups of sour cream to the pan juices and stir until well blended and heated through. Do not let the mixture boil or it will curdle. Taste for seasoning and pour over the veal. Sprinkle with chopped parsley and paprika.

## Veal Chops

Veal chops are cut from the ribs or the loin. Some people call loin chops veal *cutlets*, but so many different parts of the animal

have been referred to as cutlets that we prefer to call the cut from the loin a *chop*.

Veal chops—either rib or loin— should not be cut too thick.

## Broiled Veal Chops

We find broiled veal chops less tasty than those that are sautéed or braised. Veal is not a fat meat and when broiled tends to be coarse in texture and tough. However, if you want to broil the chops, be sure to brush them well with olive oil before cooking and continue to brush them with oil as they broil. Veal must be well done and you will find that a 1″ chop takes 15 to 18 minutes to cook through. Season with salt and pepper and serve with a dab of butter or a strip of crisp bacon.

## Veal Chops with Hearts of Palm

Hearts of palm come in tins from Brazil, Madagascar or Reunion Island. There are two sizes—very thick and much thinner. Thinner ones are best for this dish.

Allow one medium thick loin chop per serving. Dust the chops lightly with flour. Melt 3 tablespoons of butter in a large skillet and brown the chops on both sides. Salt and pepper to taste. Reduce the heat and continue cooking until the meat is tender. Cover skillet for part of cooking time.

Heat 4 hearts of palm in 3 tablespoons of butter over a low flame, turning them carefully.

When the chops are cooked, remove them to a hot platter and keep them warm. Rinse the pan with 2 tablespoons of dark rum and add ½ cup of port. Gradually add ½ cup of heavy cream and reduce the sauce a little over a low flame. Turn off the heat and add 1 tablespoon of butter, 3 tablespoons of purée of foie gras or liver pâté and salt and pepper to taste. Serve the chops covered with the sauce and garnished with the hearts of palm. You may decorate each with a slice of truffle if you want them to look extra special.

*VARIATION*

In place of hearts of palm, use sliced mushrooms sautéed in butter. Rinse the pan in which the chops were cooked with ½ cup of white wine and add 1 tablespoon of cognac. Proceed as above.

## Veal Chops, Anne de Beaujeu

Allow one chop per serving. Dip the chops in flour, then in beaten egg and again in flour. Sauté them in butter until well browned on both sides and tender. Season to taste and arrange them in a shallow oven proof pottery or metal baking dish. Top the chops with the following sauce, which has been made in advance:

For 4 servings, finely chop 1½ cups of onion. Mix with 6 tablespoons of butter in a skillet and put over low heat. Cover the pan and let the onions steam in the butter until soft and juicy. Pour off 3 tablespoons of the butter-onion liquid and blend with 3 tablespoons of flour and cook this roux until well thickened. Place the rest of the onion-butter mixture in an electric blender and blend for 1 minute, or force it through a fine sieve. Mix with the flour and onion juice and cook over a medium flame until blended and thickened. Add ⅔ cup of cream and ⅔ cup of grated Gruyère or Switzerland Swiss cheese and stir until the cheese is melted and mixed into the sauce. Add salt and pepper to taste and a dash of nutmeg.

Pour this sauce over the chops and sprinkle with a little more grated cheese. Put the baking dish in a very hot oven or under the broiler flame to melt the cheese and heat through.

## Sautéed Veal Chops

Flour the chops very lightly and sauté in a mixture of butter and olive oil as recommended for scallops. Brown the chops on both sides and cook until done and tender. These will take longer than scallops. If the chops are rather thick, cover the pan during the last few minutes.

Veal chops may be sautéed with any of the flavorings or additions which are recommended for scallops.

## Veal Chops Parmigiana

Buy quite thick rib chops. Cut all the meat away from the bone and grind or chop it very fine. Combine the ground meat with half its weight in butter and season with salt and freshly ground black pepper. Form the meat into individual portions and press these against the chop bones, patting them back into their original shape.

Dip each "ground meat chop" into flour, then into beaten egg and finally in a mixture of crumbs and grated Parmesan cheese, half and half. Sauté in butter and olive oil until delicately browned and cooked through. Garnish with strips of ham and serve with risotto.

## Veal Chop à l'Echelle

Dip 4 veal chops in flour and sauté them in butter until nicely browned and done. Season to taste. Place the cooked chops on a bed of crisp, golden, sautéed potatoes on a very hot platter, and top each chop with a poached leek.

To the pan in which the veal was cooked, add ¼ cup of sherry and 1 cup of heavy cream mixed with 2 egg yolks. Stir until the sauce thickens, but do not let it come to a boil or it will curdle. Season to taste and spoon it over the chops.

## Veal Chops in Casserole

Have the butcher cut one good size chop— either rib or loin—for each person. Dip the chops in flour and sauté them in butter and oil until nicely browned on both sides. Reduce the heat and continue cooking and turning until the meat is cooked and tender. Season to taste. Remove the chops to a lightly oiled casserole and cover with a layer of sautéed mushrooms. Surround with tiny potato balls or cubes that have been cooked and then browned in butter. Tiny new potatoes boiled and then browned are ideal for this dish. Sprinkle with chopped parsley and a bit of chopped fresh or crumbled dried tarragon and add another layer of sautéed mushrooms. Cover the casserole and cook at 350° for 15 minutes to blend the flavors and heat through.

## Veal Chops en Papillote

Buy one good size loin chop per serving. Flour the chops lightly and sauté them in butter and olive oil until nicely browned. Season to taste with salt and pepper. While the chops are cooking, sauté ½ pound of sliced mushrooms in 6 tablespoons of butter until just tender. Sprinkle the mushrooms with a few drops of lemon juice when they start to cook. Season to taste with salt and pepper.

For each chop cut a piece of aluminum foil in a heart shape large enough to fold over the chop and make a case for it. Place each cooked chop on a piece of foil, top with a very thin slice of cooked Virginia ham or prosciutto and a spoonful of mushrooms. Sprinkle with chopped parsley, and add a dab of butter. Fold the foil over the chop and crimp the edges together, making a tight envelope. Place the foiled chops on a baking sheet and cook in a 400° oven for

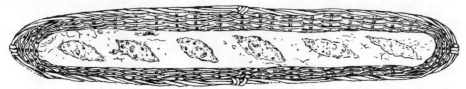

5 to 8 minutes to blend the flavors and heat thoroughly. Serve the chops in the foil cases along with crisp French fried potatoes and a green salad.

## Veal Stews

There are several special veal dishes which are lumped together as "stews" for lack of a better term. But let us assure you they are all elegant and well worth scheduling for a buffet supper party.

## Blanquette de Veau

Cut 2½ to 3 pounds of veal shoulder or breast into serving size pieces. Place them in a large skillet and cover with cold water. Bring to a boil and boil 5 minutes; then skim away any scum on top. Add 1 onion stuck with 2 cloves, 2 carrots, a sprig of parsley and a bit of bay leaf. Cover and simmer for ½ hour. Add 1½ teaspoons of salt and continue simmering for 1¼ hours.

While the veal is cooking, peel 18 small white onions and wash 12 mushroom caps. Cook the onions in 3 tablespoons of butter until lightly browned. Cover and steam until tender. Add a teaspoon or so of sugar and shake the pan to roll the onions around in the sugar-butter mixture until they caramelize a bit. Cook the mushroom caps in butter until tender and season with salt and pepper.

When the meat is tender, mix 3 tablespoons of butter with 4 tablespoons of flour in a skillet. Strain the broth from the veal and add 2 cups to the butter-flour mixture. Stir and cook until thickened. Add 1 cup of heavy cream mixed with 2 egg yolks and continue cooking and stirring until smooth and thick. Do not let the sauce boil or it will curdle. Season to taste and add 1 teaspoon of lemon juice. Arrange the pieces of veal on a large platter with a mound of cooked rice in the center. Pour the sauce over the veal and surround with the onions and mushrooms. This will serve 6 people.

## Ossi Bucchi

Buy shank bones of veal and have the butcher cut them into pieces about 3″ long. Roll the pieces in flour and sear them in hot olive oil until browned. Add 1 cup of water and ½ cup of white wine and bring to a boil. Cover the pan, lower the heat and simmer for 20 minutes. Add 1 or 2 cloves of garlic, 2 finely chopped onions, 3 or 4 peeled, seeded and chopped tomatoes, 1 teaspoon of basil and 1 teaspoon of salt. Cover and continue simmering for 1½ to 2 hours or until the meat is very tender. Remove the pieces of meat and cook the sauce down a bit. Serve 1 knuckle per person with risotto. Pour the sauce over all.

## Sauté de Veau Marengo

For 6 servings, cut 3 pounds of veal into 1½″ to 2″ cubes. Sauté 1 thinly sliced onion in ⅓ cup of olive oil until delicately colored. Add the pieces of veal and brown them on all sides. Add ⅓ cup of white wine, 2 crushed cloves of garlic, ½ teaspoon of

thyme, 1 bay leaf, a sprig of parsley, 1 cup of broth, 1 can of Italian style plum tomatoes and salt and pepper to taste. Cover and simmer until the meat is tender. This will take an hour or more. When the meat is done, remove the pieces to a hot platter. Strain the sauce and let it cook down very rapidly for about 5 minutes.

Sauté ½ pound of mushrooms in 3 tablespoons of butter. Sauté 12 to 16 small white onions in butter and then glaze them with a bit of sugar added to the pan. Mix the pieces of meat with the mushrooms and onions and pour the sauce over all. If you like a thicker sauce, you may add *beurre manié* and stir it in before pouring the sauce over the meat. Garnish the dish with chopped parsley and serve with rice or tiny new potatoes.

## Shoulder and Breast of Veal

This cut should be boned, rolled and tied. Otherwise, you will find the bones are so awkwardly placed that it is almost impossible to carve neatly. The shoulder may be prepared in any of the ways given for leg of veal or cooked as follows:

## Braised Shoulder

Sear the shoulder in butter, veal kidney fat, olive oil or a mixture of oil and butter. Add broth or white wine, allowing about 1 to 1½ cups of liquid for a 5 to 6 pound shoulder. Season. Cover, simmer from 2 to 2½ hours.

## Braised Shoulder, Italian

Heat olive oil with 2 cloves of garlic and sear the shoulder of veal in the hot oil. Remove the garlic cloves after the meat is browned on all sides. Add 1 large can of Italian plum tomatoes, 1 teaspoon of basil, 1 medium onion thinly sliced and sautéed in 2 tablespoons of olive oil, 1 grated carrot and salt and pepper to taste. Cover and simmer until the meat is tender. Remove the meat to a hot platter. Strain the juices and add ½ cup of tomato purée. Cook this sauce down until slightly thickened and add 1 tablespoon of chopped Italian parsley. Pour over the veal and serve with buttered noodles dusted with grated Parmesan.

## Braised Shoulder, Farmer's Style

Sear the veal shoulder in butter and olive oil. Add 4 or 5 thick slices of bacon cut in small dice, 2 or 3 thinly sliced onions, 2 shredded carrots and let these vegetables brown lightly. Add ½ cup of broth, cover the pan and simmer until the veal is tender. Add additional sautéed onions and 12 mushroom caps sautéed in butter.

## Stuffed Shoulder of Veal

Ask the butcher to bone a shoulder of veal and leave a pocket for stuffing. Prepare the stuffing with 2 veal kidneys finely ground with half their fat, 1 pound of ground lean pork, 2 cups of bread crumbs, 1 finely chopped or grated onion, 1 finely chopped or grated clove of garlic, 1 teaspoon of tarragon, ⅓ cup of chopped parsley and 2 eggs. Mix together and season with salt and pepper. Stuff the shoulder with this mixture and sew it up. Tie the stuffed shoulder securely so that it will hold its shape. Sear it in hot oil and butter and add 1 cup of white wine and 1 cup of broth. Cover and simmer until the veal is tender.

This dish may be served hot or cold. **To serve hot:** Remove the cooked stuffed shoulder to a hot platter and cook the sauce down 3 or 4 minutes over a brisk flame. Measure the sauce and for each cup of liquid break 2 egg yolks into a bowl and combine with a bit of the hot sauce. Gradually stir the egg mixture into the rest of

149

the broth and continue cooking and stirring until it is thickened. Do not let it boil or it will curdle. You may add a little arrowroot if you like a thicker sauce. Season to taste and serve with the veal.

*VARIATIONS*

Butter the stuffed shoulder well and roast it at 325°, basting with melted butter and white wine.

**To serve cold:** For an elaborate dish cover the cooked shoulder of veal with an aspic. An excellent aspic jelly may be made as follows: cook the shoulder bones and 1 pound of veal neck with seasonings in enough water to cover for 2 to 2½ hours. Pour the broth through a fine flannel, clarify it with egg white and then pour it through the flannel again. This will make a natural aspic. If you are afraid that it will not be firm enough, combine it with unflavored gelatin, allowing 1 envelope dissolved in ¼ cup of cold water for each 2 cups of broth. Let this set until slightly thick and then brush it over the veal shoulder. Chill for several hours and serve with herb mayonnaise.

## Chaudfroid of Veal

This rather elaborate buffet dish is not really too difficult to prepare, is spectacular to serve and goes a long way. Purchase either a breast of veal with a pocket or a boned shoulder of veal with a pocket. Ask the butcher to remove the flat bones of the breast or do it yourself with a very sharp boning knife.

If you are using the breast, trim the edges so that it has some degree of regularity. Prepare a stuffing with 1 pound ground veal, 1 pound ground pork, ½ pound ground or chopped calf's liver, 1 medium onion, grated, 2 small cloves garlic, finely

chopped, 1½ teaspoons dried basil or 2 tablespoons chopped fresh basil, ½ cup chopped parsley, 1 cup fine bread crumbs, 1 teaspoon salt, 1 teaspoon freshly ground black pepper, ¼ cup cognac, 3 eggs.

Cut 4 or 5 thick slices of cooked tongue into long square fingers. Trim 6-8 black peeled truffles into cubes, reserving the trimmings in a little Madeira or sherry to use in other dishes. Arrange ½ the stuffing in the pocket of the breast or shoulder, patting it very flat. Arrange the fingers of tongue and the cubed truffles in a pattern on the stuffing. Carefully cover with the remaining stuffing and sew the edges of the veal firmly together.

Brown the roast delicately in a very hot oven or in melted butter on top of the stove, handling with great care. When it is delicately colored, add to the pan a veal knuckle, a bay leaf, a small sprig of thyme (or ½ teaspoon dried thyme), a sprig of parsley, 1 pint of white wine or vermouth and 1 cup water. Cover tightly and roast at 325° for 1½ to 2½ hours, depending upon the size of the roast. The meat should be tender to the fork when tested. When it is tender, remove the roast to a hot platter and blaze with ⅓ cup cognac. Add the juices from the blazing to the pan juices. Allow the juices in the pan to cool, skim off the excess fat and strain the juices through cheesecloth. Allow the roast to cool thoroughly.

Meanwhile, prepare a chaudfroid sauce. Cook 6 tablespoons flour and 6 tablespoons butter together to make a roux. Cook the roux over low heat for several minutes. Gradually add to this roux the strained juices from the pan, making in all about 3 cups sauce. Stir over medium heat until the sauce is thickened. While you are making the sauce, dissolve 2 envelopes gelatin in ½ cup cold water. When the sauce is nicely thickened, taste for seasoning and add 1 cup heavy cream combined with 3 egg yolks (first add a little of the hot sauce to the cream mixture, mix well and then add this to the sauce and stir until well blended and smooth). Do not let the sauce boil after the egg yolks are added. Stir in the dissolved gelatin and stir until thoroughly mixed with the sauce. Allow this to cool until it has almost begun to set. Place the cold veal on a rack which has been placed on a platter or shallow pan and carefully spoon the sauce over the roast so that it coats it completely. The roast should be cold enough to aid the almost congealed chaudfroid to hold. You may have to give it one coat, transfer to the refrigerator to set it and coat it again.

You may decorate the coated roast with truffles cut in various shapes, fresh tarragon leaves, sliced stuffed or ripe olives, pimientos cut in various shapes or any decoration you prefer. The flower decoration on the cover photograph was made of petals cut from truffles and hard-boiled egg whites, chives (for stalks) and tarragon leaves, sieved hard-cooked egg yolk mixed with a little shortening and piped through a wax paper cornucopia to form the center of the flowers and the mimosa blossoms.

Before serving the veal, coat thinly with aspic on the point of setting, chill and, if necessary, coat again with aspic. Serve on a silver platter surrounded by finely chopped set aspic and vegetable garnishes. You can also put around the sides small aspic molds into which softened liver paté has been piped from a pastry bag.

Serves 10 or more as a buffet dish.

## Stuffed Breast of Veal

Buy a breast of veal and have the butcher make a pocket for stuffing. Prepare the stuffing with 1 pound of ground pork, 1 cup of toasted breadcrumbs, 2 finely chopped onions, 1 teaspoon of basil, 1 teaspoon of salt, 1 teaspoon of freshly ground black pepper and 2 eggs. Blend thoroughly and add ½ cup of finely chopped parsley. Stuff the breast of veal and sew it up. Melt 4 tablespoons of butter or any fat in a large heavy pot (Dutch oven is fine) and add 1 tablespoon of oil to keep the fat from burning. Brown the veal breast quickly on all sides. Add 2 cloves of garlic, salt and pepper to taste and 1½ cups of white wine. Cover and simmer for about 3 hours or until the meat is tender.

Remove the veal to a hot platter. Skim any excess fat from the pan juices and let the sauce cook down quickly. Taste for seasoning and serve it separately. Buttered noodles and peas are a good accompaniment for this.

## Saddle of Veal

This cut is the double loin including the tenderloin. If you wish, you may have the kidneys stripped of fat and rolled into the roast. A saddle will weigh from 8 to 18 or 20 pounds, depending on the size of the animal and the amount cut. It is a very decorative dish and an excellent choice for a large dinner party.

When you are ready to roast the saddle of veal, insert a meat thermometer in the fleshiest part of roast, making certain the thermometer does not touch the bone. Place the meat in a 400° oven and cook for 35 minutes. Season to taste. Then reduce the heat to 325° and continue cooking until the veal reaches an internal temperature of 170°. This will take 2½ to 3½ hours, depending on the size of the roast.

151

## Saddle of Veal with Anchovy Butter

Roast a saddle of veal as above, basting from time to time with a mixture of 1 cup of melted butter, ½ teaspoon of anchovy paste or finely chopped anchovies and 1 cup of white wine. Serve the roast with anchovy butter made as follows: cream 1 cup of butter with 6 finely chopped anchovy filets, 1 tablespoon of chopped parsley and a few drops of lemon juice.

## Rack of Veal

A rack may be cut from either the rib or the loin section. Roast as you would Saddle of Veal. Naturally, this smaller cut will take less time. Use a meat thermometer and roast until the internal temperature reaches 170°. This will take about 2 to 2½ hours.

## Leg of Veal

The center section of the leg, weighing about 7 to 8 pounds, is considered the best portion. Have the butcher tie it firmly so it will hold its shape. Roast in a low oven—about 325°—until the internal temperature reaches 170°. Baste the meat during cooking with a mixture of melted butter and white wine, melted fat and white wine, or herb-flavored olive oil and salt and pepper to taste. A 7 to 8 pound leg will take from 3 to 3½ hours. Here are ways to prepare the leg:

## Roast Leg, Fines Herbes

Roast as above, basting frequently with a mixture of ½ white wine and ½ melted butter flavored with 1 tablespoon each of chopped chives, chopped parsley and chopped tarragon.

## Roast Leg of Veal, Niçoise

Put the leg in a pan with a little olive oil and place it in a 450° oven to sear for 20 minutes. Turn the meat several times during this period to be sure it is well seared on all sides. Reduce the heat to 325° and continue cooking, basting with a mixture of 1 cup of tomato juice, ½ cup of olive oil, ½ cup of white wine, 2 finely chopped cloves of garlic, 1 tablespoon of chopped fresh basil or 1 teaspoon of dried basil and salt and pepper to taste.

When the meat has reached an internal temperature of 170°, remove it to a hot platter. Add 1 cup of tomato purée to the pan juices and cook for several minutes to heat and blend thoroughly. Then add 1 cup of ripe olives—the soft Italian or French variety if available—and let them heat through in the sauce. Pour this over the roast. Serve with sautéed eggplant, rice.

## Vitello Tonnato

*1 large onion*
*2 cloves*
*3 pounds rolled veal*
*2 bay leaves*
*2 carrots*
*2 stalks celery*
*6 sprigs parsley*
*2 teaspoons salt*
*½ teaspoon freshly ground black pepper*
*2 cans (7¼ oz.) tuna fish*
*1 can anchovy fillets*
*1 cup olive oil*
*3 tablespoons lemon juice*
*1 tablespoon chopped capers*

Stud the onion with the cloves. Put in a saucepan with the veal, bay leaves, carrots, celery, parsley, salt, pepper; add water to cover. Cover and cook over medium heat for 2 hours or until veal is tender. Drain and cool. Force the tuna fish and

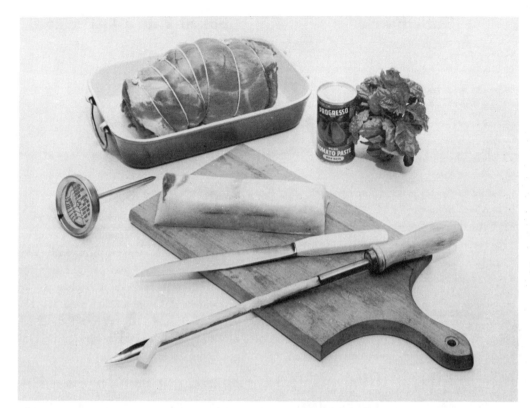

anchovies through a sieve or purée in an electric blender. Beat in the olive oil and lemon juice gradually until very creamy and smooth. Add the capers. Slice the veal very thin and place in a glass or pottery (not metal) bowl. Pour the sauce over it and let marinate in the refrigerator for 12 hours. Serve with sliced tomatoes. Serves 10-12 as an appetizer, 6-8 as main course.

## Veal Roulade

*2 pound veal steak, cut ¼″ thick*
*¼ pound butter*
*½ cup finely chopped onion*
*1 tablespoon chopped parsley*
*4 cups fresh bread crumbs*
*3 teaspoons salt*
*1 teaspoon pepper*
*¼ teaspoon thyme*
*¼ cup flour*

*1 bay leaf*
*1 cup beef consommé, fresh or canned*

Prepare the roulade the day before it is required. Have the butcher pound the veal very thin. Melt half the butter in a skillet; sauté the onion for 10 minutes, stirring frequently. Add the parsley, bread crumbs, 1 teaspoon salt, ¼ teaspoon pepper and the thyme. Mix well. Spread on the veal and roll up tightly like a jelly roll. Tie with strong thread. Mix the flour with the remaining salt and pepper. Roll the veal in it. Melt the remaining butter in a Dutch oven or heavy saucepan. Brown the veal in it on all sides. Add the bay leaf and consommé. Cover and cook over low heat for 2 hours, or until veal is tender. Remove from the saucepan and chill overnight. Slice thin and serve with a sweet mustard sauce, if desired, prepared by melting 1 cup currant jelly and mixing it with ½ cup prepared mustard. Cool. Serves 6.

## Tarte Farcie

½ pound raw veal
¼ pound cooked ham
½ pound mushrooms
½ cup soft bread crumbs
½ cup heavy cream
½ cup cracker meal
3 tablespoons grated onion
½ teaspoon salt
½ teaspoon freshly ground black pepper
½ teaspoon thyme
Rich pastry for 2 pie crusts
8 slices cooked chicken or turkey
1 egg yolk, beaten
3 tablespoons melted butter

Grind the veal, ham and mushrooms together 3 times. (Have the butcher grind the meat for you, if you prefer.) Soak the bread crumbs in the cream and combine with the ground meat mixture, cracker meal, onion, salt, pepper and thyme. Mix well. Preheat oven to 375°. Roll out half the pastry to fit an 11″ pie plate; a loaf or oval mold may also be used. Arrange half the chicken over the pastry. Turn the veal mixture onto it, arrange remaining chicken over that and cover with remaining pastry. Seal the edges well with egg white or water. Make a few slits in the top. Brush with egg yolk. Bake for 25 minutes. Pour the melted butter into the slits. Bake 40 minutes longer. If top gets too brown, cover with a piece of aluminum foil. Chill and serve in wedges or slices. Serves 6.

## Baked Pâté à la Perigord

1½ pounds calves' liver
¼ pound salt pork
2 anchovy fillets
3 eggs, beaten
2 tablespoons heavy cream
1 cup soft bread crumbs
2 tablespoons grated onion
2 teaspoons salt
½ teaspoon freshly ground black pepper

Grind the liver, salt pork and anchovies 3 times. Add the eggs, cream, bread crumbs, onion, salt and pepper. Mix until very smooth. Grease a 9″ loaf pan and turn the mixture into it. Place in a shallow pan of hot water. Bake in a 350° oven for 1½ hours. Chill and turn out carefully. Slice very thin. Serves 12-14 as an appetizer, is good with cocktails.

# POULTRY

# Poultry

When Henri IV promised his French peasants "a chicken in every pot," he created a symbol for prosperity that Herbert Hoover, some three centuries later, saw no need to improve on. (It was the same Henri who has come down in history coupled with a soup, *petite marmite Henri IV*, the prime ingredient of which is, naturally, chicken.)

Indeed, throughout the ages poultry has had a way of becoming mixed up in class distinctions and social legislation. In Venice, for example, turkey eating once was a symbol of success. A sumptuary law of 1557 ruled turkey off the tables of all but certain lofty noblemen. At the other extreme, when cackling geese warned of an approaching enemy and thereby saved the Roman Capitol, the grateful Romans accorded them the dismal distinction of being eaten only at such public festivals as the Julian games. To the Romans, first of the gourmets of the West, goes the credit for domesticating and popularizing poultry in Europe. Guinea fowl, goose, chicken, duck, turtledove and "the peacock in his pride" were all on the Roman menu.

The common barnyard fowl is probably the most determined migrant in history. Originating in southern Asia, it became part of the diet of peoples from Greece to Fiji (Captain Cook on his voyages found fowls scratching in the most remote island villages). Turkey, native to the New World, had an early press agent in Fra Agapida, confessor and historian of Cortez. He recorded that it "surpasses as food any wild bird we have found up to this time." The English, normally suspicious of foreign foods, made an exception of turkey, which soon displaced curlew, bittern and whimbrel on the fashionable bill of fare.

By the 15th century, devotees of poultry and game could buy a book which set forth the fine points of the noble art of carving. *The Boke of Keruynge* (carving) published by Wynkyn de Worde gave a list of the terms that distinguished the knowing "keruer" from the mere amateur. He admonished the artist to "rere that goose, lyft that swanne, sauce that capon, spoyle that henne, frusshe that chekynge, thye that pegyon, unbrace that malarde." A good carver might win political preferment. Ojeda, follower of Columbus, could carve a capon impaled on a fork and held aloft, and through his dexterity became Grand Carver to the King of Spain.

The virtues of poultry were solemnly proclaimed by savants. Elyot's *Castel of Helth* recommends pigeon as an antidote to "pure melancholy," and Vaughan's *Directions for Health* notes that a young fat goose "doth competently nourish." In Shakespeare's time, a fat capon was an acceptable bribe for a corrupt magistrate. By 1573, turkey was listed as essential for "Christmas husbandlie fare"; it has held the position ever since. As poet and dramatist John Gay lyrically proclaimed, "From the lowly peasant to the lord, the turkey smokes on every board."

## Roast Chicken

Any size chicken may be roasted. The baby 1-pound chickens can be roasted according to any of the recipes for roasting Rock Cornish game fowl, or just roasted plain. The larger 3½-6-pound chickens, sometimes used for stewing, are the usual size for roasting. Stuff them or not as you wish. You may use one of the good prepared stuffings on the market, any of the stuffing recipes in this cook book, or make a simple bread stuffing with soft white bread crumbs, sautéed celery and onion, melted butter, salt, pepper, thyme and chopped parsley or chives. Allow 1 cup of stuffing for each pound of chicken. Alternatively, the chicken can be stuffed with a few sprigs of fresh tarragon. Tie up, rub with softened butter, and place in a shallow roasting pan with sliced celery, carrot, onion and a little dry white wine. Roast uncovered in a moderate (350°) oven, basting several times with additional melted butter. A 2½-pound chicken will take about 45 minutes, a 4-pound chicken about 1½ hours; test by piercing leg with skewer. Strain pan juices for gravy.

## Deviled Chicken

*2 broilers, about 2½ lbs., cut up*
*Seasoned flour*
*4-6 tablespoons butter*
*¼ cup rum*
*2 green peppers, diced*
*1 large yellow onion, finely chopped*

*2 teaspoons potato flour*
*2 teaspoons tomato paste*
*2 cups strong chicken stock*
*4 pickled walnuts, chopped*
*2 tablespoons walnut juice*
*Pinch of sugar*
*Salt, pepper*

This dish is a specialty of the Colony Club in Barbados. Coat the pieces of chicken lightly with seasoned flour. Brown them slowly all over in hot butter. Brown only as many pieces at one time as will fit into the pan in a single layer, adding more butter as needed. When all the chicken is browned, pile it in the pan and flame with warmed rum. Put the chicken in an ovenproof casserole. Melt another 2 tablespoons of butter in the pan and sauté the peppers and onion until lightly browned. Blend in the potato flour and tomato paste. Pour on the stock and stir until the mixture comes to a boil. Add the chopped walnuts and juice, a pinch of sugar, salt and pepper. Pour over the chickens. Cook covered in a moderate (350°) oven until tender, about 45 minutes. Serve in the casserole. Serves 6-8.

## Fried Chicken

Frying chickens are between 2½ and 4 pounds and are usually sold cut into pieces: 2 breasts, 2 wings, 2 thighs, 2 legs and the back. Since the back has very little meat it is best to reserve it and use it for stock. The following two methods of frying chicken both produce excellent results. With Oven Fried Chicken, all the cooking is done in the oven, and the chicken needs only to be turned once. There is none of the spattering of fat that goes on when chicken is fried on top of the stove. If the directions are followed accurately, the chicken will be thoroughly cooked but still nice and moist, with a delicious crisp brown crust. Southern Fried Chicken is first steamed, then batter dipped and fried in deep fat. The steaming keeps the chicken juicy; the deep-fat frying provides a fine brown crust. Allow 2-3 pieces for each serving.

## Oven Fried Chicken

Pre-heat the oven to 450°. Put seasoned flour in a paper bag and shake 3 or 4 pieces of chicken in it at a time until evenly coated. Melt enough vegetable shortening in a large heavy pan to cover the bottom ½″ deep. Put the chicken into the hot fat, if possible in a single layer. Cook for 20 minutes at 450°. By then the bottom of each piece should be well browned. Turn the heat down to 350°. Turn the chicken and put a small piece of butter on each piece. Continue cooking for another 25 minutes. Cream gravy may be made in the pan, with 2 tablespoons of the fat and 2 tablespoons of flour for each 1½ cups of rich milk or light cream.

## Southern Fried Chicken

Put 2 cut-up frying chickens in a heavy saucepan and add 2 cups of cold water. Bring slowly to a boil. Add a celery stalk, sliced onion and carrot, and salt. Cover and steam for 30 minutes. Strain 1 cup of stock and let it cool. Beat together the cooled stock, 1 egg, a generous cup of flour, 1 teaspoon of baking powder, salt and pepper. Let stand covered for ½ hour. Dip each piece in this batter and fry in deep fat at 375° until nicely browned. maybe 5 minutes. Cook only 2 or 3 pieces at one time. Keep cooked pieces hot on a rack in a slow (275°) oven.

## Chicken Jasmine (India)

*3-pound chicken*
*½ teaspoon black pepper*
*1½ teaspoons powdered ginger*
*½ teaspoon salt*
*½ pound butter*
*1½ pints yogurt*
*Pinch chili powder (optional)*

For this recipe use pale, unsalted butter or shortening. Wash and dry the chicken. Prick it all over with a sharp pointed knife and rub the pepper and ginger inside the cavity and on the outside. Truss the chicken. Heat the butter in a very heavy skillet, and mix in the salt and yogurt. Put in the trussed chicken and raise the heat high. Cook for 3 minutes then reduce heat to medium low and cook for 45 minutes. Baste the chicken as it cooks. Cook first on one side then on the other; then on the breast side and finally turn it on its back. By this time the chicken is well done, and has a delicious pearl or jasmine white appearance, except on the parts where it is nicely mottled and reddened. Now sprinkle the chili powder over the chicken, spoon the butter-yogurt mixture over it and cook for a few minutes in a 275° oven. Serves 4.

## Chicken Curry

*1 large frying chicken, 3½-4 lbs.,*
  *cut up*
*6 tablespoons butter*
*½ cup chicken stock or water*
*1 small onion, sliced*
*1 carrot sliced*
*1 stalk celery, sliced*
*1 apple, cored and chopped*
*3-4 tablespoons curry powder*
*½ teaspoon chili powder*
*3 tablespoons flour*
*2 cups coconut or almond milk*
*Salt*
*⅛ teaspoon each mace, allspice, nutmeg,*
  *cloves, cinnamon*
*2 teaspoons red currant jelly*
*2 teaspoons chutney*

Brown the chicken slowly in 3 tablespoons of hot butter. Add the chicken stock or water, cover and steam over a slow fire until the chicken is tender, about 30-40 minutes. Remove the meat from the bones and dice it, cut the skin into small bits, and reserve the stock. Meanwhile prepare the following curry sauce. Cook the onion, carrot, celery and apple in 3 tablespoons of butter in a deep heavy saucepan until they are soft, about 20 minutes. Add the curry powder and chili powder and cook another 5 minutes. Curry powder needs thorough cooking or it will taste raw. Blend in the flour. Pour on the coconut or almond milk. (If a fresh coconut is not available for coconut milk, make almond milk by pouring 2 cups of scalded milk over ¼ pound of blanched chopped almonds and let stand for ½ hour to infuse the milk with the almond flavor.) Stir until the mixture comes to a boil, season with salt, and simmer for about ½ hour. Then put through a strainer or food mill. Put sauce into a double boiler with the chicken, skin, spices, currant jelly and chutney. Taste for seasoning and cook until thoroughly heated. Serve with boiled rice and chutney and any or all of the following condiments: chopped or whole peanuts, diced green pepper mixed with shredded orange rind, shredded coconut, chopped hard-cooked egg whites and yolks (chopped separately), diced avocado mixed with crisp bacon bits, preserved ginger, diced ripe tomato, Bombay duck. Serves 4.

## Chicken with Mushrooms and Pâté

1 3½-4 lb. chicken
3 tablespoons butter
Salt, pepper
1 small truffle, finely chopped
¼ lb. mushrooms, sliced
¼ cup sherry or dry white wine
1½ cups heavy cream
2 tablespoons pâté

Cut the chicken into 8 serving pieces. Brown slowly all over in 2 tablespoons of hot butter in a deep heavy saucepan. Season with salt and pepper. Add another tablespoon of butter, a finely chopped truffle, and the sliced mushrooms and cook for another 5 minutes. Pour over the sherry or wine and continue cooking for 3-4 minutes while the wine soaks in. Add the cream and bring slowly to a boil. Cover and simmer for 30-40 minutes, until the chicken is tender, stirring several times. Arrange the chicken on a hot serving dish. Blend the pâté into the sauce with a wire whisk. Spoon the sauce over the chicken. Serves 4.

## Chicken Kiev

Remove the skin and membranes from the breasts of young chickens weighing 2½-3 pounds. Cut the breasts in half and carefully bone them. Remove the thin white tendon and any fat around the edges. Put each half breast between two pieces of wax paper and pound the breasts to a thickness of ¼" with a wooden mallet, starting in the center. Remove the paper. Take a ¼-pound stick of butter which is very cold and hard. Cut it in half crosswise, then cut each half in quarters lengthwise, making fingers about 2½" x ⅝". Place one in the center of each half breast, season with salt and white pepper, and sprinkle with a little chopped parsley or chives. Fold one

end over the butter, then roll the breast up, tucking in the other end to completely enclose the butter. Dust with flour, brush with beaten egg and roll in dry bread crumbs. Fry in deep fat at 325° until golden brown, 2-3 minutes, then place on a cookie sheet in a hot (400°) oven for 10 minutes or so to be sure the breasts are completely cooked. Allow one for each serving.

## Chicken Breasts Château

*4 chicken breasts, boned*
*1 small can pâté de foie*
*4 paper-thin slices prosciutto*
*4 tablespoons butter*
*½ cup white wine*
*1 teaspoon tarragon*

Fill pocket in each chicken breast with pâté, then roll breasts in prosciutto, and skewer. Secure breasts on spit, and roast about 30-45 minutes basting frequently with mixed butter-wine-tarragon. When meat is tender to point of knife, chicken is done. Serves 4.

## Chicken Breasts with Tomato and Wine Sauce

*3 whole chicken breasts*
*3 tablespoons butter*
*2 tablespoons olive oil*
*1 medium-size onion, finely chopped*
*4 tablespoons flour*
*1½ cups chicken stock*
*¾ cup thick tomato juice*
*Salt, pepper*
*¼ cup sherry*
*2 tablespoons chopped parsley*

Skin and bone the breasts and cut them in half. Brown them slowly on both sides in the hot butter and oil. Remove them from the pan. Lightly brown the chopped onion in the same pan. Blend in the flour, then pour on the stock and tomato juice. Stir until the mixture comes to a boil, and season with salt and pepper. Add the chicken, sherry and parsley. Simmer covered until the chicken is tender, about 30-40 minutes. Serves 6.

## Stewed Fowl

Fowl, old hens 5-6 pounds, are full of fine flavor but require long cooking in liquid to become tender. Call it boiling, stewing, poaching, simmering, whatever you wish, as long as you don't let the liquid actually boil. Put the fowl, either whole or cut into parts, in a deep, heavy saucepan. Barely cover with cold water. Bring slowly to a boil and skim. Add a sliced onion, carrot, 1-2 celery stalks, and a few peppercorns. These are basic. A bay leaf and 2-3 whole cloves are often added although their flavor seems too pronounced to me. A sprig or two of parsley and thyme or either may also be used. Salt may be added now or after the fowl has cooked for an hour. Simmer, covered, until the fowl is tender: 1½ hours for a young chicken, 2-3 hours for a tough one. Cool the chicken, then let it stand in the cooking liquid until used. Strain and store this chicken stock in the refrigerator or freeze it. The meat may be used in recipes calling for sliced or diced cooked chicken. Turkey is stewed in the same way. Young turkeys of 12-14 pounds require only 2-2½ hours.

## Brown Fricassee of Chicken

*1 4-lb. roasting chicken, cut up*
*Salt, pepper*
*4 tablespoons butter*
*1 small onion, sliced*
*1 small carrot, sliced*
*4 cups chicken stock or water*
*1 clove*
*½ cup flour*
*1 cup cream*

*1 tablespoon lemon juice*
*2 tablespoons chopped parsley*

Season the chicken pieces with salt and pepper and brown slowly all over in the butter in a deep heavy saucepan. When they are all browned, add the onion and carrot and sauté a minute or so. Then add the stock or water, the clove, and salt and pepper. Put the chicken back for added flavor. Bring to a boil, and simmer covered until tender, about 1 hour. Arrange the pieces of browned chicken on a hot platter and keep warm. Discard the chicken back and strain off 3 cups of the liquid. Blend the flour and cream, add to the strained liquid, and stir until it comes to a boil. Add the lemon juice and parsley, and taste for seasoning. Spoon a little of the gravy over the chicken and serve the rest separately. Serves 4-6.

## Chicken Paprika

*1 6-lb. fowl*
*6 tablespoons chicken fat or butter*
*2 tablespoons paprika*
*6 tablespoons flour*
*2 cups chicken stock*
*2 cups light cream*
*Salt*

Cook the chicken according to the directions for stewing fowl. When it is tender, skin and bone it, and cut the meat into small dice. Make the following paprika sauce: Melt the chicken fat or butter in the top of a double boiler over direct heat. Blend in the paprika and cook a minute or so. Then blend in the flour. Slowly pour on the chicken stock and cream and stir over the fire until the sauce comes to a boil. Season with salt. Put the pan over boiling water and simmer for about 30 minutes to cook away the raw taste of the paprika. Add the chicken and cook until piping hot, another 10-20 minutes. This dish tastes even better if made ahead of time and reheated slowly. Serve in a rice ring made with 1½ cups rice, boiled, and blended with at least ¼ cup of melted butter, 2 cups of cooked peas, 2-3 finely diced pimentos and seasoning. Place in a well greased ring mold and bake for 10 minutes at 375°. Serves 6-8.

## Capon on a Spit (India)

*¾ pound ground lamb*
*¼ pound butter*
*¼ pound onions*
*1 teaspoon salt*
*2 tablespoons coriander*
*4-pound capon*
*2 teaspoons black pepper*
*6 pounded cardamom seeds*
*2 tablespoons mint leaves, bruised*
*1½ teaspoons turmeric*
*1½ teaspoons chili powder*

Have the meat ground very fine. Heat half the butter and brown the meat with the finely shredded onions, salt and coriander. Add ¼ cup water or so to the meat. Cook away all liquid. Wash the capon, dry it and prick all over with a sharp pointed knife. Rub it well with black pepper, cardamom, mint and turmeric. Stuff the capon with the lamb mixture. Truss it well and put on a spit. Cook for about 2 hours, basting when necessary with remaining butter mixed with chili powder. Use more butter for basting, if required. Serve hot. Serves 4.

## Capon Nob Hill

*1 capon, about 4-6 pounds*
*Salt and pepper*
*4 tablespoons butter*
*1 teaspoon chervil*
*1 cup white wine*
*½ teaspoon paprika*

Salt and pepper capon and secure on spit. Roast about 2 hours, or until meat thermometer registers "done," basting frequently with mixture of butter-chervil-wine. During last 15 minutes of roasting sprinkle with paprika. Serves 4.

*VARIATION*

Stuff bird with following: Combine ¼ cup butter, 1 diced onion, ½ pound cooked ground beef, ½ cup boiled wild rice, ¼ cup seedless raisins, 2 tablespoons cooked, diced chestnuts, salt and pepper. Roast.

## Roast Capon with Rice Stuffing

Fill a 7-8 pound capon with the following rice stuffing, and roast according to the directions for roast chicken. Capons are exceedingly tender and are usually done in about 1¾ to 2 hours. For the stuffing, cook 1 cup of white rice. Meanwhile sauté 1 medium sized onion and ½ cup of finely chopped celery in 3 tablespoons of butter until soft but not brown. Put them in a mixing bowl with all the butter. Turn up the heat, put another tablespoon of butter in the pan and when it starts to brown quickly cook the liver. Remove the liver and chop it. Blend together the rice, onion and celery, liver, 2-3 tablespoons of chopped parsley, salt, pepper, 1 cup of sour cream.

## Roast Turkey

Stuff the turkey (using either of the stuffings given below). Secure the opening with skewers, lace them up, and truss the turkey. Place breast side up in a roasting pan. Cover the breast with thin slices of salt pork. In theory a turkey should be cooked breast side down so that the juices

will flow through the breast rather than away from it. In practice this presents problems. The breast may stick to the pan or rack, breaking the skin and releasing juices. Also, starting the turkey on its breast means moving it later, which can be hazardous, if the turkey is large. If the temperature is low, the turkey well basted, and not overcooked, it can stay breast side up and still be fine. The temperature should be 350°-375°. The turkey should be basted every 15-20 minutes until it is brown and crisp, using pan juices and additional butter if needed. When the turkey is brown, aluminum foil may be placed over the top and sides and the turkey left until it is completely cooked. It is done when a meat thermometer placed in the leg registers 185°, or when the legs move up and down easily.

Most timetables for roasting turkeys allow too much time; that is why turkeys dry out. Roughly speaking, 20 minutes to the pound for a turkey up to 12 pounds, 15 minutes to the pound for larger ones, is about right. Start testing before that though, especially with large 20-24 pound birds.

Meanwhile cook the neck and giblets in water to cover with onion, carrot, celery and salt. Let simmer about 1½ hours and drain, reserving the stock. Chop the giblets fine.

Place the turkey on a hot platter and allow to stand for at least 15 minutes before carving. Pour the pan juices into a bowl. For gravy, allow 1 tablespoon of fat skimmed from the bowl of juices and 1 tablespoon flour for each cup of giblet stock; make the gravy in the roasting pan to get all the glaze, and add the pan juices (with remaining fat skimmed off), and the chopped giblets. Taste for seasoning and simmer for at least 5 minutes. Allow ¾-1 lb. of turkey, dressed weight, for each person to be served.

163

### Wild Rice Stuffing

Cook 1½ cups of wild rice. Sauté 1 cup of diced celery and 1 cup of finely chopped onion in ½ cup of butter until soft but not brown. Add ½ pound of sliced mushrooms and cook another 2-3 minutes. Melt another ½ cup of butter in the same pan. Blend together the rice, vegetables and butter, 1 cup of chopped walnuts or pecans, salt, pepper, 2 tablespoons of chopped parsley and about ½ teaspoon of dried thyme. Use to stuff the bird or cook separately. This is sufficient for a 14-15 pound turkey.

### Cornbread Stuffing

*2 eggs*
*1 cup sour milk*
*1½ cups yellow cornmeal*
*½ cup flour*
*1 teaspoon salt*
*1 teaspoon sugar*
*3 tablespoons salad oil*
*1 teaspoon baking powder*
*½ teaspoon soda*
*1 lb. sausage meat*
*1 cup finely chopped celery*
*1 cup finely chopped onion*
*1 teaspoon poultry seasoning*

Beat the eggs well. Add the sour milk, cornmeal, flour, salt, sugar and salad oil and beat thoroughly. Stir in the baking powder and soda and mix only for a few seconds to blend. Bake in a greased 9" x 13" pan for 25-30 minutes in a moderate (400°) oven until lightly browned. This makes 6 cups of cornbread for the stuffing. Meanwhile, brown the sausage meat slowly in a medium size skillet, breaking it up with a fork into small pieces as it cooks. Remove the sausage with a slotted spoon. Sauté the chopped celery and onion in the sausage fat until soft but not brown. Put the cornbread into a large mixing bowl with the sausage, 1 teaspoon salt, poultry seasoning

and the onion and celery and the sausage fat from the pan. Blend well and use to stuff the turkey or bake separately. This is sufficient for an 18-20 pound turkey.

## Roast Christmas Turkey

*1 small squab turkey, weighing no more*
*  than 8 pounds*
*Salt and black pepper*
*Melted butter*
*½ pound ground raw veal*
*3 slices trimmed white bread, soaked in milk*
*2 egg whites, unbeaten*
*1 cup light cream*
*2 cups unsweetened chestnut purée*
*2 pounds pork sausage meat*
*2 tablespoons finely chopped onion*
*2 tablespoons finely chopped parsley*
*2 large truffles*
*3 ounces salt butter*
*1½ cups dry vermouth*
*2 tablespoons brandy*
*6 cooked artichoke bottoms*
*2 tablespoons grated Parmesan cheese*

Wash the turkey well in ice water. Dry thoroughly with cheesecloth. Season the inside with salt and pepper and brush all over inside with melted butter. Put the ground veal twice through a meat chopper with the bread, which has been squeezed dry. Mix in the egg whites and slowly beat in the light cream. Season well with salt and pepper and mix in 1 cup of the chestnut purée and the sausage meat. Add the onion and parsley and set aside in a cool place.

Meanwhile, carefully loosen all the skin of the turkey without breaking it. Cut

the truffles in thin slices and lay them on the turkey meat, under the skin. Pull the skin taut over the top and fill the turkey with the stuffing. Truss for roasting. Roast in a 375° oven, allowing 20-25 minutes per pound, reducing the heat the last half of the cooking time. During roasting, baste frequently, rubbing the top of the turkey with unmelted salt butter and adding 2 or 3 teaspoons dry vermouth each time (reserve ½ cup for gravy). Should the skin get too brown, cover with heavy waxed paper or aluminum foil. To serve, arrange the turkey on a large serving dish, rub the top with a little more unmelted butter and put cutlet frills on the legs. Heat the roasting pan and add the ½ cup vermouth, a little water and the brandy. Reboil, strain and pour a little of this gravy over the turkey. Serve the rest separately in a sauceboat.

Gently reheat the artichokes in a little butter. Beat the remaining chestnut purée to a cream with a little butter, salt and pepper. When quite smooth, put in a pastry bag with a rose tube and fill the artichoke bottoms. Sprinkle with grated Parmesan cheese, dot with butter and brown quickly under the broiler. Arrange around the turkey as garnish.

## Sauteed Turkey Steak, Poulette Sauce

This is a specialty of the Treadway Inn in Rochester, New York. Cut 4 slices of cooked turkey breast ½″ thick. Coat with seasoned flour, dip in beaten egg, then in dry bread crumbs. Sauté in slightly browned butter in a large heavy skillet until golden brown on both sides. Place on a hot platter and spoon over the following poulette sauce: Melt 3 tablespoons of butter and cook ½ cup of finely chopped mushrooms until they just start to turn color. Blend in 2 tablespoons of flour. Pour on 1½ cups of milk and stir until the mixture comes to a boil.

Season with salt and white pepper and simmer for 4-5 minutes. Beat 2 egg yolks slightly; then beat in ½ cup of heavy cream. Add to the sauce and stir over a slow fire until it thickens, but do not let it boil. Just before serving add 1-2 teaspoons of lemon juice or white wine and 1 tablespoon of finely chopped parsley. Serves 4.

## Deviled Turkey

*4 slices cooked turkey breast*
*2 tablespoons melted butter*
*¾ cup dry bread crumbs*
*½ teaspoon dry mustard*
*Salt, cayenne*
*½ teaspoon curry powder*
*Parsley or watercress for garnish*

Cut 4 large neat slices of turkey breast and have them at room temperature. Brush well with melted butter. Blend together the bread crumbs, mustard, salt, cayenne and curry. Coat each slice on both sides with this mixture. Broil until nicely browned on both sides, either using a low flame or placing the turkey 4-5″ from the flame so that it will not brown too fast. Garnish with parsley or watercress; serve the following *sauce diable* separately: Into a saucepan put 2 finely chopped shallots or 1 small white onion, ½ cup of wine vinegar, 8-10 peppercorns, 1 small piece bay leaf, ½ teaspoon dry mustard, salt, and a little paprika. Simmer until reduced by half, then strain. Add to 1 cup of brown sauce, turkey gravy, or tomato sauce and heat. Serves 4.

## Barbecued Turkey

*1 small turkey, 6-7 lbs.*
*1 cup melted butter*
*½ cup fresh lemon juice*
*1 teaspoon Tabasco sauce*
*1 teaspoon dried shredded green onions*
*½ teaspoon dry mustard*
*1 teaspoon salt*
*¼ teaspoon pepper*
*1 whole clove garlic*

Have the turkey split in half and put it skin side up in a shallow roasting pan. Melt the butter in a saucepan over a slow fire. Add the rest of the ingredients and stir until the mixture comes to a boil. Simmer for a few minutes; then remove the garlic. Brush the turkey thoroughly with the sauce. Cook in a moderate oven at 375°, turning the turkey every 15 or 20 minutes and brushing and basting with the rest of the sauce. The turkey should be done in about 1½ hours. Serve covered with sauce. Serves 6-8.

## Creamed Turkey and Oysters

½ pint oysters
1 cup water
Salt, white pepper
3 tablespoons butter
3 tablespoons flour
1 cup light cream
1½ cups diced cooked turkey
Watercress for garnish

Bring the oysters slowly to a boil in 1 cup of seasoned water and simmer until their edges curl, about 2-3 minutes. Drain, reserving the stock. Melt the butter. Blend in the flour. Slowly pour on 1 cup of the oyster liquor and the cream and stir until the sauce comes to a boil. Taste for seasoning and simmer for at least 5 minutes. Just before serving add the oysters, coarsely chopped, and the turkey. Cook until piping hot. Serve with toast points or in patty shells. Garnish with watercress. Serves 4-6.

## Stuffed Turkey Legs

4 turkey legs, from 12-14 lb. birds
1 unbeaten egg white
½ lb. veal, ground three times
1½ cups light cream
Salt
4 tablespoons butter
1 cup dry white wine
1 teaspoon paprika
6 slices bacon
½ cup chopped onion
1-2 tablespoons flour

Bone the raw turkey legs and remove the white tendons—your butcher can do all this. Spread them out flat, skin side down. Make the following stuffing. Mix the egg white into the veal. Slowly beat in ½ cup cream. Season with salt. Cover the legs with mixture, roll together and tie with string. It doesn't matter if some of the stuffing is exposed; it will set when the legs are cooked. Heat the butter in a large skillet. Brown the legs slowly. When they are browned, pour the wine into the pan, blend in the paprika, cover and cook over a slow fire about 1 hour. Meanwhile dice the bacon and sauté until brown and crisp. Remove with a slotted spoon and drain on absorbent paper. Sauté the chopped onion in the bacon fat until lightly browned, then put in the pan with the legs. To serve, place the legs on a hot serving dish and keep warm. Blend the flour into the pan juices. Add 1 cup of cream and stir until the sauce comes to a boil. Taste for seasoning and simmer for 2-3 minutes. Spoon over the legs and sprinkle with crumbled bacon bits. Serves 4.

## Roast Duck

Duck is full of fat and so requires different cooking methods from other poultry. Remove all the fat you see around the openings. Do not cook with any additional fat; just put a little water in the pan to prevent burning. Don't prick and don't baste, since ducks are self basting. Pour off the fat occasionally as it accumulates in the pan. The roasting time given in the following recipes is the minimum. A 5-lb. duck will be done in 2 hours, but not well done. If you wish a drier, crisper bird, cook for another half hour. For a crisper skin, rub a little butter over it and put under the broiler for a few minutes.

It is better to cook dressing separately. If it is roasted in the duck it will get soaked with fat.

## Duck with Orange

*1 5-6 lb. duck*
*Salt, pepper*
*2 large oranges*
*1 small onion*
*2 teaspoons potato flour*
*1½ cups orange juice*
*½ cup red wine*
*1 tablespoon red currant jelly*

Season the duck lightly. Stuff with one orange, quartered, and the onion, and tie the legs together. Roast in a moderate (350°) oven breast side up for 2-2¼ hours. Keep pouring off the fat so that when the duck is cooked there are only about 2-3 tablespoons fat in the pan with the brown glaze. Meanwhile, cut thin slices of the peel from the other orange with a vegetable peeler and cut them in julienne strips. Cover with cold water, bring to a boil and drain. Section the orange. Remove stuffing from the duck place the duck on a hot serving platter and keep warm. Blend the potato flour into the pan juices. Pour on the orange juice and red wine and stir until the sauce comes to a boil. Add the currant jelly and orange rind and taste for seasoning. Simmer for a few minutes. Just before serving add the orange sections. Spoon a little of the sauce over the duck and serve the rest separately. Serves 4.

*VARIATION*

### Duck with Cherries

Follow the preceding recipe but substitute 1 cup of sour red cherries for the orange sections, cherry juice for the orange juice (or use half and half), and add a little kirsch to the red wine.

## Roast Duck with Figs
### (Canard aux Figues)

*2 Long Island ducklings, each 3½ pounds*
*Salt, freshly cracked pepper*
*2 small peeled oranges*
*2 small peeled onions*
*1 peeled garlic clove*
*1 stick butter*
*2½ cups strong chicken stock*
*1 cup mixed sliced onions, carrots, celery, leek*
*4 level tablespoons flour*
*2 teaspoons tomato paste*
*2 teaspoons meat glaze*
*1½ cups mushroom peelings and stalks (or 2 sliced mushrooms)*
*1 very ripe tomato, skinned and cut up*
*1 tablespoon red currant jelly*
*12 green, 12 black figs soaked for 24 hours in 3 cups white sauterne*
*½ cup brandy*
*1 truffle, finely chopped*
*2 cups each diced carrots, turnips, green beans*
*6 slices bread, diced and fried in a little chicken fat*

167

Wash the ducks well inside and out and dry thoroughly. Season inside with salt and pepper. Stuff each with 1 orange, 1 onion and ½ clove garlic. Tie up carefully and rub salt and pepper all over the outsides. Place on roasting racks and brush with melted butter. Pour a little stock in the roasting pan and roast at 375° for 20 minutes. Remove, baste well, add a little water to the pan and brush ducks with a little more melted butter. Reduce heat to 350° and continue roasting for a further ½ hour. Remove and cool.

Dissolve ½ stick butter in a small, heavy pan. Add sliced vegetables and cook very slowly, without browning, for 3-4 minutes. Add flour and cook slowly until dark nut-brown. Stir in, off the fire, the tomato paste, meat glaze, mushroom peelings and tomato. Pour on remaining stock and currant jelly and stir over the fire until it comes to a boil. Strain the liquid from the soaked figs and add to the sauce. Stir over fire until it comes to a boil and cook until reduced to the consistency of heavy cream. Remove legs from ducks and cut them in half. Place in bottom of a large, heavy casserole. Cut figs in four and place on top of legs. Cut off breasts of duck in one piece and slice thinly, lengthwise. Arrange slices overlapping on top of figs. Heat and flame the brandy and pour over the duck. Strain the brown sauce, add the truffle and pour over the duck. Cover casserole with wax paper and the lid and put in 350° oven for ½-¾ hour. Meanwhile, put diced vegetables in a pan and cover with water. Bring to a boil and drain. Melt a little butter in a pan and add the vegetables. Cover with wax paper and the lid and cook for 15 minutes in 350° oven.

To serve, pile up vegetables in the center of a flat serving dish. Arrange duck legs on top, then the figs, then the breast of duck. Pour over the sauce and surround with the fried croutons. Serves 4.

## Roast Duck, Spanish Style

*1 5-6 lb. duck*
*Salt, pepper*
*1 medium-sized yellow onion, finely chopped*
*4 tablespoons butter*
*½ lb. mushrooms, sliced*
*1 tablespoon Spanish paprika*
*½ teaspoon tomato paste*
*3 tablespoons flour*
*1 cup chicken stock*
*½ cup sherry*
*2 tomatoes*
*½ cup water or*
*¼ cup water, ¼ cup cognac*

Season the duck well with salt and pepper, and tie it up. Roast in a moderate (375°) oven for 2-2¼ hours, until well browned and tender. When the duck has cooked for an hour, start making the sauce. Sauté the chopped onion in 2 tablespoons of butter over a slow fire until golden brown. Add another 2 tablespoons of butter and the mushrooms and cook another 5 minutes or so. Blend in the paprika, tomato paste and flour. Pour on the stock and wine and stir until the mixture comes to a boil. Season and simmer for at least 20 minutes or until ready to use. Skin the tomatoes, remove the seedy pulp and shred the rest. Add to the sauce just before serving. Cut the duck into serving pieces. Pour off all the fat from the roasting pan, add ½ cup of water (or ¼ cup water and ¼ cup cognac) to the pan and bring to a boil to lift the glaze. Add this to the sauce. Spoon a little of the sauce over the duck and serve the rest separately. Surround the duck with small boiled buttered potatoes. Serves 4.

## Roast Duck, Chinese Style

*1 5-lb. duck*
*4 teaspoons sugar*
*4 teaspoons honey*
*3 teaspoons soy sauce*

*3 tablespoons chicken stock*
*1 green pepper, diced*
*2 tablespoons cornstarch*
*2 tablespoons water*
*2 slices canned pineapple, cut in small*
   *pieces*
*½ cup pineapple juice*
*Salt*

Wash the duck and tie it up. Put it in a small shallow roasting pan. Blend together the sugar, honey, soy sauce and chicken stock. Pour this mixture over the duck and let it stand for 45 minutes, turning several times. Before roasting, pour off about half the marinade and keep for basting. Roast the duck in a pre-heated 375° oven for about 2 hours. Turn the duck occasionally to brown all over and baste with the re-served marinade. Half an hour before the duck is to be served, make the sauce. Pour all the pan liquid into a small bowl. The fat quickly rises to the top and should be spooned off, leaving just the brown pan juices. Parboil the diced pepper in boiling water to cover for 10 minutes and drain. Blend together the cornstarch and cold water. Add to the pan juices and stir over heat in a small saucepan until the mixture thickens. Add the diced pepper and pine-apple, and season with salt. Place the duck on a hot serving platter. Add the pineapple juice to the roasting pan and dissolve the glaze—with this marinade there will be plenty of it. Add to the sauce. Serve the sauce separately. Serves 3-4.

## Broiled Duck

*1 5-5½ lb. duck*
*2 teaspoons lemon juice*
*1 teaspoon salt*
*½ teaspoon ground ginger*
*1 tablespoon butter*

Have the duck quartered and the backbone and wing tips removed. Cut off all excess fat. Sprinkle with lemon juice, salt and ginger. Let stand half an hour or so to absorb the seasoning. Place on a preheated broiler pan, skin side down, with the pan 4-5″ from the flame. Broil for 20-25 minutes on one side, turn, and cook another 20-25 minutes. Before serving brush with melted butter. Serves 4.

## Duck Casserole

*1 6-lb. duck*
*1 small onion, sliced*
*1 carrot, sliced*
*Parsley, bay leaf*
*Salt, peppercorns*
*1 medium-sized cabbage*
*3 tablespoons butter*
*3 tablespoons flour*
*2 cups duck stock*
*1 cup sour cream*

Put the duck in a large saucepan, add cold water to cover, bring slowly to a boil and skim. Add the onion, carrot, 1 or 2 sprigs of parsley, half a bay leaf, salt and a few peppercorns. Simmer covered until tender, about 1½ hours. Meanwhile core and quar-ter the cabbage and cook it until tender in boiling salted water, about 20 minutes. Drain well and chop. Remove the duck, dis-card the skin, take the meat off the bones and cut it into dice. Place it in the center of a casserole and arrange the cabbage around it. Cover with the following sauce: Melt the butter, blend in the flour. Pour on 2 cups of duck stock (strained and fat re-moved) and bring to a boil, stirring con-stantly. Simmer for 5 minutes. Blend in the sour cream and taste for seasoning. Bake uncovered in a moderate (350°) oven until thoroughly heated, about 20-25 minutes. Serves 6.

## Aspic of Duck

*1 tablespoon gelatin*
*½ cup dry white wine*
*1 cup hot chicken stock, fresh or canned*
*12 stuffed green olives*
*3 cups diced roast duck*
*¼ cup chopped green pepper*
*3 tablespoons grated onion*
*1 4-ounce can sliced mushrooms*
*2 tablespoons chopped parsley*
*2 tablespoons chopped chives or scallions*
*2 tablespoons chopped pimento*

Soften the gelatin in the wine for 5 minutes. Add the hot stock, stirring until dissolved. Barely cover the bottom of a lightly oiled 9″ loaf pan with a little of the gelatin mixture. Chill until set. Arrange the olives on it. Mix the duck, green pepper, onion, mushrooms, parsley, chives and pimento together. Add salt and pepper to taste. Lightly pack into the loaf pan; pour the remaining gelatin over it. Chill for at least 4 hours. Unmold and garnish the platter with greens. Serves 6 as a main course, 8-10 as a first course.

## Roast Stuffed Goose

*1 10-12 lb. goose*
*2 apples*
*1 orange*
*4 large yellow onions*
*1 egg*
*4 cups soft white bread crumbs*
*2-3 leaves fresh sage or*
*   about 1 teaspoon dried sage*
*1 teaspoon salt*
*½ teaspoon freshly ground black pepper*
*Nutmeg*
*Ground ginger*

Wash the goose inside and out, remove any pin feathers and rub off any down. Cut out all visible fat. Stuff with a quartered apple and orange, tie the legs together, and roast for an hour in a moderate (350°) oven. Re-move from the oven and pour off all the fat. Meanwhile, make the following sage and onion stuffing: Peel the onions and boil them in salted water for 20 minutes. Drain and chop them. Core and dice an unpeeled apple. Beat 1 egg slightly in a large mixing bowl. Add the onions, bread crumbs, apple, sage, salt, pepper, and a pinch of nutmeg. Blend well. When the goose is cool enough to handle, replace the apple and orange with sage and onion stuffing. (This pre-liminary cooking both flavors the goose and tries out a considerable amount of fat so that the stuffing won't get soaked with it.) Rub the skin with a little ground ginger, return it to the oven and continue cooking, allowing 25-30 minutes per pound for the total cooking time. Remove the fat in the pan once or twice again and do not baste the goose; it is self basting and the skin will be crisper if it is left to dry out. Brush-ing the skin once or twice with butter to-wards the end of the cooking period will also help make it darker and crisper. Mean-while, cook the giblets in seasoned water and serve the goose with a giblet gravy (see turkey gravy). Red cabbage cooked with red wine, 1-2 cloves, and a chopped apple or apple jelly, goes well with it too. Serves 8-10.

## Salmis of Goose

*1 small onion, finely chopped*
*2 tablespoons butter*
*6 thick slices cooked breast of goose*
*½ cup chopped pitted ripe olives*
*1 cup goose gravy*
*Pinch thyme*
*Salt, pepper*
*½ cup sherry*
*1 tablespoon lemon juice*

In a shallow skillet or chafing dish cook the onion in the butter until soft but not brown. Add the goose, olives, gravy, thyme, and taste for seasoning; simmer until the meat

is thoroughly heated. Just before serving add the sherry and lemon juice and cook for 2-3 minutes. This is nice served with timbales of steamed rice or on crisp toast. Serves 4.

## Squabs with Grapes

4 squabs
1 tablespoon butter
Salt and pepper
2 cups seedless grapes
4 slices bacon
½ cup vermouth

Rub birds with butter and sprinkle with salt and pepper. Stuff with grapes. Secure on spit. Cover breasts with bacon, and roast until done, about 30 minutes, or until meat is tender to tines of a sharp fork. Baste frequently with balance of butter and vermouth. Serves 4.

## Squab Casserole

6 squabs
½ cup finely diced celery
½ cup finely chopped onion
12 tablespoons butter
2 cups soft bread crumbs
1 tablespoon chopped parsley
Salt, pepper, thyme
½ pound mushrooms
1 can tiny French peas, drained
2 tablespoons sherry

Stuff the squabs and secure each with a skewer. For the bread stuffing sauté the chopped celery and onion in 4 table-

spoons of butter until soft but not brown. Combine the vegetables with the bread crumbs and parsley and season with salt, pepper and thyme. Rub the squabs with 6 tablespoons of softened butter and roast in a shallow roasting pan in a moderate (350°) oven for 30 minutes, until lightly browned. Meanwhile sauté the mushrooms in 2 tablespoons of butter. Mix with the drained peas and sherry and place in a casserole. Arrange the squabs over the peas and cover with the pan juices. Cook uncovered an additional 15-20 minutes. Serve in the casserole. Serves 6.

## Guinea Fowl
## with Sour Cream Sauce

3 guinea fowl, about 2 lbs. each
¾ pound sausage meat
6 thin slices white bread
2 tablespoons chopped parsley
¼ teaspoon dried thyme
Salt
1 cup cream
6 thin slices salt pork
2 carrots, sliced
1 small onion, sliced
1½ cups chicken stock
3 tablespoons butter
3 tablespoons flour
1 cup sour cream

Stuff the guinea fowl with the following stuffing. Cook the sausage meat slowly until well browned, breaking it with a fork into small bits. Trim the crusts off the bread, toast it, and cut into small squares. Combine the bread, sausage meat, 1-2 tablespoons of sausage fat, parsley, thyme, salt and cream. Let stand for 10 minutes or so for the bread to absorb the cream. After stuffing them, secure the fowl with skewers, and tie the birds up. Place in a shallow roasting pan, and cover with the salt pork. Put the carrots, onion and stock in the pan. Bake in a moderate (375°) oven for 45-60

171

minutes. Baste occasionally. When the birds have cooked for 30 minutes, remove the salt pork and rub birds with butter. Place the birds on a hot serving dish, strain the pan juices into a small saucepan and thicken with the flour. Blend in the sour cream and taste for seasoning. Serve sauce separately. Serves 8-10.

## Guinea Fowl Saxony

*1 guinea fowl*
*1 apple, diced*
*1 onion, diced*
*2 tablespoons butter*
*½ teaspoon powdered tarragon, chervil, or marjoram*
*Salt and pepper*
*3 strips salt pork*
*½ cup olive oil*
*½ cup sherry*

Stuff the fowl with the diced apple and onion, butter and herb of your choice. Salt and pepper, sew up opening, tie pork strips on breast, secure fowl on spit. Roast about 1½ hours, or until thermometer registers "done," basting frequently with mixed olive oil and sherry. Serves 4.

## Rock Cornish St. Loraine

*4 Rock Cornish Game fowl, each 11 ounces*
*4 tablespoons butter*
*½ teaspoon thyme, tarragon, rosemary, or marjoram*
*Salt and pepper*
*½ cup white wine*
*1 tablespoon sesame seeds*

Combine the herb of your choice with 1 tablespoon of butter and put a portion inside each bird. Put fowl on spit, tie, secure, butter well and sprinkle on salt and pepper. Cook about 45 minutes, or until leg moves freely at thigh. During cooking baste with white wine. During last ten minutes of cooking sprinkle with sesame seeds. Serves 4.

## Roast Rock Cornish Game Fowl

Allow a 1-lb. bird for each serving. If you wish, you may stuff it with the sausage stuffing for guinea fowl. Tie the bird up loosely. Season lightly with salt and rub well with softened butter, 1-2 tablespoons for each bird. Place in a shallow roasting pan. Thin slices of bacon or salt pork may be placed over the fowl, but I think butter is a less pronounced and therefore better flavor for these delicate birds. Roast uncovered in a moderate (375°) oven for about 50-60 minutes if stuffed, 35-40 minutes if not. After birds have cooked for 10 minutes, pour ¼ cup white wine in the pan. Baste every ten minutes, adding more butter if necessary. Serve with the pan juices and a tart jelly.

## Broiled Rock Cornish Fowl

Allow a 1-lb bird for each serving. Cut through the back bone with a pair of poultry shears. Spread the bird flat on a shallow roasting pan, skin side up. Season lightly with salt and pepper and rub the skin with about 2 tablespoons of softened butter. Place under the broiler at least 7-8" away from the fire and keep the heat moderate; if your broiler is shallow and hot, it is better not to cook the birds this way because the skin will get too brown before they are cooked. Broil about 10 minutes, turn over and pour over the breast a mixture of the juice of 1 lemon and ½ teaspoon of dry mustard melted in 1-2 tablespoons of butter. Continue cooking for another 20 minutes, turning twice again and basting with the pan juices. To serve, place the bird on a hot serving dish, spoon over it the pan juices, dissolve the glaze in the pan with a little white wine or water and pour this over the bird.

# GAME

# Game

We once knew a man who ate crow. He was, of course, fulfilling the conditions of a wager he had lost. But the bird was presented to him done up in a pie, in the manner of the four-and-twenty blackbirds of the nursery rhyme, and he declared it to be "not bad eating". Crow, as we all know, is hardly a delicate game bird, but this man's experience does suggest that some things we do not normally eat may be quite delectable.

Our ancestors regularly consumed most of the varieties of wild life that roam or fly over this continent. It was a matter of necessity, particularly for those who lived on the frontier. Of course, some game was always considered choice, and venison and game birds were so much in demand that they were once as common in American markets as beef and chicken. Though your grandfather undoubtedly thought of quail on toast as mighty good eating, he did not consider it a rare and almost exotic treat, as we do today.

The fact that game is a strange food to many of us reflects not only grandfather's enormous appetite and sharp shooting eye but also the urbanization of our civilization. Thanks to our strict game laws, America still is rich in wild life. Unfortunately, these came too late to save the passenger pigeon, now as extinct as the dinosaur. The wild turkey, forebear of our domesticated Thanksgiving bird, was once so scarce that few game lovers feasted on his luscious meat. But he is today happily increasing in the tangled cypress swamps of the South and the rugged hills of the Southwest. The game laws have preserved, indeed have greatly increased, for us the deer, antelope, elk, partridge, and pheasant. American hunters have a wide choice, and many of them come home with a good supply. Game is too great a treat to be wasted. Don't throw it away or give it away, but learn to prepare it properly. Here are a few general suggestions:

174

If you don't understand how to clean the animal or bird you have bagged, take it to a butcher and pay him to do the job for you; or ask an expert to show you how.

If you can't consume all that you have at once, take advantage of modern freezing methods. Use your own deep freezer or rent space in a freezer.

Most game tastes best cooked simply. The finest game of all is cooked over a charcoal fire. If you have a grill, by all means use it. For special occasions, some of the more elaborate classic game dishes are included in the recipes on the following pages. They make a superb treat. Most game birds, with the usual exception of duck and geese, tend to be dry. Wrap the breasts well with salt pork strips (this is called barding) and baste them often during cooking to keep them moist.

Opinions vary widely on how long game should be cooked. Some people like it blood rare; others prefer it cooked until the meat falls from the bones. Prepare it to suit yourself.

The practice of serving cranberries or currant jelly with game is a tradition we cannot understand. The sweetness only detracts from the subtle flavor of fine game and in some cases actually smothers it.

All game is considerably enhanced when accompanied by a fine wine, usually red, sometimes white. In most cases, we have indicated the wine we prefer to serve with the dish.

## Venison

Venison has been called "meat for princes and great estates and poor scholars when they can get it" and, we would add, for all of us when we can get it. The term "venison" is used to refer to the flesh of the deer, the antelope, the elk and the moose. They are all prepared much the same.

Venison should hang from 5 days to 4 weeks. The length of time depends on how well aged you like your meat. If you are not familiar with the process of hanging and butchering such game, you should take the animal to a good butcher and pay him to do it for you. As with beef, the cuts of venison vary in tenderness, some being suitable for broiling or roasting and others being best when treated to a slower cooking method, such as stewing.

Steaks, chops and the saddle from a young tender animal may be cooked without marinating them, but tougher cuts and meat from older animals should be soaked for at least several hours and if possible for several days in the following marinade:

### Marinade for Venison

Mix 1 bottle of red wine, 1 cup of wine vinegar, 3 cloves, 1 teaspoon of coarsely crushed peppercorns, 1½ tablespoons of salt, 3 sliced onions, 3 sliced carrots, 3 crushed cloves of garlic, 2 crushed bay leaves, a sprig of thyme and 1 cup of olive oil. Soak the venison for several hours or days, turning it frequently to be sure it is well bathed in the marinade.

## Venison Steaks and Chops

These should be cut quite thick. We like to soak them in a little olive oil (unless they have been marinated) for an hour or so. Broil over charcoal as you would beefsteak, seasoning to taste toward the end. Do not overcook them. Venison should be rare.

Serve these with a purée of chestnuts and diced yellow turnips liberally buttered. Bring out your best red wine to go with this treat.

## Venison Steak au Poivre

Crush or crack a liberal supply of peppercorns. About ½ hour before you are ready to cook the steaks, press the cracked pepper into each side of the meat with the heel of your hand. Use plenty of pepper and be sure it is embedded in the flesh.

Pan broil or sauté the steaks quickly in a very hot skillet and do not overcook them. They should be rare. Remove the steaks to a hot platter and add ¼ cup of cognac to the pan. Blend in 1 cup of sour cream and heat through but do not boil. Pour this sauce over the steaks.

Serve this with shoestring or French fried potatoes, braised celery and a bottle of good Hermitage from the Rhône Valley.

## Roast Saddle of Venison, Sauce Poivrade

If the saddle is from a young animal, it should need no marinating to tenderize it. If the meat is older and tougher, soak it for one or two days in the venison marinade before cooking.

When you are ready to cook it, wipe it dry and insert a meat thermometer in the fleshiest part. Butter the saddle well, season to taste and roast it in a 450 degree oven for 30 minutes. Then reduce the heat to 350 degrees and continue cooking until the meat thermometer registers 135 degrees. This is for rare meat, and we feel a fine saddle of venison is better eaten rare. However, if you prefer, cook the saddle until the meat thermometer registers 150 degrees and you will have a medium done roast.

Remove it to a hot platter or carving

board. Saddle should be carved in long thin slices parallel to the spinal column. Serve with tiny turnips and mushrooms, a purée of chestnuts and the following sauce:

### Quick Sauce Poivrade

This is a short-cut method for making the famous sauce. In ½ cup of dry vermouth simmer 6 chopped shallots or green onions, 1 chopped carrot and a bay leaf. Season with salt, a dash of cayenne pepper, 1 teaspoon (or more) of freshly ground black pepper and ½ teaspoon of dry mustard. Stir in 1 can of beef gravy and heat thoroughly. Add 2 ounces of butter and a dash of lemon juice, blend and strain. Serve with the venison.

## Roast Leg of Venison

If the leg is from a young animal it will not need marinating. Otherwise, soak it in the venison marinade for one or two days. Roast the leg as you do the saddle (see above) until the internal temperature registers 135-140 on the meat thermometer. This is for rare meat.

Roast some potatoes in the pan with the meat and with these and the venison serve cauliflower dressed with black butter, and a good Médoc wine.

*Note:* The loin and tenderloin may also be roasted in the same manner.

## Rotisserie Leg of Venison

*1 leg of venison, about 6 pounds, boned*
*1 cup olive oil*
*1 cup dry red wine*
*½ teaspoon garlic powder*
*2 crushed juniper berries or ½ bay leaf,*
*   or ½ teaspoon powdered cloves, cumin*
*   seed, or basil*

Combine the olive oil, wine and garlic powder with the seasoning of your choice, and marinate meat overnight or for several hours, turning frequently. Reserve marinade. Bring meat to room temperature before securing on spit. Roast about 1½ to 2 hours, or until thermometer registers "done." Baste with marinade. Serves 6.

## Ragout of Venison

For 4 people cut 3 pounds of venison (using the less tender cuts) into pieces about 1 to 1½ inches square. Soak these for a day or two in the marinade, using one half the marinade recipe.

Render about ½ cup of salt pork cut in fine strips and brown the drained pieces of

venison in the fat. When all the meat is browned, add the marinade and 2 cups of canned tomatoes to the pan. Cover tightly and simmer for 1 to 1½ hours, or until the venison is tender. If the liquid evaporates too much during the cooking add red wine and stock mixed.

When the meat is done, thicken the broth, if you like, with small balls of butter and flour kneaded together.

Serve this ragout with noodles dressed with buttered crumbs, and a red cabbage. A red Burgundy goes well with this.

## Wild Rabbit or Hare

In some areas of this country it is dangerous to eat rabbit or hare unless it is carefully handled. If you are not sure, seek the advice of local authorities. Certainly, if you are not experienced in skinning and cleaning these animals, you should ask an expert to do it for you or show you how.

A tender young rabbit or hare may be broiled, spitted or sautéed as you would cook a chicken. Older animals with tougher fibers demand long, slow cooking methods. Use these for terrines or pâtés.

## Sautéed Young Hare or Rabbit

Wash and disjoint the rabbit and dredge the pieces well with flour. Brown them in 4 tablespoons of butter and when all the pieces are nicely colored, season to taste with salt and pepper, cover the pan and simmer for 15 to 20 minutes, or until the meat is tender and cooked through. Remove the rabbit pieces and arrange them around the edge of a hot platter.

To the pan add 1 cup of sour cream, 2 teaspoons of paprika and a little salt. Stir until the cream and pan juices are blended and heated through but do not let the sauce boil. Pour into the center of the platter and sprinkle chopped parsley on the meat and sauce. Serve with mashed potatoes and braised endive.

*VARIATIONS*

### Rabbit Tarragon

Brown the rabbit as above and add 1 teaspoon of tarragon and ½ cup of white wine before covering and simmering. Just before you take the rabbit from the pan, add more white wine, a good piece of butter and some chopped parsley. Heat and blend and dish the rabbit up in the sauce.

### Rabbit with Carrots

Brown the rabbit as above and add ½ cup of grated carrots and ½ cup of white wine before simmering. Serve with buttered young carrots and sautéed potatoes.

### Rabbit with Mushrooms

Brown rabbit as above and add 2 tablespoons of chopped shallots or green onions and ½ cup of white wine before simmering. When the rabbit is just tender, remove the cover and add ½ pound of sliced mushrooms, sautéed, ¼ cup of chopped parsley and 4 tablespoons of cognac. Heat through and serve with buttered noodles garnished with croutons and a celery salad with a mustard dressing.

## Saddle of Hare

This is a classic dish that takes time and trouble, but when well done it is a memorable treat. In this country, hares are not as large as the European variety, and you may need one saddle per person. Put the saddles in a deep bowl and cover them with red wine. Add 1 teaspoon of dried thyme, 1 bay leaf, an onion stuck with cloves, 1 sliced carrot, a few sprigs of parsley, 1 teaspoon of crushed peppercorns and 1 teaspoon of salt. Soak the meat in this marinade for several days—at least three, if possible—turning it often to bathe evenly.

When you are ready to cook, remove the saddles, dry them and insert pieces of larding pork in the flesh. Sear them quickly in butter until brown on all sides, lower the heat and continue cooking for 15 minutes until they are cooked just to the rare stage. Remove the saddles to a hot platter and rinse the pan with ¼ cup of cognac. To this add 3 or 4 tablespoons of gooseberry jelly and allow this to caramelize. Then add ½ cup of Sauce Poivrade for each saddle and heat through. (Use the Quick Sauce Poivrade recipe under Saddle of Venison.)

Serve the saddles of hare with the sauce and puréed chestnuts.

## Hare a la Royale

This is another classic French dish—difficult but superb. Prepare the marinade used for Saddle of Hare (see above) adding 1 cup of Madeira and ½ cup of cognac to the red wine. Soak a whole cleaned hare in this mixture for two days, turning it frequently.

Prepare the following stuffing: grind ½ pound of fresh lean pork with ½ pound of chicken livers and season to taste with salt, freshly ground black pepper and a bit of thyme. Stuff the hare and sew it up.

Line a large casserole with slices of salt pork and over this place 6 to 7 cloves of garlic finely chopped. Add 4 chopped onions and some chopped parsley. Place the stuffed hare on this bed of seasonings and cover it with slices of bacon or salt pork. Cook slowly in a low 200-degree oven for about 12 hours. Cool overnight.

Strain the marinade, add ½ bottle of red wine and reduce it over a brisk flame to ⅓ its original amount. Take the hare from the casserole, skim the grease from the liquid and strain the pan juices. Return the hare to the casserole, pour the pan juices and the reduced marinade over it and heat for 15 or 20 minutes. Thicken the sauce with small balls of butter and flour kneaded together and stirred into the liquid slowly.

Serve from the casserole.

## Wild Duck

We are blessed with many varieties of wild duck in this country. The larger kinds, such as mallard, will serve two persons. Smaller birds, such as teal, will serve only one. You will have to judge for yourself.

Duck is better when it has hung for a few days. Bleed it soon after killing and hang it by the head, not the feet. If it is impossible to let the bird hang, at least wait a few hours before eating it.

Do not pluck the bird until you are ready to cook it unless you plan to put it in a deep freezer. When you pluck it, you may find you have a tedious job, but you will find a thorough job well worth the work. Pluck it dry. Next, go after the pin feathers and be sure you get them all out. Use tweezers and pick and pick. Then singe the bird thoroughly.

We like to turn back the skin around

the neck and cut the neck out. We think it makes a neater looking bird when roasted. Draw the duck, as you would any fowl, and wash it well. Then rub with a piece of lemon.

Some ducks, because of the region in which they live or their feeding habits, develop a fishy or muddy taste. There are supposed to be various ways to eliminate this undesirable flavor. After rubbing the duck thoroughly, inside and out, with lemon, soak it for several hours in acidulated water. (To 1½ quarts of water, add 1 tablespoon of vinegar or lemon juice.) Or marinate the duck in red wine seasoned with a little grated garlic and onion. Personally, we do not think a muddy or fishy duck can ever be made tasty.

There are various opinions on how long wild duck should be cooked. When we were young, there were three different cooking times for this game bird in our family. One person liked it rather well done; another preferred medium rare duck; and still another wanted it really rare. If we had guests, the situation could be even more complicated. Suit yourself about the cooking time.

One of the best wild ducks we ever ate was prepared by Helen Evans Brown, the West Coast food authority, and her husband. Here is the recipe:

## Charcoaled Duck

For 4 persons, use 4 small ducks. Rub them well inside and out, with lemon and olive oil, and put a stalk of celery and a few juniper berries in the cavity of each duck. Spit the birds all on one long spit, running it through them crosswise, from side to side. Alternate the birds, one breast up and next down. Then fasten them securely with two long skewers, one run through them near the tails, and the other near the necks. Season to taste and roast them over a medium

charcoal fire for about 20 minutes. (Give them less time if you want them blood rare.) At the last minute, bring the fire up close to the ducks to sear them and crisp the skin.

Remove the birds from the spit to a carving board. Pour cognac over and blaze.

Serve these elegant ducks with a fine risotto in which you have mixed buttered almonds, and an orange and onion salad. This calls for a good red wine: a great St. Emilion, a Château Cheval Blanc or a Château Ripeau. With excellent cheese and crisp bread this is a delicious dinner.

### VARIATION

Baste the ducks with equal parts of olive oil and orange juice and when done, blaze them with gin instead of cognac.

## Oven Roasted Duck (Rare)

Put a stalk of celery, an onion, a half orange and a few juniper berries in the cavity of each duck, and cover the breasts of the bird with thinly sliced salt pork. Roast in a 475 degree oven for 15 to 18 minutes, basting with the pan juices or with melted butter and red wine mixed. Four minutes before the ducks are done, remove the salt pork to brown the breasts and baste frequently at the last.

To serve, cut the ducks in halves or quarters with poultry shears. This olive sauce is a good accompaniment:

**Olive Sauce**

Sauté ½ cup of chopped shallots or green onions in butter until just soft. Add 1 cup of broth (make this with the duck giblets, wing tips and neck), 1 teaspoon of freshly ground black pepper, ½ teaspoon of tarragon and simmer for 4 minutes. Add 1 cup of tiny Spanish olives and let them heat through. Taste for seasoning.

## Oven Roasted Duck (Well Done)

If you like duck stuffed and roasted well done, here's the way to do it. For 4 ducks, make the following stuffing:

¼ lb. butter
1 cup chopped green onions, scallions or shallots
½ cup chopped parsley
Gizzards and hearts, ground
2 cups crumbs
1 teaspoon thyme
1 teaspoon freshly ground black pepper
1 teaspoon salt
4 tablespoons cognac

Melt the butter and sauté the chopped onion and parsley until they are just soft. Add the ground gizzards and hearts and crumbs and toss to mix thoroughly. Then add the seasoning and cognac. Stuff the ducks lightly and cover the vents with pieces of foil. Wrap the breasts with thinly sliced salt pork and roast in a 400 degree oven for 35 to 45 minutes or until the ducks are done to your taste. Baste from time to time with melted butter mixed with broth or vermouth.

## Pressed Duck or Duckling

Pressed duck has always been considered a luxury, probably because you need a duck press to prepare it, and this little gadget costs around $200. Actually, pressed duck is easy to make.

Place an onion, a stalk or so of celery, a sprig of thyme and a few juniper berries in the cavity of each duck. Cover the breasts with thinly sliced salt pork. Roast in a 425 degree oven for 18 to 20 minutes. Meanwhile, in a saucepan put 1 cup of red wine for each duck and boil it until it is reduced to ¼ of its original volume.

When the ducks are done, remove the breasts and cut them in thin slices. Place the sliced breast meat in a pan or chafing dish and pour the reduced wine over it. Keep it warm over a low flame. Remove the legs and thighs and broil them briefly under a medium flame to crisp the skin. Cut the duck carcasses in chunks and press these thoroughly in the duck press to extract the juices. To the juice add ¼ cup of red wine and 2 tablespoons of cognac for each duck and heat these together just to the boiling point. Add a large lump of butter and let it melt and blend in. Taste for seasoning, pour over the sliced breast meat. Reheat.

Serve the breast meat in the sauce with the crisped thighs and legs, tiny French peas and glazed onions. With this meal drink a fine Burgundy—a Clos Vougeot or a Musigny—and follow with cheese, celery, bread and more wine.

## Wild Duck with Cognac

2 wild ducks
½ cup cognac
1 cup dry white wine
1 teaspoon each: parsley, marjoram
4 tablespoons butter
1 teaspoon garlic powder
Salt and pepper

Marinate the ducks in the cognac, wine and herbs (except garlic powder) for 2-3 hours. Combine 2 tablespoons butter with ½ teaspoon garlic powder and put half in each duck, truss and secure on spit. Sprinkle ducks with salt and pepper and rub with balance of butter and garlic powder. Roast about 45 minutes, or until meat thermometer registers "done." Baste with balance of marinade during cooking. Serves 2.

## Wild Duck Chaucer

*2 wild ducks*
*¼ cup soy sauce*
*½ teaspoon one of the following: garlic powder, ground cardamom, ground cloves, cumin seed, marjoram or oregano*
*4 tablespoons butter*

Rub the ducks with soy sauce, inside and out, then combine the herb of your choice with the butter and put in cavity of each duck. Rub outside of ducks with a little more butter, tie securely on spit, and cook about 45 minutes, until meat thermometer registers "done" (reduce cooking time if you prefer duck rare). For extra flavor add about 2 ounces cognac, bourbon, or white wine to drippings and baste.
*Note:* If birds are lean, it is advisable to wrap breasts with bacon strips. Serves 2.

## Dove

The dove is common all over the country and is prized as a game bird. It is a delicious morsel with a delicate flavor. Allow at least one per person, and two for those with hearty appetites.

## Sautéed Dove

Clean the doves as you would any other fowl. Dust them with seasoned flour and brown them in butter or bacon fat, turning them often to cook evenly on all sides.

When the birds are browned, add 1½ teaspoons of tarragon leaves and turn the doves to coat them with the herb. Continue cooking, turning occasionally, until the birds are tender and done to your taste.

Remove them to a hot platter, rinse the pan with a little white wine and pour the juices over the doves.

Serve these with crisp French fried or shoestring potatoes and cole slaw. Instead of the usual red wine I prefer a good white wine with a delicate dish of dove.

## Roast Dove

Rub the doves well with butter and dust them with flour. Roast in a 375 degree oven for about 35 minutes, or until tender. During the roasting baste every 10 minutes with melted butter mixed with white wine and season to taste with salt and pepper.

Serve roast doves with tiny new potatoes dressed with parsley butter, asparagus and a pleasant white wine, such as Meursault or a Chassagne Montrachet.

## Grouse

Some people like their grouse hung until it is quite high. We agree the bird should be hung for some time, but we do not enjoy it when it is overripe.

The flesh of grouse is so delicately flavored it needs no fancy saucing. Simple buttered crumbs and a bit of bread sauce will do. We deplore particularly the use of currant jelly with this bird. A great St. Émilion or Médoc is the right accompaniment.

In our opinion, there are only two ways to cook grouse, broiling and roasting. Allow one bird per person.

## Broiled Grouse

Clean and split the birds and rub them well with seasoned butter or olive oil. Broil over charcoal or in a broiler at medium heat for 12 to 15 minutes, turning them once or twice during the cooking.

Serve broiled grouse with chopped sautéed giblets on toast, chip or shoestring potatoes and a big bowl of watercress.

## Roast Grouse

Clean and draw the birds and bard them well with thin slices of salt pork. Roast them in a 425 degree oven for 20 to 25 minutes, basting often with melted butter and white wine mixed. Serve with the chopped, sautéed giblets on toast, shoestring potatoes and green peas dressed with butter.

## Partridge

Partridge has been a popular game bird for centuries. The first partridges of the season in France mark the opening of a major food event and people feast on them just as they feast on the first asparagus or the first strawberries.

We feel that a whole bird will serve one person, though some are satisfied with a half.

## Broiled Partridge

Partridge broiled over charcoal is especially delicious. Clean and split the birds and flatten them out. Brush them well with butter or oil and broil for about 15 minutes, turning once during the cooking. Baste with butter and season to taste with salt and pepper.

Serve broiled partridge with chopped parsley, shoestring potatoes and sautéed corn. With it drink a good Burgundy.

## Roast Partridge

Clean the birds well and bard the breasts with thinly sliced salt pork. Roast them in a 400 degree oven for 25 to 28 minutes. (A large bird will take a slightly longer time.) The giblets may be chopped and sautéed and served on toast with the roast partridges. The traditional accompaniments are chip potatoes and watercress, green peas or turnips. We also enjoy braised celery or endive with roast partridge. Drink a good red wine with it—a Corton, a red Chassagne Montrachet or a fine Châteauneuf du Pape.

## Partridge with Cabbage

This is a good way to prepare older partridges that may be tough. For 4 people clean 4 birds thoroughly. Heat 4 tablespoons of butter in a large skillet and brown the partridges on all sides. Remove them to a deep casserole and add a ½ pound piece of salt pork, 3 carrots cut in rounds, 4 medium onions and salt and pepper to taste. Simmer over a low flame for a few minutes to blend the flavors.

While the birds are simmering, blanch 1 large or 2 small cabbages in boiling water for 20 minutes. Drain and chop the cabbage fairly fine and add it to the casserole, spreading it over the partridges. Add 1 cup of bouillon or game broth, cover the casserole and cook gently over a low flame for about 3 hours. One half hour before it is done, add a garlic sausage, Italian sausages or Spanish sausages.

183

To serve, cut the salt pork in slices and arrange these on the bottom of a large platter. Place the partridges on top and surround them with the cabbage. Garnish with slices of sausage.

## Partridges with Orange

For 4 people clean 4 partridges and bard them with salt pork. Roast them in a 425 degree oven for 25 to 30 minutes. Remove the salt pork and keep the birds hot on a platter or in a casserole.

Melt 2 tablespoons of butter in a skillet, add 1 tablespoon of chopped shallots or green onions and ½ teaspoon of tarragon and cook for 2 or 3 minutes, stirring occasionally. Add 1 cup of broth or stock and salt and pepper to taste and cook until the liquid is reduced to ⅓ of its volume. Add ¼ cup of Grand Marnier, ½ cup of orange juice and the grated rind of an orange. Let the sauce cook down and mellow for a few minutes; then add ½ cup orange sections.

Arrange the cooked partridges on toast and pour the sauce over them. Serve with a risotto, green beans and buttered almonds and a rosé wine.

## Partridge en Brochette

*4 partridge*
*Salt and pepper*
*4 strips salt pork*
*4 tablespoons butter*
*4 juniper berries, or ½ teaspoon chervil or*
  *rosemary.*

Salt and pepper birds and cover breasts with strips of salt pork. In each bird put 1 teaspoon butter combined with either juniper berries (1 per bird) or with herb of your choice. Secure birds on spit. Truss and roast. Use balance of butter for basting. Birds will be done in about 30 minutes,

but test to be sure (meat will be tender to a sharp fork). Serves 4.

## Cold Stuffed Partridge

For 4 people clean 4 partridges and stuff them with the following mixture: Sauté 1 pound of chicken livers and the partridge livers in 6 tablespoons of butter. Also sauté ¼ cup of chopped green onion. When the livers are brown but still rare, remove them from the pan and chop them coarsely. Add 1 teaspoon of salt, ½ teaspoon of freshly ground black pepper, 4 tablespoons of bread crumbs, the sautéed onions, ½ teaspoon of thyme, ¼ cup of chopped parsley and 3 tablespoons of cognac. Mix well and bind with 3 lightly beaten eggs.

Stuff the partridges and cover the vents with foil or sew them up. Bard the breasts of the birds and roast them in a 425 degree oven for 20 minutes. Remove the salt pork and reduce the oven temperature to 350 degrees. Continue roasting for another 20 minutes. Cool to room temperature.

Using a sharp knife or poultry shears, cut each bird in half. Arrange the halves, cut side up with the stuffing on top, on a platter. Serve with a Russian salad, sliced tomatoes, herbed French bread and a chilled Meursault. Hot chicken broth with a dash of sherry is an excellent first course.

## Pheasant

Pheasant is the most popular game bird with the general public. The demand is so great that numerous pheasant farms flourish near large eastern cities to supply the markets and restaurants.

Our favorite pheasant dish is the one served in our home when we were young. It is simple, but we have never had pheasant that tasted better no matter how elaborately prepared. We always called it Pioneer

Fashion, which it probably was. We sometimes make one change in the original recipe, substituting butter for bacon fat. We have never decided which we like better.

One pheasant will serve 2 to 4 persons, depending on the size of the bird and the size of the appetites.

## Pheasant Pioneer Style

Clean 2 pheasants and cut them in quarters or disjoint them as you would a chicken. Dredge the pieces in seasoned flour.

Sauté 6 slices of good smoked bacon—the limp, tasteless variety won't do—until it is crisp. Remove the bacon from the pan and keep it hot. Brown the pieces of pheasant in the bacon fat, turning them to cook on all sides. When they are all browned, reduce the flame, cover the pan and simmer for about 15 minutes or until the pheasant is tender. Remove the cover, increase the heat and crisp the skin of the birds. Remove them to a hot platter and garnish with the bacon strips. Pour off all but 3 tablespoons of the fat in the pan and add 3 tablespoons of flour. Blend well and cook for a few minutes. Gradually stir in 1½ cups of heavy cream and continue stirring and cooking until the sauce thickens. Taste for seasoning and serve with the sautéed pheasant.

With this serve mashed potatoes, braised celery and a Châteauneuf du Pape.

## Plain Roast Pheasant

A word of warning: roast pheasant tends to be dry. Bard the breasts well and baste the birds often during roasting.

When you have cleaned and barded the bird, add a piece of butter to the cavity and roast in a 350 degree oven for about 45 minutes, basting frequently.

Serve with chip or shoestring potatoes, buttered turnips mixed with sauteed mushrooms, and a fine Burgundy, such as a Chambertin, or an excellent claret.

*VARIATION*
Put tarragon butter instead of plain butter in the cavity and baste with tarragon butter mixed with white wine.

## Braised Pheasant with Sauerkraut

This is an excellent method for preparing an older bird. For 4 persons buy 2 to 3 pounds of sauerkraut. You will have a little left over but it is even better reheated the next day. Wash the kraut, put it in a large pan and add 1½ teaspoons of freshly ground black pepper, 2 finely chopped cloves of garlic and ½ pound of salt pork cut in thick slices. Cover with 2 cups of white wine and simmer for 3 hours.

Clean 2 pheasants and brown them in butter or bacon fat until they are colored on all sides. Add them to the pan with the sauerkraut, spreading some of the kraut over the top of the birds. Simmer for 1½ to 2 hours or until the pheasants are tender. One half hour before they are done, add a large garlic sausage or small Italian or Spanish sausages to the pan.

Cut the pheasants into serving pieces and arrange these on a platter with the sausage and salt pork. Surround the meat with the sauerkraut. Serve boiled potatoes and a white wine. We like an Alsatian wine or a Moselle.

## Pheasant Souvaroff

This is a classic dish and a truly elegant way to prepare pheasant. Here is the recipe from the famous Maxim's in Paris. For 4 persons cut 5 to 6 truffles into thin slices and sauté them in butter. Season to taste with salt and pepper. Add 4 ounces of cognac, 2 ounces of port and 1 teaspoon of meat glaze. Then add the livers of 2 pheasants and enough chicken livers to make ½ pound. Cook for 2 minutes. Stuff 2 pheasants with this mixture and cover the vents with foil or sew them up. Bard with salt pork.

Make a bed of slices of salt pork in a roasting pan and place the birds on top. Roast in a 350 degree oven for 30 to 40 minutes, basting frequently. Remove the barding pork and put the pheasants in an ovenproof casserole with a tight cover.

Pour off the fat from the roasting pan and rinse pan with cognac or port. To pan juices add ¼ cup of double chicken or veal broth (reduce 1 cup of broth to ¼ cup volume) and boil the mixture for 2 minutes. Pour this over the pheasant in the casserole, cover tightly and seal the cover with a flour and water paste. Return it to the oven for 15 more minutes.

Carry the covered casserole to the table. The wonderful odor when the cover comes off must not be missed.

## Italian Braised Pheasant

For 2 pheasants, prepare the following stuffing: Sauté the pheasant livers and ½ pound of chicken livers in ¼ cup of olive oil. Add 2 finely chopped cloves of garlic, a leaf or two of thyme, 1 cup of dry bread crumbs and salt and pepper to taste. Blend in 3 tablespoons of butter and bind with 2 lightly beaten eggs. Stuff the birds and truss them firmly.

Brown the stuffed pheasants in olive oil, turning them to cook evenly. When they are browned, add 2 carrots cut in rounds and 1 medium onion, sliced. Place the pan in a 375 degree oven for 30 minutes and then reduce the heat to 350 degrees and continue cooking for another 30 minutes. Baste every 5 minutes with a mixture of 1 cup of white wine, ½ cup of rich broth and 3 tablespoons of tomato purée.

Serve the pheasants with the pan sauces poured over them and accompany them with a fine risotto mixed with mushrooms, and broccoli dressed with lemon butter. For drink, try a Barbera from Italy.

## Pheasant Pompadour

The fastidious Madame Pompadour may or may not have favored this recipe, but for generations it has carried her name.

For 4 people clean and prepare 2 pheasants for roasting. Put about 2 tablespoons of butter in the cavity of each bird and bard their breasts well. Place them in a roasting pan and add 1 sliced onion, 2 carrots cut in rounds and ½ teaspoon of thyme. Roast in a 425 degree oven for 20 minutes, basting after 10 minutes with melted butter. Reduce the heat to 350 degrees and continue cooking for another 20 minutes basting twice with a mixture of melted butter and claret. Add ¼ cup of capers and 1½ cups of small green olives and cook another 10 minutes.

Serve these roast pheasants on fried toast with the sauce poured over them. Garnish with plenty of chopped parsley. With this dish serve cornmeal soufflé and a purée of spinach with mushrooms.

## Pheasant with Triple-Sec

*2 pheasants*
*2 ounces brandy*
*2 3-ounce cans mushroom crowns*

*3 cups croutons*
*½ teaspoon each: chervil, marjoram*
*Salt and pepper*
*½ cup orange juice (frozen concentrate)*
*6 strips bacon*
*½ cup red wine*
*2 ounces Triple-Sec*

Rub birds well with brandy. Combine mushrooms, croutons and seasonings, moisten with orange juice and balance of brandy. Stuff birds, truss, tie bacon strips onto breasts of birds. Secure on spit and roast about 1 hour, basting with wine, until tines of fork can easily penetrate meat. Warm Triple-Sec, ignite and pour flaming over birds. Serves 4.

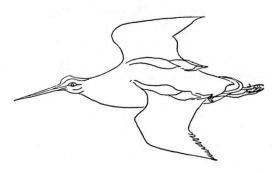

## Snipe

Snipe are rarely served in this country, though we have eaten them often on the West Coast. This is one of the game birds usually cooked with the intestines left inside. As with quail, after the birds are cooked, the entrails are removed, chopped, mixed with butter and cognac and spread on toast.

## Broiled Snipe

Clean the snipe but do not draw or split them. Butter them well and broil at a little higher than medium heat—around 400 degrees—for 12 to 15 minutes. Turn the birds often to cook them evenly, and season them to taste. Serve on fried toast, with or without chopped intestines. Buttered crumbs, crisp potato chips and braised celery are excellent accompaniments.

## Spitted Snipe

Clean the birds and spit them, running them through crosswise and alternating them head to tail. If necessary tie them together to make them secure. Roast them over coals for 12 to 15 minutes, basting them once or twice with butter. Season to taste with salt and pepper.

Remove the snipe to a hot platter, pour 3 ounces of cognac over them and blaze. Remove the intestines, chop them and mix them with the juices and cognac from the platter. Spread this on toast. We like shoestring or chip potatoes with this and thin slices of zucchini, dusted with flour and deep fat fried.

## Roast Snipe

Clean and draw the snipe and place a few leaves of tarragon and a cube of butter in the cavity of each one. Bard the breasts with salt pork strips. Roast in a 425 degree oven 12 to 15 minutes, basting frequently.

## Wild Goose

Wild goose, another rare game bird, is often disappointing. It can be very tough and hardly worth the effort. If you do bag one, treat it as you would wild duck. Or cook it according to the directions for Pheasant Pioneer Style.

## Goose au Madeira

Clean and draw the goose and stuff it with peeled apple halves lightly dusted with sugar, nutmeg and dipped in melted butter, prunes that have soaked in Madeira for 2 days and whole boiled (canned) chestnuts.

Roast the goose in a 350 degree oven,

basting frequently with Madeira, until the internal temperature reaches 160 degrees, or until the legs can be easily moved back and forth. The skin should be crisp and the meat not quite as rare as duck.

Serve goose with sauerkraut seasoned with juniper berries and black pepper and simmered for 4 hours in white wine.

## Wild Turkey

The wild turkey is America's traditional game bird. It was so highly prized during Colonial times, that Benjamin Franklin suggested it be used as our national symbol. Fortunately, this unique bird, once very scarce, is now on the increase.

If you manage to bag a wild turkey, do *not* treat it as you do the farmyard variety, roasted in the oven and dressed up with the usual stuffing, gravy and cranberry sauce. It should be cooked on a spit.

## Spitted Wild Turkey

Clean and draw the turkey and rub it well with butter inside and out. Season with salt and pepper and place a sprig or two of celery, some parsley, a touch of thyme and a lump of butter in the cavity. Spit it and roast it, basting often during the cooking with melted butter. It is done when the legs can be moved back and forth easily.

Serve this simple delicacy with potatoes mashed and beaten to a froth with butter and cream, dried corn (if you can find

it) cooked and liberally buttered, or corn on the cob, and paper thin slices of tomato. Drink in honor of the occasion a New York State or California wine, red or white.

## Quail

The term "quail" means different things in different regions of the country. In some areas, quail and partridge are the same thing. In others, quail is the tiny bob-white. The number of birds per serving will depend on the type of quail you are preparing. Incidentally, this miniature bird is one form of game that we prefer to eat cold.

Some people cook quail with the entrails left in the birds. After cooking, they are removed, chopped and spread on toast. The quail are placed on top. We happen to like this dish; you may not.

Although red wine is traditional with game birds, we suggest you try one of the white Burgundies with these delicate morsels. Try a great Meursault or Montrachet or a white Musigny.

## Broiled Quail

These tiny birds broil in a very short time. Clean them, split them, and if you are adept with a knife, remove the pointed part of the breastbones. If you can not manage this, flatten the birds with a cleaver as much as you can. Butter them well and broil them for 8 to 10 minutes, beginning bone side down and then turning them to cook skin side down. Season to taste and brush often during the cooking with butter. Be sure the skin is crisp and brown. Sauté the giblets in butter and oil, chop them and serve them on toast under the quail.

Serve at least 2 of these to a person and with them serve fried grits, green peas and if sticking to tradition, a light red wine like Julienas or a Fleurie from the Beaujolais district of Burgundy.

## Roast Quail

Clean the birds and draw them or not, as you choose. Bard the breasts well with salt pork and roast in a 425-450 degree oven for 18 to 25 minutes, basting frequently. Remove the salt pork a few minutes before the birds are done, to brown the breasts. Serve on toast with the chopped entrails, or on squares of crisp fried scrapple; or serve roast quail on fried toast covered with slivers of Virginia ham—a delicious combination of flavors.

*VARIATIONS*

1. Draw the quail and stuff them with oysters and a lump of butter. Roast as above and serve on toast with fried parsley.

2. Before barding the quail, rub the breasts with tarragon butter and put a few leaves of tarragon in each cavity.

3. Chop ½ pound of mushrooms very fine. Sauté them slowly for 1 hour in ¼ pound of butter with 1 finely chopped clove of garlic. Sprinkle with 1 teaspoon of flour and salt and pepper to taste. Place a spoonful of this mixture in the cavity of each bird and roast. Serve with creamed mushrooms and turnips and shoestring potatoes.

## Caille d'Octobre par Alain

A colorful little restaurant in Paris, Le Relais de Porquerolles, serves a most elegant dish of quail. Here is the recipe:

Clean and draw 6 quail and reserve the heads, wing tips and feet. Stuff each bird with 1 large truffle and 2 tablespoons of foie gras. Place them in a bowl and grind some pepper over each. Pour over 1 cup armagnac or cognac and let stand 1 hour.

Cook the heads, feet and wing tips with a bouquet garni in 1½ cups of chicken broth for 1 hour. Strain, season with salt and pepper and add a little of the armagnac or cognac. Return to the stove and reduce over a brisk flame until the broth is ⅓ of its original volume.

Sprinkle a little rosemary on each quail, place a slice of salt pork over each breast and wrap the birds in grape leaves. Truss them firmly. Heat 6 tablespoons of butter in a casserole and place the birds in it. Roast in a 450 degree oven 15 minutes.

Prepare 6 pieces of fried toast and seed ½ pound of muscat grapes. Place the toast in the bottom of a large oven-proof serving dish and place one quail on each piece of toast. Add the grapes, cover tightly and keep hot. Pour the pan juices from the casserole in which the quail were roasted into a skillet and rinse the casserole with ½ cup of muscatel. Add this to the skillet and reduce it quickly over a hot flame. Add the reduced broth and blend thoroughly and heat through. Taste for seasoning, add 1 teaspoon of lemon juice, pour over the quail and serve at once.

## Quail with Chestnuts
### (Caille aux Marrons)

*4 quail*
*1 stick butter*
*¼ cup brandy*
*1 teaspoon tomato paste*
*1 teaspoon meat glaze*
*1 teaspoon potato flour*
*1¼ cups chicken stock*
*1 tablespoon black raspberry jelly*
*8 artichoke bottoms, cooked*
*Salt, black pepper*
*2 cups unsweetened chestnut purée*
*6 rounds of bread*

189

Tie up the quail and brown them slowly all over in melted butter. Flame with brandy. Cover the pan and braise in a 375° oven for 20 minutes. Remove, set quail aside and stir into the pan the tomato paste, meat glaze and potato flour. Pour on the stock, add the jelly and stir over the fire until mixture comes to a boil. If too thick, add a little more stock. Strain over the quail and keep warm.

Heat artichoke bottoms in a little butter with salt and pepper and set aside. Melt 1 or 2 tablespoons butter in a pan, add the chestnut purée, salt and pepper and beat over the fire until hot. Fry the rounds of bread in a little butter until golden brown on each side.

To serve, arrange the bread rounds on a long serving dish. Fill artichoke bottoms with chestnut purée, forcing it through large round tube on a pastry bag. Put a quail on top of each alternate artichoke. Pour sauce on and serve. Serves 4.

## Quail with Cognac

*4 quail*
*½ cup cognac*
*½ cup dry red wine*
*1 pound fresh mushrooms, sliced*
*½ teaspoon powdered thyme*
*Salt and pepper*

Marinate quail in cognac and red wine for 2-3 hours; remove and stuff with mushrooms sprinkled with thyme, salt and pepper. Secure birds on spit, truss, and roast for about 30 minutes, or until meat is tender when tested with a fork. Serves 4.

# BARBECUE and ROTISSERIE

# Barbecue
# and Rotisserie

**P**robably the first genuinely good meal the Pilgrims had in this country was a fresh-killed turkey, spitted and roasted— barbecued, that is—over an open fire. The word barbecue, which is an offshoot of the Spanish *barbacoa* (a wood frame used as a drying rack or cooking grill), came into currency among the earliest settlers of the Southern and Western states. A Frenchman visiting Mississippi in the eighteenth century recorded the curious American equivalent of a *fête champêtre* when a whole pig, roasted over charcoal, was the main dish. Wily Southern politicians enticed waverers to their meetings with free-for-all barbecues and considered it to be the duty of a good voter "to holler right, vote straight and eat as much barbecue as any man in the county." Today, following the custom of their forebears, millions of Americans are cooking in this same simple fashion, for outdoor cookery has rapidly developed from a sometime sport indulged in by campers, fishermen and Boy Scouts into a nation-wide family pastime. Indeed, an ironic chronicler might view the history of indigenous American cookery as a progress from outdoor cookin' to outdoor grilling.

Spit roasting, ancient and honorable ancestor of modern rotisserie cooking, has never been bettered as a means of bringing out the full flavor and succulence of meat and fowl. Ever since primitive man discovered how to apply fire to food, the crusty brown roast, done to a turn, has been a symbol of hearty eating. Saxon drawings in the Cotton library preserved in the British Museum show serving men presenting roasts of meat, still on their spits, to guests at a banquet. Each guest took a huge knife and hacked off what he fancied.

During the next eight or nine hundred years spits were powered by every means human ingenuity could devise: boys, dogs, clockwork, twisted string and the draught from the chimney. The original cook boy or turn-spit gave way in Elizabethan times to a turn-spit dog, a small, patient, bandy-legged animal which galloped in a wheel to keep the spit turning. This reliance on boy—or dog—power persisted into the 18th century. An advertisement in Benjamin Franklin's *Pennsylvania Gazette* offered for sale "several dogs and wheels, much preferable to any jacks for roasting any joints of meat." The clockwork-operated spit was an invention eagerly adopted by the novelty-seeking noblemen of Charles II's day. Many of these clockwork devices were artfully designed not only to turn the spit but to time the roast; others were geared to music but the chef needed a musical education to count the bars that timed the meat or fowl. Today, thanks to automatic spits built into the new ranges, to portable rotisseries and electric spits for outdoor barbecues, toil and trouble have been banished from spit-roasting and the tempting smell of fresh-roasted meat once more rouses the American appetite.

Modern grills have made outdoor cooking as easy as indoor cooking. The choice in equipment is very wide: everything from small portable bucket grills to the huge indoor or outdoor grill with an electric spit and large enough to take a whole baby lamb or an enormous roast.

If you are buying outdoor equipment for the first time, or replacing old equipment, select a grill with a movable firebox that will enable you to control the heat source.

One obvious but very important suggestion: Always keep your grill spotless and clean the equipment after every use. Old odors and flavors from last week's steak do not enhance this week's broiled chicken.

## Beef: General Rules

Beef is sold in several grades. The purple U. S. Government stamp on the outside layer of fat states whether it is PRIME, CHOICE, GOOD or UTILITY. Prime is the finest; it is distinguished by a good covering of fat. Choice is almost as fine. If well aged, these two grades may be dark red and even moldy on the outside but, when cut into, brilliant on the inside. The fat is creamy in color and flaky.

When you buy beef for roasting on a spit or grilling over coals, it is wise to select a cut from the top two grades. There is one exception: a filet from Good or even Utility grade may be tender and well flavored and, of course, will be far less expensive.

Here are the various beef cuts most commonly used in outdoor cooking. When you buy a roast or steak, allow 12 to 16 ounces of meat per person.

**Porterhouse and T-Bone:** These two steaks are very similar. Both come from the short loin and both have a section of filet. They are choice cuts for broiling and should be 2 to 3 inches thick.

**Club Steak:** This is next to the porterhouse and T-bone. It should be 2 to 2½ inches thick.

**Rib Steak or Entrecote:** This cut from the first few ribs is a favorite with many. It should be 1½ to 3 inches thick. In some places a boneless rib steak is called a Spencer.

**Strip or Shell Steak:** This is also called New York cut and, in some parts of the country, sirloin. It comes from the short loin with the filet removed. It may be boneless. A very thick strip or shell steak will serve a number of people. Slice it on the diagonal.

**Sirloin Steak:** There are several types of sirloin: pin bone, wedge bone and whole sirloin. They sometimes cost less per pound than other cuts, but often have a large amount of bone. They should be 2 to 3 inches thick. If you are entertaining a large number, have a whole sirloin cut even thicker and serve it sliced on the diagonal.

**Top Sirloin:** This comes from the end of the loin and is a boneless cut.

**Filet or Tenderloin:** This is sometimes cooked whole over charcoal and then sliced into serving pieces; or it is cut into individual portions and then grilled. Either way it is highly prized by most people. Individual cuts of filet are:

1. Chateaubriand: a thick diagonal cut.

2. Tournedos: thick slices tied with larding fat around them.

3. Filet mignon: cut from the smaller ends of the filet. They are sometimes almost triangular in shape.

**Rump Steak:** A boneless rump steak is a great favorite in Europe and England. It can be delicious and tender.

**Flank Steak:** This is a little used cut since most people think it will be tough. If it is broiled quickly over a hot fire, just until crusty brown on the outside but still very rare inside and then sliced on the diagonal into thin strips, it is excellent. Many restaurants serve this with a sauce as London Broil.

**General Suggestions
for Broiling Beef:**

The secret of all good broiling is a steady, even fire. Be sure you have an even bed of coals before you start. Spread them out over an area at least as large as the piece of beef you are going to cook. Sear the steak quickly on both sides close to the coals. Then move it farther away from the heat to finish cooking more slowly. If you have an adjustable firebox, you can raise or lower it as needed. If you like a charred, burnt exterior on meat, just before serving bring the steak so close to the coals that it actually catches fire. Let it burn for a scant minute.

Many people argue that steak should not be salted until after it is cooked. We have never found that it made any difference. Experiment for yourself and make your own decision. Pepper or various herbs may be applied before grilling.

**Cooking timetable:**

*1-inch steak:*

Very rare — 8 minutes
Rare — 9 minutes
Medium — 12 minutes
Well done — 15-18 minutes

*1½-inch steak:*

Very rare — 8-10 minutes
Rare — 10-12 minutes
Medium — 13-15 minutes
Well done — 15-20 minutes

*2-inch steak:*

Very rare — 14-18 minutes

Rare — 18-25 minutes
Medium — 25-32 minutes
Well done — 30-45 minutes

*2½-inch steak:*

Very rare — 20-27 minutes
Rare — 25-35 minutes
Medium — 35-40 minutes
Well done — 45-60 or more minutes

The steak 3 or more inches thick should be cooked with a meat thermometer inserted in the thickest part. Use the following temperature table:

Very rare — 120°-130°
Rare — 125°-135°
Medium — 145°-155°
Well done — 160°-170°

The only way to be absolutely sure whether a steak is cooked the way you want it is to use the age-old knife test. With a sharp knife cut a small incision in the flesh next to the bone and see how red it is.

## Churrasco

This South American version of beef steak is wonderfully good eating. For 6 persons, buy a large sirloin of 7 pounds or more: about 3 inches thick. Or you can use two steaks with a combined weight of 7 or more pounds. Broil the steak according to previous instructions and during the cooking baste once or twice with butter seasoned to taste with dried rosemary. Cook the meat just to the rare state and char it at the last minute.

Meanwhile prepare the following sauce: Sauté 2 cups of finely chopped green onions in ½ pound of butter until just soft. Add a dash or two of dried rosemary, 1½ teaspoons of salt, 1 tablespoon of freshly ground black pepper, 1 cup of white wine and ½ cup of wine vinegar. Bring this to a boil, lower the heat and simmer for 5 minutes. Taste for seasoning and add another large lump of butter.

When the steak is ready, cut it in rather thin diagonal slices and put these in the sauce for a minute. Serve each person some of the sauce with the meat. Good accompaniments for this steak dish are home fried potatoes, sautéed or roasted onions, and French bread with butter. For a drink, beer is the best choice, since the vinegar in the sauce will kill a good wine.

*VARIATION*

Substitute any other steak cut; or slice rare rib roast of beef and serve it in the same manner.

## Beefsteak Jerome LePlat

In spite of the French name, this dish was originally Italian. The secret is in the sauce.

Prepare your favorite Sauce Hollandaise, and when it is thickened add the juice of 1 lemon, 2 tablespoons of tomato purée, 1 teaspoon of freshly ground black pepper, and a touch of Worcestershire Sauce. Just before serving add ¼ cup of finely chopped parsley. (These amounts are for 1 cup of Hollandaise.)

Broil steak in your favorite manner, slice it diagonally and bathe the slices in the sauce.

## Beefsteak Pizzaioula

This is another Italian version of steak, popular with those who like the flavor of tomatoes.

Grill 2-inch sirloin steak, or entrecote for 4 persons according to instructions. Meanwhile prepare the following sauce: Sauté 4 chopped cloves of garlic in ¼ cup of olive oil. Add 1 large tin of Italian tomatoes (those canned with basil) and cook this down to half the original amount. Season to taste with salt, fresh black pepper and 1 teaspoon of oregano.

When the steak is done to your satisfaction, remove it to a hot platter, pour the sauce over it and top with chopped Italian parsley and sautéed mushrooms. With this serve a tossed salad, dressed with olive oil, wine vinegar and a touch of garlic, and crusty bread. To drink: an earthy Italian red wine, such as Barbera.

## Sliced Larded Filet on French Bread

For hearty appetites allow 1 pound of filet for each guest. Be sure to get whole, not sliced, filet. Ask the butcher to lard the filets for you, or if you have a larding needle you can do it yourself. For each filet, soak 3 thin strips of salt pork in cognac for 2 hours. Run them through the edges of the beef with the larding needle.

Roll the filets in coarsely crushed black pepper and broil over coals for about 25 minutes, to 120° on thermometer, turning often. Season to taste with salt. Or you can spit the filets and roast them over charcoal for the same length of time. If you use a meat thermometer, remove the filets when it registers 120°. This is for very rare, but filets are best at this stage.

To serve: cream ½ pound of butter and blend it with 1½ to 2 teaspoons of rosemary. Heat French bread and split the loaf. Spread each half liberally with the rosemary butter. Cut the filet in paper thin slices and arrange these on the hot buttered French bread. Let guests eat these as sandwiches, or with knife and fork.

## Chateaubriand Marchand de Vin

This is a special party dish, elegant and costly. Select large Chateaubriands of about 1 pound each per serving. Buy marrow bones and have the butcher cut them so the marrow can be extracted in one piece.

Broil the Chateaubriands. During the cooking, brush them frequently with melted butter and turn them often. Meanwhile, extract the marrow and slice it in thin rounds. Poach these for about 1 minute in boiling salted water.

Prepare the following sauce: Sauté ⅔ cup of finely chopped green onions in ¼ pound of butter until just colored. Add 1 cup of red wine (preferably a good Bordeaux) and cook this down to one half its volume. Add 1 can of brown gravy, a dash of cognac, a large pat of butter and the juice of a lemon. Sprinkle the sauce heavily with chopped parsley.

When the meat is done to your satisfaction, remove it to hot plates, pour the sauce over each portion and top with slices of poached marrow. With this serve lyonnaise potatoes, watercress, crisp French bread, fruit and cheese. Try a fine bottle of Bordeaux with this.

*VARIATION*

Use the Maxim's frozen Sauce Marchand de Vin instead of making your own. Simply follow the instructions on the package, adding 2 tablespoons of red wine.

## Saté with Steak

*2 pounds sirloin steak*
*½ cup peanut oil*
*¾ cup soy sauce*
*2 ground onions*
*1½ cloves garlic, ground*
*2 tablespoons sesame seeds*
*¾ tablespoon cumin seeds*
*1 teaspoon lemon juice*
*1 teaspoon black pepper*
*½ teaspoon salt*

Have the steak cut into thin pieces about 4″ long and 1½″ wide. Make a marinade of the oil and soy, ground onions and garlic, and the sesame seeds which have been roasted in a skillet. Marinate the beef for 1 to 2 hours. Remove and thread on skewers. Brush with pounded cumin mixed with lemon juice. Broil over a hot fire, or under broiler and cook until done, turning the skewers. Add salt and pepper before serving. Serves 4.

## Kebabs

Traditionally, kebabs are made of lamb or mutton, but beef, veal and even pork tenderloin are delicious cooked in this manner. Here are several versions, adaptable to any kind of meat.

1. String cubes of meat on skewers, brush well with olive oil and broil, turning often. If you crowd the cubes together, you will have rare, juicy meat. If the cubes are placed farther apart, you will have medium well done meat. (Remember, pork must be well done.) Salt and pepper the kebabs to taste as they cook.

Serve these plain kebabs with rice mixed with pistachio nuts and a plate of crisp French fried onion rings.

2. Marinate meat cubes in a mixture of olive oil, lemon juice and a pinch of dried thyme. Let the meat soak for 2 hours or more. Alternate the cubes on skewers with tiny tomatoes, tiny whole onions that have been parboiled for a few minutes and strips

of green pepper. Broil as above, brushing with the marinade during the cooking.

3. Soak the meat in a marinade of olive oil, lemon juice, oregano and plenty of coarse black pepper. Proceed as above.

4. Alternate lamb cubes with pieces of sweetbread and marinate in olive oil, lemon juice and several crushed bay leaves. Proceed as above.

5. Alternate cubes of lamb or beef with squares of eggplant. Marinate in olive oil, lemon juice, grated garlic and black pepper. Broil as above.

## Roast Leg of Lamb

You may have the leg of lamb boned or not, as you choose. Make several gashes in the outside flesh and insert slivers of garlic. Rub the meat well with salt and pepper and then arrange it on a spit. Be sure you balance it evenly. It is wise to use a meat thermometer with a roast; simply stick the sharp end of the thermometer in the fleshiest part of the leg. Roast over medium heat until the thermometer registers 150°. Then remove the roast and let it stand 20 minutes before carving. The meat will continue to cook during that time. This gives you a rare leg of lamb, and in my opinion a tastier, more tender dish than lamb cooked to the well done stage. If you must have well done lamb roast to 165°-170°.

Serve this roast with a fresh green vegetable, some hot French bread and a delicate rosé wine.

## Shoulder of Lamb

This is delicious and tender, but the shoulder must be boned and rolled. Insert garlic in the flesh and rub the roast with salt, pepper and dried tarragon. Roast in the same way as the leg. Serve with plenty of melted butter seasoned with tarragon, and

a white bean salad. To make this salad, boil white dried beans until tender. Drain and dress with salt, pepper, olive oil, wine vinegar and grated onion to taste.

## Lamb Steaks

Buy steaks from the leg or the shoulder cut about 1½ inches thick. Rub each steak with a cut clove of garlic and brush with melted butter or oil. Grill over coals, turning to brown evenly, until the steaks are nicely browned on the outside but still pink and rare in the middle. Season to taste with salt and pepper as they cook.

## Oriental Lamb Steaks

Marinate lamb steaks in soy sauce seasoned with chopped garlic and grated ginger. Let the meat stand in this mixture for 5 or 6 hours and turn it often. Grill as for lamb steaks, brushing with the marinade during cooking. Omit salt and pepper.

Serve with fried rice and broiled pineapple fingers.

## Ham Steak

Buy center slices of ham about **1 to 1½** inches thick. Gash the fat on the edges and cook slowly. Grill for about 15 minutes before turning, then turn and grill for another 10 minutes or so. During the last few minutes of cooking brush with honey mixed with dry mustard and turn to glaze both sides with this mixture.

Serve with broiled peach halves and fried potatoes.

## Plain Hamburgers

Buy lean ground beef with no more than 25 to 30 per cent fat and allow at least ½ pound per person. If you are serving hamburgers on buns, make two patties of ¼ pound each for each person. The less you handle the raw meat, the juicier the cooked hamburger will be, so form the patties gently, with a light touch. **Brush with melted butter or oil. Sear them well on both sides and then continue grilling, turning often, until they are as well done as you like them. We like them crusty brown on the outside, but still juicy and rare in the middle. Season with salt and pepper as you turn.**

Serve on hot toasted buns, or hot toasted French bread with a choice of good relishes and pickles. Don't forget the mustard (a sharp English type or one of the excellent French imports) and freshly grated horseradish for those who prefer something hot instead of the customary pickle condiments.

## Savory Hamburgers

To each pound of ground beef add 1 medium onion chopped very fine, ½ cup of chopped ripe olives and 1 tablespoon of Spice Islands mushroom powder. Grill as above, seasoning to taste with salt and pepper as the meat cooks. Serve these hamburgers with crisp fried potatoes and a salad of sliced tomatoes dressed with olive oil and wine vinegar and garnished with black olives and strips of anchovies.

## Frankfurters

Many people think all frankfurters are the same. Nothing could be more wrong. Too often the frankfurter in the market display case is a dreary hunk of pressed meat. There is not much you can do to give it flavor. Hunt out German shops, Greek or Kosher delicatessens for the well-seasoned franks and big knockwurst.

1. Cut a gash in the side of each frankfurter. Spread prepared mustard inside; add a strip of cheese and push the frankfurter back in shape. Wrap a strip of bacon around it. Fasten with a toothpick. Grill until cheese melts and bacon is crisp.

2. Cut gashes in the frankfurters and spread the inside with garlic· butter to which you have added chopped chives and parsley. Wrap with bacon strips and grill.

3. Mash blue cheese with a little grated onion and blend in chopped chives and parsley. Gash the frankfurters and stuff them with this mixture. Wrap with bacon strips and grill.

4. Cut frankfurters in 1-inch pieces. Alternate these on skewers with tiny whole tomatoes and strips of green pepper. Grill. Serve with a good hot Mexican chili.

## Grilled Italian Sausages

Sweet and hot Italian sausages are delicious grilled over charcoal. Poach them in water or white wine for 5-8 min. before grilling, to cook out excess fat. They then grill quickly and to a delicious brownness. Have both sweet and hot sausages. Serve with crisp Italian bread and if you wish a great bowl of green noodles with butter and grated cheese.

## Spitted Roast Chicken

Put a good square of butter and a little salt and pepper in the cavity of each chicken. Truss well and brush them with melted butter or oil seasoned to taste with salt, pepper and paprika. Spit them carefully. Run the spit through the backbone just above the tail and guide it to the top part of the breast at the base of the neck. In this way you achieve a good balance.

When your fire has burned down to a good bed of coals, make a ring of the briquets or charcoal leaving the center area directly under the chickens clear to catch the drippings. Arrange the spitted chickens over this space and roast, basting them frequently with equal parts of melted butter and white wine or dry vermouth. The cooking time will take from 45 minutes to 1¼ hours, depending on the size of the birds. Test according to instructions above to see whether they are done.

Plain roast chicken goes best with crisp sautéed potatoes and a fresh green salad with a minimum of dressing. As for wine, most people prefer a white, such as a Pinot Blanc from California, or a Meursault or Pouilly Fuissé from France.

## Chicken Tarragon

Put 2 sprigs of fresh tarragon and a sprig of parsley into the cavity of the bird along with butter, salt and pepper. Truss the bird and then slip a few tarragon leaves under the skin of the breast, working down from the neck and being careful not to puncture the skin as you separate it from the flesh. Brush the bird with seasoned melted butter in which you have steeped a few tarragon leaves. Roast according to directions above, basting with more tarragon butter during the cooking.

Serve with tarragon butter and potatoes that have been wrapped in foil and roasted in the coals. A bowl of fresh raw vegetables is an excellent accompaniment.

## Garlicked Chicken

Mash 2 cloves of garlic and blend with ¼ pound of butter. Let this stand for ½ hour. Meanwhile, chop 2 more cloves of garlic very fine and sprinkle them inside the cavity of a chicken. Add a large sprig of parsley, a cube of butter and close the vent with foil. Truss the chicken well.

Melt the garlic butter, add the juice of 1 lemon and salt and pepper to taste. Roast the chicken on a spit, basting it frequently with the melted butter mixture.

Serve this highly flavored fowl with noodles dressed with butter and cheese, celery sticks and toasted herbed bread. Split a loaf of French bread and spread it with butter to which you have added parsley, chives and rosemary. Toast until heated through and crisp. Choose a robust Chianti to drink with this garlicky chicken.

## Ginger Chicken

Take a piece of fresh ginger about the size of a finger and chop it fine or grate it on a coarse grater. Combine it with 1 finely chopped clove of garlic and a sprig or two of fresh coriander or Chinese parsley (also known as cilantro). Put this mixture in the cavity of a chicken and add a dash or two of soy sauce. Close the vent with foil, truss the bird and brush it with a mixture of soy sauce, peanut oil and ground ginger. Spit it and roast, basting during the cooking with more soy, oil and ginger.

Serve this chicken with a good chutney, hot mustard and additional soy sauce. Rice, of course, is the perfect accompaniment. Dress the rice with plenty of butter, chopped toasted almonds, salt and freshly ground black pepper. To drink with this there is nothing better than iced or hot tea.

Finish the dinner with vanilla ice cream topped with chopped preserved ginger. This is an amazing combination of flavors and sensations: tangy, hot, sweet and mellow.

## Baby Chickens on the Spit

These little delicacies are called *poussin*, squab chicken or baby pullets. Plan at least one to a person, and those with hearty appetites could consume as many as three. Spit them, brush them with plenty of seasoned butter and roast them quickly, being careful not to overcook them. Brush frequently during the cooking with melted butter.

Serve these tender bits with tiny new potatoes dressed liberally with butter and chopped parsley, a pleasant summer salad and an Alsatian wine, chilled. French bread, cheese and fresh fruit are a fitting final course. (These tiny chickens are too delicate to be accompanied by foods of strong flavor.)

## Saté Ajam-Chicken on the Spit (Indonesia)

*2-pound chicken boned*
*¾ teaspoon vinegar*
*¾ cup water*
*½ teaspoon powered cumin*

*½ teaspoon minced garlic*
*¼ teaspoon salt*

Cut the boned chicken into 1½" pieces. Thread on 6" skewers. Mix the vinegar, water, cumin, garlic and salt. Dip the chicken in this. Cook over an open fire for about 15 to 20 minutes. Serve hot with the following sauce:

Cook until smooth and thickened 5 tablespoons peanut butter, ½ cup bouillon, 1 teaspoon sugar, ½ teaspoon minced garlic, 1 teaspoon soy sauce, ½ cup milk, ½ teaspoon paprika, 1 bay leaf. Serves 3-4.

## Grilled Chicken Hearts

Buy 2 to 3 pounds of chicken hearts and marinate them in the following mixture: to equal parts of soy sauce and sherry wine add 2 crushed cloves of garlic, 1 teaspoon of freshly ground black pepper and 1 teaspoon of ground ginger. Let the hearts soak for an hour or two before cooking. Arrange 3 to 4 chicken hearts on each small skewer and grill them until nicely brown on all sides. Bamboo chopsticks can be whittled down to make excellent skewers. Soak them in water for an hour before using or they will burn and char. This will serve 25 as an appetizer course.

## Epicurean Broiled Turkey

Turkeys weighing 4 to 7 pounds will be excellent broiled. They must be split and cooked over low heat—far from the coals—for the first 40 minutes. Then they may be moved closer to the heat to finish cooking and browning.

Arrange the turkey halves bone side down on the grill and cook slowly for 25 minutes. Season to taste and turn skin side down. Continue cooking for 15 to 20 minutes, or until almost done. To finish cooking, bring meat close to the coals to brown. Baste during the cooking with melted but-

201

ter and white wine or with seasoned oil.

Serve this broiled turkey with the following sauce:

### Epicurean Sauce

Chop ½ pound of mushrooms very fine and cook them slowly with ¼ pound of butter until they are black and thoroughly mellow. This will take about 2 hours. The mushrooms should be very concentrated with a strong mushroomy odor. Add more butter if necessary during the cooking.

When the mushrooms are thoroughly done add 6 more tablespoons of butter and 3 tablespoons of flour. Blend this well and continue cooking the mixture for ½ hour more. Season to taste with salt and pepper and keep warm.

Sauté 1 pound of chicken livers in 4 tablespoons of butter until they are lightly browned but not too well done. Shake the pan so the livers brown on all sides. When they are done, mash them thoroughly or put them through a food mill. Combine the mashed livers with the mushroom mixture. Rinse out the pan in which the livers were cooked with ¼ cup of cognac and add this to the mixture. Taste for seasoning and add a pinch of nutmeg and a little chopped parsley. Keep this sauce warm and serve it with the turkey.

Good accompaniments for this broiled turkey with Epicurean Sauce are heated potato chips, a bowl of watercress and well buttered toasted protein bread. Add a bottle of red wine, not too heavy. A fine dessert might be a bowl of giant fresh cherries and some fine small cakes. Finish with strong black coffee and cognac.

## Broiled Turkey Flambé

This dish has an exceptionally delicious sauce and makes fine party fare. Have a turkey broiler split. Cook the turkey giblets in 1½ cups of water to which you have added an onion stuck with 2 cloves and salt and pepper to taste. When the giblets are tender, remove them and chop them very fine. Let the broth cook down for 10 or 15 more minutes.

Broil the turkey halves according to the instructions for Epicurean Broiled Turkey, basting them well with melted butter and white wine. When the turkey is done, remove it to a hot flameproof platter or a board. Heat ⅓ cup of cognac slightly, pour it over the turkey and ignite. When the flame dies down, pour off the juices into a cup. Keep the turkey warm. Sauté the chopped giblets briefly in 4 tablespoons of butter. (Do this in a pan on the grill, in an electric skillet, or in a chafing dish.) To the giblets add the reserved juices and a little of the giblet broth. Taste for seasoning, blend well and heat thoroughly. Stir in 1½ cups of sour cream, blend and heat, but do not allow this mixture to boil or it will curdle. Add another dash of cognac and serve with the turkey.

With this delectable dish, serve potatoes wrapped in foil and baked in the coals, cucumber salad and fine chilled white wine. A perfect dessert is a platter of cheese and fresh peaches and pears.

## Broiled Duckling

Have duckling split in halves for broiling. Be sure to spread the coals in a circle leaving the center under the duckling clear. Duckling is fat and the drippings blaze up quickly; if the fat drips on the coals, you will have a roaring fire instead of hot ashes. A dripping pan in the center helps.

Arrange the duckling on the grill, bone side down, and cook for about 20 minutes. Turn, and continue turning occasionally until the duck is done and the skin brown and crisp. Baste the skin side during cooking with any of the following glazes:

1. The traditional Chinese glaze of honey mixed with soy sauce. You can add any seasonings to this you like.

2. Equal parts of honey and lemon juice, orange juice, pineapple juice or white wine. Season to taste with salt.

3. Equal parts of honey and any citrus fruit juice seasoned with soy sauce, sherry wine, crushed garlic and ginger.

4. Apricot puree or orange marmalade, cut with a little lemon juice and seasoned to taste.

## Broiled Whole Fish

Small fish, such as a small trout, can be grilled whole without splitting. A larger, thick fish should be split. Rub the inside with lemon, sprinkle with salt and pepper and arrange on a well greased grill (or use a greased hinged grill). Cook on both sides to brown evenly and baste with melted butter and lemon juice or white wine. Fish cooks quickly. A small whole fish will only take 15 to 20 minutes. Larger ones take a half hour or more. Test with a fork or toothpick. The fish is cooked when the flesh flakes easily.

Serve with more melted butter and lemon juice or white wine, or with parsley butter. Fried potatoes and a crisp green salad or cucumber salad are excellent with fish dishes. Serve a fine dry white wine, chilled of course.

## Fish Mixed Grill

For each person serve one filet of sole or haddock (or frozen filet), one rock lobster tail (cut the soft part of the shell away with scissors to expose the meat), one skewer with 3-4 shrimp alternated with scallops and, if you like, one King crab leg.

Start with plenty of melted butter. Use a large grill for the filets, lobster tails and crab legs. The skewers of shrimp and scallops can broil right on the regular grill. Dip the filets in melted butter and then in sesame seeds. Brush the lobster tails and the crab legs well with butter. Clean the shrimp as for Broiled Shrimp Appetizer and alternate them on skewers with the scallops. Brush these well with butter.

The filets and lobster tails will take about 7-8 minutes, so start them first. Allow 5-6 minutes for the skewered shrimp and scallops and about 5 minutes for the crab legs. These only need to heat through. Brush everything liberally with butter during the cooking process, and sprinkle additional sesame seeds on the filets. Season to taste with salt and pepper and serve on hot plates, with small bowls of melted butter, lemon wedges and Dill Sauce.

### Dill Sauce

Mix ⅔ cup of mayonnaise with ⅔ cup of sour cream. Add 2 tablespoons of finely chopped green onion, 2 tablespoons of finely chopped parsley, 1 tablespoon of finely chopped fresh dill (or 1 teaspoon of dried dill weed), and salt and pepper to taste.

## Spit roasting

Whether you are roasting beef, lamb or pork it is important that the meat be centered and balanced on the spit. If the meat is not balanced, the spit will not turn properly. Keep trying different locations of the spit until you get it balanced, and don't worry about losing meat juices. The holes will seal themselves as soon as the meat begins to sear. Be sure to press the spit forks securely into the ends of the roast and tighten their locking screws.

When the meat is done, lift the spit from the rotisserie, using mitts. Place meat on a cutting board and remove all twine and any skewers. Then loosen both of the lever locking screws of the meat forks, raise spit so pointed end is on board and with a carving fork press against meat fork so both forks slide off the spit. Then withdraw forks from meat.

All the recipes here can be used on an outdoor barbecue if it has an electric spit. If you want to save juices for basting, form a small pan out of foil and put it under the meat on the charcoal cooker, and the drippings will be caught in the pan. Buy a good basting brush, or a small paint brush, and baste with it frequently during rotisserie cookery. The food will have a much better flavor.

## Trussing

Turkey, chicken, in fact all fowl, should be trussed. Use "butchers" twine, for it will not burn or char. Use stainless steel skewers to pin loose parts together.

Cut off the neck and the wing tips (which you can use with the giblets and liver for gravy), and tie the wings securely against the breast by placing a loop, or several loops, around the bird. Tie the drumsticks together, then tie them again to the spit. This will prevent the legs from straightening as they roast. Lastly, run additional cord over and around the bird and tie to the spit. Be sure you tie the string tightly, for there will be a slight shrinkage during cooking and the string will tend to loosen.

## Timing

All times given in the following recipes are approximate. This is because of the variance in the different types of rotisseries with different types of heating elements. The only sure guide is a meat thermometer. Buy a good one and use it on all meats, fish and fowl. (Skewer cookery does not require a thermometer, because it is a simple matter to pierce small cubes of meat to gauge whether they are done.)

After the meat has been placed on the spit and in the rotisserie, insert the thermometer. Make certain that the thermometer does not touch the spit or any bone in the meat or it will not register accurately. If you are cooking fowl, a good test is to pull the leg gently. If the joint moves easily at the thigh, the meat is cooked.

It is also important to remember that once the meat starts to cook it naturally retains heat and will continue to cook even with the heat off. This interim period is called "coasting." If you want a rare roast, the heat should be turned off before the liquid in the thermometer reaches "rare" on the gauge. Let the meat continue to rotate and the liquid will gradually reach the "rare" mark on the thermometer.

## Seasoning

Many of the recipes in this cook book give you a variety of herbs and spices to choose from. All have an affinity for the particular dish, but try only one at a time. Next time, use another for a different flavor. The amounts given are for dry herbs. If fresh herbs are used, multiply the given amount by four.

## Rotisserie Veal With Kidneys

*2 veal kidneys, sliced*
*4-pound veal shoulder, boned*
*4 strips salt pork, or 4 strips bacon*
*Salt and pepper*
*1 teaspoon of basil, coriander seed, cumin*
*seed or two crushed juniper berries*
*½ cup white wine*

Place kidneys inside veal and roll up. Tie salt pork or bacon strips to roast. Secure roast on spit, season with salt, pepper and herb of your choice. Roast about 1½ hours, or until meat thermometer registers "done;" baste frequently with wine. Serves 6.

## Roast Leg of Lamb Hong Kong

*6-pound leg of lamb, boned*
*2 tablespoons lemon juice*
*½ cup red wine*
*½ cup seedless raisins*
*¼ teaspoon mace*
*2 tablespoons soy sauce*

Marinate lamb in lemon juice and red wine for at least 2 hours. Sprinkle inside of meat with raisins and mace, roll and tie. Secure on spit and rub with soy sauce. Roast about 2 hours, or until meat thermometer registers "done;" baste with marinade. Serves 6.

## Shish Kebab

*2 pounds leg of lamb, cut into 2" chunks*
*½ cup olive oil*
*¼ cup white wine*
*1 tablespoon lemon juice*
*1 clove garlic, crushed*
*Salt and pepper*
*½ teaspoon any of the following: curry*
*powder, caraway seed, basil, mace, soy*
*sauce, thyme, cinnamon or oregano*
*5 strips bacon*
*1 pound large fresh mushrooms*
*Green peppers, sectioned*
*Onion wedges*

Marinate the meat in the oil, wine, lemon juice, garlic, salt and pepper and seasoning of your choice from 3-4 hours, or overnight. When ready to roast, wrap lamb chunks in bacon strips. Spit, alternating with mushroom crowns, pepper and onion. Roast, basting with marinade. Serves 4.

205

## Pork Loin with Sherry

6-pound loin of pork
4 tablespoons dried apricots, diced
1 cup croutons
1 cup sherry
Salt and pepper

Soak apricots and croutons in sherry, drain. Season loin with salt and pepper. Make a pocket in loin and stuff with apricot-crouton mixture and skewer. Secure loin on spit and tie so stuffing will not fall out. Roast about 3 hours, basting with reserved sherry, or until meat thermometer registers "done." Serves 6.

## Pork Shoulder Robert

3-4 pound canned pork shoulder (picnic)
1 tablespoon Dijon mustard
½ cup dark brown sugar
½ cup sweet vermouth

Rub pork shoulder well with mustard, then secure on spit. Roast for about 1 hour, basting with mixed sugar and vermouth. (Canned picnics, already cooked, require less time than regular hams.) Serves 4.

*VARIATION*

Substitute pineapple juice for the sweet vermouth.

## Loin of Pork California Style

6-pound loin of pork
½ cup olive oil
½ cup water
1 cup catsup
¾ cup wine vinegar
2 tablespoons Worcestershire sauce
1 cup onion, minced
3 tablespoons brown sugar
1 teaspoon oregano
2 teaspoons paprika
½ teaspoon garlic powder

½ teaspoon ground cloves
1 teaspoon pepper
1 teaspoon dry mustard
½ bay leaf

Have the butcher separate backbone from ribs. Mix ingredients (except pork) together in a saucepan, bring to a boil, lower heat and simmer for 45 minutes. Secure meat on spit and tie with string. Roast meat about 3 hours, basting frequently with hot barbecue sauce, or until meat thermometer registers "done." Serves 6.

## Pork Tenderloin Orleans

4-5 pound smoked pork tenderloin
1 teaspoon caraway seed
2 ounces kümmel

Press caraway seed into roast, then center and secure on spit. Roast for about 2 hours, or until meat thermometer registers "done." Warm the kümmel just before serving, ignite and pour over roast and serve flambé. Serves 4-5.

## Spareribs Island Style

3 pounds spareribs
½ cup soy sauce
1 small can crushed pineapple
¼ cup brown sugar
2 tablespoons molasses
½ teaspoon caraway seed

Marinate spareribs in soy sauce for 2 to 3 hours, then weave on spit. Combine other ingredients and baste meat frequently while roasting. Roast about 1½ hours. Serves 2.

## Spareribs German Style

3 pounds spareribs
1 can sauerkraut
1 teaspoon caraway seeds
Salt and pepper

Marinate spareribs in other ingredients for 2 to 3 hours. Thread ribs on spit and roast for 1 hour. Then gradually begin to baste with marinade, allowing pieces of sauerkraut to cling to meat. Roast another ½ hour. Serves 2.

Sprinkle pig inside and outside with salt, pepper and herb of your choice. Secure pig on spit, tie well, and roast about 3 hours, basting with wine, until meat thermometer registers "done." When ready to serve, insert apple in pig's mouth, and cherries for eyes.

*To carve,*
First, cut off the hams, then slice down the backbone and carve off chops from the loin and ribs. Serve both to each person with some of the crisp skin. Serves 8.

## Roast Chicken Pierre

*1 chicken, about 5 pounds*
*Salt and pepper*
*1 teaspoon meat tenderizer*
*1 cup sherry*
*1 teaspoon of one of these: tarragon, oregano, ginger, rosemary or thyme*
*4 tablespoons melted butter*

Sprinkle bird with salt and pepper and meat tenderizer, and marinate in sherry and herb of your choice for 2-4 hours. Secure on spit, rub with butter, and roast, basting with marinade, for about 2 hours, or until meat thermometer registers "done." Serves 4.

## Suckling Pig on a Spit

*10-pound suckling pig*
*Salt and pepper*
*1 tablespoon of one of the following: allspice, basil, caraway seed, horse-radish, marjoram or oregano*
*1 cup white wine*

## Chicken Far East

*2 broilers, about 2 pounds each*
*Salt and pepper*
*½ cup chopped cashew nuts*
*4 tablespoons peanut butter*
*½ cup white wine*

Salt and pepper broilers, and fill cavities with cashew nuts. Lightly spread peanut butter on each bird, secure on spit and cook 1 hour and 15 minutes, or until leg moves easily at thigh joint. Baste with drippings and white wine. Serves 4.

## Long Island Duckling Gourmet

*1 Long Island duckling, 4-6 pounds*
*2 tablespoons soy sauce*
*4 tablespoons butter*
*½ teaspoon ginger, fenugreek, or curry powder*
*½ cup orange juice (frozen concentrate)*
*2 ounces Triple-Sec or brandy*

Rub duckling with soy sauce and 3 tablespoons butter. Tie bird on spit and roast for about 1½ hours, or until meat thermometer registers "done." Combine remaining tablespoon butter with preferred seasoning, and baste bird frequently with this mixture, warmed in drip pan and combined with orange juice. When ready to serve, warm Triple-Sec or brandy, ignite and pour over duckling. Serves 4.

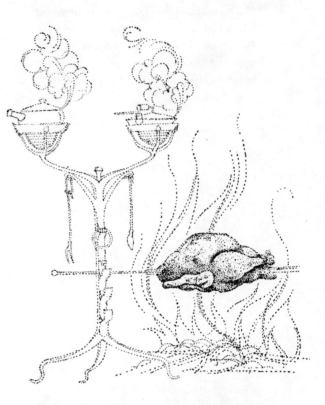

## Goose Montmartre

*1 junior goose, about 6-8 pounds*
*Salt and pepper*
*3 crushed juniper berries, or 2 ounces gin, or 1 teaspoon marjoram, rosemary, sage or thyme*
*1 cup white wine*

Rub cavity with salt, pepper and half of chosen herb or gin, using the other half to rub the outside. Secure on spit, tie, and roast about 2 hours, or until meat thermometer registers "done." Pour off drippings from drip pan regularly, and baste with white wine. Serves 4.

# SAUCE

# Sauce

Sauces are the *sine qua non* of gourmet cooking and their meticulous preparation is the mark of a good cook. Famous Ritz chef Louis Diat stated that in the best restaurants the *saucier* (sauce chef) is surpassed in importance only by the *chef des cuisines*, acknowledged autocrat of the kitchen. The *Dictionary of Jovial Gastronomy* stipulates that the *saucier* must be "adroit and sensitive to the most delicate nuance, as sauce making includes chemistry, harmony, flavor, voluptuousness, vigilance and other virtues, all crossed by the lightning stroke of genius." Sauces have had a long and illustrious history. Many of the "cunning sauces" of Imperial Rome might be considered outlandish today, and the early English sauces (the word was introduced by the Norman conquerors) were no more than spicy relishes to make food more palatable, yet they were in many instances a merciful disguise. The classic sauces we use today are in great part due to the fine palates and epicurean tastes of French noblemen (history credits Cardinal de Richelieu with the discovery of Mayonnaise, the Marquis de Nointel, Lord Steward of the Household of Louis XIV, with Béchamel Sauce), and they have inspired a legion of variations. Larousse in his epic dictionary of gastronomy counts 200 sauces, Ali Bab, the French housewife's Fanny Farmer, 287. Yet all these sauces derive from but a few foundation sauces, called by the French *Grandes Sauces* or *Sauces Mères*, which are soon mastered. First is the basic Brown Sauce (in the refined version Sauce Espagnole or Demi Glace). Second, the white sauces, Béchamel, Velouté and Allemande (so named to distinguish its blondness from the swarthy Espagnole). Hollandaise is the chief butter sauce and Mayonnaise, the classic cold sauce. A good sauce requires good ingredients: fresh butter, milk, cream, vegetables and wine that is worthy to be served at the table. Brown stock is the traditional basis for brown sauces but canned beef broth is often substituted today (allow, however, for its extra saltiness). For brown sauces, a brown *roux* (the amalgamation of fat and flour) is required. This should be cooked over low heat to prevent burning. For white sauces, the *roux* is white, cooked only until it is golden in color. When liquid is added, the sauce should be thin, to allow for the long cooking and reduction which blend flavors and make the sauce smooth. Butter sauces, which are thickened by egg yolks instead of the fat and flour mixture, take a little more care as they must be cooked over water beneath the boiling point to prevent the curdling of the yolks. Sauces such as these are the springboard to thousands of superb dishes and inspired menus.

## Brown Stock

3 pounds beef and veal bones
1 pound short ribs
1 cup sliced onions
½ cup sliced carrots
5 quarts water
2 teaspoons salt
4 peppercorns
Bouquet garni

Spread the bones, meat, onions and carrots in a shallow pan. Roast in a 375° oven until very brown. Transfer to a deep kettle and add the water, salt, peppercorns and bouquet garni.* Bring to a boil; cover and cook over low heat 4 hours. Strain, cool and remove all the fat. Pour into jars, cover tightly and refrigerate or freeze. Keeps a week in the refrigerator, 6 months in freezer. Makes about 3 quarts. As a substitute, use canned beef consommé.

*For bouquet garni, tie a sprig of parsley, thyme, bay leaf and celery top in a small cheesecloth bag.

## Glace de Viande
### (Meat Glaze)

Glace de Viande is unsurpassed for enriching brown sauces or any meat gravy. Many fine food shops have it available or you can make your own. Start with 3 cups Brown Stock; be sure all the fat is removed. Cook over low heat until very thick and syrupy and reduced to about 1 cup. Stir frequently. Pour into a clean jar, cover tightly and keep in the refrigerator. Use a tablespoon or two in stews, pot roast or other brown sauces.

## Brown Sauce

Serve with beef dishes or as base for sauces.

½ cup beef fat
3 onions, diced
1 carrot, sliced
⅓ cup flour
2 quarts Brown Stock
Bouquet garni
3 tablespoons canned tomato sauce

Melt the fat in a heavy saucepan; cook the onions and carrot until brown. Sprinkle the flour over the vegetables and cook, stirring constantly until dark brown. Gradually add the stock, stirring constantly. Add the bouquet garni. Cook over low heat 2 hours. Stir in the tomato sauce and cook 1 hour longer. Strain and correct seasoning. Makes 5 cups.

## Simplified Brown Sauce

¼ cup minced shallots or onions
2 tablespoons butter
1 tablespoon flour
2 cups canned beef consommé
⅛ teaspoon pepper
⅛ teaspoon thyme
1 bay leaf
2 teaspoons tomato paste

Cook the shallots or onions in the butter for 5 minutes; stir in the flour and cook over low heat, stirring constantly until browned. Gradually add the consommé, stirring until it reaches the boiling point. Add the pepper, thyme, bay leaf and tomato paste. Cook over low heat 20 minutes. Strain. Makes 1½ cups. Serve with beef dishes or use as a base for other sauces.

## Sauce Espagnole
### (Demi-Glace)

Serve with beef, ham or game

¾ cup chopped mushrooms
2 tablespoons butter
¼ cup dry sherry
2 cups Brown Sauce
1 tablespoon Glace de Viande

Cook the mushrooms in the butter for 3 minutes. Stir in the sherry and cook until reduced to half. Stir in the Brown Sauce and Glace de Viande; cook over low heat 15 minutes. Makes about 2 cups.

## Sauce Chasseur

Serve with chicken or veal

*½ pound mushrooms, sliced*
*2 tablespoons olive oil*
*4 tablespoons minced shallots or onions*
*½ cup dry white wine*
*1½ cups Brown Sauce*
*2 tablespoons tomato paste*
*¼ teaspoon freshly ground black pepper*
*1 tablespoon butter*
*1 tablespoon minced parsley*

Sauté the mushrooms in the oil 5 minutes. Add the shallots and sauté 2 minutes long-er. Add the wine and cook over low heat until reduced to half. Stir in the Brown Sauce, tomato paste and pepper. Cook 5 minutes. Blend in the butter and parsley. Makes about 1½ cups. You may serve the sauce separately or cook sautéed chicken or veal in it.

## Bordelaise Sauce

Serve with steak or roast beef

*Large marrow bone*
*2 tablespoons minced shallots or onions*
*¼ cup dry red wine*
*1 cup Brown Sauce*
*1 tablespoon cognac*
*1 teaspoon minced parsley*

Have the butcher crack the bone; carefully remove the marrow. (You need about 3 tablespoons.) Dice it and place in lukewarm water for 5 minutes, then drain.

Cook the shallots and wine for 5 minutes. Stir in the Brown Sauce and cognac; cook over low heat 10 minutes. Add the marrow and parsley just before serving. Heat. Correct seasoning. Makes about 1¼ cups.

## Sauce Romaine

Serve with game, tongue or ham

*½ cup seedless raisins*
*¼ cup sugar*
*⅓ cup tarragon vinegar*
*2 cups Brown Sauce*

Soak the raisins in boiling water for 10 minutes. Drain. Cook the sugar and vinegar until it caramelizes. Add the Brown Sauce and raisins; cook over low heat 10 minutes. Makes about 2¼ cups.

## Sauce Lyonnaise

Serve with game or beef

*¼ cup minced onions*
*2 tablespoons butter*
*1 cup dry white wine*
*1½ cups Brown Sauce*

Cook the onions in the butter until reduced to half. Add wine, Brown Sauce; cook over low heat 5 minutes. Makes 2 cups.

## Sauce Bigarade

Serve with duck or game birds

*3 tablespoons grated orange rind*
*3 tablespoons minced shallots or onion*
*½ cup dry red wine*
*1½ cups Brown Sauce*
*½ cup orange juice*
*1 tablespoon red currant jelly*
*2 tablespoons cognac*

Pour boiling water over the rind and let soak 5 minutes. Drain. Cook the shallots in the wine until reduced to half; stir in the Brown Sauce, orange juice, jelly and cognac. Cook over low heat 10 minutes, stirring frequently. Add the orange rind. Makes about 2 cups.

## Sauce Poivrade

Serve with game

*¼ cup minced onions*
*¼ cup grated carrots*
*3 tablespoons minced parsley*
*2 tablespoons olive oil*
*½ cup dry red wine*
*¼ cup cider vinegar*
*2 cups Brown Sauce*
*Dash ground cloves*
*¼ teaspoon freshly ground pepper*

Sauté the onions, carrots and parsley in the oil for 5 minutes. Add the wine and vinegar, cooking until reduced to half. Add the Brown Sauce; cook over low heat 30 minutes. Strain the sauce and return to a clean saucepan; stir in the cloves and the pepper. Cook over low heat for 5 minutes. Makes about 2¼ cups.

### VARIATION

#### Sauce Venaison

Add 3 tablespoons red currant jelly, 3 tablespoons heavy cream and 1 teaspoon lemon juice to Sauce Poivrade. Cook 10 minutes. Serve with venison.

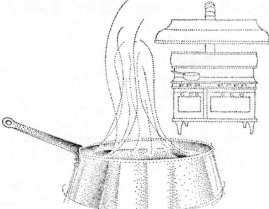

## Sauce Fines Herbes

Serve with eggs or fish

*2 teaspoons mixed dried herbs (tarragon, chervil, chives, thyme)*
*½ cup dry sherry*
*1½ cups Brown Sauce*
*⅛ teaspoon lemon juice*
*2 teaspoons butter*
*1 tablespoon minced parsley*

Cook the herbs and wine until reduced to half; strain. Add the strained wine to the Brown Sauce with the lemon juice. Cook over low heat 5 minutes. Add the butter and parsley, stirring until butter dissolves. Makes about 1¾ cups.

## Sauce Robert

Serve with pork or ham

*2 tablespoons minced onion*
*2 tablespoons butter*
*¼ cup wine vinegar*
*1 cup Brown Sauce*
*¼ cup chopped gherkins*
*1 teaspoon prepared mustard*
*2 teaspoons minced parsley*

Cook the onion in the butter for 5 minutes; add the vinegar and cook until reduced to half. Add the Brown Sauce and cook over low heat 15 minutes. Stir in the gherkins, mustard and parsley just before serving. Makes about 1⅓ cups.

## Sauce Portugaise

Serve with beef or poultry

*1 tablespoon minced shallots or onions*
*2 tablespoons butter*
*½ cup dry red wine*
*½ cup peeled and diced tomatoes*
*1 cup Brown Sauce*
*1 tablespoon tomato paste*

Cook the shallots in the butter for 5 minutes. Add the wine and cook until reduced to half. Add the tomatoes, Brown Sauce and tomato paste. Cook over low heat 15 minutes. Taste for seasoning. Makes about 1½ cups.

## Sauce Madère

Serve with filet mignon, escalope of veal or other beef dishes

*¾ cup Madeira or Amontillado sherry*
*2 teaspoons Glace de Viande (or 2 teaspoons beef extract)*
*1 cup Brown Sauce*
*1 tablespoon cognac*
*1 tablespoon butter*

Cook the wine until reduced to half; stir in the Glace de Viande and Brown Sauce. Cook over low heat 5 minutes. Add the cognac, and then the butter, stirring only until dissolved. Makes about 1½ cups.

*VARIATION*

### Perigueux Sauce

Add 3 tablespoons chopped truffles to the Sauce Madère. Serve with pheasant, guinea hen, partridge or beef.

## Sauce Rouennaise

Serve with wild or domestic duck

*3 duck livers or 6 chicken livers*
*2 tablespoons minced onion*
*1 tablespoon butter*
*¼ cup red wine*
*1½ cups Brown Sauce*
*1 tablespoon cognac*

Wash the livers carefully, removing any discolored areas. Chop the livers and then force through a fine sieve. Refrigerate until needed.

Cook the onion in the butter for 5 minutes. Add the wine and cook until reduced to half. Stir in the Brown Sauce and cognac; cook over low heat 10 minutes. Just before serving, mix ¼ cup of the hot sauce with the liver. Return to the saucepan; heat but do not let boil. (This is an extremely rich sauce.) Makes about 2¾ cups.

## Sauce Diable

Serve with broiled chicken or red meat

2 tablespoons minced shallots or onions
1 tablespoon butter
¼ cup cognac
1 cup Brown Sauce
1 teaspoon Worcestershire sauce
Dash cayenne pepper

Cook the shallots in the butter for 5 minutes. Add the cognac and cook until reduced to half. Stir in the Brown Sauce, Worcestershire and cayenne pepper; cook over low heat 5 minutes. Strain. Makes about 1 cup.

## White Stock

1½ pounds veal bones
3 quarts water
2 teaspoons salt
2 whole onions
2 carrots
Bouquet garni

Cover the bones with water; bring to a boil and cook 10 minutes. Drain, carefully removing the scum.

Put the bones, 3 quarts water, salt, onions, carrots and bouquet garni into a deep saucepan. Bring to a boil, cover loosely, and cook over low heat 3½ hours. Strain, cool and remove fat. Pour into jars, cover tightly and refrigerate or freeze until needed. Keeps 5 days in refrigerator, 6 months in freezer. Makes about 1½ quarts. For an adequate substitute, use canned chicken broth.

## Fish Stock

1 carrot, sliced
2 onions, sliced
1 bay leaf
6 cups water
Heads and bones of 2 fish (salmon, white-fish, pike, perch, etc.)
1½ teaspoons salt
3 tablespoons white wine

Combine all the ingredients in a saucepan. Bring to a boil and cook over low heat 1 hour. Strain. Makes about 4 cups.

## Béchamel Sauce

Serve with any creamed dish and use as a base for other white sauces.

3 cups milk (or 1½ cups milk and 1½ cups White or Fish Stock).
2 tablespoons minced onion
1 bay leaf
4 tablespoons butter
⅓ cup flour
½ teaspoon salt
Dash white pepper

Bring the milk, onion and bay leaf to a full boil. Let stand 10 minutes and strain.

Over low heat melt the butter in a saucepan; stir in the flour, cooking over low heat until flour turns golden. Gradually add the milk, or milk and stock (use Fish Stock when sauce is for fish dishes; White Stock for white meat, poultry, etc.), stirring constantly until the boiling point. Stir in the salt and pepper. Cook over low heat 20 minutes, stirring frequently. If not completely smooth, strain. Makes about 2 cups.

## Sauce Soubise

Serve with sweetbreads, veal or fish.

1 cup minced onions
2 tablespoons butter

*2 cups Béchamel Sauce*
*1 cup heavy cream*

Pour boiling water over the onions and let stand 5 minutes; drain. Cook the onions in the butter over low heat until soft, but do not let brown. Add Béchamel Sauce; cook 15 minutes. Slowly stir in cream; strain. Correct seasoning. Makes about 2¾ cups.

## Sauce Aurore

Serve with fish, eggs, vegetables and meat.

*3 tomatoes, peeled and diced*
*2 cups Béchamel Sauce*
*3 tablespoons heavy cream*

Cook the tomatoes in 2 tablespoons water over low heat until very soft. Force through a sieve (or substitute 2 tablespoons tomato paste). Combine with Béchamel Sauce; cook over low heat 5 minutes. Stir in cream. Makes 2½ cups.

## Sauce Nantua

Serve with fish or sea food.

*1 cup Béchamel Sauce*
*¼ cup heavy cream*
*¼ cup shrimp or lobster, ground fine*
*¼ cup chopped shrimp or lobster*

Cook the Béchamel Sauce and cream over low heat for 5 minutes, but do not let boil. Stir in the ground and chopped sea food. Taste for seasoning, heat, but do not let boil. Makes about 1½ cups.

## Sauce Smitane

Serve with chicken croquettes, game birds or veal.

*2 tablespoons minced shallots or onions*
*½ cup dry sherry*
*2 tablespoons beef extract*
*2 cups Béchamel Sauce*
*¾ cup heavy cream*
*¼ teaspoon lemon juice*

Cook the shallots and sherry until reduced to half. Stir in the beef extract, Béchamel Sauce and cream. Bring to a boil; cook 1 minute stirring constantly. Stir in lemon juice; taste for seasoning. Makes 3 cups.

## Sauce Mornay

Serve with pastas, eggs, vegetables, gratins and fish.

*2 cups Béchamel Sauce*
*3 tablespoons grated Parmesan cheese*
*3 tablespoons grated Gruyère or Swiss cheese*
*2 tablespoons heavy cream*

Heat the sauce and stir the cheese into it until melted. (If it looks too thick, add a little milk.) Stir in the cream and taste for seasoning. Makes about 2¼ cups.

For a richer sauce, beat 2 egg yolks in a bowl. Gradually add the Sauce Mornay, stirring constantly. Return to the saucepan and cook over low heat until the boiling point, but do not let boil.

## Velouté Sauce

Use as a base for other sauces and serve with chicken.

*4 tablespoons butter*
*4 tablespoons flour*
*2½ cups White Stock*

Over low heat melt the butter in a saucepan; stir in the flour until it turns golden. Gradually add the stock, stirring constantly to the boiling point. Cook over low heat 20 minutes, stirring occasionally. Makes about 2 cups. For Fish Velouté, substitute Fish Stock for White Stock.

## Sauce Chivry

Serve with chicken, eggs or fish.

*1 cup chopped spinach*
*2 tablespoons chopped fresh tarragon (or ¼ teaspoon dried)*
*2 tablespoons chopped fresh chervil (or ¼ teaspoon dried)*
*3 tablespoons chopped chives or scallion*
*2 cups Velouté Sauce*

Cook the spinach, tarragon, chervil and chives in a little water for 5 minutes. Drain and force through sieve. Combine with the Velouté Sauce and cook 2 minutes. Makes about 2 cups.

## Sauce Suprême

Serve with veal, chicken or egg dishes.

*1 cup chopped mushrooms*
*2 cups White Stock*
*1 cup Velouté Sauce*
*1 cup heavy cream*

Cook the mushrooms and stock for 20 minutes or until reduced to one half the original quantity. Stir in the Velouté Sauce and cook over low heat 10 minutes. Very gradually stir in the cream. Cook 5 minutes. Taste for seasoning and strain. Makes 2¼ cups.

## Sauce Porto Vino

Serve with duck or game birds.

*1 cup port*
*½ cup orange juice*
*⅛ teaspoon thyme*
*2 teaspoons potato flour or cornstarch*
*1 cup White Stock*
*2 teaspoons grated orange rind*

Cook the port, orange juice and thyme until reduced to half. Mix the potato flour and stock until smooth. Stir into the wine. Cook over low heat, stirring constantly to the boiling point. Add rind; cook 5 minutes. Taste for seasoning. Makes about 1½ cups.

## Mustard Sauce

Serve with fish.

*2 tablespoons flour*
*¼ teaspoon salt*
*½ teaspoon powdered mustard*
*1 teaspoon sugar*
*Dash turmeric*
*½ cup Fish Stock*
*2 tablespoons tarragon vinegar*
*2 egg yolks*

Mix the flour, salt, mustard, sugar and turmeric in the top of a double boiler. Mix the Fish Stock and vinegar together, stir into the flour mixture. Place over hot water and cook, stirring until it begins to thicken.

Beat the egg yolks in a bowl; gradually add the hot mixture, stirring constantly to prevent curdling. Return the sauce to the top of the double boiler and cook, stirring constantly until thickened. Makes about 1¼ cups.

## Newburg Sauce

Serve with shellfish and fish.

*2 tablespoons minced shallots or onions*
*2 tablespoons butter*

*½ cup sherry (Amontillado)*
*1 cup heavy cream*
*1 cup Fish Velouté Sauce*
*2 egg yolks*

Cook the shallots, butter and ¼ cup sherry for 10 minutes. Stir in cream, Velouté Sauce. Cook over low heat 5 minutes.

Beat the egg yolks and remaining sherry together; gradually add the hot sauce, stirring constantly to prevent curdling. Return to saucepan and cook over low heat; continue stirring until it reaches the boiling point, but do not let it boil. Taste for seasoning. Makes about 2 cups. Add 2 cups lobster meat for Lobster Newburg.

## Horse-radish Sauce

Serve with boiled beef or chicken.

*1 tablespoon potato flour or cornstarch*
*1½ cups milk*
*½ cup freshly grated horse-radish*
*2 tablespoons butter*
*1 teaspoon salt*
*⅛ teaspoon white pepper*
*1 teaspoon lemon juice*

Mix the potato flour and milk until smooth. Cook over low heat, stirring constantly until it reaches the boiling point. Stir in the horse-radish; cook over low heat 10 minutes. Add the butter, salt, pepper and lemon juice, stirring until butter melts. Makes about 1¼ cups.

## Allemande Sauce

Serve with boiled chicken or veal.

*2 egg yolks*
*⅓ cup heavy cream*
*2 cups Sauce Suprême*

Beat the egg yolks and cream in a saucepan. Gradually stir in the Sauce Suprême. Cook over low heat, stirring constantly until thickened, but do not let boil. Makes about 3 cups.

*VARIATIONS*

### Sauce Albert

To 3 cups Allemande Sauce add 4 tablespoons sautéed shallots or onions, 1 tablespoon freshly grated horse-radish and 2 tablespoons minced parsley.

### Sauce Fines Herbes

To 3 cups Allemande Sauce add 4 tablespoons minced fresh herbs (tarragon, chervil, parsley, etc.) or 2 teaspoons dried herbs soaked in water for 10 minutes, then drained. Serve with eggs, fish or poultry.

## Sauce Vin Blanc

Serve with poached or broiled fish.

*1 cup dry white wine*
*3 tablespoons minced shallots or onions*
*3 peppercorns*
*½ bay leaf*
*⅛ teaspoon mace*
*3 tablespoons butter*
*1 tablespoon flour*
*¾ cup fish stock*

*½ cup light cream*
*1 tablespoon tarragon vinegar*
*½ teaspoon salt*
*⅛ teaspoon pepper*

Cook the wine, shallots, peppercorns, bay leaf and mace until liquid is reduced to half. Strain. Melt 1 tablespoon butter, stir in the flour, then the stock and cream, mixing steadily until it reaches the boiling point. Add the vinegar, salt and pepper. Combine mixtures. Cook 5 minutes; stir in remaining butter. Makes 1¼ cups.

## Mushroom Sauce

Serve with chicken, fish, eggs or pasta.

*1 cup mushrooms, sliced fine*
*½ teaspoon salt*
*3 tablespoons butter*
*2 cups Béchamel Sauce*

Sauté the mushrooms and salt in the butter for 5 minutes. (If any liquid remains, turn up heat until it evaporates.) Add the Béchamel Sauce. Heat and taste for seasoning. Makes about 2½ cups.

## Hollandaise Sauce

Serve with vegetables or fish

¼ *pound sweet butter*
*4 egg yolks*
*1 tablespoon lemon juice*
⅛ *teaspoon salt*
*2 tablespoons heavy cream*

Divide the butter in 3 pieces. In the top of a double boiler, beat the egg yolks and lemon juice with a wooden spoon. Add 1 piece of butter, place over hot water, and cook, stirring constantly until butter melts. (Never let the water boil, and add a little cold water to keep it under the boiling point if necessary.) Add the second piece, still mixing steadily, until melted and absorbed, then add the third piece. When thickened, remove from heat, stir in the salt and cream. Serve as soon as possible. Makes 1¼ cups.

## Mousseline Sauce

Serve with fish or vegetables

Fold 1¼ cups whipped cream into the Hollandaise Sauce. Heat over hot water. Makes about 2½ cups.

## Maltaise Sauce

Serve with asparagus, artichokes or leeks

Blood (red) oranges are customarily used, but ordinary orange juice is good too. Add 3 tablespoons orange juice, 1 teaspoon grated orange rind, 1 drop red food coloring to Hollandaise Sauce. Makes about 1⅓ cups.

## Anchovy Butter Sauce

Serve with fish

*3 anchovy filets*
¼ *pound butter*
¼ *cup dry sherry*

*1 tablespoon capers, washed, drained and chopped*
*2 teaspoons minced parsley*
*1 teaspoon lemon juice*

Pound the anchovies very fine. Combine with the butter and sherry. Bring to a boil and cook over low heat 10 minutes. Stir in the capers, parsley and lemon juice. Taste for seasoning. Makes about ¾ cup.

## Caper Butter Sauce

Serve with fish or vegetables

¼ *pound sweet butter*
⅓ *cup capers*
*2 teaspoons lemon juice*
½ *teaspoon salt*

Melt the butter and add the capers, lemon juice and salt. Makes about ¾ cup.

## Meunière Butter

Serve with fish or shellfish

¼ *pound butter*
*1 tablespoon lemon juice*
*2 teaspoons minced parsley*

Melt the butter and cook over low heat until brown. Stir in the lemon juice and parsley. Makes about ½ cup.

## Polonaise Butter

Serve with vegetables

Add ⅓ cup dry bread crumbs to Meunière Butter. Pour over the vegetables and garnish with chopped hard-cooked egg yolk. Makes about ⅔ cup.

## Maître d'Hôtel Butter

Serve with broiled meat, poultry or fish

¼ *pound sweet butter*
*2 tablespoons lemon juice*

*1 teaspoon minced parsley*
*½ teaspoon salt*
*⅛ teaspoon white pepper*

Have the butter at room temperature; cream it with the lemon juice, parsley, salt and pepper. Chill. To serve, put a teaspoon or so on the hot food. Makes about ½ cup.

## Colbert Butter

Serve with fish

Add 1 teaspoon melted Glace de Viande or beef extract to Maître d'Hôtel Butter.

## Marchand de Vin Butter

Serve with steaks or chops

*½ cup dry red wine*
*4 tablespoons minced shallots or onion*
*Maître d'Hôtel Butter (omit lemon juice)*
*2 teaspoons minced parsley*

Cook the red wine and shallots until reduced to one third. Cool. Mix this with the parsley into the Maître d'Hôtel Butter. Makes about ⅔ cup.

## Béarnaise Sauce

Serve with beef or fish

*3 tablespoons tarragon vinegar*
*¾ cup dry white wine*
*2 peppercorns*
*1 tablespoon shallots or onion, chopped fine*
*1 tablespoon fresh tarragon, chopped fine*
  *(or 1 teaspoon dried)*
*1 tablespoon fresh chervil, chopped fine*
  *(or 1 teaspoon dried)*
*3 egg yolks*
*½ teaspoon salt*
*1 cup melted butter*
*2 teaspoons minced parsley*
*Dash cayenne pepper*

Combine the vinegar, wine, peppercorns, shallots, tarragon and chervil in a sauce-pan; cook over low heat until reduced to half. Beat the egg yolks and salt in a bowl; gradually add the wine mixture, beating steadily to prevent curdling. Still beating steadily, gradually add the butter until it is the consistency of very thick cream. Place over hot water and beat for a minute. Strain and add the parsley and cayenne pepper. If fresh herbs are used, add 1 teaspoon of each, chopped, before serving. Makes about 1½ cups. 1 teaspoon of melted Glace de Viande may be added for a darker sauce, called Valoise, to serve with eggs, broiled chicken.

### VARIATION

#### Choron Sauce

To 1 cup Béarnaise Sauce add ¼ cup tomato purée. Use on meat, chicken or fish.

## Hot Ravigote Sauce

Serve with fish

*2 egg yolks*
*1 cup hot water*
*4 tablespoons butter*
*1 tablespoon flour*
*3 tablespoons tarragon vinegar*
*2 tablespoons minced shallots or onion*
*½ teaspoon salt*
*⅛ teaspoon pepper*
*1 teaspoon prepared mustard*
*1 teaspoon chopped fresh chervil*
  *(or ⅛ teaspoon dried)*
*1 teaspoon chopped tarragon*
  *(or ⅛ teaspoon dried)*
*2 teaspoons chopped chives*

Beat the yolks and gradually add the hot water, stirring steadily to prevent curdling. Melt 1 tablespoon of butter in a saucepan; stir in the flour and then the yolk mixture all at once. Stir steadily to the boiling point but do not let boil. Add remaining butter in small pieces, mixing steadily.

Cook the vinegar and shallots until reduced to half. Strain. Add to the sauce with the salt, pepper, mustard, chervil, tarragon and chives. Makes about 1½ cups.

Note: If dried herbs are used, soak in hot water for 10 minutes before adding.

## Almond Butter Sauce

Serve with fish or sea food

¼ *pound butter*
¾ *cup blanched sliced almonds*
⅛ *teaspoon minced garlic (optional)*
*1 teaspoon lemon juice*
¾ *teaspoon salt*
⅛ *teaspoon white pepper*

Melt the butter and when hot, add the almonds. Cook over low heat stirring occasionally, until almonds brown. Stir in the garlic, lemon juice, salt and pepper. Pour over the fish. Makes about 1 cup.

## Mayonnaise

*2 egg yolks*
½ *teaspoon salt*
*Dash cayenne pepper*
¼ *teaspoon dry mustard*
*1 tablespoon lemon juice*
*1 cup olive or salad oil or a mixture of both*
*1 tablespoon white wine vinegar*

Make small quantities of Mayonnaise at a time, as it is best when fresh. The above proportions will make about 1¼ cups. Have all the ingredients the same temperature—it lessens the danger of curdling.

Be sure the gelatinous thread of the egg is removed. Place yolks, salt, cayenne pepper and mustard in a bowl. Use a wire whisk, fork or wooden spoon. Beat the yolks and add a little lemon juice. Now drop by drop beat in about ¼ cup oil. Add a little lemon juice and vinegar. (If you don't have white wine vinegar, use all lemon juice.) Add more oil, a little more quickly, beating all the while. Use up the lemon juice

and vinegar, then the oil, beating constantly until thick. If the Mayonnaise should curdle, beat it into another egg yolk, but if you're careful it won't be necessary.

## Mayonnaise Sauce Niçoise

Serve with cold shellfish or fish

½ *cup finely chopped green pepper*
*1 tablespoon tomato paste*
⅛ *teaspoon minced garlic*
*1 teaspoon minced fresh tarragon*
1½ *cups Mayonnaise*

Mix all ingredients together. Makes about 1¾ cups.

## Mayonnaise Ravigote

Serve with crab meat and fish

*2 tablespoons minced parsley*
*4 tablespoons minced shallots or onions*
*2 tablespoons minced capers*
¼ *cup dry sherry*
*1 teaspoon anchovy paste*
*1 cup Mayonnaise*

Cook the parsley, shallots, capers and sherry until reduced to half. Strain and chill. Mix the anchovy paste, Mayonnaise, sherry mixture. Makes about 1⅛ cups.

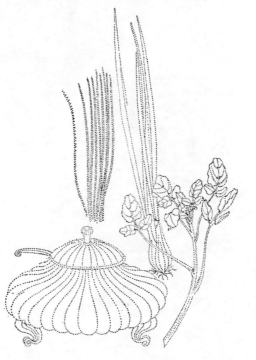

### Sauce Verte

Serve with cold fish, particularly salmon

*1 cup chopped spinach*
*2 tablespoons chopped fresh chervil*
*2 tablespoons chopped fresh tarragon*
*2 tablespoons minced parsley*
*1 cup Mayonnaise*
*2 tablespoons heavy cream*
*Drop green food coloring (optional)*

Cook the spinach, chervil, tarragon and parsley for 5 minutes in a little water. Drain thoroughly and force through a sieve. Cool and stir into the Mayonnaise with the cream and food coloring. Makes 1¼ cups.

## Mayonnaise Chaud Froid

To coat fish or chicken

*1 tablespoon gelatin*
*2 tablespoons water*
*1 cup Mayonnaise*

Soften the gelatin in the water; stir over hot water until dissolved. Cool and stir into the Mayonnaise. Coat food and chill. For a White Chaud Froid Sauce, substitute Velouté Sauce for Mayonnaise.

## Aïoli

Serve with boiled beef, fish, bouillabaisse

*2 egg yolks*
*3 cloves garlic, mashed very fine*
*½ cup olive oil*
*1¼ teaspoons lemon juice*
*¾ teaspoon salt*
*¼ teaspoon freshly ground black pepper*

Beat the egg yolks and garlic in a bowl; add the oil drop by drop, beating steadily until half is used up. Beat in a little lemon juice and then the remaining oil, still beating steadily. Season with salt and pepper. Chill. Makes ¾ cup.

## Vinaigrette Sauce

Serve with vegetables, salads or hors d'oeuvre

*¾ cup olive oil*
*½ cup tarragon vinegar*
*¾ teaspoon salt*
*¼ teaspoon freshly ground black pepper*
*2 teaspoons minced chives*
*2 teaspoons minced fresh chervil (or ⅛ teaspoon dried)*
*2 teaspoons minced capers*
*1 hard-cooked egg yolk, mashed*

Beat all the ingredients together. Makes about 1 cup.

## Vanilla Sauce

Serve with fruits or cake

*5 egg yolks*
*½ cup sugar*
*1 teaspoon cornstarch*
*⅛ teaspoon salt*
*2 cups light cream, scalded*
*1 teaspoon vanilla extract*

Beat the egg yolks, sugar, cornstarch and salt together until thick and light. Gradually add the cream, stirring constantly to prevent curdling. Cook over hot water, stirring steadily until the mixture is custardy and coats the back of a silver spoon. Strain; stir in the vanilla. Cool, stirring occasionally. Makes about 2¾ cups. Fold in ½ cup whipped cream for a richer sauce.

## Parisienne Sauce

Serve with berries, on cakes or puddings

*1 cup strawberries*
*2 tablespoons cognac*
*1 cup Vanilla Sauce*
*1 cup heavy cream, whipped*

Mash berries with cognac. Fold into Vanilla Sauce with whipped cream. Makes 3 cups.

## Caramel Sauce

Serve with ice cream or puddings

*1 cup water*
*1 cup sugar*
*¼ cup heavy cream*

Cook the water and sugar together until syrupy and caramel colored. Remove from heat and place saucepan in cold water to prevent burning. Stir in the cream. Serve hot or cold. Makes about 1¼ cups.

## Sabayon Sauce

Serve with fritters or puddings

*3 egg yolks*
*½ cup sugar*
*¾ cup Marsala or sweet sherry*
*1 tablespoon cognac*

Beat the egg yolks and sugar together in the top of a double boiler until thick and light. Add the wine and place over hot water. Cook, stirring constantly until thickened. Stir in cognac. Serve hot. Makes 1½ cups.

## Apricot Sauce

Serve with ice cream, fruit or fritters

*2 cups apricot jam*
*1 cup water*
*2 tablespoons sugar*
*¼ cup Cointreau or curaçao*

Cook the jam, water and sugar together over low heat for 10 minutes, stirring frequently. Force through a sieve. Stir in the liqueur. Makes about 2 cups.

## Berry Sauce

Serve with fruit, ice cream or soufflés

*2 cups strawberries or raspberries, fresh or frozen*
*½–¼ cup sugar*

*1 tablespoon lemon juice*
*2 teaspoons cornstarch*
*2 tablespoons cognac*

Cook the berries, sugar (½ cup for fresh, ¼ cup for frozen) and lemon juice until soft, about 10 minutes. Force through a sieve. Mix the cornstarch and cognac together until smooth. Add to the hot fruit juice; cook the mixture over low heat, stirring constantly, until it is clear and thickened. Sauce may be served hot or cold. Makes about 1¼ cups.

## Jubilee Sauce

Serve with ice cream

*1 can (#2) pitted black bing cherries*
*2 teaspoons cornstarch*
*¼ cup cognac*

Drain the cherries, reserving 1 cup of the juice. Mix the cornstarch and juice together; cook over low heat, stirring constantly until clear and thickened. Add the cherries. Warm the cognac and set it aflame. Pour over the sauce. Makes about 2 cups.

# PASTA and RICE

# Pasta and Rice

**R**ice, the most venerable of cultivated crops, has been a vital element in the history of mankind since the beginning of civilization. For centuries, rice alone saved Asia's millions from starvation, and even today half the world's population gets 80 per cent of its calories from this tiny but puissant grain. Perhaps our familiarity with rice has bred a kind of culinary contempt for this inexpensive but invaluable food, yet in China, around 2800 B.C., rice was so revered that the ceremonial right to sow it was reserved for the Emperor; lesser members of the royal household sowed four other types of grain. Although the origin of rice is obscured by early migrations (the first recorded mention of its cultivation is about 5000 years old), it is generally accepted as a native of the monsoon countries of Southeast Asia.

Rice has been assimilated into the cuisine of every country, each producing its own distinctive rice dish such as the Spanish paella (shown on the preceding page), Italian risotto, Indian pellao, Mid-East pilaff, Swedish risgrynsgröt, Southern jambalaya. Yet there are still many misconceptions about the nature and treatment of rice. There are over 7000 cultivated varieties of rice, which is a member of the grass family called *Orza sativa*. (Wild rice, found in the Great Lakes region, is not a true rice but a related genus.) Brown rice is rice that has been hulled. When both the hull and kernel are removed, the rice is classified as white. The final milling process removes a thin coating, known as the polish, on the rice grain. Contrary to what many people think, milled white rice does not have to be washed before cooking. Washing or boiling in large quantities of water only deprives the rice of much of its valuable vitamin content. Rice should be cooked in only as much water as it can absorb.

The protean properties of pasta were summed up by a 19th-century Italian poet, Antonio Viviani, in these words, "From this

228

dough you get the little bows, The spiral fanfares and the stardust, The organ pipes and furbelows, The roller coasters and pie crust." Among the countries where pasta is rumored to have originated, Italy's claim is the strongest. Despite the apocryphal story about Marco Polo's discovering spaghetti in China, a manuscript on the life of the Blessed Hermit William, published in 1200, records, "He invited William to dinner and served macaroni." The delightful names the Italians give to pasta attest their affectionate regard for it. Spaghetti (which means little strings) and macaroni, most familiar to our ears, are just two of the immense pasta family. Each has a descriptive name such as little pipes, butterflies, needle points, stars, turbans, rings, sea shells, little hats and fancy bows. Pasta takes many forms: spiral, tubular, flat, stringlike, ribbed and rounded. It was Thomas Jefferson who first imported such fine Italian products as Lombardy poplars, Tuscan wine and a spaghetti-making machine. Even then pasta was much abused. A recipe of 1792 calls for spaghetti to be boiled for 3 hours in water, cooked for 10 minutes in broth and then mixed with bread in a soup tureen. Today, Americans still prefer their spaghetti softer than the Italians, who serve it *al dente* (to the tooth), or just biteable, neither too hard nor too soft. Our recommended way to cook pasta is to put 7 or more quarts of water and 2 tablespoons salt in a large spotless pot and bring to a violent, rolling boil before adding 1 pound of pasta. (Do not break long strands but nudge them in gently with a wooden spoon as the ends soften.) When the water begins to boil over, reduce heat for a moment and then return to full boil. Do not cover or stir. For a very smooth pasta, add 1 teaspoon olive oil to the pot. If you follow the manufacturer's cooking time, be careful not to overcook. After the first four minutes, test a strand by biting and keep on testing until it reaches the stage you prefer. Drain thoroughly in a colander to get rid of all water before serving.

229

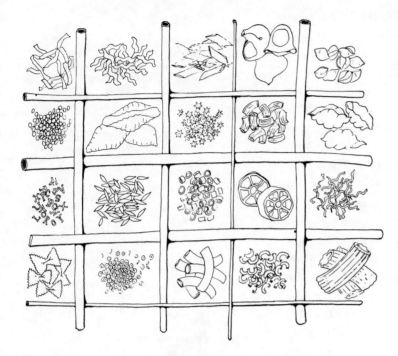

Make a paste (pesto) by pounding in a mortar the garlic, basil leaves, parsley, salt, Parmesan cheese and enough olive oil to thin the mixture. Mix it with the spaghetti, cooked *al dente*.

## Spaghetti with Olive and Cheese Sauce

*2 tablespoons butter*
*2 tablespoons olive oil*
*2 tablespoons flour*
*2 cups milk*
*1 teaspoon salt*
*2 cups grated American cheese*
*1 cup sliced, stuffed olives*
*1 pound spaghetti, cooked and drained*

Combine the butter and olive oil in a saucepan. Melt over low heat, and add the flour, stirring until smooth. Gradually add the milk, stirring constantly until the sauce reaches the boiling point. Add the salt and cheese; cook over low heat for 5 minutes, stirring frequently. Add the olives and mix. Pour the sauce over the spaghetti, toss lightly, and serve.

## Spaghetti al Burro

Cook 1 pound of spaghetti *al dente* (firm to the tooth), drain and mix with 4 or 5 ounces melted butter and 2 cups freshly grated Parmesan cheese.

## Spaghetti Olio e Aglio

Cook spaghetti as above. Melt ¼ cup (½ bar) butter and heat with 4 crushed cloves garlic and ¼ cup olive oil. Discard garlic and mix sauce into spaghetti. Pass plenty of freshly grated cheese.

## Creamed Noodle Ring

*5 eggs*
*1 cup light cream*
*1 teaspoon salt*
*¼ teaspoon freshly ground black pepper*
*1 pound broad noodles, cooked and drained*
*3 tablespoons melted butter*

Beat the eggs; add the cream, salt and pepper. Beat together very well and combine with the noodles.

Butter a 9″ ring mold thoroughly. Pour mixture into it, sprinkle with the butter.

Bake in a 325° oven for 50 minutes, or until set. Carefully run a knife around the edge, and unmold onto a platter. The center may be filled with any desired mixture.

## Spaghetti al Pesto

*3 cloves garlic*
*½ cup (packed) fresh basil leaves*
*¼ cup minced parsley*
*1 teaspoon salt*
*1 cup freshly grated Parmesan cheese*
*Olive oil*
*1 pound spaghetti*

## Swiss Spaghetti

*4 tablespoons butter*
*1 onion, chopped*
*1 green pepper, chopped*
*1 pound ground beef*
*2 cups canned tomatoes*
*1½ teaspoons salt*
*½ teaspoon pepper*
*¾ pound Swiss or Gruyère cheese, cubed*
*1 pound spaghetti, cooked and drained*
*½ cup grated Swiss or Gruyère cheese*

Melt the butter in a saucepan. Add the onion and green pepper; sauté for 5 minutes. Add the beef and cook over high heat, stirring constantly until brown. Add the tomatoes, salt and pepper. Cover and cook over low heat for 1 hour. Add the cubed cheese and cook for 5 minutes. Add the spaghetti and mix thoroughly but lightly.

Serve with the grated cheese.

## Spaghetti alla Papalina

*8 egg yolks*
*½ cup heavy cream*
*¼ pound butter, broken into small pieces*
*1 teaspoon salt*
*1 teaspoon freshly ground black pepper*
*½ cup grated Parmesan cheese*
*1 pound spaghetti, cooked and drained*

Beat the egg yolks in a saucepan. Add the cream, butter, salt, pepper and cheese. Mix all together very well. Add the spaghetti, tossing lightly. Place over very low heat and continue tossing until butter melts and spaghetti is well coated.

## Cheese and Bacon Noodles

*½ pound bacon*
*1 pound broad noodles, cooked and drained*
*1 pound pot cheese*
*1½ cups sour cream*

Fry the bacon until crisp. Drain, but re-serve 2 tablespoons of fat. Crumble bacon.

Place the 2 tablespoons of bacon fat in a saucepan. Add the noodles, tossing lightly. Add the cheese and sour cream. Cook over very low heat until the ingredients are very hot, stirring occasionally.

Arrange the noodle mixture on a platter, and sprinkle crumbled bacon on top.

## Spaghetti with White Clam Sauce

*36 Little Neck clams*
*¾ cup olive oil*
*3 cloves garlic, chopped*
*½ teaspoon salt*
*¼ teaspoon dried ground red peppers*
*¼ cup chopped parsley*
*1 pound spaghetti, cooked and drained*

Wash and scrub the clams thoroughly. Place in a large skillet with 2 tablespoons of the olive oil. Cook over high heat, stirring frequently, until the clams open. Remove the clams from the shells. Strain and reserve the juice.

Heat the remaining oil in a skillet and sauté the garlic for 3 minutes, stirring frequently. Add the clam juice, salt and dried peppers. Cook over low heat for 2 minutes. Add the clams and parsley and cook for 1 minute only. Do not overcook. Pour the sauce over the spaghetti and serve.

## Spaghetti with Spicy Tuna Sauce

*4 tablespoons butter*
*2 onions, chopped*
*1 clove garlic, chopped*
*2   7¾-ounce cans tuna fish, flaked*
*½ teaspoon salt*
*¼ teaspoon freshly ground black pepper*
*2 cups chili sauce*
*2 tablespoons chopped parsley*
*1 pound spaghetti, cooked and drained*

Melt the butter in a skillet. Sauté the onions and garlic for 10 minutes, stirring frequently. Add the tuna fish and cook over medium heat until lightly browned. Add the salt, pepper, chili sauce and parsley. Cook for 5 minutes over low heat, stirring occasionally. Correct seasoning.

Place the spaghetti on a platter, pour the sauce over it and serve.

## Shrimp and Macaroni in Chili Sauce

½ cup olive oil
4 onions, chopped
1 clove garlic, minced
2 green peppers, cut into julienne strips
3 cans tomato sauce
1 teaspoon salt
¼ teaspoon dried ground chili peppers
1 teaspoon sugar
1 pound cooked shrimp, shelled and cleaned
½ pound elbow macaroni, cooked and drained
3 hard-cooked eggs, quartered

Heat the olive oil in a saucepan. Add the onions, garlic and green peppers. Sauté for 10 minutes. Add the tomato sauce, salt, chili peppers and sugar. Cook over low heat for 1 hour, stirring occasionally. Add the shrimp and macaroni. Mix lightly and heat thoroughly over low heat. Correct seasoning.

Arrange the macaroni on a platter, and serve garnished with the quartered eggs.

## Vermicelli and Anchovies

3 tablespoons olive oil
3 tablespoons butter
1 onion, chopped
8 tomatoes, peeled and chopped
1 teaspoon salt
½ teaspoon freshly ground black pepper
1 teaspoon basil
6 anchovies, mashed

2 tablespoons chopped parsley
1 pound vermicelli, cooked and drained
½ cup grated Parmesan cheese

Heat the olive oil and butter. Add the onion and sauté for 10 minutes, stirring frequently. Add the tomatoes, salt, pepper and basil. Cook over low heat for 1 hour, stirring occasionally. Force the mixture through a sieve, and return it to the saucepan. Add the anchovies and parsley; mix well. Correct seasoning.

Add the vermicelli, and mix well together. Serve with the grated Parmesan cheese.

## Spaghetti and Lobster Fra Diavolo

⅓ cup olive oil
1 onion, grated
2 cloves garlic, minced
1 #2½ can Italian-style tomatoes
1½ teaspoons salt
¼ teaspoon dried ground red peppers
1 teaspoon oregano
2 lobsters (uncooked), split in half
2 tablespoons chopped parsley
1 pound spaghetti, cooked and drained

Heat ¼ cup of the olive oil in a saucepan. Sauté the onion and garlic for 10 minutes, stirring frequently. Add the tomatoes, salt, dried red peppers and oregano. Cook over low heat for 30 minutes, stirring occasionally.

Remove and slice the uncooked meat from the lobsters. Heat the remaining olive oil in a skillet. Add the lobster meat and sauté for 10 minutes, stirring frequently. Add to the tomato sauce with the parsley. Cook for 10 minutes. Correct seasoning.

Arrange the spaghetti on a platter or serving dish. Pour the lobster and sauce over it, and serve immediately.

## Chicken-Spaghetti Casserole

*3 tablespoons olive oil*
*1 onion, chopped*
*1 green pepper, chopped*
*1 cup sliced mushrooms*
*2 cans tomato sauce*
*1 teaspoon salt*
*½ teaspoon freshly ground black pepper*
*½ teaspoon oregano*
*1 pound spaghetti, cooked and drained*
*2 cups cooked chicken or turkey, diced*
*½ pound mozzarella cheese, grated*

Heat the olive oil in a skillet. Sauté the onion and green pepper for 10 minutes, stirring frequently. Add the mushrooms, tomato sauce, salt, pepper and oregano. Cook over low heat for 30 minutes, stirring occasionally. Correct seasoning.

In a buttered casserole, arrange successive layers of the spaghetti, poultry, sauce and mozzarella cheese.

Bake in a 375° oven for 30 minutes.

## Chicken Livers and Spaghetti

*¼ cup olive oil*
*2 onions, chopped*
*2 cups canned tomato sauce*
*1½ teaspoons salt*
*¼ teaspoon dried ground red peppers*
*½ cup grated Parmesan cheese*
*4 tablespoons butter*
*1 pound chicken livers*
*½ pound mushrooms, sliced*
*1 pound spaghetti, cooked and drained*

Heat the olive oil in a saucepan. Sauté the onions for 10 minutes. Add the tomato sauce, ½ teaspoon of the salt and the red peppers. Cook over low heat for 15 minutes. Gradually add the cheese. Cook over low heat while preparing the livers and mushrooms.

Melt the butter in a skillet. Add the livers and mushrooms. Sauté for 5 minutes, or until the livers are done. Sprinkle with the remaining salt. Combine with the tomato mixture and stir together.

Pour over the spaghetti, toss lightly.

## Lasagna, Bologna Fashion

*¼ pound salt pork, diced*
*½ pound ground beef*
*½ pound ground pork*
*½ pound ground veal*
*2 onions, sliced thin*
*1 carrot, chopped*
*2 cups stock or canned consommé*
*2 teaspoons tomato paste*
*1 teaspoon salt*
*¼ teaspoon freshly ground black pepper*
*½ pound mushrooms*
*3 chicken livers, coarsely chopped*
*½ cup heavy cream*
*1 pound lasagna, or*
*    very broad noodles cooked and drained*
*½ pound ricotta cheese*
*1 cup grated Parmesan cheese*

In a saucepan, fry the salt pork until there are at least 2 tablespoons of fat. Add the beef, pork, veal, onions and carrot. Brown well, stirring constantly. Add the stock, tomato paste, salt and pepper. Cover, and cook over low heat for 1 hour. Add the mushrooms, livers and cream. Cook for 15 minutes. Correct seasoning.

In a buttered baking dish, arrange as many layers as possible of lasagna, ricotta cheese, meat sauce and Parmesan cheese, ending with Parmesan cheese.

Bake in a 375° oven for 15 minutes.

## Lasagna

¼ cup olive oil
2 onions, finely chopped
1 clove garlic, minced
1 #2½ can Italian-style tomatoes
1½ teaspoons salt
¼ teaspoon dried ground red peppers
8 Italian sweet sausages, sliced thin
1 pound ricotta cheese
½ pound mozzarella cheese, diced
1 pound very broad noodles,
    cooked and drained
1 cup grated Parmesan cheese

Heat the olive oil in a saucepan. Sauté the onions and garlic for 10 minutes, stirring frequently. Add the tomatoes, salt and dried red peppers. Bring to a boil. Cover, and cook over low heat for 1 hour. Correct seasoning. Sauté the sausages until brown; drain well. Mix the ricotta and mozzarella cheese together.

Pour ½ cup of the tomato mixture on the bottom of a buttered, square baking dish. Arrange half the noodles over it. Add successive layers of half of the sausage, half of the mixed ricotta and mozzarella cheeses, half of the remaining tomato sauce, and the Parmesan cheese. Repeat with the remaining sausage, cheeses, tomato sauce and Parmesan cheese.

Bake in a 350° oven for 25 minutes. Cut into squares and serve with additional grated cheese, if desired.

## Stuffed Lasagna, Naples Style

Cook ½ lb. lasagna in plenty of salted water to which a little olive oil has been added. This will keep it from sticking together. Butter an oblong glass baking dish gener-

ously, and line it with a layer of cooked lasagna, the strips all going in one direction. Cover this with a layer of sauce (2 small cans beef gravy combined with 1 small can tomato sauce and 1 cup bouillon seasoned with salt, pepper and oregano and simmered to desired consistency), then with a layer of cooked and coarsely chopped Italian sausage, and then with spoonfuls of ricotta cheese, some chopped hard-boiled egg, and a layer of grated cheese or sliced mozzarella cheese. Now arrange another layer of lasagna, in the other direction. Continue the layers until the dish is filled, with grated cheese as the top layer. Put in a 350° oven for 25 minutes, or until hot and brown. Serves 8.

## Noodles with Spanish Mushroom Sauce

2 tablespoons olive oil
2 onions, chopped
1 cup canned tomato sauce
1 tomato, chopped
1 teaspoon salt
½ teaspoon freshly ground black pepper
3 slices bacon, chopped
¼ pound ham, cut into julienne strips
2 sausages (Spanish type) sliced thin
1 cup chopped mushrooms
1 cup stock or canned consommé
¾ pound medium noodles,
    cooked and drained
1 cup grated American, Cheddar
    or Parmesan cheese

Heat the olive oil in a saucepan. Sauté the onions for 10 minutes, stirring frequently. Add the tomato sauce, tomato, salt, pepper, bacon, ham and sausages; stir well. Cover, and cook over low heat for 20 minutes. Mix the mushrooms and stock together and add. Cover and cook over low heat for 15 minutes. Correct seasoning.

Arrange successive layers of cooked

noodles, grated cheese and the sauce in a buttered baking dish. Arrange as many layers as possible, ending with the sauce. Bake in a 375° oven for 25 minutes, or until delicately browned on top.

Serve hot, directly from the dish.

## Italian Sausages and Spaghetti

*1 pound sweet italian sausages,*
*    sliced into ¼″ pieces*
*3 onions, chopped*
*1 clove garlic, minced*
*1 pound mushrooms, sliced*
*1 #2½ can tomatoes*
*1 teaspoon basil*
*½ teaspoon salt*
*¼ teaspoon freshly ground black pepper*
*½ cup chopped black olives*
*1 pound spaghetti, cooked and drained*

Fry the sausages for 5 minutes. Pour off most of the fat. Add the onions and garlic, and sauté for 10 minutes. Add the mushrooms and sauté for 5 minutes. Add the tomatoes, basil, salt and pepper. Cover, and cook over low heat for 45 minutes, adding water if sauce becomes too thick. Correct seasoning. Add the olives, and stir.

Pour over the spaghetti, toss lightly, and serve.

## Italian Macaroni Custard

*1 #2½ can tomatoes*
*2 onions, chopped*
*1½ teaspoons salt*
*¼ teaspoon freshly ground black pepper*
*¼ pound butter*
*2 tablespoons breadcrumbs*
*1 pound macaroni, cooked and drained*
*⅓ pound Parma ham, coarsely shredded*
*½ pound mushrooms, sliced*
*2 cups grated Parmesan cheese*
*3 eggs*
*1½ cups light cream*

Cook the tomatoes, onions, salt and pepper for 10 minutes. Force through a sieve.

Grease a casserole with 1 tablespoon of the butter, and dust it with the breadcrumbs. Using half the ingredients, arrange successive layers of macaroni, ham, mushrooms, cheese and tomato mixture. Dot with half of the remaining butter. Repeat layers.

Beat the eggs and cream together. Pour over the top. Bake in a 350° oven for 35 minutes.

## Spaghetti, Syracuse Style

*½ cup olive oil*
*1 onion, chopped*
*2 cloves garlic, minced*
*2 green peppers, cut into julienne strips*
*8 tomatoes, peeled and chopped*
*    or 3 cups canned tomatoes*
*1 eggplant, peeled and diced*
*12 black olives, sliced*
*    (Italian or Greek type, if available)*
*1 tablespoon capers*
*1 teaspoon basil*
*4 anchovies, mashed*
*¼ teaspoon dried ground red peppers*
*1 pound spaghetti, cooked and drained*

235

Heat the oil in a skillet. Sauté the onion, garlic and green peppers for 10 minutes, stirring occasionally. Add the tomatoes and eggplant. Cook over low heat for 30 minutes, stirring frequently. Add the olives, capers, basil, anchovies and red peppers. Cover, and cook over low heat for 10 minutes. Correct seasoning.

Arrange the spaghetti on a platter, pour sauce over it. Serve immediately.

## Spinach Noodle Pudding

*4 egg yolks*
*2 pounds cooked spinach, or 1 package*
*frozen spinach, cooked, drained and*
*chopped*
*2 tablespoons grated onion*
*1 teaspoon salt*
*¼ teaspoon freshly ground black pepper*
*¼ teaspoon nutmeg*
*½ pound fine noodles, cooked and drained*
*4 egg whites*

Preheat oven to 350°.

Beat the egg yolks in a bowl. Add the spinach, onion, salt, pepper and nutmeg. Mix together very well. Add the noodles, and mix lightly. Correct seasoning.

Beat the egg whites until stiff but not dry. Fold them into the mixture carefully.

Pour into a buttered baking dish. Bake in a 350° oven 25 minutes. Serve at once.

## Kraut Fleckerl
### (Noodles and Cabbage)

*1 large head cabbage (about 3 pounds)*
*1½ teaspoons salt*
*½ pound butter*
*2 teaspoons sugar*
*½ teaspoon freshly ground black pepper*
*1 pound broad noodles, broken in half,*
*cooked and drained*

Wash the cabbage and cut it as fine as possible, discarding all imperfect leaves and the core. Place the shredded cabbage in a bowl and add the salt, mixing well. Allow to stand for at least 1 hour, preferably 2 hours. Rinse and drain well, squeezing out all the liquid.

Melt half the butter in a saucepan. Add the cabbage, sugar and pepper. Cook over low heat for 1½ hours, or until browned, stirring frequently. Add the remaining butter at intervals until all has been used. Correct seasoning.

Add the noodles to the cabbage, and stir together until well mixed. Heat for a few minutes, stirring frequently. Serve with roast meats or poultry.

## Zucchini with Spaghetti

*½ cup olive oil*
*2 onions, chopped*
*2 cloves garlic, minced*
*1 pound zucchini, sliced thin*
*2 green peppers, cut into julienne strips*
*4 tomatoes, chopped*
*3 tablespoons water*
*2 teaspoons salt*
*⅛ teaspoon dried ground red peppers*
*1 pound spaghetti, cooked and drained*

Heat the olive oil in a skillet. Sauté the onions, garlic, zucchini and green peppers for 15 minutes, stirring occasionally. Add the tomatoes, water, salt and dried red peppers. Cook over low heat for 15 minutes. Add the spaghetti, mixing lightly. Correct seasoning, and serve.

## Spaghetti with Artichoke Hearts

*4 tablespoons butter*
*3 onions, chopped*
*3 tablespoons flour*
*2 cups consommé*
*1 #2 can tomatoes*
*2 teaspoons salt*

½ teaspoon freshly ground black pepper
1 teaspoon oregano
4 tablespoons olive oil
2 cloves garlic, minced
½ pound mushrooms
6 artichoke hearts, cooked or canned
½ pound chicken livers
1 pound spaghetti, cooked and drained
½ cup grated Parmesan cheese

Melt the butter in a saucepan and sauté the onions for 10 minutes, stirring frequently. Add the flour, stirring until smooth and browned. Add the consommé, stirring constantly until it reaches the boiling point. Stir in the tomatoes, 1 teaspoon salt, ¼ teaspoon pepper and the oregano. Cook over low heat for 1 hour.

Heat the olive oil in a skillet. Sauté the garlic, mushrooms and artichokes for 5 minutes, stirring frequently but gently. Add the livers and sauté for 10 minutes. Add the remaining salt and pepper. Mix lightly with the previous mixture.

Place the spaghetti on a platter and pour the sauce over it. Sprinkle with the cheese and serve.

## Luncheon Salad

6 sausages (Italian style) sliced 1″ thick
2 red onions, sliced thin
1 green pepper, cut into julienne strips

2 tablespoons chopped parsley
½ pound elbow macaroni, cooked,
     drained and cooled
3 hard-cooked eggs, quartered
2 cups canned kidney beans, drained
½ cup olive oil
3 tablespoons wine vinegar
1 clove garlic, minced
½ teaspoon salt
¼ teaspoon freshly ground black pepper
⅛ teaspoon oregano

Fry the sausages until browned. Drain well. Combine the onions, green pepper, parsley, macaroni, eggs, beans and sausages in a salad bowl. Toss lightly.

Combine the olive oil, vinegar, garlic, salt, pepper and oregano. Beat or shake together vigorously. Pour over the salad, and mix together lightly.

## Macaroni and Bacon Salad

½ cup olive oil
2 tablespoons wine vinegar
½ teaspoon salt
¼ teaspoon freshly ground black pepper
2 tablespoons ketchup
1 teaspoon capers, drained
½ pound elbow macaroni, cooked,
     drained and cooled
8 slices bacon, crisply cooked, chopped
2 tablespoons grated onion
½ cup mayonnaise
3 tomatoes, cut into eighths
3 hard-cooked eggs, quartered

Combine the olive oil, vinegar, salt, pepper and ketchup. Beat or shake together very well. Add the capers and set aside.

Combine the macaroni, bacon, onion and mayonnaise in a salad bowl, and toss together lightly. Arrange the tomatoes and eggs around the edge. Pour the dressing over the salad, and serve.

## Ravioli with Cheese

2 cups sifted flour
6 egg yolks
¾ teaspoon salt
½ cup warm water
1 pound ricotta cheese
1 cup grated Parmesan cheese
2 tablespoons grated onion

Sift the flour onto a board; make a well in the center. Place 3 of the egg yolks in it. Add ¼ teaspoon of the salt and 3 tablespoons of the water. Work in the flour, and knead until a stiff dough is formed, adding a little more warm water if necessary. Knead until smooth and elastic. Cover the dough and let stand for 15 minutes. Divide the dough in half, and roll out one of the halves as thin as possible. Mix the remaining egg yolks, the ricotta cheese, Parmesan cheese, onion and remaining salt together. Place 1 teaspoonful of the mixture on the dough; repeat, spacing teaspoonfuls 2" apart in each direction. Roll out the remaining dough and place on top carefully, moistening the outside edges. Press the two layers of dough together around each mound of the cheese mixture. Cut the squares apart with a pastry wheel or a sharp knife. Drop into boiling, salted water, and boil for 10 minutes. Drain well.

Serve with melted butter and grated Parmesan cheese.

## Potato Gnocchi

4 potatoes (about 1 pound),
  peeled and boiled
¾ cup sifted flour
1½ teaspoons salt
1 egg
1 egg yolk

Force the potatoes through a ricer, or mash until completely smooth. Add the flour, salt, egg and egg yolk, mixing until thoroughly blended. Shape into small sausages, about 2" long. Drop into boiling, salted water. Cook until they float, about 8 minutes. Drain.

Serve with Tomato Sauce (see recipe under Sauces) and grated Parmesan.

## Green Gnocchi

8 potatoes (about 2½ pounds),
  boiled and mashed
1½ cups cooked puréed spinach
⅓ cup sifted flour
2 tablespoons grated Parmesan cheese
2 egg yolks, beaten
½ teaspoon salt

Beat the potatoes, spinach, flour, cheese, egg yolks and salt together until light and smooth. Roll into long, even rolls about the thickness of a cigar, on a lightly floured board. Break or cut off 2" lengths. Drop into boiling, salted water (do not cook too many at once). Boil until they rise to the surface, about 5 minutes. Drain well.

Serve with Tomato Sauce and grated cheese, or with melted butter and grated cheese.

## Lasagna Verde with Shrimp

¼ cup olive oil

2 onions, finely chopped

1 cup canned tomato sauce

2 teaspoons salt

½ teaspoon pepper

1 teaspoon oregano

4 cups sifted flour

1 cup spinach purée

2 eggs

2 pounds shrimp, shelled,
    cleaned and cooked

½ pound mozzarella cheese, thinly sliced

1 cup grated Parmesan cheese

Heat the olive oil in a skillet. Sauté the onions for 5 minutes. Add the tomato sauce, 1 teaspoon of the salt, the pepper and oregano. Cover, and cook over low heat for 1 hour, adding a little water if the sauce becomes too thick.

Sift the flour and remaining salt into a bowl. Make a well in the center and place the spinach purée and eggs in it. (The spinach should be very smooth and fine.) Work in the flour until a dough is formed, adding a little water if necessary. Roll out ¼″ thick on a lightly floured board. Cut into 4″ squares. Boil a few squares of dough at a time in salted water for 10 minutes. Drain well.

In a buttered baking dish, arrange successive layers of the boiled dough (lasagna), shrimp, sauce, mozzarella and Parmesan cheese. Make at least 3 layers, using the ingredients in the same order.

Bake in a 350° oven for 25 minutes.

## Cappelletti with Beef

2 cups sifted flour

2 teaspoons salt

3 eggs

2 tablespoons water

1 tablespoon olive oil

½ pound ground beef

1 pound ricotta cheese

¼ teaspoon freshly ground black pepper

⅛ teaspoon nutmeg

1 cup grated Parmesan cheese

Sift the flour and 1 teaspoon of the salt onto a board. Make a well in the center. Place 2 of the eggs and the water in the center. Work in the flour gradually, kneading until the dough is smooth and pliable. Add a little more flour or water if necessary. Set aside while preparing the filling.

Heat the olive oil in a skillet. Sauté the beef until browned, stirring constantly. Mix with the ricotta cheese, pepper, nutmeg, remaining salt and egg.

Roll out the dough as thin as possible. Cut into 2″ circles. Place a teaspoonful of the filling on each. Fold over the dough, sealing the edges with the tines of à fork. Drop into boiling, salted water, or stock. Cook about 8 minutes, or until they rise to the top. Do not cook too many at one time. Drain well. Serve with the grated cheese or in soup.

## Homemade Soft Noodles

2 cups sifted flour

1 teaspoon salt

1 egg

¾ cup water

Sift the flour and salt into a bowl. Beat the egg and add to the flour, together with the water. Mix together until a soft dough is formed.

Place half the dough on a board, and flatten it as much as possible with the hands (the dough will be too soft to roll). Cut into 1″ squares with a wet knife. Repeat the process with the remaining half of the dough.

Drop into boiling, salted water. Cook until they rise to the surface. Remove immediately and drain well.

Serve with melted butter or with grated cheese. The noodles may also be served with meat or poultry dishes.

## Chinese Pork Balls in Noodle Wrappers

2½ cups sifted flour
3 eggs
½ teaspoon baking soda
2 tablespoons water
½ pound ground cooked pork
2 tablespoons chopped ham
¼ cup chopped mushrooms
2 teaspoons soy sauce
½ teaspoon salt
¼ teaspoon pepper
8 cups stock or canned consommé

Sift the flour onto a board and make a well in the center. Place the eggs in it. Dissolve the baking soda in the water and add to the well. Work in the flour, kneading until a stiff dough is formed. Roll out, fold over and roll out again, repeating each step 10 times. Roll out as thin as possible, and cut into 2″ squares.

Mix together the pork, ham, mushrooms, soy sauce, salt and pepper. Place a teaspoon of the mixture on each square. Fold over the dough, and seal the edges well.

Drop into the boiling stock, and boil for 15 minutes. Serve in the soup.

## Pizzaiola Sauce

¼ cup olive oil
2 cloves garlic, minced
1 #2½ can tomatoes
½ teaspoon salt
¼ teaspoon dried ground red peppers
1 teaspoon oregano
2 tablespoons chopped parsley

Heat the olive oil in a saucepan. Add the garlic, and sauté for 3 minutes, stirring frequently. Add the tomatoes, salt, dried peppers and oregano. Cook over high heat for 15 minutes, stirring frequently. Remove sauce from the heat and add the parsley. Serve with pasta, fish or steak.

## Marinara Sauce

½ cup olive oil
2 cloves garlic, minced
2 pounds tomatoes, peeled and chopped
3 tablespoons chopped parsley
1½ teaspoons salt
½ teaspoon freshly ground black pepper
½ teaspoon oregano

Heat the olive oil in a saucepan. Sauté the garlic for 5 minutes, stirring frequently. Add the tomatoes, parsley, salt, pepper and oregano. Cook over very low heat for 30 minutes, stirring occasionally. Correct seasoning. Serve with any pasta.

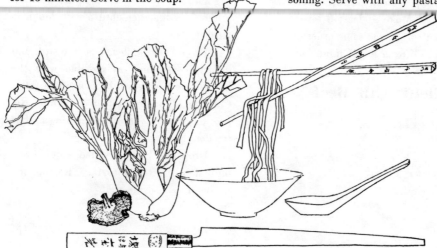

## Meat Sauce

½ cup olive oil
3 onions, chopped
2 cloves garlic, minced
½ pound ground beef
1 #2½ can tomatoes
   (Italian style, if available)
2 tablespoons tomato paste
2 teaspoons salt
½ teaspoon freshly ground black pepper
⅛ teaspoon dried ground red peppers
⅛ teaspoon sugar
1 bay leaf
½ teaspoon basil
3 tablespoons chopped parsley

Heat the olive oil in a saucepan. Sauté the onions and garlic for 5 minutes, stirring frequently. Add the beef. Sauté until brown, stirring constantly to prevent lumps from forming. Add the tomatoes, tomato paste, salt, pepper, red peppers, sugar, bay leaf, basil and parsley.

Cook over low heat for 2 hours, stirring frequently. Add a little water if the sauce becomes too thick.

## Tomato Sauce

¼ cup olive oil
2 onions, chopped
2 cloves garlic, minced
1 stalk celery, chopped
2 tablespoons chopped parsley
1 #2½ can tomatoes
   (Italian style, if available)
1 can tomato paste
1 teaspoon salt
½ teaspoon dried ground red peppers
1 teaspoon basil
1 bay leaf
½ pound mushrooms, chopped
¼ pound spinach, chopped
2 tablespoons white wine

Heat the oil in a saucepan. Sauté the onions, garlic, celery and parsley for 10 minutes. Add the tomatoes, tomato paste, salt, dried red peppers, basil and bay leaf. Cook over low heat for 3 hours, adding a little water if the sauce becomes too thick. Add mushrooms, spinach, wine. Cook 30 minutes longer. Correct seasoning. Serve with ravioli, gnocchi or spaghetti.

## Balkan Goulubsky

12 cabbage leaves
5 tablespoons butter
1 onion, chopped
½ pound lean ground pork
¼ pound ground veal
2 hard-cooked eggs, chopped
1½ cups cooked rice
4 tablespoons red wine
3 tablespoons tomato paste
¼ teaspoon black pepper
⅔ cup sour cream

Carefully remove cabbage leaves and place in salted warm water for 2 minutes. Remove and drain well. Melt 2 tablespoons butter and fry onion with pork, veal, chopped hard-cooked eggs and cooked rice for 5 minutes on medium heat. Put some of the mixture on each cabbage leaf, roll up and tie well.

Melt rest of butter in heavy cast-iron casserole and brown cabbage rolls. Sprinkle with wine and cover casserole. Braise very slowly for 40 minutes. Meanwhile mix tomato paste with black pepper and sour cream. Simmer 7 minutes in heavy skillet. Pour over cabbage rolls and serve immediately. Serves 4-6.

## Indonesian Nasi Goreng

6 tablespoons butter
¾ cup chicken livers
1¾ cups rice
1 teaspoon chili powder
1 teaspoon salt
2½ cups water

*1 cup mixed sliced celery and onion*
*½ cup sliced zucchini or similar vegetable*
*1 medium cucumber, sliced*
*¾ cup shrimp, cooked*
*5 fried eggs*

Melt butter in casserole and add chicken livers. Fry for 3 minutes and add rice. Cook, stirring often, till rice has absorbed butter. Sprinkle on chili powder and salt. Pour on water. Put lid on casserole and cook on low fire for 25 to 30 minutes. Halfway through cooking, add sliced vegetables and shrimp and cover again.

Before serving, add eggs, fried hard, under and on rice. This is one variation of nasi goreng. Serves 4-6.

## Liver and Rice

*3 tablespoons butter*
*2 pounds calves liver or chicken livers*
*3 onions, cut in rings*
*1¼ pounds rice*
*¾ teaspoon salt*
*½ teaspoon oregano*
*¼ teaspoon black pepper*
*½ pound lean bacon, fried*

Melt butter, and fry well washed and dried liver. After 10 minutes add ¾ cup water and simmer till tender. Reserve. Fry onions and also reserve.

Cook rice in water with salt. In a casserole arrange a layer of liver, sprinkle over it a pinch of oregano and pepper, a few onion rings, a few chips of bacon and rice. Repeat till all ingredients are used. Bake in a preheated 350° oven for ¼ hour. Serve hot. Serves 6.

## Risotto Milanese

*1 medium size onion*
*½ cup butter*
*¼ cup chopped beef marrow*
*1 lb. rice*

*⅛ teaspoon powdered Spanish saffron*
*¼ cup white wine*
*3 cups rich chicken stock*
*Salt, pepper*
*1 cup grated Parmesan cheese*

Chop onion and cook until golden in ¼ cup butter with the beef marrow. Add rice and cook, stirring, until lightly colored—about 15 minutes. Add saffron dissolved in white wine and chicken stock. Salt and pepper to taste. Simmer until the rice is soft and the liquid absorbed. Remove from heat and stir in another ¼ cup butter and the Parmesan cheese. Serves 6.

## Risotto Parmigiana

*½ lb. chicken livers*
*½ cup chopped onion*
*½ cup butter*
*1 lb. rice*
*3 cups chicken stock*
*Salt, pepper*
*1½ cups freshly grated aged Parmesan*

Cut chicken livers in quarters and cook with chopped onion in ¼ cup of butter. Add rice and cook 5 minutes, stirring. Stir in stock and cook until the rice is tender and the liquid absorbed. Correct seasoning and stir in another ¼ cup of butter and the aged Parmesan. Serves 6.

## French Piemontaise Risotto Gourmet

*6 tablespoons butter*
*2 medium onions, minced*
*1 pound rice*
*1 quart consommé*
*¼ teaspoon pepper*
*½ teaspoon salt*
*8 tablespoons Parmesan cheese*

Warm 4 tablespoons butter in a casserole. Add minced onion, cook and stir till brown. Add rice and cook it till it has absorbed butter. Add consommé to rice in four parts, stirring and cooking till it has absorbed consommé each time, also adding salt and pepper. When all consommé has been added, cook rice covered—this is the authentic way to make a risotto. When rice is done, add remaining butter and cheese. Finish this recipe, if desired, with delicate slivers of white truffles or smoked ham.

Prepare the Piemontaise. Mash 3 tablespoons white truffles, and arrange with risotto in a timbale mold.

Thoroughly wash and thinly slice 6 kidneys. Season with salt and pepper, dredge with flour and sauté in butter. Remove kidneys, scrape pan and add to scrapings 5 to 6 tablespoons demi-glacé sauce (stock reduced to a thick semi-liquid consistency) and 2¼ tablespoons Madeira. Mix well and arrange on top of risotto Piemontaise. Sprinkle on 1½ tablespoons melted butter. Place some sliced black truffles on top. Bake in 375° oven for 9 to 12 minutes. Serves 6.

Mushrooms of two different kinds can be substituted for truffles, but use the latter if you can get them. There is a big difference.

## Arroz Con Pollo

*4 tablespoons olive oil*
*1 large clove garlic, diced*
*2 medium onions, chopped*
*3-pound chicken, cut in 12 pieces*
*3 tomatoes, diced*
*Pinch of cayenne*
*1 teaspoon salt*
*¾ pound rice*
*1¾ cups water*
*Pinch of saffron*

Melt 2 tablespoons oil and sauté diced garlic. When brown, remove and discard garlic. Put in onions and fry until dark gold. Add rest of oil and fry chicken for 15 minutes. Remove and place in Dutch oven with onions on top. Add diced tomatoes, sprinkle on cayenne and salt. Add rice, 1¾ cups water and saffron. Cover and simmer over low heat until chicken is tender. Remove cover, let rice dry off a little and serve hot. Serves 4-6.

## Paella à la Valenciana

*2 pounds lobster (whole or claws only)*
*1 pound raw mussels, in shells*
*20 small clams, in shells*
*½ cup olive oil*
*1½ cloves garlic, minced fine*
*6 medium onions, sliced*
*8 medium tomatoes*
*Pinch of oregano*
*2 sweet green peppers, chopped*
*3 cups rice*
*Chicken stock or water*
*½ teaspoon saffron strands*
*¼ teaspoon black pepper*
*½ teaspoon salt*
*½ pound raw shelled shrimp*
*½ pound cooked crab meat, fresh or frozen*
*4 canned pimentos, cut in strips*
*1 package frozen peas, cooked*

Cook lobster briefly until it turns red. Crack claws and reserve. Scrub mussels and clams well with a wire brush under cold running water. Heat oil in a deep flameproof casserole or Dutch oven and add garlic. Put in lobster and fry over fairly high heat, turning continually. After 5 minutes add onions, sliced medium, tomatoes, cut in wedges, oregano and chopped green pepper and cook for a few minutes. Add rice and enough stock or water to cover by 1". Add saffron, pepper and salt and cook for 10 minutes. Add mussels, clams and shrimp, adding more liquid if necessary, cover and cook over very low heat for 10 minutes. Now place crab meat deep in center of rice. Cover tightly and leave over lowest heat for 8 minutes. Serve with strips of pimento and cooked peas on top of rice. Serves 10. This is one version of paella, which differs in various regions of Spain. Other recipes call for the inclusion of sliced hot Spanish sausage (chorizo), diced ham, chicken cut in serving pieces and sautéed, artichoke hearts. The paella can be cooked in a deep earthenware casserole or in the large shallow Spanish steel pan called a *paella*, such as the one which is shown in the cover photograph.

## Elena's Rice-Cheese-Chili Casserole

*3 cups cooked rice*
*2 cups sour cream*
*½ teaspoon salt*
*½ lb. Monterey Jack cheese*
*4-ounce can peeled green chili peppers*
*Butter*

Mix rice with sour cream and salt and arrange half of it in a layer in a well-buttered 8" x 8" baking dish. Cut Monterey Jack cheese in small oblongs (about 1½" x 1" x ½") and wrap each piece in a strip of peeled green chili pepper. Each chili should be rinsed of seeds and cut into 3 lengthwise strips. Arrange cheese and chili bundles in a layer on the rice, cover with the remaining rice mixture, sprinkle the top with a little more grated cheese and dot with butter. Bake at 350° for about ½ hour, or until well heated. Serves 6.

# VEGETABLE

# Vegetable

The powerful virtues of vegetables were recognized by the Greeks and Romans to whom the pungency of a vegetable was a guarantee of its effectiveness. Nero ate leeks to improve his voice and garlic was given to soldiers to excite their courage, to gamecocks to make them fight and to laborers for strength. (The Egyptians were evidently of same opinion, for we are told that the building budget for the Great Pyramid included 1,600 talents' worth of garlic, onions and radishes for the workers.) Cabbage, the people's panacea for anything from drunkenness to baldness, practically put the Roman physicians (who doubled as barbers) out of business, and Tiberius introduced the forcing of vegetables because of his fondness for cucumbers out of season. Beans had their own peculiar powers in the fields of religion and politics. Light and dark broad beans were used to elect magistrates in an early version of the blackball. Centuries later the Massachusetts Bay Colony fathers found this a handy means of balloting. Their records state, "It is ordered that for the yearly choosing of assistants, the freemen shall use Indian beans, the white to manifest election, the black for blank."

Most of the vegetables we know today are mentioned in John Gerard's sixteenth-century *Herbal or Historie of Plantes* (peas were considered "a dainty dish for a lady—they come so far and cost so dear") and were highly prized by our ancestors. Notable exceptions were the tomato, eggplant and potato which belong to the nightshade family and were therefore supposed to cause death or insanity (the eggplant was nicknamed the "mad apple"). It was left to the French, true vegetable lovers, to save the tomato and the potato from ill repute and oblivion. The tomato was christened *pomme d'amour* or love apple (a happy translation of the Italian, *pomo de Mori*, apple of the Moors, and a far cry from the original Aztec *tomatl*) and became the rage of the salons. Parmentier, the 18th century physician

246

and agronomist whose name is synonymous with potato in France, popularized the disdained root. It received a royal accolade when Louis XVI wore a potato flower as a boutonnière.

This tender regard of the French for the virtues of the vegetable is shown in their cuisine. The freshest and youngest vegetables are chosen to be blanched, braised or gently simmered until they reach the point of perfection, never savagely boiled to a soggy death in the Anglo-Saxon manner. The Chinese, also respecters of vegetables, precook them rapidly in hot fat and then steam them with a little water to preserve their crispness and flavor.

Half the success of vegetable cooking lies with the vegetables themselves. A stale vegetable is a sad and sorry thing of little or no worth. It is false economy to buy old, stale or wilted vegetables when there are young, fresh ones to be had. You can always judge the freshness of a vegetable by its texture and appearance. It should be crisp, plump and well-colored rather than dry, soft, bruised and faded. The younger the vegetable, the less time it takes to cook. All vegetables are best boiled quickly in a small amount of salted water with perhaps a little lemon juice added to green vegetables to keep the color and vitamin content, except for cauliflower. This needs to be cooked uncovered in large amounts of boiling water to eliminate cooking odors.

We are often admonished to be kind to animals. Let us also be kind to vegetables and enjoy at every meal the rewards of our benevolence.

## Asparagus with Maltese Sauce

*1 large bunch of asparagus*
*2 large slices of bread, fried in bacon fat*
*3 egg yolks*
*Salt, cayenne pepper*
*2 tablespoons tarragon vinegar*
*2 tablespoons cream*
*2 tablespoons whipped cream*
*1 tablespoon orange juice*
*Grated rind of a large orange*
*6 ounces butter*

Scrape the asparagus stalks and cut off the hard ends. Tie securely and cook until tender in boiling salted water (about 15 minutes). Drain carefully. Place the fried bread on a hot flat oval serving dish. Carefully place the asparagus on the top, remove the string. Make following sauce:

Put into a china bowl the egg yolks, salt, cayenne pepper and the vinegar. Beat well. Stir in the cream and whipped cream, orange juice and rind. Place the bowl in a pan of hot water and beat with a whisk over a low fire until it begins to thicken. Add the butter bit by bit. Pour over the asparagus. Brown quickly under the broiler and serve. Serves 4.

## Peas à la Bonne Femme

*Heart of lettuce*
*3-4 lbs. peas*
*3 tablespoons butter*
*2 ounces bacon, sliced*
*1 dozen scallions*
*1 tablespoon flour*
*1½ cups stock*
*Bouquet of herbs*
*Salt and pepper*

Shred the lettuce and shell the peas. Melt the butter in a casserole, put in the sliced bacon and the scallions, and shake over the fire until scallions just turn golden. Stir in

the flour, add the lettuce, pour on the stock, and bring to a boil. Simmer for a few minutes, put in the peas with the herb bouquet and seasonings. Cook gently 20-30 minutes, stirring frequently. Remove the bouquet and serve in the casserole. Serves 4.

## Peas Scoville

*1 cup small pearl onions*
*2 cups shelled peas*
*½ lb. small white mushrooms*
*Lemon juice*
*4 tablespoons olive oil*
*Salt and pepper*

Put the onions in cold water, bring to a boil and drain. Blanch peas in the same way. Wash the mushrooms in lemon juice and water, cut in thick slices and sauté in the hot oil. Add the peas, onions, salt and pepper. Cover with the lid and cook over a slow fire for 10-15 minutes, shaking occasionally, until the peas are soft but not mushy. Serve in a casserole. Serves 4.

## Braised Endive with Ham

8 stalks endive
6 slices bacon
1 cup finely sliced onion, carrot, celery
Bay leaf, peppercorns, salt
2 cups strong beef stock
8 slices boiled ham
Lemon juice
3 ounces sweet butter
4 level tablespoons flour
Salt and pepper
1¼ cups creamy milk
1 cup freshly grated Gruyère cheese
2 egg yolks
¼ cup light cream
1 cup whipped cream

Bring the endive to a boil in water with a little vinegar. Drain and dry well. Place 3 slices of bacon on the bottom of a deep dish. Scatter half the sliced vegetables over the bacon. Arrange the drained endive on top of the vegetables. Cover with the rest of the vegetables. Scatter over them a few peppercorns, bay leaf and a little salt. Place the rest of the bacon on top. Pour on the strong stock, cover with greased wax paper. Braise in a 400° oven for 1 hour, basting frequently. Remove the endive, strain the stock, boil it down to 1 tablespoon and set aside. Carefully wrap each endive in a slice of boiled ham. Arrange down the length of a hot serving dish. Sprinkle with a little lemon juice and pour over the following sauce:

Melt 2 tablespoons of butter in a pan, stir in the flour, off the fire, season with salt and pepper. Pour on the creamy milk and stir over the fire until the mixture comes to a boil. Add the reduced beef stock and half the grated cheese. Simmer 5 minutes. Mix the egg yolks with the light cream and add to the sauce with the whipped cream. Pour sauce over the endive and sprinkle with the remaining cheese. Dot with butter and brown quickly under the broiler. Serves 4.

## Celery Amandine

4 cups young celery stalks, diced
Salt and pepper
8 tablespoons butter
2 tablespoons finely chopped fresh chives
2 tablespoons grated onion
1 cup blanched, shredded almonds
½ teaspoon finely chopped garlic
2 tablespoons dry white wine

Dice the celery stalks, wash and drain and put them into a pan. Season lightly with salt and pepper and add 4 tablespoons of butter. Cover the pan closely and cook very slowly until the celery is tender, shaking the pan frequently to prevent scorching. During cooking, sprinkle the celery with the chives and onion. When celery is cooked, arrange it on a small oval serving dish. Melt the rest of the butter in a shallow, heavy pan, add the blanched, shredded almonds and shake them over a medium fire until brown. Then add the chopped garlic, salt, pepper, and the white wine. Cook for 1 minute, pour over the celery and serve at once. Serves 4.

## Stuffed Artichokes Barigoule

6 tender young artichokes
3 ounces salt butter
½ lb. finely chopped bacon
1 cup finely chopped onions
¼ cup finely chopped shallots
4 cloves garlic, minced
½ lb. finely chopped mushrooms
1 teaspoon meat glaze (Bovril or B-V or glace de viande)
Salt, pepper, nutmeg
2 tablespoons chopped parsley
4 tablespoons moist bread crumbs
2 egg yolks
12 slices bacon
¼ cup olive oil
1 sliced white onion

*2 small carrots, diced*
*½ cup dry white wine*
*1 cup water*
*1 tablespoon flour*
*1 tablespoon tomato paste*
*1 tomato, skinned, seeded, shredded*
*6 whole sautéed mushroom caps*
*Chopped parsley*

Cut the tips off the artichoke leaves, turn them leaf side up on a chopping board and press the leaves open. Carefully remove the choke. Put the artichokes into boiling water for 2 minutes. Drain and dry. Spread leaves out around the center, season inside with salt and pepper and put a small lump of butter inside each artichoke. Heat a shallow, heavy skillet and put the chopped bacon, onion, shallots and 2 cloves of garlic in it. Cook until they are about half done, add the chopped mushrooms and cook for 2-3 minutes longer. Add the meat glaze and season with salt, pepper and nutmeg. Add the chopped parsley, bread crumbs and the egg yolks. Mix well and fill center of artichokes with this mixture. Tie one strip of bacon around the middle and one over the top of each artichoke. Put a few spoonfuls of oil in the bottom of a heavy casserole, add the sliced onion and the carrots and place the artichokes on top. Sprinkle with salt, pepper, nutmeg and a little more olive oil. Cover the casserole. Bake in a 300° oven, shaking occasionally. When the vegetables begin to brown, add 2 more cloves of minced garlic, white wine and water. Cook covered until the artichokes are tender. Remove from oven, take off the bacon, arrange on a hot, flat serving dish and pour over the following sauce:

Melt 3 tablespoons of butter in a pan. Stir in the flour and the tomato paste off the fire. Strain and add the liquid from the vegetables and stir over the fire until it comes to a boil. Add the rest of the butter, bit by bit, and if you want, a little more

chopped garlic. Add the tomato and pour sauce over the stuffed artichokes. Garnish the tops with the mushroom caps and finely chopped parsley. Serves 6.

## Fennel with Mustard Sauce

*4 stalks fennel*
*1½ tablespoons butter*
*Salt and pepper*
*1 tablespoon flour*
*2 teaspoons dry mustard*
*1 cup fennel liquid*
*2 teaspoons chopped, fresh dill*
*1 tablespoon cream*
*Parmesan cheese, grated*

Split the fennel in half, blanch and drain, reserving the liquid. Return fennel to pan with ½ tablespoon butter, salt and pepper. Cover and cook slowly until tender.
Sauce: Melt 1 tablespoon butter, stir in flour, mustard, salt and pepper. Pour on 1 cup reserved liquid. Stir over the fire until the sauce comes to a boil. Add chopped dill and cream.

Arrange fennel on a flat serving dish, pour over the sauce, sprinkle with cheese. Brown under the broiler. Serves 4.

## Corn Fritters

*6 fresh ears of corn*
*4 rounded tablespoons flour*
*¼ teaspoon baking powder*
*½ teaspoon nutmeg*
*Salt, cayenne pepper to taste*
*2 large eggs*

1 cup sour cream
2 tablespoons melted butter, cooled
½ teaspoon German mustard

Remove all the green leaves and silk from the corn cobs, then place on the bottom of a deep, hot pan, and moisten with boiling water. Rub the corn with a little salt and place it on top of the greens and silk. Cover the pan and steam very quickly for 5-6 minutes, shaking frequently. Remove the corn cobs and carefully take off all the corn kernels. Set aside, and allow to get quite cold. Put the flour, baking powder, nutmeg, salt and pepper in a small bowl with 1 whole egg and the yolk of 1 separated egg, half of the cream, and the cold melted butter. Beat with a wire whisk until quite smooth. It should have the consistency of thick cream. If too thick, thin with a little milk. Mix in the German mustard, chill for ½ hour. Mix in the corn, and lastly mix in the well beaten egg white. Heat a heavy cast-iron or aluminum skillet. When very hot, rub with a piece of well-buttered paper. Drop in teaspoons of the mixture about the size of a silver dollar, brown on one side (they brown very quickly), turn over and brown on the other side. Drain on paper towels and keep hot in the oven with the door open. Serve at once on a hot flat serving dish. Serves 4.

## Lima Beans Poulette

3 lbs. young lima beans
2 tablespoons butter
1 tablespoon flour
¾ cup stock
Lemon juice
1 tablespoon cream
1 egg yolk
1 tablespoon finely chopped parsley

Shell the beans and simmer in salted water for about 15 minutes. Strain and return to the pan. Melt the butter in a saucepan, add the flour, pour on the stock and lemon juice, and bring to a boil. Take off the fire and stir in the cream, yolk and parsley. Season well, pour over the beans, and shake over the fire for a few minutes without boiling. Serves 6.

## Green Beans Parisienne

1 lb. young green beans
3 ounces butter
4 tablespoons water
1 teaspoon lemon juice
1 teaspoon salt
½ teaspoon cayenne pepper
1 cup blanched shredded almonds
1 teaspoon chopped fresh garlic

Top and tail the beans. Cut in very thin slices diagonally. Put in cold water and bring slowly to a boil. Drain. Melt half the butter in a very heavy pan. Add the water, lemon juice, salt and pepper. Add the beans, cover and cook gently, stirring occasionally, until just soft (approximately 20 minutes). In another pan melt the rest of the butter, add the blanched shredded almonds and brown slowly. Add the chopped garlic. Put the beans in a serving dish and pour over the almonds, garlic and butter. Serves 4.

## Cucumbers Neapolitan

3 tablespoons butter
1 onion, chopped
12 scallions
2 small cucumbers

*Salt and pepper*
*3 tablespoons flour*
*½ cup stock or water*
*2 teaspoons chopped mint*
*4 tomatoes*

Melt the butter in a casserole, add the chopped onion, the scallions, the cucumbers, peeled and cut in half lengthwise and then into ½" pieces, salt and pepper. Cover and simmer very slowly, stirring frequently, for 7 minutes. Remove from fire and stir in the flour. Moisten with the stock, add the mint and simmer for 15 minutes more. Skin, quarter and seed the tomatoes; add them and cook for another minute or two. Serve in the casserole. Serves 4.

## Eggplant Bordelaise

*3 medium eggplants*
*1½ cups olive oil*
*1 ounce dried mushrooms*
*½ cup finely chopped shallots*
*4 large cloves of garlic, chopped*
*Salt, black pepper*
*1 tablespoon French mustard*
*½ cup chopped Hamburg parsley*
*6 firm tomatoes, skinned*
*¼ cup melted butter*
*1 cup fried bread crumbs*

Skin the eggplants, cut them into slices a little less than ½" thick, spread them on a platter, sprinkle well with salt and leave for half an hour. Rinse under cold water and dry well on a cloth. Heat a little of the oil in a shallow, heavy skillet and fry the eggplant slices until golden brown on each side, a few at a time. Remove and keep warm on a hot flat serving dish. Soak the dried mushrooms in a little water. When soft, drain and chop finely. Add these chopped mushrooms to the olive oil in the skillet. Then add the shallots, garlic, and seasoning. Cook for 5-6 minutes, then add

the Hamburg parsley (a type of flat-leaf parsley with a slight celery flavor). Cut the tomatoes in thirds, and arrange them on top of the eggplant. Add ¼ cup of melted butter to the mixture in the skillet and pour it over the tomatoes. Sprinkle with the fried bread crumbs and bake for 10 minutes in a 400° oven. Serve hot. Serves 4-6.

## Eggplant with Mushroom and Cheese Filling

*2 eggplants*
*Salt and pepper*
*4 tablespoons oil*
*2 sliced onions*
*6 tablespoons butter*
*3 tablespoons flour*
*Cayenne pepper*
*¾ cup milk*
*4 tablespoons grated Gruyère and Parmesan cheeses, mixed*
*¼ cup cream*
*1 teaspoon dry mustard*
*6 sliced mushrooms*

Cut the eggplants in half and make a few incisions in the pulp with a sharp knife. Sprinkle well with salt and let stand for half an hour. Drain out the water and salt and dry on a cloth. Dust the cut surface lightly with flour. Heat oil in frying pan and add eggplants, cut side down. Cover with lid and cook slowly for 10 minutes on each side.

Cook the onions slowly in a little butter, salt and pepper until soft, but not brown. Melt 2 tablespoons butter in a pan. Remove from the fire and add the flour, salt and cayenne pepper. Stir in the milk and stir over the fire until boiling. Add 2 tablespoons grated cheese, 3 tablespoons cream and the dry mustard. Add to the onions. Add a little extra cheese and the mushrooms, sautéed in a little butter.

Scoop out the meat from the fried egg-plants, chop roughly in a wooden bowl and add to the mixture. Fill the eggplant skins. Sprinkle well with the remaining grated cheese. Melt the remaining butter and pour over the top. Brown under the broiler. Just before serving pour over the remaining cream, seasoned with a little salt. Serves 4.

## Zucchini Provençale

*2 lbs. small zucchini*
*¼ cup finely chopped shallots*
*3 ounces salt butter*
*6 small tomatoes, skinned,*
  *seeded and quartered*
*2 tablespoons olive oil*
*Salt and pepper to taste*
*2 teaspoons chopped garlic*
*1 finely chopped green pepper*
*½ cup grated Parmesan cheese*
*2 tablespoons chopped parsley*

Wash the zucchini and cut them into slices about ½″ thick. Place in cold water, bring to a boil and drain. Slowly sauté the shallots in a little butter in the bottom of an earthenware casserole until golden. Arrange the tomatoes on top and pour over the olive oil. Sprinkle with salt and pepper, garlic and green pepper. Cover the casserole and cook over a very low flame for 15 minutes. Re-

move the cover and arrange the zucchini on the top. Melt the remaining butter and pour half over the zucchini. Cover again and cook gently over a low flame until the zucchini is just tender. Sprinkle the top with the Parmesan cheese and the chopped parsley. Pour over the rest of the melted butter and serve in the casserole. Serves 4.

## Baked Acorn
## Squash Martinique

*4 medium sized acorn squash*
*3 ounces butter*
*Salt, freshly cracked pepper*
*Ground ginger*
*1½ cups warm chicken stock*
*2 large beef marrow bones*
*½ cup cognac*
*2 tablespoons creamed butter, mixed with*
  *1 tablespoon German mustard*

Wash the squash but do not peel. Cut in half and carefully remove the seeds. Coat the insides heavily with melted butter, and season with salt, pepper and a little ginger. Put the prepared squash cut side up in a shallow baking dish and pour the warm stock around it. Bake in a 350° oven for 1 hour or until the squash is very brown and tender. Meanwhile cook the marrow bones in boiling salted water for

253

20 minutes, cool, and carefully remove the marrow. Cut marrow into 1″ slices. About 8 minutes before removing the squash from the oven, garnish each half with 3-4 slices of the marrow. Pour over each a little cognac, sprinkle with a little more salt and freshly ground black pepper. Just before serving, dot with the creamed butter mixed with the mustard. Serve very hot. Serves 4

## Squash Rice Bombe

2 cups cooked rice
1 tablespoon Madeira
3 tablespoons butter
2 onions, minced
2 tablespoons shredded green pepper
½ teaspoon pepper
8 big zucchini or similar squash
2 tablespoons heavy cream
4 tomatoes, chopped
¾ teaspoon salt

When cooking rice, add 1 tablespoon Madeira. Reserve rice. Melt butter and sauté minced onions, shredded pepper and cooked rice seasoned with pepper. Cut zucchini in halves lengthwise, and hollow out, reserving pulp. Stuff zucchini with rice and onion mixture, adding a little cream to stuffing. Skewer halves tightly or tie together.

Mix chopped tomatoes with zucchini pulp and salt, add just enough water to enable mixture to ½ cover zucchini (for acorn squash, use enough water to ⅔ cover). Bring mixture to a boil in a heavy cast-iron casserole, put in zucchini and cook covered till almost dry. Serve hot. Serves 8.

## Stuffed Peppers

6 small green peppers
Butter
Salt, black pepper

2 ounces butter
1 cup raw rice
2½ cups chicken stock
2 cups finely chopped sautéed onion
1 cup chopped, sautéed mushrooms
1 cup chopped, cooked ham
2 cups cooked vegetables (carrots, green beans, turnips) diced, chopped and mixed
2 cups light beef stock
1 tablespoon flour
2 tablespoons tomato paste
¼ teaspoon sugar
1 clove of garlic, crushed
1 tablespoon chopped parsley

Carefully remove the tops of the peppers. Remove seeds. Put peppers into boiling water and leave for 5 minutes. Drain and dry. Place a small lump of butter in the bottom of each pepper and season with salt and pepper. Fill with the following mixture: Melt 1 ounce butter in a pan. Add the rice and cover with the chicken stock. Season with salt and pepper. Stir over the fire until the mixture comes to a boil; reduce the heat, cover the pan, and cook slowly for 35 minutes. Mix in the onions, mushrooms, ham and vegetables. Season well and use to fill the peppers. Replace the pepper caps and arrange on a flat, fireproof dish. Pour over the beef stock and bake in a moderate oven for 30-35 minutes, basting frequently. Arrange the peppers on a dish. Melt the rest of the butter in a pan; stir in the flour and the tomato paste. Add the strained beef stock. Stir over the fire until the sauce comes to a boil; add the sugar, crushed garlic and a small lump of butter. Simmer for 5 minutes; pour over the peppers, sprinkle with chopped parsley. Serves 6.

## Spinach with Mornay Sauce

2 lbs. spinach
4 tablespoons butter
Salt and pepper

*1 cup croutons (small bread cubes, fried in
    butter until golden)*
*2 tablespoons flour*
*Cayenne pepper*
*1 cup milk*
*½ teaspoon dry mustard*
*3 tablespoons Parmesan cheese*
*2 tablespoons Gruyere cheese*
*3 tablespoons cream*

Wash the spinach well. Drain well and put into a pan with 1 tablespoon butter, salt and pepper. Cook slowly for 6 to 7 minutes, stirring occasionally. Drain well. Chop coarsely in a wooden bowl; mix in the croutons; arrange on a flat dish. Melt 2 tablespoons butter in a pan. Stir in the flour, salt and cayenne pepper until the mixture is smooth; add the milk. Stir over the fire until the mixture comes to a boil. Add mustard, 2 tablespoons Parmesan cheese, Gruyère cheese and cream. Simmer slowly for 8 to 9 minutes. Pour over the spinach and sprinkle the top with the remaining Parmesan cheese. Dot with butter and brown quickly under the broiler. Serves 4.

## Braised Lettuce

*4 firm heads of Boston lettuce*
*3 tablespoons butter*
*2 slices fat bacon*
*1 finely chopped small onion*
*1 finely chopped small carrot*
*¾ cup strong stock*
*Salt and pepper*
*Chopped parsley*

Remove the outside leaves of the lettuce and wash the heads. Place in a pan, cover with cold water and bring to a boil. Drain and put into ice water. Dry with a cloth and cut in half. Butter a fireproof dish well and place the bacon on the bottom. Sprinkle the onion and carrot over the bacon. Place the lettuce on top; pour the stock over the lettuce. Add salt and pepper. Cover with

buttered waxed paper. Cook in a 350° oven for 45 minutes. Remove the lettuce and arrange on a hot dish for serving. Strain and reduce the liquid in which lettuce was cooked. Pour it over the lettuce and sprinkle with chopped parsley just before serving. Serves 4.

## Broccoli Sauce Béarnaise

*1 bunch broccoli*
*Juice ½ lemon*
*3 egg yolks*
*1 tablespoon tarragon vinegar*
*2 tablespoons cream*
*Salt and cayenne pepper*
*4 tablespoons butter*
*2 tablespoons mixed fresh herbs—parsley,
    tarragon, chives, thyme, basil*
*¼ teaspoon finely chopped garlic*
*1 teaspoon finely chopped onion*
*1 teaspoon finely chopped green olive*
*¼ teaspoon meat glaze (Bovril or B-V)*

Wash the broccoli well. Drop into a pan of boiling salted water with the lemon juice. Cook until just soft. Drain well and arrange carefully on a hot serving dish. Make the following sauce:

    Mix well in a bowl the egg yolks, tarragon vinegar, cream, salt and cayenne pepper. Place this bowl in a shallow pan of hot water over a slow fire. Stir until the mixture begins to thicken. Add bit by bit, the butter. Mix in the herbs, garlic, onion, olive and meat glaze. Pour over the broccoli and serve at once. Serves 4.

## Brussels Sprouts and Braised Chestnuts

*1½ lbs. chestnuts*
*4 tablespoons oil*
*1 sliced onion*
*1 sliced carrot*
*1 small stalk celery, sliced*
*1 sliced clove garlic*
*3 tablespoons flour*
*A few mushroom peelings and stalks*
*1 teaspoon tomato paste*
*2 cups strong stock*
*¼ cup red wine*
*1 tablespoon sherry*
*1 tablespoon red currant jelly*
*1 bay leaf*
*Salt and pepper*
*Butter*
*1 lb. Brussels sprouts*
*1 teaspoon lemon juice*

Put the chestnuts in a pan and cover with cold water. Bring to a boil and boil for 6 to 7 minutes. Then remove both inner and outer skins and brown quickly in a little hot oil. Remove from the oil. Place the onion, carrot, celery, and garlic in the pan and brown slowly. Add flour and brown very slowly. Add the mushroom peelings and stalks and cook for another 1 to 2 minutes. Add the tomato paste and stock and stir until smooth. Stir over the fire until the mixture comes to a boil. Add the red wine, sherry, jelly and bay leaf. Simmer until reduced to a creamy consistency; add salt and pepper. Strain the mixture and put the chestnuts in it. Simmer very gently until the chestnuts are just cooked. If the liquid becomes too thick, add a little more stock.

Wash the Brussels sprouts well and bring to a boil in cold water. Drain and return to the pan with a little butter, lemon juice and 2 tablespoons water. Season, cover with the lid and cook gently until just soft. Do not overcook. Add them at the last moment to the chestnuts. Serve in a casserole. Serves 4.

## Carrots Flamande

*1 lb. tiny, new carrots*
*¼ cup cold water*
*4 ounces salt butter*
*Salt and sugar to taste*
*3 large egg yolks*
*½ cup heavy cream*
*2 tablespoons melted sweet butter*
*1 tablespoon finely chopped parsley*
*Few drops of lemon juice*

Blanch the carrots in boiling water for 5 minutes. Hold them under cold, running water and slip off the thin skins. Trim carrots, leaving them whole. Put them into a well buttered casserole. Add the water and 4 ounces salt butter and season with salt and sugar. Cover the casserole and bring to a boil. Reduce the heat and continue to cook the carrots for 25 minutes or longer—until they are tender. Shake the carrots every 5 minutes to prevent scorching. Mix the egg yolks with the heavy cream and the melted sweet butter. Add the chopped parsley and lemon juice and mix well together. Add to the casserole, stir gently, and serve at once. Serves 4.

## Carrots Vichy

*1 lb. young carrots*
*Salt, pepper*
*Sugar*
*¼ cup butter*
*½ cup finely chopped parsley*
*Juice of 1 lemon*

Scrape the carrots, soak in ice water for 1 hour. Drain and dry. Cut into very thin slices. Drop in boiling water and leave for 5 minutes. Drain well. Butter a casserole, put half of the sliced carrots in it, season with salt, pepper and sugar and add a small amount of water. Dot with half the butter and add half the chopped parsley. Add the rest of the carrots, dot with the rest of the butter and pour over the lemon juice. Cover the casserole and cook very slowly until the carrots are just tender. Add the rest of the parsley, a little more sugar, mix well, and serve in a hot vegetable dish. Serves 4.

## Oyster Plant Italienne

*8 sticks oyster plant*
*Juice ½ lemon*
*2 tablespoons butter*
*1 chopped onion*
*2 chopped mushrooms*
*2 tablespoons cooked chopped ham*
*1 tablespoon flour*
*1 teaspoon tomato paste*
*Salt and pepper*
*¼ cup white wine*
*1 cup stock*
*2 skinned and quartered tomatoes*
*Chopped herbs or parsley*
*Grated Parmesan cheese*

Wash the oyster plant well, trim and scrape. Simmer in boiling salted water with the lemon juice until tender (about 45 to 50 minutes). Melt the butter in a casserole. Add the onion, mushrooms, and ham. Cook slowly for 7 to 10 minutes, stirring frequently. Remove from the fire, mix in the flour, tomato paste, seasoning, wine and stock. Bring slowly to a boil and simmer for 15 to 20 minutes with the lid off. Add the oyster plant and tomatoes and cook for 5 minutes. Sprinkle with the chopped herbs or parsley. Serve with Parmesan cheese. Serves 4.

## Stuffed Onions

*6 small Spanish onions*
*Salt, pepper*
*4 tablespoons butter*
*4 tablespoons flour*
*2 cups cooked, strained spinach*
*½ cup cooked, strained sorrel*
*½ cup sour cream*
*4 mushrooms*
*1 cup heavy cream*
*2 tablespoons butter*
*1 egg yolk*
*1 level teaspoon potato flour*
*1 tablespoon brandy*
*¼ cup grated Gruyère cheese*
*¼ cup grated Parmesan cheese*
*Bread crumbs*
*Chopped parsley*

Skin the onions and parboil them. Remove the center carefully. Season the inside with salt, pepper and a small piece of butter. Melt the rest of the butter in a pan and stir in the flour. Brown slowly and add the spinach and sorrel purées. Add the sour cream, salt and pepper. Cook 5 minutes. Fill the onions with the mixture and arrange them on a hot flat serving dish. Rub the raw mushrooms through a strainer, add to the heavy cream with 2 tablespoons of butter, salt and pepper. Bring quickly to a boil. Mix the egg yolk with the potato flour and brandy. Pour on the cream mixture. Stir until it thickens but do not let it boil. Pour half of this mixture over the onions, sprinkle the top with the grated Gruyère cheese, pour over the rest of the sauce. Sprinkle with the Parmesan cheese and bread crumbs, dot with butter. Brown under the broiler and garnish with chopped parsley. Serve at once. Serves 6; 3 if served as separate course.

## Onions Amandine

½ cup sweet butter
½ cup blanched, shredded almonds
1 tablespoon dark brown sugar
2 teaspoons chopped garlic
½ teaspoon salt
¼ teaspoon black pepper
A little dry white wine
4 dozen small white onions

Melt the butter in a heavy casserole; stir in the almonds and sugar. Add garlic, seasonings and wine. Put in the onions and stir until they are well coated. Cover pan and bake in a 350° oven for 1 hour, shaking every 15 minutes. Serve in the casserole. Serves 6-8.

## Orange Potatoes

2 lbs. old potatoes
Grated rind of 1 large orange
1 large egg
Salt
Black pepper
2 tablespoons butter
2 tablespoons hot milk

Peel the potatoes and cut them in half. Place in a pan and cover with cold water. Season well and bring to a boil. Simmer slowly until soft. Drain and return to the pan to dry over the fire. Put through a ricer or fine strainer. Add the orange rind. Beat in thoroughly one whole egg, salt, black pepper, butter and hot milk. Take a pastry bag with a rose tube attachment, fill with potato mixture and pipe out in small rosettes onto a well greased cookie sheet. Bake in a 400° oven until golden brown. Remove from the oven, carefully slide a spatula under each rosette, and arrange on a hot serving dish. Note: This recipe can also be finished in the following manner: with well-floured hands form the potato mixture into small cork shapes, roll in flour, brush with beaten whole egg, roll in white, dry bread crumbs and fry in hot fat until golden brown. Serves 4.

## Potatoes Anna

2 lbs. old potatoes
Salt and pepper
¾ cup melted butter
French mustard

Butter a shallow tin. Peel the potatoes and cut enough of them in thin slices to line the bottom of the pan, slightly overlapping. Sprinkle with salt and pepper and dot with melted butter. Put a second layer of finely sliced potatoes on top and a little French mustard. Arrange in seasoned layers, until the pan is full. Bake in a 400° oven for 40 to 50 minutes, or until the potatoes begin to come away from the side of the pan. Remove. Slide a thin knife carefully around the side of the pan, give it a small knock on the side of the stove, and turn out on a hot, flat dish. Serves 4.

## Potatoes Mousseline

2 lbs. potatoes
2 egg yolks
2 tablespoons butter
Salt, pepper
½ cup hot milk

Peel the potatoes and cut in half. Put in a pan of cold water with plenty of salt and bring to a boil. Simmer until soft, drain and return to the pan. Dry over the fire. Rice or rub potatoes through a fine strainer. Thoroughly beat in the egg yolks, butter, salt, pepper and milk. The mixture should be of a fairly soft consistency. Serves 4.

## Chef's Potato Cakes

Grate 2 cups of raw potatoes, add two tablespoons of onion chopped fine, a dash each of salt, pepper, thyme, and one well beaten egg. Shape into cakes and either bake on a well greased griddle or fry in deep fat. Serves 4.

## Austrian Potato Cake

1½ lbs. potatoes, boiled
2 tablespoons chopped parsley
1 tablespoon chopped mint
1 tablespoon chopped chives
½ teaspoon dried sage
Dash of dried sweet marjoram
1 tablespoon butter
Salt to taste
Pinch of pepper
½ cup grated cheese
2 eggs, separated

Mash potatoes while still warm. Sauté parsley and herbs in butter. Add to potatoes with salt, pepper and cheese. Gradually stir in egg yolks. Beat egg whites until stiff and fold into potato mixture. Pour into a greased and floured 7″ spring form cake pan. Bake in moderate (375°) oven 35 minutes. Serves 4.

## Italian Potatoes

2 lbs. small potatoes
2 cloves garlic
1 medium onion
1 bunch parsley
2 tablespoons dill
2 tablespoons fat

Wash and peel potatoes. Boil in salted water until almost tender; drain. Chop fine the garlic, onion, parsley, and dill and add to potatoes; sauté in hot fat over a low heat until the potatoes are lightly browned. Serves 6.

## Lorraine Potatoes

2 lbs. potatoes
½ cup hot shortening
1 tablespoon salt
½ cup grated cheese
2 eggs, slightly beaten
1½ cups milk
½ teaspoon nutmeg

Peel and slice potatoes thin. Sauté in fat in a covered saucepan, stirring frequently to prevent burning. Season with salt and place in greased 1½ quart baking dish. Combine cheese, eggs, milk and nutmeg. Pour over potatoes. Cover dish and bake in hot (400°) oven for 10 minutes, or until the bottom is golden brown. Serves 4-6.

## Potato and Onion Casserole

6 medium potatoes
6 medium onions
1 tablespoon chopped parsley
Salt and pepper
Pinch of thyme and sage
2 tablespoons butter or margarine

Peel and slice the potatoes and onions thin. Place a layer of potatoes and onions in a well greased casserole, sprinkling each layer lightly with seasoning and herbs; dot with butter. Repeat until the dish is full. Cover and bake in a slow (300°) oven 1 hour. Uncover; brown under broiler. Serves 6.

## Baked Potato with Herbs

4 *baking potatoes*
4 *tablespoons butter*
2 *tablespoons cream (sweet or sour)*
½ *teaspoon thyme*
½ *teaspoon chervil*
½ *teaspoon chives*
*Salt, pepper*

Bake potatoes until well done. Melt butter, add cream, herbs, salt and pepper. Scoop out inside of potato—mix well with the herb-butter mixture. Refill potatoes lightly and top with either a light sprinkling of paprika or grated cheese. Reheat thoroughly and serve hot. Serves 4.

## Herb Potatoes

10-12 *small new potatoes*
*cooked in their skins*
3 *tablespoons butter or bacon fat*
1 *clove garlic*
1 *teaspoon each of chives, minced **dill**, parsley*
*Freshly ground pepper, salt*

Peel potatoes. Heat the fat with the garlic. Remove garlic clove and brown potatoes evenly. Sprinkle with herbs and seasonings and serve very hot. Serves 4-6.

## Green Potatoes

6 *medium potatoes*
1 *cup finely chopped raw spinach*
1 *cup chopped parsley*
2 *tablespoons shortening*
*Salt, pepper*

Wash, peel and slice potatoes. Boil in salted water until almost tender; drain and dry over heat. Combine spinach and parsley and steam 7 to 10 minutes. Drain and add them to the potatoes. Sauté in hot shortening about 5 minutes. Season well with salt and pepper. Serves 6.

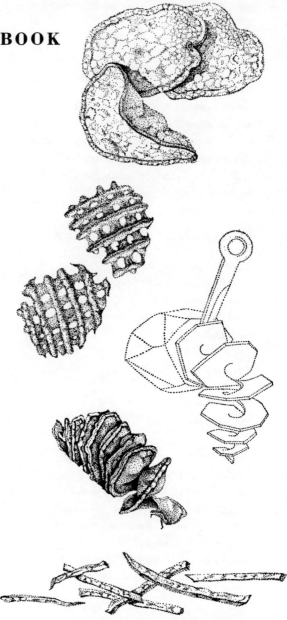

## Garlic-Herb Fried Potatoes

3-4 *medium size potatoes*
4 *tablespoons olive oil*
2 *cloves garlic, crushed*
1 *teaspoon rosemary*
*Salt and freshly ground pepper*
*Dash cayenne pepper*

Peel and slice potatoes. In a skillet heat together the olive oil and garlic. Fry the potato slices a few at a time in the bubbling oil. Push one batch aside to make room for another. Brown slices well on both sides.

Season each batch as it fries with rosemary, salt, pepper. Cooked this way in small amounts potatoes cook quickly. When potatoes are all cooked and tender, drain well on paper and serve very hot. Serves 4.

## Savory Scalloped Potatoes

4 cups sliced cooked potatoes
¼ cup diced onion
¼ cup celery leaves
2 sprigs parsley
3 tablespoons flour
¼ cup butter
1½ teaspoons salt
¼ teaspoon pepper
1½ cups milk
¼ cup grated cheese
Paprika

Place potato in a greased 1-quart baking dish. Place onion, celery, parsley, flour, butter, seasonings, and milk in electric blender. Mix until thoroughly blended, about 1 minute. Pour blended mixture over the potatoes. Sprinkle with grated cheese and paprika. Bake in moderate (350°) oven until bubbling and brown, about 50 minutes. Serves 6.

## Potatoes Chantilly

4 medium size Idaho potatoes
½ cup heavy cream
3 tablespoons butter
Salt and pepper
Chopped parsley
½ cup grated sharp cheese

Peel and cut potatoes into thin strips as for French fries. Place in center of large piece of aluminum foil. Pour over the cream, dot with butter and sprinkle with seasonings, parsley and cheese. Bring foil up over potatoes and seal all edges together to make a tight package. Place on cookie sheet or other shallow pan and bake in a hot (425°) oven for 40 minutes. Serve in the aluminum foil. Potatoes will be deliciously soft with the cream and cheese practically absorbed. Serves 4-6.

## Country Creamed Potatoes

1½ cups light cream
2 tablespoons butter
1 teaspoon onion juice
½ teaspoon salt
⅛ teaspoon pepper
3 cups diced cooked potatoes
Minced parsley

Add cream, butter, onion juice, salt and pepper to potatoes. Cover and simmer 20 to 30 minutes, or until slightly thickened, stirring occasionally. Sprinkle with parsley. Serves 6.

## Caramel Potatoes

2 tablespoons butter
2 tablespoons flour
2 cups milk
½ teaspoon salt
Freshly ground pepper
3 cups raw potatoes, shredded

Make a thin well seasoned white sauce with the butter, flour, milk and seasonings. Add shredded raw potatoes to the hot sauce and pour into a well buttered casserole. Sprinkle with ½ teaspoon salt, pepper and dot generously with butter. Bake at 325° for 3-4 hours or until a caramel-like glaze forms on the potatoes. Serves 4-6.

## Casserole Niçoise

6 potatoes, peeled
  and sliced thin
3 carrots, grated
4 tomatoes, chopped coarsely
2 onions, chopped fine
2 green peppers, sliced thin

2 cloves garlic, minced
3 tablespoons chopped parsley
1½ teaspoons salt
½ teaspoon pepper
½ teaspoon basil
2 cups water
¼ cup olive oil

Arrange the potatoes in a buttered shallow baking dish. Mix the carrots, tomatoes, onions, green peppers, garlic, parsley, salt, pepper, and basil together. Spread over the potatoes and add the water. Bake in a 375° oven for 45 minutes. Sprinkle the olive oil on top and bake 15 minutes longer. Chill and serve in wedges or squares. Serves 6.

## Sweet Potato Soufflé

2 cups of mashed, cooked sweet potatoes
1 cup sour cream
¼ cup cognac
4 tablespoons melted butter
¼ teaspoon cayenne pepper
¼ teaspoon grated nutmeg
½ teaspoon salt
Grated rind of half a lemon
4 egg yolks, well beaten
5 egg whites

Put the potatoes in a bowl and gradually mix in the sour cream and cognac. Add the butter and beat the mixture until quite smooth. Beat in the cayenne pepper, nutmeg, salt and lemon rind. Then mix in the egg yolks. Beat the egg whites until very stiff and carefully fold into the mixture. Pour into a buttered soufflé dish and bake in a 400° oven for 25-30 minutes, or until lightly browned. Serve at once. Serves 4.

## Sherried Sweets

6 medium-size sweet potatoes
¼ cup sugar
Dash of powdered cloves
1 teaspoon grated lemon peel
3 tablespoons butter
¼ cup boiling water
¼ cup sherry

Peel and slice potatoes lengthwise into ½" strips. Arrange in a greased baking dish, sprinkle with sugar, cloves and lemon peel, then dot with butter. Add boiling water, cover and bake until done—about 30 minutes. Ignite sherry and add just before serving. Serves 6.

## Hot Beets with Tarragon

24 baby beets
2 ounces butter
Salt and black pepper
1 teaspoon sugar
2 tablespoons tarragon vinegar
3 tablespoons flour
2 cups beet tops, cooked, drained and strained
4 tablespoons sour cream
1 tablespoon chopped fresh tarragon

Boil the beets until soft. Skin carefully. Heat half of the butter, add the skinned beets with salt, pepper, sugar, vinegar, and shake over brisk fire until hot. Put in the rest of the butter. Add the flour and brown very slowly. Then add the strained beet tops, sour cream and tarragon. Arrange on a hot serving dish. Serves 4-6.

# SALAD

# Salad

## RECIPE FOR POTATO SALAD

*By the Reverend Sydney Smith  (1771-*

*1845),  the "Witty Canon of St. Paul's"*

Two large potatoes passed through kitchen sieve
Smoothness and softness to the salad give;
Of mordent mustard, add a single spoon,
Distrust the condiment that bites too soon;
But deem it not, thou man of herbs, a fault
To add a double quantity of salt;
Four times the spoon with oil of Lucca crown
And twice with vinegar procured from "town",
True flavor needs it, and your poet begs
The pounded yellow of two well boiled eggs.
Let onion's atoms lurk within the bowl
And scarce suspected, animate the whole;
And lastly in the flavor'd compound toss
A magic spoonful of Anchovy Sauce.
Oh! great and glorious, and herbaceous treat
'Twould tempt the dying anchorite to eat,
Back to the world he'd turn his weary soul,
And plunge his fingers in the salad bowl.

Although Caesar never knew the piquant dish of romaine, anchovy, cheese and egg that bears his name, it was the Romans who introduced salad to the world. The plebs dipped their humble *cichorium* (chicory) and *lactuca* (lettuce) in salt and so from *salata* (salted) came salat. Even French dressing had its forbear in the Roman *Jus Simplex* or Greek Sharp Sauce compounded of oil, wine or vinegar, and seasonings. For centuries, the virtues of a simple green salad were ignored by the rich, who regarded uncooked vegetables as harmful and indigestible. But the 17th century diarist John Evelyn came to its defense in his *Acetaria or a Discourse on Salats* and called for "a mess of raw vegetables" instead of the oiled, boiled or pickled concoctions of the day. By 1758 the therapeutic qualities of salad were solemnly lauded by a German doctor who prescribed a different salad for each of the four classical divisions of humanity: Temperamentum Sanguineum, Cholericum, Phlegmaticum and Melancholicum. Many of today's salads have ancient precedents. Potato salad is mentioned as early as 1597 and a 17th century recipe for chicken salad requires that the meat be sliced thin, soaked in vinegar, mixed with capers, anchovies and "a little long grass" minced together and served with a garnish of lemons, oranges, or barberries.

The tender nature of young salad greens is frequently taken advantage of by uncouth cooks. Wilted, soggy lettuce or an indiscriminate sprinkling of leftovers will take the heart out of any salad bowl. To be worthy of the name, a salad should be made of only the best and freshest ingredients, mingled with a deft hand and a feeling for proportion. The Spanish proverb recommends "a spendthrift for the oil, a miser for the vinegar, a counselor for the salt and a madman to stir them up."

## Boeuf Marinade

Lean roast beef, well done, is the proper base for this dish, but boiled beef or roast lamb may also be used. Serve it with a bowl of raw vegetables—scallions, radishes, carrot sticks, celery, fennel, cauliflowerets, strips of green pepper and spears of French endive—with coarse ground salt, French bread and a bottle of red wine.

*1 tablespoon prepared Dijon or*
  *herb mustard*
*½ teaspoon salt*
*½ teaspoon garlic salt*
*1 tablespoon cider vinegar*
*2 tablespoons olive oil*
*1 teaspoon chopped basil (with beef)* **or**
  *rosemary (with lamb)*
*8-10 thin slices of roast beef or lamb*
*Salt and pepper*
*4 tablespoons minced parsley*
*Grated onion (optional)*

Dissolve the mustard, salt and garlic salt in the vinegar, then gradually beat in the oil. Add the basil or rosemary. Shave the meat very thin, salt and pepper lightly and slip it into the marinade a few slices at a time, turning so that each slice is thoroughly coated. Let stand for several hours—preferably 24—occasionally turning the meat over in the marinade. If it absorbs all the marinade, add more in the proportions given. To serve, sprinkle with parsley and, if you wish, grated onion. Serves 4.

## Salade Boulangère

*1½ cups diced cooked potatoes*
*3 cups diced cooked beef, chicken or turkey*
*1 cup cooked green beans*
*1 cup watercress, coarsely shredded*
*6 radishes, sliced*
*2 tablespoons chopped scallions or onions*
*1 cup chili sauce*

*¼ cup mayonnaise*
*¼ cup wine vinegar*

Combine the potatoes, meat, green beans, watercress, radishes and scallions in a salad bowl. Mix together the chili sauce, mayonnaise and vinegar. Pour over the salad and toss together until well blended. Serve on shredded lettuce. Serves 6 as a luncheon main course.

## Meat and Vegetable Salad

*½ cup each of cooked peas, string beans, carrots, limas, beets, parboiled cauli-flowerets*
*½ cup chopped raw cabbage*
*3 cups diced meat—veal, ham, beef or lamb*
*¾ cup French dressing made with lemon juice*
*1 clove garlic*
*1 tablespoon capers*

*2 tablespoons minced green pepper*
*1 teaspoon grated onion*
*½ cup mayonnaise*
*Lettuce*
*Slivers of cheese*
*Strips of salami*
*Anchovy fillets or smoked salmon strips*

Leftover vegetables may be used if they have not been buttered. Marinate the meats and all the vegetables together in the French dressing, except for the beets, which must be marinated separately and added at the last. Tuck in the garlic clove, stuck with a toothpick so you can find and remove it before final assembling.

When ready to serve the salad, add the capers, green pepper, onion, and mix well. Add the mayonnaise, and last of all, the beets. Serve the salad on a bed of lettuce, and garnish it with cheese, salami, anchovy or smoked salmon. Serves 6-8.

## Corned Beef Salad

*2 tablespoons gelatin*
*¼ cup cold water*
*1½ cups boiling water*
*1 bouillon cube*
*1 can corned beef*
*2 cups celery, diced*
*3 hard-cooked eggs, chopped small*
*1 small onion, minced*
*½ cucumber, diced small*
*½ teaspoon salt*
*1 cup mayonnaise*
*1 green pepper*
*Lettuce*

Soak the gelatin in the cold water. Melt the bouillon cube in the boiling water and dissolve the gelatin in it. Cut and flake the **corned beef into small bits and mix it with the** remaining ingredients (except the green pepper and lettuce). Add the gelatin mixture. Make a design of green pepper

strips in the bottom of a mold rinsed out with cold water. Spoon in the corned beef mixture and set the mold, covered, in the refrigerator to chill. When ready to serve, unmold on lettuce bed. Serves 6-8.

## Chicken Liver Salad

### For each serving:

*2 pairs of chicken livers*
*1 slice onion*
*1 stalk celery*
*2 sprigs parsley*
*¼ teaspoon peppercorns*
*1 teaspoon salt*
*Lettuce*
*Curly endive*
*1 small tomato*
*2 slices bacon*
*¼ cup Russian dressing*

Simmer the chicken livers for 10 minutes in a bouillon of boiling water, onion, celery, parsley, peppercorns and salt. Let the livers drain, dry and chill. Lay them whole in a nest of lettuce and curly endive. Peel and quarter the tomato, and tuck the quarters in among the livers. Garnish with the bacon slices, cooked until crisp and dry, and spoon Russian dressing over all.

## Sweetbread Salad

*2½ cups sweetbreads*
*Court bouillon*
*2 slices lemon*
*½ cup chopped celery*
*½ cup cooked peas (or canned petits pois)*
*½ teaspoon onion juice*
*¼ cup French dressing made with*
  *wine vinegar*
*2 tablespoons mayonnaise thinned with*
  *2 tablespoons cream*
*Lettuce*
*2 slices crisp bacon*
*2 hard-cooked eggs*

*Ripe olives*
*Tomato quarters*

Soak the sweetbreads in cold water for half an hour to whiten them; then parboil them gently for 20 minutes in court bouillon (see instructions under Chicken Liver Salad) with two slices of lemon. Drain. Plunge the sweetbreads into cold water and let them stand until cool enough to handle. Remove all fat and membrane from the cooked sweetbreads and separate them into small chunks. Add the celery and peas and sprinkle with onion juice. Marinate for at least one hour in the French dressing. Then cover sweetbreads with the thinned mayonnaise. Serve in lettuce cups with hot crisp bacon crumbled on top. For garnish, use quartered hard-cooked eggs, ripe olives and quartered tomatoes. Serves 4-6.

## Hedwig's Herring Salad

*2 lbs. lean veal*
*1 lb. (4) celery root*
*6 potatoes*
*6 beets*
*12 salt herring*
*2 onions*
*2 dill pickles*
*6 hard-cooked eggs*
*2 tablespoons capers*
*1 cup vinegar*
*½ cup red wine*
*2 tablespoons prepared mustard*
*Lettuce*

Boil veal, celery root, potatoes and beets separately. Dice. Rinse the herring in cold water then chop them. Mix together the veal, potatoes, herring and celery root. Chop in the onions, dill pickles and eggs, then add the beets and capers. Mix the vinegar and wine with the mustard for dressing. Stir well, then chill. Serve the herring salad in a big bowl lined with let-

tuce. Makes about 2 quarts or sufficient for 12-14 servings.

## Sardine Salad Plate

*12 large skinless, boneless sardines*
*24 asparagus tips*
*4 curried eggs*
*Lettuce*
*1 hard-cooked egg, riced*
*½ can pimento, minced*
*1 teaspoon chopped chives*
*2 teaspoons chopped parsley*
*1 teaspoon chopped sweet pickle*
*½ cup French dressing made with tarragon*
*vinegar*
*Lemon wedges*
*Ripe olives*

Arrange the sardines, asparagus and halves of curried eggs (see recipe under Cheese and Egg) on a bed of lettuce. Add the riced egg, pimento, chives, parsley and pickle to the French dressing and pour over the asparagus. Garnish the platter with lemon wedges for the sardines and ripe olives. Serves 4.

## Crab Meat Salad

*1 clove garlic*
*2 cups fresh cooked crab meat*
*1 cup chopped celery*
*¼ cup chopped green pepper*
*2 tablespoons chopped chives*
*¼ cup French dressing*
*½ teaspoon curry powder*

½ *cup mayonnaise*
*Shredded lettuce and watercress*
*2 teaspoons capers*
*2 tomatoes*

Rub a kitchen bowl with a cut clove of garlic. Mix crab meat, celery, green pepper, chives and French dressing in the bowl and let marinate until time to assemble the salad. Then blend the curry powder into the mayonnaise and stir into the crab mixture. Serve the salad on a bed of shredded lettuce and watercress. Garnish with the capers and the tomatoes, peeled and cut into eighths. Serves 4.

## Lobster Tails with Dill

*4 frozen lobster tails*
*2 teaspoons salt*
*12 heads of dill (or 3 tablespoons dill seed)*
½ *teaspoon dry mustard*
*2 tablespoons chopped chives*
½ *cup French dressing made with*
*wine vinegar*
*Watercress*
*Hard-cooked eggs*
*Ripe olives*
*Lemon wedges*

Plunge the lobster tails, still frozen, into a quart of boiling water. Add the salt and eight heads of dill (or 2 tablespoons of dill seed). Let simmer for 8 minutes, or as package directs; then let the lobster tails cool in the liquid. Drain and dry them well; split each tail in half, lengthwise, and crosscut the flesh into bite-size slices. Fold the tails together again, wrap and chill. Add the mustard, chives and remainder of the dill, chopped fine, to the French dressing. Let it stand, covered, for at least half an hour.

To serve, arrange the tails, opened flat, on a bed of watercress. Use hard-cooked eggs, ripe olives and lemon wedges,

as garnish. Pass the French dressing separately. Serves 4.

## Crab Meat Stuffed
## Artichoke Salad

**For each serving:**

*1 artichoke*
¼ *cup fresh cooked crab meat*
¼ *cup chopped celery*
*1 tablespoon chopped green pepper*
*Few drops of onion juice*
*2 tablespoons mayonnaise thinned with a*
*teaspoon of cream*
⅛ *teaspoon nutmeg*
*Salt*
*Paprika*
½ *teaspoon capers*

There's an art to preparing artichokes for the table. The stem should be cut flush with the base and, the tight top leaves of the artichoke sliced off to remove the prickly leaf tips. Each side leaf should have its prickle snipped off with scissors. Then boil for 35 to 40 minutes in salted water. The artichoke is done when an outer leaf pulls out easily. Drain well upside down, and while still warm from the cooking, prepare for salad.

Press the leaves gently back so that the artichoke lies open like a flower. Pull out the cone of undeveloped white leaves. Scrape out choke with a spoon. Chill.

Mix the crab meat, celery, green pepper, onion juice and mayonnaise together; add nutmeg, salt and paprika. Heap this on the artichoke heart and decorate with the capers. Pass a bowl of mayonnaise at table.

## Tuna Fish Salad Plate

*1 can white meat tuna fish*
*1 hard-cooked egg*
*2 tablespoons chopped green pepper*

½ cup diced cucumber
2 chopped scallions
2 teaspoons lemon juice
½ teaspoon nutmeg
½ teaspoon salt
¼ teaspoon pepper
⅓ cup mayonnaise
*Watercress*
*Lettuce, spinach, escarole*
*Radishes, sweet gherkins*
*Rolled watercress sandwiches*

Flush the oil from the can of tuna by holding it under cold running water, then drain and flake. Combine fish and the next nine ingredients, mixing lightly with a fork. Serve in a nest of shredded greens—lettuce, watercress, spinach, escarole. Garnish with radishes, sweet gherkins, and rolled watercress sandwiches. Serves 3-4.

## Romaine Caesar Salad

*1 clove garlic*
*6 anchovy fillets*
*3 tablespoons Parmesan cheese*
*1 egg*
*3 tablespoons olive oil*
*1 tablespoon wine vinegar*
*4 slices bread, cut thin*
*2 tablespoons butter*
*2 heads of romaine*

Mash the garlic in a large wooden salad bowl, rubbing it well around the sides. Let it stand thus for a few minutes, then scrape out and discard the garlic pulp. Put the anchovy fillets and cheese into the bowl and mash them to a smooth paste. Coddle the egg by cooking it in fast-boiling water for one minute, just enough to cut the edge of rawness. Add this to the anchovy-cheese mixture and work smooth. Blend in the oil and vinegar. Neither salt nor pepper is needed.

Make croutons by buttering the bread on both sides, cubing it small, and browning the croutons in the oven until crisp.

Wash the romaine well, dry and crisp it. Break it into the bowl, sprinkle on the croutons and toss lightly in the dressing until every leaf is coated and the dressing absorbed by the croutons.

For a memorable outdoor meal on a warm summer evening, serve an outsize bowl of Caesar salad with grilled steak sandwiches followed by peach shortcake. Serves 4-6.

In doubling or tripling this recipe, you can put all the ingredients for the dressing into a blender (cutting the amount of garlic in half) for a quick whirl. Store the dressing in a screw-cap jar until the salad is ready to be tossed. The flavor is the same, but the texture of the dressing is creamy and looks less attractive on the romaine.

## Tossed Green Salad
## with Herbs

This aristocrat of the salad family is usually considered to belong properly to dinner, accompanying the main entrée, or even better, as a separate course to refresh the palate. But why not, on a hot summer day, feature the big bowl of cool greens for itself? The accompaniment can be hearty—cheese muffins or sandwiches—but let the salad have the center of the stage.

*1 clove garlic*
*1 head lettuce*
*Salad greens: curly endive, celery cabbage,*
*leaves of spinach, rhubarb chard, sprigs*
*of watercress*
*1 teaspoon each fresh cut dill, basil,*
*marjoram, chervil*
*8 tablespoons olive oil*
*2 tablespoons wine vinegar*
*1 teaspoon salt*
*½ teaspoon pepper*
*1 tablespoon chopped chives*

The lettuce may be Bibb or Boston, romaine or leaf; the greens may be a few leaves of any or all of those listed above, or you may select others of your choosing. The prime requisite is that they be fresh and crisp, well washed and thoroughly dried. No drop of water should be allowed to lurk in the fold of a leaf, or the salad will be watery and quick to wilt.

Rub an outsize salad bowl with the garlic, peeled and halved, until there is a good coating well up on all sides. Break the lettuce and greens into the bowl. Snip the herbs small and crush them lightly as you add them to the greens. Measure the oil into a big spoon and sprinkle it over the salad. Dissolve the salt and pepper in the vinegar in the same spoon, and sprinkle this on the salad. Then begin a light and rhythmic tossing, which is more a gentle turning of the greens over and over until every leaf is coated and the seasonings well distributed. Add the chives, taste to see if more salt is needed, then serve. Serves 6-8.

## Belgian Tomatoes

*1 Spanish onion*
*4 well ripened tomatoes*
*½ teaspoon salt*
*¼ teaspoon sugar*
*Fresh ground pepper*
*1 tablespoon each chopped fresh chives,*
*basil, dill*

*1 teaspoon celery seed*
*¼ cup French dressing*

Prepare this salad on a large flat platter from which it can be served. First slice the onion and separate it into rings. Spread these on the platter. Slice the tomatoes, almost ½ inch thick, onto the onion rings and dust them with the salt and sugar. Sprinkle each slice with a grind of fresh pepper and chopped herbs. Sprinkle all with celery seed and French dressing. Cover the platter with aluminum foil and set it in the refrigerator to gain flavor until supper time. Serve Belgian Tomatoes with cold cuts, cheese and crusty garlic bread for a snack supper. Serves 4.

## Surprise Salad

*½ teaspoon dry mustard*
*½ teaspoon onion juice*
*¾ cup French dressing*
*1 cup cooked diced potatoes*
*1 cup cooked diced green beans*
*1 cup cooked diced beets*
*⅓ cup mayonnaise*
*Lettuce*
*1 hard-cooked egg*
*2 tablespoons chopped chives*
*1 teaspoon chopped fresh dill*

Add the mustard and onion juice to the French dressing. While the vegetables are still warm, marinate them separately, each in ¼ cup of the dressing. Set to chill for at least an hour.

To serve, combine the potatoes and beans with the mayonnaise, and put them in a bowl lined with lettuce. Arrange the diced beets over the beans and potatoes. Rice the egg over these and sprinkle all with the chives and dill. Serve with marinated herring, or with thin rye bread sandwiches of cream cheese and anchovy paste Serves 4-6.

271

## Salade de Boheme

1 large bunch watercress
½ celery cabbage
½ cucumber
4 hard-cooked eggs
4-6 small boiled beets
1 tablespoon chives
½ teaspoon marjoram
6 anchovy fillets, chopped small
*½ cup Spiced Salad Dressing

Line a bowl with watercress and on this bed arrange cross-cut slices of celery cabbage, intermingled with thin slices of unpeeled cucumber. Arrange slices of the eggs and beets on top of this. Sprinkle with the herbs and anchovy. When ready to serve, pour on Spiced Salad Dressing and toss well. Serves 6.
*See recipe under Salad Dressings.

## Zucchini Salad

8 zucchini
1 cup French dressing with
½ teaspoon oregano added

1 large onion, sliced
2 cloves garlic, sliced
Lettuce
2 tomatoes
Mayonnaise
Parmesan cheese
Salt

Choose tender zucchini about 4 inches long. Parboil them, unpeeled, in salted water for about 6 minutes, then cool. Cut the zucchini in half, lengthwise, and scoop a shallow hollow from the center. Lay the zucchini, cut sides up, on a flat dish; pour a generous amount of French dressing over them and cover with slices of onion and garlic. Cover the plate tightly with aluminum foil and let it stand for a day in the refrigerator to marinate.

When ready to serve, remove the onion and garlic and drain off the French dressing, which can be strained and used to toss a green salad. Arrange the zucchini halves on crisp lettuce. Fill the hollows with thin crescents of tomato. Top with a spoonful of mayonnaise and sprinkle generously with Parmesan cheese. Serves 8.

## Artichoke Salad Plate

**For each serving:**

1 artichoke
½ teaspoon lemon juice
2 tablespoons mayonnaise
1 teaspoon chopped chives
Small bunch watercress
Radish rosettes

Prepare the artichoke as described in Crab Meat Stuffed Artichoke Salad (see recipe under Fish). Sprinkle the heart with lemon juice and a dash of salt; heap with mayonnaise and top with chives. Arrange the watercress in a loose bunch at one side of the artichoke and tuck the radishes among the watercress sprigs.

## Potato Salad

6 large potatoes
½ teaspoon dill
½ cup French dressing made with cider
   vinegar plus ½ teaspoon dry mustard
¼ cup minced onion
2 red apples, unpeeled but cored and diced
1 cup diced celery
6 hard-cooked eggs, chopped
4 tablespoons chopped parsley
1½ cups mayonnaise
½ cup sour cream
Salt and pepper

Cook the potatoes in their skins with the dill; peel and dice them and marinate them while still hot in the French dressing. Add the onion and let stand until cold—at least an hour—while you prepare the rest of the ingredients. Combine potato-onion mixture with remaining ingredients, including mayonnaise blended with sour cream. Season with salt and pepper to taste. Makes about 2 quarts.

## Potato Salad with
## Piquant Salad Dressing

1 quart (4 cups) diced cooked cold potatoes
1½ teaspoons salt
3 tablespoons French dressing
1 tablespoon fresh lemon juice
⅛ teaspoon ground black pepper
⅛ teaspoon garlic powder (optional)
1½ cups diced celery
½ cup diced green pepper
2 hard-cooked eggs, chopped
*⅓ cup Piquant Salad Dressing
Lettuce or watercress
6 to 8 frankfurters
2 tablespoons butter
Radishes, parsley or paprika

Combine the first six ingredients. Marinate 1 hour or more. Add celery, green pepper, eggs, and salad dressing. Mix lightly.

Serve on lettuce or watercress with frankfurters heated in butter. Garnish with radishes, parsley or paprika. Serves 6 to 8.
*See recipe under Salad Dressings.

## German Potato Salad

8 slices bacon
3 tablespoons flour
4 teaspoons chopped onion
⅔ cup vinegar
⅔ cup water
½ cup sugar
4 teaspoons salt
½ teaspoon ground black pepper
1 teaspoon powdered dry mustard
½ teapsoon crumbled rosemary leaves
2 quarts cooked diced potatoes
½ cup chopped fresh parsley

Fry bacon until crisp. Remove from pan, drain and crumble. Add flour and onion to the bacon fat left in the pan. Stir in vinegar, water, sugar, salt and spices. Cook only until mixture is of medium thickness. Add to potatoes, parsley and crumbled bacon. Mix carefully to prevent mashing the potatoes. Serves 8-10.

## Potato and Shrimp Salad,
## Provençale

2 pounds potatoes
3 pounds shrimp, cooked and cleaned
6 hard-cooked eggs, sliced
1 pound (or 1 package frozen) French style
   green beans, cooked
1 can anchovy fillets
1 cup dry white wine
¼ cup cognac
1 cup olive oil
⅓ cup lemon juice
1 teaspoon salt
¼ teaspoon freshly ground black pepper
¼ teaspoon dry mustard

Prepare the salad the day before it is to be served. Boil the unpeeled potatoes in salted water until tender but firm. Peel and slice them. In a bowl arrange successive layers (starting and ending with the potatoes) of potatoes, shrimp, eggs, green beans and anchovies. Pour the wine over all. Cover and chill overnight. Beat together the cognac, olive oil, lemon juice, salt, pepper and mustard. Pour over the salad just before serving. Serves 6.

## Celery Root Salad

*1 lb. celery root*
*1 teaspoon onion juice*
*¼ teaspoon dry mustard*
*2 tablespoons cream*
*½ cup French dressing made with lemon juice*
*2 tablespoons parsley, minced*
*2 teaspoons chervil, minced*
*1 hard-cooked egg, riced*

Scrub the celery root and cook it in salted water until tender, which may take anywhere from 20 minutes to 2 hours, depending upon the age of the root. When tender, cool, peel and slice into small julienne strips. Add onion juice, mustard and cream to the French dressing. Beat well. Let the celery root chill in this for several hours. If it absorbs all the marinade, add more to moisten. Serve sprinkled with the parsley, chervil and riced egg. Serves 4.

## Dill-Spiced Carrots

*8 young carrots*
*1 cup dill pickle juice*
*2 tablespoons fresh cut dill*
*1 tablespoon minced chives*
*1 cup sour cream*

Scrape and trim the carrots and quarter them lengthwise. Simmer them in the dill pickle juice until they can be easily pierced with a fork, about 20 to 25 minutes. They will not soften, but will stay pleasantly crunchy. Chill overnight in the pickle juice.

To serve, drain off the liquid and sprinkle the herbs on the carrots. Pass the sour cream in a separate bowl. Dill-Spiced Carrots should not be served on lettuce, but used as a salad garnish for cold chicken or a platter of cold cuts. Serves 4.

## French Bean Salad

*1 cup dry baby limas or navy beans*
*1 carrot*
*1 stalk celery*
*½ small onion*
*1½ teaspoons salt*
*½ cup French dressing made with red wine vinegar*
*2 tablespoons onion, minced very fine*
*3 tablespoons parsley, minced fine*
*1 tablespoon fresh chopped chervil*
*1 tablespoon fresh chopped marjoram or thyme*
*Fresh ground pepper*

Soak the beans overnight in cold water, then drain. Simmer them with the carrot, celery and ½ onion in salted water until just tender (25-30 minutes). Drain; remove the carrot, celery and onion and stir the French dressing into the beans. Chill for several hours, stirring occasionally to distribute the marinade.

When ready to serve, taste for salt, then put the beans in a bowl and sprinkle with minced onion, the herbs and fresh ground pepper. This salad is usually served as a salad hors d'oeuvre. It fits well in a salad supper, as accompaniment to cold cuts and sliced tomatoes. Makes 1 pint.

## Arabic Green Bean Salad

*½ cup olive oil*
*1 cup chopped onions*

*2 pounds fresh or 2 packages frozen*
    *green beans*
*1 cup canned tomatoes*
*1½ teaspoons salt*
*½ teaspoon pepper*
*½ teaspoon oregano*

Heat the olive oil in a saucepan; add the onions and sauté for 10 minutes but do not allow to brown. Add the beans. Cover and cook over low heat 10 minutes, stirring occasionally. Add the tomatoes, salt, pepper and oregano; cook 20 minutes. Chill and serve with lemon wedges. Serves 6.

## Sour Cream Cucumbers

*½ teaspoon salt*
*1 scant tablespoon sugar*
*2 tablespoons cider vinegar*
*1 cup sour cream*
*2 tablespoons chopped chives*
    *or a grating of onion*
*2 tablespoons chopped fresh dill,*
    *head and fronds*
*1 teaspoon celery seed*
*2 firm fresh cucumbers*

Dissolve the salt and sugar in the vinegar, add the sour cream and stir smooth. You may like more or less vinegar, salt or sugar, but don't make the dressing too sweet. Add the chives, dill and celery seed. Slice the unpared cucumbers paper-thin and combine with the dressing. Chill for 1 hour or more. Sour cream cucumbers improve in taste as they stand. The flavor of the cucumbers seeps into the dressing. Serves 4-6.

## Choucroute Froide

*2 tablespoons salad oil*
*1 cup chopped onions*
*3 cups sauerkraut*
*1 cup chicken stock, fresh or canned*
*½ cup olive oil*
*3 tablespoons wine vinegar*

*1 teaspoon salt*
*¼ teaspoon freshly ground black pepper*
*¼ teaspoon minced garlic*
*2 hard-cooked eggs, chopped*

Heat the salad oil in a saucepan; sauté the onions for 5 minutes. Add the sauerkraut and stock. Cook over low heat for 1 hour, stirring occasionally. Chill. Beat together the olive oil, vinegar, salt, pepper and garlic. Add the eggs. Pour over the sauerkraut and toss until well blended. Serve in mounds. Serves 6.

## Curried Egg Salad

*6 hard-cooked eggs*
*6 tablespoons mayonnaise*
*½ teaspoon seasoning salt*
*¼ teaspoon salt*
*½ teaspoon curry powder*
*2 dozen cooked asparagus tips*
*Leaf lettuce*
*4 tablespoons grated Parmesan cheese*
*½ cup French dressing*
*2 tablespoons chopped chives*
*Cherry tomatoes*
*Ripe olives*

Split the eggs lengthwise. Mash the yolks with the mayonnaise and seasonings and use as stuffing for the whites. Use a well spiced mayonnaise or add a little mustard or lemon juice to make it sharper. You may wish to increase the amount of curry, but the aim of this recipe is to produce a bland, elusive flavor. For each serving arrange 3 of the curried egg halves and half a dozen asparagus tips on a bed of leaf lettuce. Sprinkle the asparagus with grated cheese and French dressing, and garnish with chives. Use cherry tomatoes and ripe olives as garnishes. Serves 4.

## Cottage Cheese Salad

*Soft cottage cheese*
*Shredded lettuce*
*Garnishes*
*Salt*
*Sour cream*

Spoon the cottage cheese into a bowl lined with shredded lettuce—iceberg, for preference, because of its crispness. Set it forth on a tray surrounded with little bowls of various garnishes: chopped green peppers; chopped sweet red peppers; chopped scallions; and if you like dill, celery and caraway seed mixed; chopped nuts; chopped stuffed olives; sweet pickle relish. Pass the salt shaker and a bowl of sour cream, and let each person season and garnish to his own taste.

## Cheese-Stuffed Tomato Salad

*½ lb. diced sharp Cheddar cheese*
*3 hard-cooked eggs, chopped*
*¼ cup chopped sweet pickles*
*¼ cup chopped pimento*
*1 teaspoon minced onion*
*¼ cup French dressing*
*6 firm, ripe tomatoes*
*Lettuce*
*Mayonnaise*

Combine the first five ingredients and marinate for an hour in the French dressing.

Peel the tomatoes and hollow them out carefully. Fill the hollows with the cheese mixture and chill. To serve, put the tomatoes in lettuce cups, and give each a topping of mayonnaise. Serves 6.

## Patio Salad

*1 can kidney beans*
*2 cups drained diced tomatoes*
*1 diced cucumber*
*½ cup chopped green pepper*
*½ cup chopped green onion*
*2 cups diced cheese*
*Mayonnaise*
*Salt, pepper*
*Crisp bacon*

Combine kidney beans, tomatoes (peeled and with seeds discarded), cucumber, green pepper, onion, cheese and enough mayonnaise to moisten. Salt and pepper to taste and chill, then arrange in a lettuce-lined bowl, and sprinkle the top with crisp crumbled bacon. This is a good salad to serve at barbecues, with charcoal-grilled hamburgers. Serves 8.

## Farmer's Salad

*2 cups diced cucumbers*
*1 cup unpeeled diced radishes*
*½ cup diced red onions*
*½ pound diced hoop cheese*
*1 cup sour cream*
*Salt, pepper*
*Chopped fresh dill or dill seed*

Mix together cucumbers, radishes, onions, hoop cheese, sour cream, add salt and pepper to taste, and a sprinkling of chopped fresh dill or dill seed. Add more sour cream if needed, and serve with rye or pumpernickel bread. Serves 8.

## Fruit Salad Buffet

An added pleasure of this salad lunch is that you can mix your own. Take a large tray and line it with grape leaves or large flat leaves of leaf lettuce. In the center place a shallow dish piled high with heart leaves of lettuce, watercress and spikes of French endive. Around this dish, on the grape leaves, arrange fruits according to your liking, such as:

*Crescents of peeled cantaloupe*
*Crescents of peeled honeydew*
*Bartlett pears, unpeeled, cut in eighths*
*Clusters of stemmed seedless grapes*
*Apples with red skin left on, cut in eighths*
*Half-rounds of fresh pineapple*
*Bananas split and quartered*
*Pitted Bing cherries*
*Mounds of strawberries or raspberries*
*Sections of orange*
*Sections of grapefruit*
*Sprigs of lemon mint*
*\*Celery Seed Dressing*
*\*Honey-Cream Dressing*
*Mayonnaise and whipped cream, half and half*

Decorate the tray with sprigs of lemon mint. Flank it with bowls of the various dressings. Let each guest compile a salad with dressing of his own choosing. With this you might serve date-nut sandwiches filled with cream cheese, hot cheese or herb biscuits, Melba toast, buttered scones, garlic bread.
\*See recipe under Salad Dressings.

## Fruit Salad
## with Poppy Seed Dressing

*1 grapefruit*
*2 oranges*
*2 avocados*
*¼ cup lemon juice*
*Watercress*
*2 heads French endive*
*\*Poppy Seed Dressing*

Cut the grapefruit and oranges in half and into skinless sections. Peel and slice the avocado and put the slices into the lemon juice to prevent their darkening. Arrange the fruits on watercress and tuck spears of the endive around. Pour the Poppy Seed Dressing upon the fruit, but do not cover the endive, which may be eaten with the fingers. Serve with balls made of the Spiced Cheese Salad mixture (see recipe under Cheese and Egg). Serves 4.
\*See recipe under Salad Dressings.

### Honeydew Salad Plate

*1 large honeydew melon*
*1 cantaloupe*
*2 cups raspberries*
*2 cups seedless grapes*
*Bibb lettuce*
*Sprigs of mint*
*\*Celery Seed Dressing*

Cut six circular slices from the center of the honeydew; peel them and make melon balls from the remainder. Scoop balls from the cantaloupe. Stem the grapes. Lay the honeydew rings upon leaves of Bibb lettuce; pile the other fruits in the ring and decorate with mint sprigs. Pass Celery Seed Dressing in a separate bowl. Accompany this salad with cream cheese balls rolled in ground nuts, and blueberry muffins. Serves 6.

*See recipe under Salad Dressings.

### Avocado Mousse

*1 tablespoon gelatin*
*½ cup cold water*
*½ cup boiling water*
*2½ cups mashed avocado*
  *(4-5 medium avocados)*
*3 tablespoons parsley, minced fine*
*1 tablespoon lemon juice*
*½ teaspoon onion juice*
*1 teaspoon Worcestershire sauce*
*1 teaspoon salt*
*½ cup whipping cream*
*½ cup mayonnaise*
*Watercress*

Soak the gelatin in the cold water, then dissolve it in the boiling water. Let it stand until cool. Mash the avocados with a silver fork, add the parsley, lemon and onion juices, Worcestershire sauce and salt. Whip the cream stiff; fold in the mayonnaise and add the dissolved gelatin. Combine this with the avocado mixture and pour into a quart mold rinsed out with cold water. Chill until firm.

Unmold the salad on a platter and surround with watercress. Avocado mousse may be served with tomato quarters and sliced hard-cooked eggs, or with fruits of your choice. For a suggestion: sections of orange and grapefruit and plump strawberries.

Leftover mousse will keep its color if it is packed so no air reaches it. Serves 6-8.

### French Dressing or Basic Marinade

*2 teaspoons salt*
*1 teaspoon pepper*
*½ teaspoon dry mustard*
*½ teaspoon sugar*
*½ cup lemon juice or vinegar*
*2 cups olive oil*

Prepare this dressing in a screw-top jar. Dissolve the salt, pepper, mustard and sugar in the lemon juice or vinegar. Add the oil gradually, shaking vigorously as you do so. Keep the jar in a cool place. This basic dressing may be used plain or with herbs for a tossed green salad; it may be spiced with onion and garlic for marinating meat, vegetables or fish; or it may be sweetened with honey or sugar as a dressing for fruit salads. Use it whenever one of the recipes in this cook book calls for French Dressing. Shake well before using. Makes 1½ pints.

### Spiced Salad Dressing

*2 cups olive oil*
*½ cup wine vinegar*
*2 teaspoons granulated sugar*
*1 teaspoon salt*
*¼ teaspoon pepper*
*2 tablespoons tomato sauce*
*2 tablespoons chili sauce*

½ *teaspoon oregano*
1 *green pepper, sliced*
2 *slices onion*
½ *clove garlic*

Put all the ingredients into a blender, blend for 1 minute. Pour into a screw-top jar. This dressing is excellent for fish or vegetable salads, or for mixed greens as a piquant change from the classic French dressing. It may be prepared ahead of time, kept cold in an air-tight jar, and used as desired. Makes 1½ pints.

## Green Mayonnaise

1½ *cups mayonnaise*
½ *cup sour cream*
1 *tablespoon wine vinegar*
4 *scallions*
½ *teaspoon tarragon leaves,*
  *preferably fresh*
2 *tablespoons chopped parsley*
¼ *teaspoon nutmeg*
4 *cups raw spinach*

Put all ingredients into a blender in the order given, feeding in the spinach gradually as the machine whirs. Blend for 1 minute.

This is a good dressing to keep handy for fish or vegetable salads or to spread on bread for sandwiches. Makes 1½ pints.

## Roquefort Cream Dressing

¾ *cup olive oil*
2 *tablespoons wine vinegar*
3 *tablespoons cream*
½ *clove garlic*
¼-*inch slice of onion*
3-*ounce package of Roquefort cheese*
1 *teaspoon salt*
½ *teaspoon pepper*
*Dash of cayenne*

Put all ingredients into a blender in the order given. Blend for half a minute. If you like a lumpy dressing, blend only half the cheese; mash the rest and add it later. If you do not use a blender, beat the oil, vinegar, salt and pepper in a bowl until thoroughly blended. Mince the garlic fine and use 1 tablespoon of grated onion. Mash the cheese with this, adding the cream. Then combine the two mixtures and beat hard. This dressing may be kept on hand in the refrigerator; it solidifies as it chills, but readily softens at room temperature. Makes about 1¾ cups.

## Piquant Salad Dressing

3 *tablespoons butter*
2 *tablespoons flour*
1½ *teaspoons salt*
1 *teaspoon powdered dry mustard*
1 *tablespoon sugar*
½ *teaspoon paprika*
1¼ *cups milk*
2 *egg yolks*
⅓ *cup cider vinegar*
*Dash of onion and garlic powder (optional)*

Melt 3 tablespoons butter in a saucepan. Mix flour, salt, mustard, sugar and paprika and blend with the butter. Add 1 cup milk. Cook mixture to medium thickness, stirring constantly. Mix the remaining ¼ cup milk with the egg yolks; stir into the hot mixture. Add remaining ingredients. Cook over low heat until thickened. Chill. Serve over vegetable, sea food and meat salads. Makes 1½ cups.

## Honey-Cream Dressing for Fruit Salad

*2 tablespoons strained honey*
*3 tablespoons lemon juice*
*1 teaspoon lemon rind, grated*
*¾ cup olive oil*
*½ teaspoon salt*
*Cayenne pepper*
*3-ounce package cream cheese*

Put all the ingredients in a blender, cream cheese last and blend for 30 seconds. If you do not use a blender, mash the honey, lemon juice and cheese together until smooth. Add the rind and beat the oil in gradually. Add the salt and a dash of cayenne. If the dressing tends to separate, beat it gently with a spoon before serving. Makes 1¼ cups.

## Celery Seed Dressing for Fruit Salad

*¹/₃ cup sugar*
*1 teaspoon dry mustard*
*1 teaspoon salt*

*2 teaspoons onion juice*
*¹/₃ cup vinegar*
*1 cup olive oil*
*1 teaspoon paprika*
*1½ tablespoons celery seed*

Put the sugar, mustard, salt, onion juice and vinegar into a pint jar and shake well. Add the oil and continue shaking vigorously until all are well blended. Add the paprika and celery seed and give the dressing a final shaking. Makes 1½ cups.

## Poppy Seed Dressing for Fruit Salad

*¹/₃ cup sugar*
*1 teaspoon salt*
*1 teaspoon dry mustard*
*¹/₃ cup wine vinegar*
*2 teaspoons onion juice*
*1 cup olive oil*
*1½ tablespoons poppy seed*

Dissolve the sugar, salt and mustard in the vinegar. Add the onion juice and oil. Beat until the dressing is well blended. Stir in the poppy seed and shake well. Makes 1½ cups.

# DESSERT

# Dessert

When it comes to dessert, most people play favorites. Some plump for the forthright all-American apple pie, others prefer flamboyant crêpes Suzette or a chocolate-laden Austrian torte. In this we are only following the precedent of famous people, who all had their weaknesses for some delectable dessert. The Empress Josephine had a nostalgic fondness for bananas Creole, probably a reminder of her youth in Martinique. Two such dissimilar characters as the Empress Poppaea, wife of Nero, and Cardinal Wolsey were partial to strawberries, although she liked hers served on a bed of rose petals and he preferred a blanket of fresh heavy cream. Henry VIII, an advocate of stouter fare, gave his cook a manor for inventing a particularly good pudding. This partisan attitude applies to countries as much as to people. That famous American dessert, ice cream, actually had a long history of migration from China to Italy and France (where ices were sold as "frozen niceties") before it found a lasting welcome and home in the land of the refrigerator. Its frosty charms have never palled, though they are often masked by an overcoat of hot chocolate or baked meringue. Spain's favorite dessert is *flan*, a flavored custard. The Chinese and Japanese take only a little preserved fruit or a cooky. In Thailand dessert is a drink, a sweetened liquid made from fruit. The English cleave characteristically to steamed puddings with an occasional trifle or gooseberry fool. Understandably, it is in France, stronghold of the *haute cuisine*, that dessert gained not only its name (from *desservir*, to clear the table) but its true glory. French chefs elevated the simple sweet to a full-scale production which suitably concluded an epicurean meal. Flaming fruits, honeyed mounds of tiny cream puffs, ephemeral soufflés and iced concoctions molded to majestic proportions help close a meal with a flourish. Yet many good cooks who are eager to experiment with new entrées will stick to a few tried-and-true recipes when it comes to serving dessert to family and friends. Be a little more adventurous and you will discover how the right dessert can be the perfect balance to your menus. Consider the dessert in relation to the foods which come before it, their flavors and textures. If the first course is fruit, choose a chocolate torte or a coffee cream rather than a fruit dessert. Fruit is an excellent contrast to a heavy meat course and, according to the season, can be served flambéed or chilled (but not too cold as overchilling destroys delicate flavor). Rich creamy desserts taste best after a light entrée like squab. A spectacular dessert is not so much of a problem as you may think, because it can often be prepared ahead of time. Delicate little crêpes can be made up in batches, stored in the refrigerator, then warmed and served in a suave sauce at the last minute. A soufflé mixture can be on hand, ready for the final addition of egg whites. Frozen desserts, made days in advance, are good stock for your freezer. They lend themselves to decorative forms and designs, so rather than serving the conventional wedge of ice cream, prepare them in a bombe mold. The recipes on the following pages will give you new ideas for that grand finale which makes a meal linger in the memory of your guests.

## Snow Apples

*2 cups water*
*½ cup brown sugar*
*2 tablespoons grated lemon rind*
*6 large apples, peeled and cored*
*½ cup chopped mixed candied fruit*
*1 tablespoon melted butter*
*3 tablespoons orange juice*
*2 egg whites*
*4 tablespoons sugar*
*Chocolate sauce*
*(see recipe under Dessert Sauces)*

Combine the water and brown sugar in a saucepan; cook over low heat for 10 minutes. Place the lemon rind and apples in it and cook 15 minutes, turning them frequently. Drain and arrange fruit in a baking dish. Preheat oven to 350°.

Mix the candied fruit, melted butter and orange juice together and stuff apples.

Beat the egg whites until peaks form; gradually add the sugar, beating until stiff but not dry. Force through a pastry tube or pile on top of the apples. Bake 5-10 minutes or until delicately browned. Serve hot or cold, with chocolate sauce. Serves 6.

## Crème aux Pommes

*4 apples*
*½ cup cognac*
*½ cup sifted flour*
*2 cups milk*
*3 eggs, beaten*
*⅛ teaspoon salt*
*½ cup sugar*

Peel the apples, cut in quarters, then slice ⅛″ thick. Pour the cognac over them and let soak while preparing the batter. Preheat the oven to 275°.

Mix the flour with a little milk until smooth. Add the eggs, salt and sugar. Mix well. Stir in the remaining milk. Pour into a buttered 9″ pie plate. Arrange the drained apples over it in an overlapping design.

Bake 40 minutes or until just set. Serve warm or cold. Serves 6.

## Baked Apple and Noodle Casserole

*6 apples, peeled and sliced*
*¼ cup brown sugar*
*1 teaspoon cinnamon*

½ teaspoon salt
¼ cup melted butter
¼ pound cream cheese
3 cups cooked and drained noodles

Combine the apples, brown sugar, cinnamon, salt and butter in a bowl. Toss together lightly. Mash the cream cheese and add to the previous mixture. Add the noodles, mixing lightly.

Pour into a buttered 2-quart casserole. Bake in a 350° oven for 40 minutes.

Serve hot or cold. Serves 6.

## Apple Rice Pudding

1¼ pounds apples, cooked
2½ cups milk
¾ pound rice
3½ teaspoons grated lemon rind
2 eggs, separated
5 tablespoons sugar
¼ teaspoon nutmeg

Peel, core, slice and cook apples with a little sugar for about 7 minutes. Boil milk and mix in the rice and lemon rind. Cook briskly for 20 minutes. Add the thoroughly beaten egg yolks. Arrange apples in layers in a baking dish, pour rice and any liquid over them. Sprinkle on sugar and nutmeg. Beat egg whites till they form peaks. Stir in very gently. Bake in a 350° oven till brown. Serve hot. Serves 6-8.

## Riz à la Compagne

2 cups milk
¼ cup rice, washed and drained
2 teaspoons gelatin
⅓ cup orange juice
¼ cup sugar
1 apple, peeled and diced
½ cup sliced strawberries

1 tablespoon cognac
¼ cup heavy cream, whipped

Combine the milk and rice in a saucepan. Cook over low heat 25 minutes or until rice is very soft.

Soak the gelatin in the orange juice for 5 minutes. Add to the hot rice mixture with the sugar and stir until dissolved. Cool for 30 minutes. Fold in the apple, berries, cognac and whipped cream.

Pour into a lightly oiled ring mold. Chill until set. Turn out carefully and fill the center with sweetened berries or fruit sauce (see Dessert Sauces). Serve 4-6.

## Peach Pudding

1¼ cups sugar
2 tablespoons lemon juice
3 cups sliced peaches, fresh or frozen
⅔ cup butter
4 eggs
1 teaspoon vanilla
24 ladyfingers, split

Sprinkle ¼ cup sugar and the lemon juice on the peaches. Cream the butter, gradually adding the remaining sugar. Add 1 egg at a time, beating well after each addition. Add the vanilla and fold in the peaches. Line a buttered oblong mold with ladyfingers, reserving a few for the top. Fill with the peach mixture and cover with remaining ladyfingers. Chill for 24 hours. Carefully unmold. Serves 6.

## Pêches Sabayon

4 egg yolks
½ cup sugar
¾ cup Marsala
1 tablespoon cognac
6 peaches
2 tablespoons lemon juice

Beat the egg yolks and sugar in the top of a double boiler. Add the wine, place over hot water and cook, stirring constantly until thick and foamy. Stir in the cognac. Chill. Peel and slice the peaches and sprinkle them with the lemon juice. Chill 15 minutes and drain. Place the peaches in a glass serving dish or individual dishes and cover with the sauce. Serves 6.

*Note:* Other fruits may be served in the same manner.

## Poires aux Crème Caramel

*6 firm pears*
*¾ cup sugar*
*2 tablespoons butter*
*1 cup heavy cream*

Preheat the oven to 475°. Peel and quarter the pears. Arrange them in a buttered shallow baking dish (not glass, as the cream would crack it when added). Sprinkle with the sugar and dot with the butter.

Bake 15 minutes, or until the sugar is dark brown, basting once or twice. Pour the cream over all and stir gently. Bake 2 minutes longer. Serve hot. Serves 6-8.

## Pineapple Rice Bavarian

*½ cup canned pineapple, puréed*
*2 cups sugar syrup*
*2 cups cooked rice*
*Juice of 3 lemons*
*1½ ounces gelatin*
*2 cups whipped cream*
*8 fresh pineapple slices, pared and peeled*

Mix fruit purée with sugar syrup and cooked rice. Add lemon juice, dissolved and strained gelatin and whipped cream. Mix well and pour in mold well oiled with sweet almond oil. Chill till set. Turn out and arrange pineapple around rice. Serves 4.

Another way to serve this recipe is to pour mixture into silver dish or individual timbales. Surround dish or timbales with well packed crushed ice. Do not unmold. Serve in dish or timbales.

## Strawberries Romanoff

*½ cup Cointreau or Curaçao*
*1 quart strawberries, hulled and washed*
*½ cup heavy cream*
*½ pint vanilla ice cream*
*1 teaspoon lemon juice*

Pour half the liqueur over the strawberries and chill for 1 hour. Whip the cream. Beat the ice cream until soft. Add the lemon juice and remaining liqueur. Fold in the whipped cream and berries. Serve at once. Serves 6.

## Strawberry Rice Mold

*¾ cup rice*
*1 quart milk*
*½ teaspoon salt*
*1¼ cups sugar*
*2 tablespoons gelatin*
*½ cup Cointreau or Curaçao*
*1 teaspoon vanilla*
*1 cup heavy cream*
*1 quart strawberries, hulled, washed*

Wash the rice in several waters. Combine in a saucepan with the milk, salt and ¾ cup sugar. Bring to a boil and cook over low heat 30 minutes, or until very soft. Force through a sieve. Soften the gelatin in ¼ cup of the liqueur and add to the rice mixture, stirring until dissolved. Add the vanilla. Cool for 30 minutes. Whip the cream and fold it into the rice mixture. Pour into a ring or melon mold. Chill for at least 3 hours, or until firmly set. While the mold is chilling, sprinkle the remaining sugar and liqueur on the berries and chill. Carefully turn out the rice mold and either fill center or arrange berries around it. Serves 6.

## Austrian Rice and Chestnut Dessert

*2½ pounds chestnuts*
*1 pound rice*
*1 cup milk*
*¾ cup water*
*1 cup sugar*
*4 tablespoons brandy*
*1 egg white*
*3 cups heavy cream, whipped*

Cook chestnuts in water and remove skins. Purée chestnuts and reserve. Cook rice in milk and water. Reserve. Make a syrup of water and sugar, cooking until a thread forms. Pour in brandy and mix. Add, off fire, rice and chestnut purée. Mix these together with stiffly beaten egg white. Arrange mixture in a dome in center of a platter, ring with whipped cream. Serves 6-8.

## Mont Blanc

*1 lb. fresh chestnuts, shelled*
*2 cups milk*
*1″ stick vanilla bean*
*¾ cup sugar*
*¼ cup water*

*2 tablespoons butter*
*2 teaspoons vanilla extract*
*1½ cups heavy cream*
*4 tablespoons grated sweet chocolate*

Combine the chestnuts, milk and vanilla bean in a saucepan. Bring to a boil and cook over low heat 30 minutes, or until the chestnuts are very soft. Drain and force the chestnuts through a sieve. Boil the sugar and water together until the mixture is syrupy and a soft ball forms when a little is dropped in cold water. Blend into the chestnut purée with the butter and vanilla extract. Mix well. Form into a mound (or pour into a mold) and chill. Whip the cream and cover the mound using a pastry tube. Sprinkle with the chocolate. You can also make individual mounds. Serves 6.

## Crêpes

*2 eggs*
*2 tablespoons salad oil*
*1 cup milk*
*1 tablespoon cognac*
*¾ cup sifted flour*
*½ teaspoon salt*
*6 tablespoons butter*

Beat the eggs, oil, milk and cognac together. Sift in the flour and salt, beating until smooth. Chill for 30 minutes. The batter should have the consistency of heavy cream, so add a little milk if necessary. Melt 1 teaspoon of the butter in a 6″ skillet. Pour enough batter into the pan to coat the pan evenly, tilting the pan in a circular motion as you pour. Turn when brown. Stack cooked pancakes and add butter to the skillet as needed. Makes 18 crêpes.

## Crêpes Suzette

*6 lumps sugar*
*1 large orange*
*1 tablespoon lemon juice*

*2 teaspoons grated lemon rind*
*6 tablespoons butter*
*⅓ cup Cointreau or Curaçao*
*⅓ cup Grand Marnier*
*Crêpes*
*⅓ cup cognac*

Rub the lumps of sugar on the orange rind. Squeeze the orange and grate the rind. Combine the sugar, orange juice, lemon juice, orange and lemon rinds and the butter in a skillet or in the flat pan of a chafing dish. Bring to a boil and add the Cointreau and Grand Marnier. Place the crêpes in the pan and turn until moistened. Fold into quarters. Pour the warmed cognac over them and set aflame.

## Crêpes Normande

*3 apples, peeled and sliced*
*¼ cup sugar*
*½ teaspoon cinnamon*

*Crêpes*
*⅓ cup melted butter*
*2 tablespoons brown sugar*
*½ cup apple brandy*

Combine the apples, sugar and cinnamon in a saucepan. Cook over low heat for 10 minutes, stirring frequently. Cool for 15 minutes. Prepare the crêpes but cook only on one side, stacking them as they are made. Place a tablespoon of the mixture on cooked side of each crêpe and roll up carefully. Arrange in a buttered baking dish. Sprinkle with the butter and brown sugar. Bake in a 375° oven 15 minutes. Pour the warmed brandy over the top and set aflame.

## Apple Fritters

*⅓ cup sugar*
*3 large apples, peeled, cored and diced*
*¾ cup sifted flour*
*Dash of salt*
*¼ cup milk*
*1 tablespoon melted butter*
*2 tablespoons cognac*
*1 egg yolk, beaten*
*1 egg white, stiffly beaten*
*Fat for deep frying*

Sprinkle the sugar (reserving 1 tablespoon) on the apples. Cover and set aside for 1 hour. Mix the flour, salt, milk, butter and cognac until smooth. Add the egg yolk. The batter should be the consistency of heavy cream, so add a little water if too thick. Fold in the egg white. Heat the fat to 370°. Drain the apples and dip into the batter. Fry a few pieces at a time until well browned. Drain and sprinkle with sugar. Place in a 450° oven until glazed. Pineapple may be prepared in same way. Serves 6.

## Beignets

A *beignet*, or fritter, must be properly prepared to be successful. Appliance companies have been of great help in recent years. The new thermostatically controlled deep fryers are excellent for this purpose. If you don't own one, use a deep, heavy saucepan, a frying basket, and an accurate thermometer. The temperature of the fat is all-important, and should be maintained at the recommended heat level at all times. Never crowd the basket if you want crisp, well browned fritters. Use sweet, fresh fat and save it for future use. Never fry any strong-flavored foods in it if you want to use it for fritters again.

## Beignets Soufflés

*¼ lb. butter*
*1 cup water*
*½ teaspoon salt*
*1 tablespoon sugar*
*1 cup sifted flour*
*4 eggs*
*1 tablespoon cognac*
*Fat for deep frying*
*Confectioners' sugar*

Combine the butter, water, salt and sugar in a saucepan. Bring to a boil and when butter melts add all the flour at once, stirring constantly over low heat until mixture leaves the sides of the pan. Remove from heat, and add one egg at a time, beating well after each addition. Add the cognac. Heat the fat to 370° and drop the mixture into it by the tablespoon. Do not fry too many at once. Fry until browned on all sides. (There is no need to turn the *beignets*, as they turn themselves when brown on one side.) Drain and sprinkle with confectioners' sugar. Serve hot. Serves 6.

### VARIATIONS

#### Beignets Dauphine

Split the fritters and fill with sweetened whipped cream, flavored with almond extract. Sprinkle with confectioners' sugar.

#### Beignets Grandmère

Split the fritters and fill with strawberry jam. Sprinkle with confectioners' sugar.

#### Medicis

Split the fritters and fill with chocolate Bavarian cream. Serve with chocolate sauce. (See recipe under Dessert Sauces.)

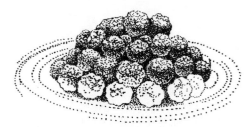

## Crème Frite Flambé

*3 egg yolks*
*¼ cup sugar*
*Dash of salt*
*4 tablespoons cornstarch*
*½ cup cognac*
*2 cups heavy cream, scalded*
*1 tablespoon lemon juice*
*½ cup vanilla wafer crumbs*
*1 egg, beaten*
*¼ cup ground almonds*
*Fat for deep frying*

Beat the egg yolks in the top of a double boiler. Stir in the sugar and salt. Mix the cornstarch and half the cognac to a smooth paste. Add to the egg yolk mixture. Gradually add the cream, stirring constantly. Place over hot water and cook, stirring constantly until thick. Add the lemon juice. Pour into a well buttered oblong dish (about ¾″ to 1″ deep). Cool until firm. Cut into 2″ squares. Dip in the crumbs, then the egg and then the almonds. Heat the fat to 370° and fry a few at a time until browned. Drain. Place in a heated serving dish, pour the remaining cognac over them and set aflame. Serves 6.

## Black Bottom Pie

20 gingersnaps, crushed fine
½ cup melted butter
4 egg yolks
1½ tablespoons cornstarch
2 cups milk, scalded
1 cup sugar
2 squares (ounces) unsweetened chocolate,
    melted
1 teaspoon vanilla
1 tablespoon gelatin
¼ cup cold water
2 tablespoons cognac
4 egg whites
1 cup whipped cream
3 tablespoons shaved chocolate

Preheat oven to 325°. Mix the gingersnaps and butter together. Press on the bottom and sides of a buttered 11″ pie plate. Bake 10 minutes. Cool. Lightly beat the egg yolks and cornstarch in the top of a double boiler. Gradually add the milk, mixing steadily. Add ½ cup of sugar. Place over hot water and cook, stirring frequently until mixture coats the spoon. Measure 1½ cups of the custard mixture and add the melted chocolate and vanilla, mixing until well blended. Cool slightly and pour into prepared pie plate. Chill. Soften the gelatin in water and add to the remaining custard, stirring until dissolved. (If custard is too cool to dissolve gelatin, heat slightly over hot water.) Cool slightly. Add cognac. Beat the egg whites until peaks form. Gradually add remaining sugar, beating until stiff. Fold into the custard. Pour this over the chocolate mixture in the pie plate. Chill. Cover with the whipped cream and sprinkle with the shaved chocolate. Serves 8-10.

## Chocolate Angel Pie

3 egg whites
Dash of salt
⅛ teaspoon cream of tartar
¾ cup sifted sugar
¾ cup ground blanched almonds
1 teaspoon almond extract
¼ pound sweet chocolate
3 tablespoons brewed coffee
1 tablespoon cognac
1 cup heavy cream

Beat the egg whites until foamy. Add the salt and cream of tartar. Beat until peaks form. Beat in the sugar, a spoonful at a time, beating until stiff. Fold in the almonds and extract. Pile on the bottom and sides of a 9″ buttered pie plate. Bake in a 275° oven for 45 minutes or until firm and lightly browned. Cool. Melt the chocolate in the coffee. Add the cognac, stirring until smooth. Whip the cream and fold in the chocolate mixture thoroughly. Pour into the prepared pie plate. Chill at least 3 hours before serving. Serves 6-8.

## Omelette Norvégienne

3 egg whites
¼ teaspoon cream of tartar
¾ cup sugar
1 teaspoon vanilla
1 sponge cake (9″ round or 8″ square)
¼ cup Curaçao
1 quart vanilla ice cream (firm)

Preheat the oven to 450°. Beat the egg whites and cream of tartar until peaks form. Gradually beat in half the sugar, continuing to beat until stiff but not dry. Fold in the remaining sugar and the vanilla. Cover a board with brown paper and place the cake on it. Sprinkle with the Curaçao. Spread the ice cream to within 1″ of the edges. Cover with the meringue right to the edges of the cake. Sprinkle with a little granulated sugar. Bake 5 minutes. Transfer to a chilled dish and serve at once. Serves 6.

## Baked Melon Glacé

*3 small cantaloupes*
*½ cup cognac*
*6 egg whites*
*1¼ cups sifted sugar*
*1 quart vanilla ice cream (very firm)*
*Crushed ice*

Preheat oven to 475°. Cut the melons in half; cut the pulp into balls or squares and pour the cognac over them. Reserve the shells. Beat the egg whites until stiff but not dry; fold the sugar in very gradually. Half fill the shells with the melon balls. Cover with the firm ice cream, and then pile the meringue over it, being sure the edges are well covered. Place the ice in a baking pan with the melons on top of it. Bake until meringue is just browned, about 3 minutes. Serve immediately. Serves 6.

## Baked Alaska Pie

*3 egg whites*
*Few grains of salt*
*¼ teaspoon cream of tartar*
*¾ cup powdered sugar*
*1 teaspoon vanilla*
*1 prebaked pie shell, chilled*
*1 quart hard ice cream*

Preheat oven to 450°. Beat the egg whites, salt and cream of tartar until stiff but not dry. Add 1 tablespoon of sugar at a time, beating constantly until ⅓ cup is added. Fold in the remaining sugar and vanilla. Fill the pie shell with the ice cream and cover with the meringue, being sure the edges are well covered. Sprinkle with a little sugar. Place the pie plate on a board and bake 5 minutes. Serve immediately. Serves 6.

## Refrigerator Chocolate Almond Torte

The torte is prepared in layers:

1. Cream ½ lb. sweet butter, gradually adding 1 cup sugar. Beat until light and fluffy. Add ½ lb. sweet chocolate, melted and cooled, and 1 teaspoon vanilla. Mix well. Spread on bottom of a buttered 9″ spring form. Chill for 2 hours before adding the next layer:

2. Cream ½ lb. sweet butter, gradually adding 1 cup sugar. Beat until light and fluffy. Add 1½ cups ground blanched almonds and 2 tablespoons heavy cream. Mix well. Spread over the chocolate mixture. Chill and then cover with the following icing:

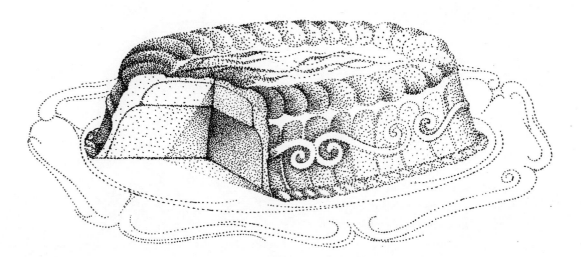

3. Melt ¼ lb. sweet chocolate in 3 tablespoons brewed coffee. Add 2 tablespoons cream. Spread over the nut filling. Chill. To serve, carefully run a knife around the spring form and remove sides. Serves 8-10.

## Biscuit Tortoni

¼ cup water
¾ cup sugar
5 egg yolks
1 tablespoon cognac
1 teaspoon vanilla
1 cup ground, toasted almonds
1 pint heavy cream whipped

Set refrigerator at coldest point.

Boil the water and sugar together until syrupy, about 5 minutes.

Beat the egg yolks in the top of a double boiler; gradually add the syrup, beating steadily. Place over hot water and stir until thick. Add cognac and vanilla. Cool. Fold in half the almonds and all of the whipped cream.

Pour into 6 large or 12 small individual paper cups. Sprinkle with the remaining almonds. Freeze for 3 to 4 hours.

## Banana Bombe

1½ pints heavy cream
3 bananas, sliced
1 teaspoon vanilla
¼ cup sugar
1 quart chocolate ice cream

Whip the cream; add the bananas, vanilla and sugar.

Spread the ice cream around a chilled bombe mold and pack it down with the back of a spoon. Fill with the banana mixture. Cover with a piece of buttered waxed paper and then the mold cover. Freeze in the refrigerator freezing compartment or home freezer for 3-4 hours. Unmold onto a chilled serving dish. Serves 6.

## Tri-color Bombe

1½ tablespoons gelatin
3 tablespoons cold water
3 cups heavy cream
4 tablespoons raspberry or strawberry jelly, melted
3 tablespoons sweet cocoa
2 tablespoons crème de cacao
2 tablespoons ground almonds
3 tablespoons Grand Marnier or Curaçao

Soften the gelatin in the water; place over hot water and stir until dissolved.

Whip the cream until stiff; remove ⅓ of the cream and combine with jelly and ⅓ the gelatin. Pour into a lightly oiled mold. Divide the remaining cream and combine one half with the cocoa, crème de cacao and half the remaining gelatin. Carefully spoon over the raspberry mixture. Combine the almonds and Grand Marnier with the remaining cream and gelatin. Pour over the chocolate mixture. Chill at least 4 hours. Carefully unmold. Serves 6.

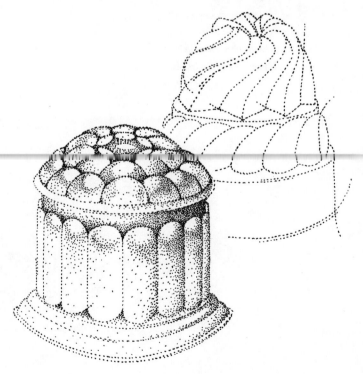

## Ice Cream Rollup

*1 cup sifted confectioners' sugar*
*¼ cup sifted flour*
*¼ cup unsweetened cocoa*
*½ teaspoon salt*
*5 egg yolks*
*1 teaspoon vanilla extract*
*5 egg whites, stiffly beaten*
*1 pint vanilla ice cream*

Grease a jelly roll pan (about 11″ x 16″), line it with waxed paper and grease the paper. Preheat oven to 400°. Sift the sugar, flour, cocoa and salt together. Beat the egg yolks until thick and lemon colored. Stir in the dry ingredients, stirring just enough to blend together. Add the vanilla. Fold in the egg whites. Spread the mixture in the lined pan. Bake 15 minutes or until a cake tester comes out clean. Turn out onto a damp cloth and carefully peel off the paper. Roll up in the cloth and cool. (If you have a freezer, you can unroll the cake as soon as it has cooled, spread it with ice cream and roll up again. Keep in the freezer until ready to serve.) If you haven't a freezer, keep the cake rolled up in the cloth until needed; then spread with the ice cream and roll up again. Cut into diagonal slices. If desired, serve with hot chocolate sauce and whipped cream. Serves 8-10.

## Bavarian Cream

*1 tablespoon gelatin*
*2 tablespoons water*
*4 egg yolks*
*½ cup sugar*
*½ cup light cream, scalded*
*½ cup milk, scalded*
*1 teaspoon vanilla*
*1 cup heavy cream, whipped*

Soften the gelatin in the water. Beat the egg yolks in the top of a double boiler with a wooden spoon, gradually adding the sugar. Add the cream and milk slowly, beating steadily. Place over hot water and cook, stirring constantly until thick and smooth. Remove from hot water. Add the vanilla and gelatin, stirring until gelatin dissolves. Cool, mixing occasionally. Strain. Fold in the whipped cream. Pour into a mold and chill until set. Serve with strawberries, raspberries or chocolate sauce. Serves 6.

For chocolate Bavarian Cream: add 2 squares of melted unsweetened chocolate when adding the gelatin.

## Coffee Cream

*½ cup brewed coffee*
*1 cup sugar*
*8 egg yolks*
*½ teaspoon coffee extract*
*½ teaspoon vanilla extract*
*1½ pints heavy cream*

Cook the coffee and sugar over low heat until the mixture is syrupy and a thread forms when a fork is lifted from the pan. Beat the egg yolks, coffee extract and vanilla in a bowl, and gradually add the syrup, beating steadily until thick and cold. Whip the cream and fold into the coffee mixture. Pour into a mold and place in the freezing compartment (control set at coldest point), or in the freezer. Freeze for 3-4 hours, or until firm. Serves 8-10.

## Apricot Cream

*1 tablespoon gelatin*
*3 tablespoons cold water*
*1 can (#2) apricots, drained and pitted or*
*    3 jars puréed apricots (baby food)*
*2 tablespoons lemon juice*
*⅓ cup sugar*
*1½ cups heavy cream*

Soften the gelatin in the water; place over hot water and stir until dissolved. Combine with the applesauce, lemon rind and mace. Chill ½ hour. Whip the cream and fold it into the apple mixture. Spoon into individual serving dishes and chill. Serves 6.

## Apple Fromage

*1 tablespoon gelatin*
*2 tablespoons cold water*
*3 cups applesauce, fresh or canned*
*2 teaspoons grated lemon rind*
*⅛ teaspoon mace*
*1 cup heavy cream*

Soften the gelatin in the water; place over hot water and stir until dissolved. Combine with the applesauce, lemon rind and mace. Chill ½ hour. Whip the cream and fold it into the apple mixture. Spoon into individual serving dishes and chill. Serves 6.

## Pots de Crème (Vanille)

*6 egg yolks*
*½ cup sugar*
*2 cups heavy cream, scalded*
*1 teaspoon vanilla powder or extract*

Preheat the oven to 300°. Beat the egg yolks until thick. Beat in the sugar, and gradually add the cream, stirring constantly. Stir in the vanilla. Strain and pour into 6 custard cups. Place in a pan of warm water and cover the pan. Bake 15 minutes or until a knife inserted in the center of the custard comes out clean. Chill.

## Pots de Crème (Chocolat)

*4 ounces sweet chocolate*
*2 tablespoons brewed coffee*
*10 egg yolks*
*¼ cup sugar*
*2 cups heavy cream, scalded*

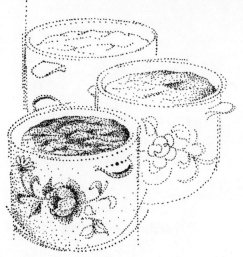

Melt the chocolate in the coffee, stirring until smooth. Beat the egg yolks in the top of a double boiler, gradually adding the sugar. Add the cream, beating constantly. Beat in the chocolate. Place over hot water and cook, stirring constantly until thickened. Strain into 8 custard cups. Chill.

## Crème Caramel

*¾ cup water*
*3 cups sugar*
*¼ teaspoon cream of tartar*
*6 eggs*
*Dash of salt*
*1 cup milk, scalded*
*1 cup light cream, scalded*
*1 teaspoon vanilla*
*Whipped cream*

Combine the water, sugar and cream of tartar in a saucepan. Bring to a boil and cook over high heat until it begins to turn light brown. Cool for 15 minutes. Measure 1 cup of the syrup and reserve the rest. Preheat oven to 350°. Butter a 9″ ring mold and dust it with sugar. Beat the eggs and salt thoroughly; gradually add the 1 cup syrup, beating steadily. Add the milk, cream and vanilla. Pour into the mold. Place it in a shallow pan of hot water. Bake 35 minutes or until a knife comes out clean. Chill. Carefully unmold and fill center with whipped cream. Serve the remaining syrup separately. Serves 6-8.

## Cheese Cake

16 graham crackers
¼ lb. melted butter
¾ cup sugar
1 lb. cream cheese
2 teaspoons vanilla
½ cup cream
2 beaten eggs
1 cup sour cream mixed with 1 tablespoon
    sugar and 1 teaspoon vanilla

Make a crust by rolling graham crackers into crumbs, and mixing them with melted butter and ¼ cup of sugar. Press into the sides and bottom of a lightly buttered 10″ pie pan, and bake 5 minutes at 450°. Make the filling by combining cream cheese with the ½ cup sugar, vanilla, and cream. Beat well, blend in eggs and mix thoroughly. Pour into the crust and bake at 350° for 20 minutes. Remove pie from the oven and cover with sour cream-sugar-vanilla mixture. Bake another 5 minutes and cool before serving. Serves 6-8.

## Sicilian Cassato

1 large pound or sponge cake
1½ lbs. ricotta cheese
½ cup sugar
1 teaspoon vanilla
2 tablespoons cognac or rum
¼ cup chopped semi-sweet chocolate bits.
1 tablespoon chopped candied orange peel
Salt
Powdered sugar

Split cake into four layers, and put together with ricotta filling. Allow to ripen in the refrigerator for several hours. Dust the top with powdered sugar before serving. Serves 8-10.

### Ricotta Filling

Mix cheese, sugar, and vanilla flavoring in an electric blender or mixer until smooth and creamy. Add remaining ingredients and extra sugar if your palate dictates.

## Coeur à la Crème

1 lb. cream cheese
¼ cup cream
¼ teaspoon salt
2 tablespoons powdered sugar

This is one of the most famous and pleasant of cheese desserts. A simple version is made by mixing the cream cheese with the cream, salt and sugar. Line a heart-shaped *coeur à la crème* basket (or mold) with wet cheesecloth, pour in the cheese mixture, and chill. Turn out on a dish, surround with *bar-le-duc* or strawberry preserves, and serve with butter biscuits. Serves up to 12.

## Chocolate Soufflé

5 tablespoons sweet butter
3 tablespoons sifted cake flour
6 ounces dark sweet chocolate
1½ cups light cream
1″ vanilla bean
4 egg yolks
4 tablespoons granulated sugar
**6 egg whites**
**Pinch of salt**
*Granulated sugar*
*Confectioners' sugar*

Melt 3 tablespoons butter in pan. Stir in flour off fire. Cut up chocolate in small pieces, put into saucepan with light cream and stir over slow fire until it dissolves. Pour this mixture slowly onto butter and flour. When smooth, stir over fire until it just comes to a boil. Remove, add scraped vanilla bean, cool and cover. Beat egg yolks with granulated sugar until light and fluffy. Add this to soufflé mixture. Beat egg whites with the salt in a metal bowl with a whisk until stiff, and carefully fold into the soufflé mixture. Grease inside of an 8″ soufflé dish with remaining butter, dust with coarse granulated sugar, fill with soufflé mixture and sprinkle top with fine granulated sugar. Stand in pan of hot water and bake in 350° oven for 30 minutes; increase heat to 375° for another 15 minutes, or until firm to the touch. Sprinkle with confectioners' sugar and serve at once. Serve with chocolate sauce. Serves 6.

## Soufflé Demoiselle

8 egg yolks
2 tablespoons flour
⅓ cup sugar
¾ cup heavy cream
1 teaspoon vanilla
¼ cup Grand Marnier or Curaçao
12 ladyfingers, split
8 egg whites
⅛ teaspoon salt

Beat the egg yolks, flour and sugar together in the top of a double boiler. Add the cream. Place over hot water and cook, stirring constantly until thick and smooth. Add the vanilla and liqueur. Let cool for 15 minutes, stirring occasionally.

Preheat the oven to 350°. Line a buttered 2 quart soufflé dish with the lady fingers.

Beat the egg whites and salt until stiff but not dry and fold into the cooled mixture. Pour into the prepared soufflé dish. Bake 30 minutes. Serve at once. Serves 6-8.

## Brazil Nut Soufflé

4 egg yolks
¼ cup sugar
3 tablespoons flour
¼ teaspoon salt
1 cup ground Brazil nuts
1 cup heavy cream
3 tablespoons melted butter
2 tablespoons cognac
4 egg whites

Beat the egg yolks, gradually adding the sugar, flour and salt. Mix well.

Combine the nuts and cream in a saucepan. Cook over low heat until bubbles form. Gradually add the sugar mixture, stirring constantly until thick, about 5 minutes. Add butter and cognac. Let cool for 15 minutes.

Preheat the oven to 350°. Beat the egg whites until stiff but not dry and fold into the nut mixture. Pour into a buttered 1½ quart soufflé dish. Bake 30 minutes. Serve at once. Serve with cognac-flavored whipped cream if desired. Serves 6.

## Chestnut Soufflé

4 eggs
3 egg yolks
½ cup granulated sugar
2 tablespoons plain gelatin
¼ cup brandy
1 cup sweet chestnut purée
2 cups whipped cream
8 marrons glacés
½ cup chopped browned almonds

Put eggs and egg yolks into an electric mixer with granulated sugar. Beat until thick. Melt gelatin in brandy over a slow fire. Carefully fold into egg mousse with a wooden spoon. Mix in sweet chestnut purée and one cup whipped cream.

Tie a band of oiled paper around a 7″ soufflé dish. Pour in mixture and put in refrigerator to set for 2 hours. Remove and

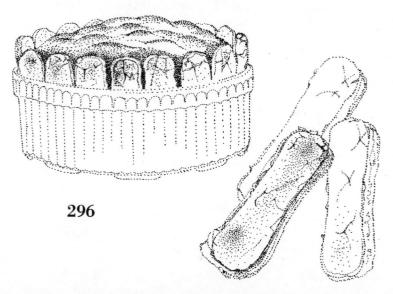

decorate top with rest of whipped cream forced through rose tube of pastry bag. Arrange marrons glacés on top of cream. Carefully remove paper and stick chopped almonds around the edge. Serves 8-10.

## Apricot Soufflé

*2 tablespoons butter*
*3 level tablespoons flour*
*¾ cup milk*
*2 teaspoons lemon juice*
*½ cup apricot jam or*
  *1 cup cooked apricot pulp*
*4 egg yolks*
*4 tablespoons sugar*
*5 egg whites, beaten stiff*
*Confectioners' sugar*

Melt butter and stir in flour off fire. When blended, pour on milk. Stir over fire until thick; it must not boil. Then add lemon juice and apricot jam or cooked apricot pulp. Mix in egg yolks and sugar, and lastly fold in beaten egg whites.

Grease an 8″ soufflé dish. Dust with sugar and tie wax paper outside to form a cuff. Fill with mixture and bake for ½ hour in a 350° oven. Remove paper, dust with confectioners' sugar and serve immediately. Serves 6.

## Strawberry Soufflé Glacé

*1 cup sugar*
*1 cup water*
*2 cups strawberries, fresh or frozen*
*4 egg yolks*
*2 cups light cream, scalded*
*2 cups heavy cream, whipped*

Combine ½ cup sugar and the water in a saucepan. Cook until syrupy, about 5 minutes. Add the berries and cook 5 minutes. Force through a sieve.

Beat the egg yolks and remaining sugar in the top of a double boiler. Gradually add the light cream, stirring steadily. Place over hot water and cook, stirring constantly until thick. Strain. Add to strawberry syrup. Cool. Fold in the whipped cream.

Butter a band of wax paper and tie it around the top of a buttered 1½ quart soufflé dish so that it extends 2″ above the top. Pour the mixture into dish.

Place in the freezing compartment and freeze for 3-4 hours. Carefully remove collar and serve. Serves 6.

## Lemon Soufflé

*1 large lemon*
*4 level teaspoons cornstarch*
*¾ cup creamy milk*
*3 teaspoons sweet butter*
*4 egg yolks*
*6 tablespoons fine granulated sugar*
*6 egg whites*
*Pinch of salt*
*2 teaspoons vegetable shortening*
*Granulated sugar*
*Confectioners' sugar*

Grate lemon and squeeze juice. Add cornstarch to juice and mix until smooth. Scald milk and mix carefully into cornstarch. Stir over slow fire until it comes to a boil and allow to boil gently 2 or 3 minutes, stirring all the time. Add butter, bit by bit. Then add grated lemon rind. Beat egg yolks with granulated sugar until very light and fluffy. Add carefully to sauce. Beat egg whites with salt in a metal bowl with a whisk until stiff. Fold carefully into lemon mixture.

Grease an 8″ soufflé dish with vegetable shortening, dust with coarse granulated sugar and fill to top of dish with soufflé mixture. Sprinkle top with fine granulated sugar and stand in pan of hot water. Bake in 375° oven for 40 to 45 minutes or until firm to the touch. Remove, dust with confectioners' sugar and serve at once. Serve with lemon sauce. Serves 6.

## Orange Soufflé

4 eggs
3 egg yolks
6 tablespoons sugar
1½ tablespoons plain gelatin
2 teaspoons lemon juice
3 tablespoons water
2 large oranges
2 cups heavy cream, whipped
½ cup strained red currant jelly

Put eggs, egg yolks and sugar in electric mixer. Beat until thick. Dissolve gelatin in lemon juice and water over slow fire. Carefully stir this into egg mousse with grated rind and juice of one orange. Mix in whipped cream.

Tie a band of oiled paper around an 8″ soufflé dish. Pour in mixture and put to set in refrigerator for about 2 hours. Remove and arrange around the edge skinned sections of other orange. Dip a soft brush into red currant jelly and carefully cover top of whole soufflé with red currant jelly. Chill again and remove the paper just before serving. Serves 8-10.

## Hot Chocolate Sauce

½ pound sweet chocolate
½ cup brewed coffee
1 tablespoon cognac
1 teaspoon vanilla
3 tablespoons heavy cream

Break the chocolate into small pieces and combine with the coffee in a saucepan. Place over low heat and stir until melted and smooth. Add the cognac, vanilla and cream. Hold over hot water until needed.

## Fruit Sauce

¼ cup sugar
2 tablespoons water
2 cups fresh or frozen strawberries or raspberries
½ cup heavy cream, whipped
½ teaspoon vanilla

Combine the sugar, water and berries in a saucepan. Bring to a boil and cook over low heat 5 minutes, stirring occasionally. Force through a sieve and cool. Fold in the whipped cream and vanilla.

## Lemon Sauce

¾ cup sugar
3 tablespoons sifted flour
3 egg yolks
¾ cup cold water
2 tablespoons sweet butter
¾ cup lemon juice
Grated rind of one lemon
1 teaspoon grated orange rind
1 teaspoon grated lime rind

Put sugar and flour in top of double boiler and add egg yolks. Mix in cold water; stir over hot water for about 10 minutes. Add butter bit by bit. Mix in lemon juice and lemon, orange and lime rinds. Mix well and serve hot or cold. Makes 2½-3 cups.

# CAKE, COOKIE, and BREAD

# Cake, Cookie and Bread

At different periods in history, cakes have been credited with propitiating the fates, inspiring vigor and sparking a Revolution. They occasioned a warning from the prophet Jeremiah and nostalgic reminiscences by authors as diverse as Charles Dickens and Marcel Proust. Traditionally regarded as rewards and prizes, they are the proper symbols for feasts, festivals, celebrations and all happy occasions. Cake recipes were jealously guarded in early England. One of the most famous, the Nun's Cake, was said to be an invention of Hilda, the great Abbess of Whitby Abbey, where learning and culture flourished. At the court of Charles II, most sought-after was the Countess of Rutland's recipe for Banbury Cake, which included cinnamon, mace, 2 pounds of butter and 10 of currants. Cooking temperatures and times in those days were decidedly vague. An oven was too hot if it scorched the inquiring hand. A cake was cooked in the time in which a *Miserere* could be repeated slowly.

The cake as a success symbol became an American adoption. The expression "to take the cake" came from the custom of presenting a cake to the winner of the cake walk—a contest held in the South which gave its name to a popular dance. Cookie is an anglicization of *koekje*, a diminutive St. Nicholas cake put in

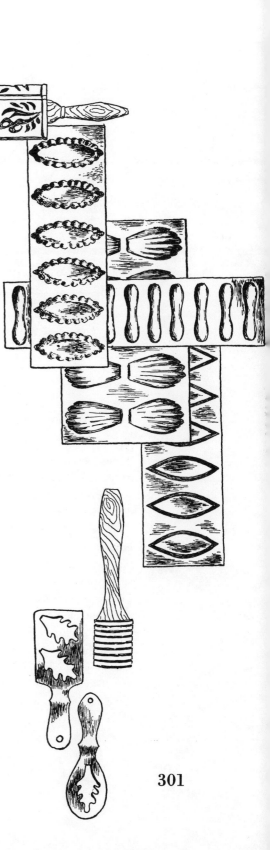

children's stockings by the Dutch settlers. Specialties which have delighted Americans and their European ancestors over the years: the superb Viennese *torten* with their rich fillings and frostings; the fluted *kugelhoff*, baked in a tube mold, which goes so well with coffee; Germany's festive *baumkuchen*, a white-frosted edifice tiered like a skyscraper which only expert hands can produce; little cup cakes; roly-poly melon cake; sugary cookies. Also deserving of praise are the small, melting cakes of France such as the delicate scallop-shaped *madeleines* beloved of Proust.

In these days of prepackaged, presliced and even pre-digested foods, bread making, that other ancient and most honest art, is having a welcome revival. Down through the ages bread has held its place as man's most precious food. Loaves of bread were made tens of thousands of years ago in the Stone Age. By the time of the Pharaohs, bread making was big business. Every village had its public ovens, every man of wealth his private baker. In twelfth-century England, snobbism required a distinction between breads. The makers of rye bread for the poor were called Brown Bakers while those who made fine wheaten loaves for the rich were known as White Bakers. Every country has its own specialties. In France, a three-foot-long *flûte* of bread thrusts from every woman's marketing bag. Italy has her crisp breadsticks and festive *panettone*, Sweden the delicate *limpa*.

If the baking and eating of cakes and bread is one of the oldest, it is also one of the most constant of life's pleasures. With French sociologist François Fournier, we can anticipate that "instead of by battles . . . the rival portions of humanity will one day dispute each other's excellence in the manufacture of little cakes."

301

## Génoise

*6 eggs*
*1 cup sugar*
*1 teaspoon vanilla*
*1 cup sifted cake flour*
*¼ pound butter, melted and cooled*

Butter a cake pan 9″ in diameter and dust it lightly with flour.

Beat the eggs and sugar in the top of a double boiler. Place over hot water and continue beating with a wire whisk or rotary beater for about 15 minutes. Remove from the heat and beat until mixture is thick and a ribbon forms when beater is lifted. Preheat oven to 350°.

Gently mix in the vanilla; sift the flour over the mixture a little at a time and fold in carefully. Add the lukewarm butter gradually in a folding motion. Pour into pan.

Bake 40 minutes, or until a cake tester comes out clean and cake leaves the sides of the pan. Turn out immediately onto a cake rack to cool.

This is a very versatile cake—it can be iced, or split and put together with a butter cream, or served plain.

## Butter Cream

*¼ pound butter*
*2 cups confectioners' sugar*
*3 egg whites*
*1 teaspoon vanilla*

Cream the butter until soft and smooth. Gradually add 1 cup sugar.

Beat the egg whites until stiff; gradually fold in the remaining sugar and the vanilla. Combine the 2 mixtures.

For chocolate butter cream, add 3 squares of melted unsweetened chocolate when combining the butter mixture with the egg-white mixture.

For mocha butter cream, add 2 teaspoons coffee extract and 1 tablespoon cocoa instead of the vanilla.

## Delicate Spice Cake

¼ pound butter
2 cups dark brown sugar, packed
3 eggs
2¼ cups sifted cake flour
¼ teaspoon salt
1 teaspoon baking soda
2 teaspoons cinnamon
2 teaspoons ginger
½ teaspoon nutmeg
¼ teaspoon ground cloves
1 cup sour cream

Cream the butter, gradually adding the brown sugar. Add 1 egg at a time, beating well after each addition. Preheat the oven to 350°.

Sift together the flour, salt, baking soda, cinnamon, ginger, nutmeg and cloves. Add to the butter mixture alternately with the sour cream. Divide between 2 buttered 8″ layer cake pans.

Bake 30 minutes or until a cake tester comes out clean. Cool on a cake rack, and ice with the following:

¼ cup melted butter
2 cups sifted confectioners' sugar
¾ cup heavy cream

Mix the butter and sugar together. Add just enough cream to make the mixture spreadable. Ice the cake when it has completely cooled.

## Nut and Honey Cake

2 eggs
½ cup sugar
¼ cup brewed coffee
1 cup honey
1 tablespoon salad oil
2 cups sifted cake flour
⅛ teaspoon salt
¾ teaspoon baking powder
½ teaspoon baking soda
1 cup shelled filberts (hazelnuts)
2 tablespoons cognac

Oil a 10″ loaf pan and line it with waxed paper or aluminum foil. Preheat the oven to 325°.

Beat the eggs; gradually add the sugar. Beat until light and fluffy. Add the coffee, honey and oil, mixing well. Sift together the flour, salt, baking powder and baking soda; add the nuts. Add gradually to the honey mixture, stirring steadily. Add the cognac. Pour into the pan.

Bake 55 minutes, or until a cake tester comes out clean. Cool in the pan or on a cake rack. This is a moist cake and will keep well.

## Mocha Melon Cake

3 cups sifted cake flour
⅛ teaspoon salt
1 tablespoon baking powder
¾ cup (6 ounces) butter
2 cups sugar
3 eggs
½ cup milk
½ cup light cream
1 teaspoon vanilla extract
1 tablespoon cognac

Grease a 2-quart melon mold and dust it lightly with flour. Preheat oven to 375°.

Sift the flour, the salt and the baking powder together.

Cream the butter, gradually adding the sugar. Beat until light and fluffy. Beat in one egg at a time.

Mix the milk, cream, vanilla and cognac together. Add to the butter mixture alternately with the flour mixture. Turn into the mold.

Bake 35 minutes, or until a cake tester inserted in the center comes out clean. Unmold very carefully. Cool on a cake rack. When completely cold, cut a 2″ piece from the flat bottom of the cake and reserve it.

Carefully scoop out the center of the cake. Fill with 2 cups sweetened whipped cream or vanilla ice cream. Replace bottom. Quickly cover with Mocha Frosting which should be made while cake is cooling. Chill until ready to serve.

## Mocha Frosting

½ cup brewed coffee
⅔ cup sugar
¾ cup (6 ounces) soft butter

Boil the coffee and sugar together until syrupy, about 10 minutes. Cool 15 minutes.

Cream the butter, gradually adding the sugar. Beat vigorously until mixture is smooth. Cover the cake with it.

## Gateau Favorite

1 cup water
8 tablespoons sweet butter
⅛ teaspoon salt
½ cup flour
3 large or 4 small eggs
1 beaten egg
1½ cups blanched, shredded almonds
Chocolate pastry cream

Put the water and butter in a small, heavy pan and bring slowly to a boil. As it bubbles, add the salt and flour. Remove from the fire and beat until smooth. Beat in the 3 large or 4 small eggs, one at a time. Grease a cookie sheet and mark on it an 8″ circle. Fill a pastry bag with a large plain round tube with the paste and pipe onto the cookie sheet, covering the circle. Brush the top with the beaten egg and sprinkle generously with the shredded almonds. Bake in a 375° oven for 25-30 minutes, or until well risen and golden-brown all over. Remove and cool. Carefully split across in half and fill the bottom of the cake with Chocolate Pastry Cream.

## Chocolate Pastry Cream

Put in a bowl 1 whole egg and 1 egg yolk, 3 tablespoons flour and 3 tablespoons granulated sugar. Beat until smooth. Add 2 teaspoons plain gelatin, mix well, and pour on ¾ cup hot rich milk. Stir over the fire until the mixture comes just to a boil, then stir over ice until it is on the point of setting. Add 4 ounces dark sweet chocolate which has been melted with 3 tablespoons water. Stir into the egg mixture. When mixture is cool and thick, add 1 stiffly beaten egg white, 4 tablespoons whipped cream and 2 tablespoons dark rum. Fill into a pastry bag with a plain tube and cover the bottom of the cake. Cover the top with whipped cream (about 1¾ cups) forced through the rose tube of a pastry bag. Cover with other half of cake, sprinkle well with confectioners' sugar, chill in the refrigerator before serving.

## Nougat Cake

2¼ cups coarsely chopped mixed nuts
  (almonds, walnuts, filberts)
1½ cups chopped mixed candied fruits
¾ cup sifted cake flour
4 tablespoons unsweetened cocoa
1 teaspoon ginger
1 tablespoon cognac
½ cup honey
⅓ cup sugar

Line an 8″ square pan with waxed paper. Grease it heavily. Preheat oven to 300°.

Mix together the nuts, fruit, flour, cocoa, ginger and cognac.

Boil together the honey and sugar, stirring constantly until it reaches the soft ball stage (use a candy thermometer or drop a little into cold water. If it forms a ball, it is ready). Add to the previous mixture, stirring well. Spread evenly in the pan.

Bake 35 minutes. Cool and carefully remove waxed paper. Sprinkle with confectioners' sugar. This cake keeps very well wrapped in aluminum foil.

## Chocolate Flake Cake

½ pound butter
1 cup powdered sugar
6 egg yolks
4 ounces sweet chocolate, grated
1 cup ground almonds
⅔ cup dry bread crumbs
1 teaspoon vanilla extract
6 egg whites

Grease a 9″ spring form and dust lightly with flour. Preheat the oven to 375°.

Cream the butter, gradually adding the sugar. Beat until light. Beat in one egg yolk at a time. Add the chocolate, almonds, bread crumbs and vanilla, beating lightly.

Beat the egg whites until stiff but not dry. Fold into butter mixture carefully but thoroughly. Turn into the spring form.

Bake 35 minutes, or until a cake tester inserted in the center comes out clean. Remove sides of pan and cool. Cover with chocolate frosting or whipped cream.

## Orange Mousseline Cake

½ cup sifted cake flour
½ cup sifted potato flour
4 egg yolks
½ cup sugar
2 tablespoons grated orange rind
3 egg whites, stiffly beaten

Grease a 9″ layer cake pan and dust lightly with flour. Preheat oven to 300°.

Sift the flour and potato flour together.

Beat the egg yolks, sugar and rind until very light and fluffy. Fold in the flour and egg whites alternately. Use a very light touch to preserve the lightness of the cake. Turn into the pan.

Bake 40 minutes, or until a cake tester comes out clean. Cool on a cake rack. Ice with the following:

2 egg whites
¾ cup powdered sugar
3 tablespoons orange juice
½ teaspoon cream of tartar
⅛ teaspoon salt
1 teaspoon orange extract
1 tablespoon grated orange rind

Combine the egg whites, sugar, orange juice, cream of tartar and salt in the top of a double boiler. Place over hot water and beat with a rotary beater until peaks form. Stir in extract and rind.

## Open Fruit Cake

2⅓ cups sifted cake flour
½ teaspoon baking powder
¼ teaspoon salt
¾ cup sugar
6 ounces (¾ cup) butter
3 tablespoons heavy cream
2 egg yolks
Sliced peaches, halved apricots or plums

Sift the flour, baking powder, salt and 6 tablespoons sugar onto a board. Cut in the butter thoroughly. Make a well in the center and place the cream and egg yolks in it. Work in the flour mixture, kneading until a dough is formed. Chill for 1 hour.

Preheat the oven to 350°. Roll out the dough to fit an 11″ x 17″ pan. Butter the pan and dust lightly with flour. Place the dough in it and form a rim on all sides. Arrange the fruit in rows. (If apricots or plums are used, place them skin side down.) Sprinkle with the remaining sugar. Bake 40 minutes or until fruit is tender. Cut into strips while warm.

## Party Cake

1 cup almonds
6 ounces (¾ cup) butter
⅔ cup sugar
¼ pound sweet chocolate, melted
7 egg yolks
¾ teaspoon baking powder
7 egg whites stiffly beaten

Grind the almonds as fine as possible. Preheat oven to 350°.

Cream the butter, gradually adding the sugar. Beat in the chocolate, and then 1 egg yolk at a time. Add the nuts and baking powder, mixing well. Fold in the egg whites carefully but thoroughly. Divide evenly between 2 9″ buttered and floured layer cake pans. Bake 30 minutes or until a cake tester comes out clean. Cool. Prepare the following filling:

3 eggs
3 tablespoons sugar
1 teaspoon cornstarch
6 tablespoons softened butter
3 ounces sweet chocolate, melted
½ cup ground filberts or walnuts
1 tablespoon cognac

Beat the eggs in the top of a double boiler. Add sugar and cornstarch. Place over hot water and cook, stirring constantly until thickened. Remove from heat and add the butter and chocolate, stirring until well blended. Add nuts, cognac. Cool until thick enough to spread between layers.

## Kugelhoff

1 cake or package yeast
¼ cup lukewarm water
2½ cups sifted flour
2 eggs
2 cups scalded milk, cooled to lukewarm
6 tablespoons butter
½ teaspoon salt
4 tablespoons powdered sugar
½ cup currants
½ cup ground blanched almonds
3 tablespoons grated lemon rind
1 teaspoon cinnamon
¼ cup sifted confectioners' sugar

A kugelhoff pan is a fluted tube-like pan. If you do not have one use a 9″ tube pan.

Butter pan generously. Soften the yeast in the water in a large bowl. Sift ½ cup flour over it and blend in. Sift remaining flour over the yeast-flour blend, without mixing. Cover bowl with towel. Set in a warm place until the yeast mixture rises through the flour. Mix with the hand until blended and then mix in eggs, one at a time, and milk. Beat until very smooth. Cream the butter, salt and 2 tablespoons of the powdered sugar and beat into the first mixture (the resulting mixture should be softer than dough but a little firmer than batter). Turn half this mixture into the pan. Sprinkle over it the currants, almonds, lemon rind, cinnamon and remaining powdered sugar and cover with the remaining dough. Cover and set aside to rise until double in bulk.

Preheat oven to 400°. Bake kugelhoff for 40 minutes, or until browned. Cool in pan for 5 minutes, then carefully remove

⅔ *cup sugar*
3 *egg yolks*
⅔ *cup ground almonds*
⅔ *cup sifted cake flour*
3 *egg whites, stiffly beaten*
1 *cup heavy cream, whipped*

Melt the chocolate in the water. Preheat the oven to 325°. Butter an 8″ square pan and dust it lightly with flour.

Cream the butter, gradually adding the sugar, egg yolks and chocolate. Mix very well. Add almonds and beat well again. Add the flour, mixing lightly. Fold in the egg whites thoroughly.

Bake 35 minutes, or until a cake tester comes out clean. Cool.

Serve with the whipped cream, flavored with 2 tablespoons cocoa and 2 tablespoons sugar, if desired.

## Linzer Torte

1¼ *cups sifted cake flour*
½ *teaspoon baking powder*
6 *ounces (⅔ cup) sweet butter*
⅔ *cup sugar*
1¾ *cups ground blanched almonds*
4 *egg yolks*
1 *teaspoon vanilla*
1 *tablespoon lemon juice*
1 *teaspoon grated lemon rind*
4 *egg whites, stiffly beaten*

Sift the flour and baking powder together. Butter an 8″ square pan and dust it lightly with flour. Preheat oven to 350°.

Cream the butter. Gradually add the sugar, beating until light and fluffy. Add the almonds. Mix. Add 1 egg yolk at a time, beating well after each addition. Beat in the vanilla, lemon juice and lemon rind. Fold in the egg whites and then the flour mixture. Spread evenly in the cake pan.

Bake 40 minutes or until a cake tester comes out clean. Cool and dust with confectioners' sugar or spread with raspberry jam. Cut into squares.

and cool on a cake rack. Serve sprinkled with the confectioners' sugar.

## Cheese Torte

1 *pound cream cheese*
1 *cup sugar*
4 *tablespoons sifted cake flour*
¼ *teaspoon salt*
4 *egg yolks*
1 *cup light cream*
1 *teaspoon vanilla*
4 *egg whites, stiffly beaten*

Preheat oven to 325°.

Beat the cream cheese until light and fluffy. Add the sugar, flour and salt, beating well. Add 1 egg yolk at a time, beating after each addition. Beat in cream and vanilla. Fold in the egg whites.

Pour into a 9″ spring form pan. Bake 1 hour, or until a knife comes out clean. Cool for 3 hours and remove sides of pan.

## Chocolate Torte

¼ *pound sweet chocolate*
2 *tablespoons water*
¼ *pound butter*

## Orange Torte

*6 tablespoons butter*
*⅔ cup sugar*
*⅓ cup orange juice*
*2 tablespoons grated orange rind*
*3 hard-cooked egg yolks, mashed*
*4 egg yolks*
*½ cup sifted cake flour*
*½ teaspoon baking powder*
*2 egg whites, stiffly beaten*

Butter a 9″ layer cake pan and dust with flour. Preheat oven to 325°.

Cream the butter, gradually adding the sugar. Beat until light and fluffy. Add the orange juice, rind, the hard-cooked egg yolks, and one raw yolk at a time. Beat well. Add the flour and baking powder, mixing lightly. Fold in the egg whites, carefully but thoroughly.

Pour into the pan. Bake 45 minutes, or until a cake tester comes out clean. Cool. Cover with whipped cream flavored with 1 teaspoon orange extract, 2 teaspoons grated orange rind and 1 tablespoon sugar.

## Meringue Almond Torte

*8 egg whites*
*1¼ cups powdered sugar*
*1¼ cups finely ground blanched almonds*

Heavily grease 3 9″ layer cake pans (with slip bottoms if possible) and dust with flour. Preheat the oven to 350°.

Beat the egg whites until stiff. Combine the sugar and almonds; fold into the egg whites carefully but thoroughly. Divide among the three pans.

Bake 30 minutes, or until delicately browned. Carefully remove from pans and cool. Put together with Mocha Cream:

*½ cup sugar*
*⅓ cup water*
*4 egg yolks*
*¼ pound butter*
*2 tablespoons coffee extract*
*½ cup whipped cream*

Boil the sugar and water together until syrupy, about 7 minutes.

Beat the egg yolks in the top of a double boiler; gradually add the syrup, stirring steadily to prevent curdling. Place over hot water and cook, stirring until mixture coats spoon. Cool for 10 minutes.

Cream the butter and coffee extract together; gradually add the egg yolk mixture. Fold in the whipped cream. Spread between the layers. Chill before serving. Dust the top with confectioners' sugar. Make the cake the day before it is to be served.

## Walnut Roll

*5 egg yolks*
*½ cup sugar*
*1¼ cups ground walnuts*
*½ teaspoon baking powder*
*5 egg whites, stiffly beaten*

Preheat the oven to 375°. Butter a jelly roll pan (11″ x 17″), line with wax paper and butter again.

Beat the egg yolks, gradually adding the sugar. Add the walnuts and baking powder, mixing well. Fold in the egg whites. Spread evenly in the pan. Bake 15 minutes or until a cake tester comes out clean. Cover with a damp cloth and place in the refrigerator for ½ hour. Now prepare the filling:

½ cup hot milk
1½ cups ground walnuts
¼ pound butter
⅔ cup sugar
2 tablespoons cognac
1 cup heavy cream, whipped
½ cup confectioners' sugar

Pour the milk over the walnuts; cool. Cream the butter, gradually adding the sugar. Cream until light and fluffy. Beat in the nut mixture and cognac. Fold in the whipped cream.

Sprinkle the confectioners' sugar on a piece of wax paper. Loosen the bottom of the cake, and turn out. Peel paper from the cake. Spread filling on it, and carefully roll up like a jelly roll. Chill.

If desired, the roll may be filled with sweetened whipped cream.

## Chocolate Roll

6 ounces sweet chocolate
3 tablespoons brewed coffee
1 teaspoon coffee extract
1 teaspoon vanilla
5 egg yolks
⅔ cup sugar
5 egg whites, stiffly beaten
½ cup cocoa
2 cups whipped cream

Butter a jelly roll pan (11″ x 17″), line it with wax paper and butter again.

Melt the chocolate in the coffee; add the coffee extract and vanilla, mixing until smooth. Preheat oven to 350°.

Beat the egg yolks; add the sugar, beating until thick and light. Stir in the chocolate mixture. Fold in the egg whites carefully but thoroughly.

Spread evenly on the prepared pan. Bake 15 minutes, or until a cake tester comes out clean. (The cake should be fairly moist, so do not overbake.) Cover with a damp cloth and place in the refrigerator for 1 hour. Loosen from the pan.

Sprinkle the cocoa on a piece of wax paper and turn cake out onto it. Peel the paper away. Spread with whipped cream and roll up like a jelly roll. Chill.

## Lady Fingers

2 egg whites
Few grains salt
¼ cup sifted powdered sugar
2 egg yolks
1 teaspoon vanilla
½ cup sifted cake flour
3 tablespoons granulated sugar

Line a cookie sheet with heavy brown paper or aluminum foil.

Beat egg whites and salt until peaks form, then beat in the powdered sugar, a spoonful at a time. Preheat oven to 350°.

Beat egg yolks until thick; fold into the egg whites with the vanilla. Sift the flour over it and fold in carefully. Press through a pastry bag (with plain tip) onto the paper in 2″ strips, leaving space between each. Sprinkle with the granulated sugar.

Bake about 10-12 minutes, or until golden in color. Cool for 5 minutes and remove from the paper.

Lady fingers may be put together like sandwiches or served singly. If sandwiches are desired, brush one lady finger with egg white and cover with another. Makes about 24 single fingers.

## Madeleines

8 eggs
1¼ cups sugar
2 cups sifted cake flour
1 tablespoon lemon juice

½ teaspoon grated lemon rind
¼ pound plus 2 tablespoons melted sweet
    butter

Madeleine tins are scallop shaped, deep grooved molds. Cup cake or muffin tins may be used instead, however. Butter 16 tins and dust lightly with flour. Preheat oven to 350°.

Beat the eggs in the top of a double boiler. Add the sugar, place over hot water and beat steadily until the mixture thickens. Remove from heat; stir in the flour, lemon juice, rind and butter. Pour into the tins.

Bake 20 minutes, or until delicately browned. Cool on a cake rack and serve sprinkled with confectioners' sugar.

## Dutch Butter Cakes

3⅓ cups sifted cake flour
¼ teaspoon salt
1 cup sugar
½ teaspoon cinnamon
½ teaspoon ginger
½ teaspoon mace

1½ cups ground almonds
½ pound butter
½ cup milk
1 egg, beaten
½ cup poppy seeds

Sift the flour, salt, sugar, cinnamon, ginger and mace into a bowl. Add the almonds. Work in the butter with the hand. Add milk, kneading until a dough is formed. Preheat oven to 400°.

Press into a buttered 11″ x 17″ pan. Brush top with egg and sprinkle with the poppy seeds.

Bake 20 minutes or until browned. Cut into squares.

## Fudge Squares

¾ cup (6 ounces) butter
3 squares (ounces) unsweetened chocolate
½ cup sifted cake flour
½ teaspoon salt
½ teaspoon baking powder
3 eggs
1 cup powdered sugar
1 teaspoon vanilla
1 cup coarsely chopped walnuts

Grease an 8″ square pan and dust lightly with flour. Preheat the oven to 350°.

Melt the butter and chocolate over hot water. Cool for 15 minutes.

Sift the flour, salt and baking powder together. Beat the eggs, gradually adding the sugar. Continue to beat until light and fluffy. Stir in the chocolate mixture, then the flour mixture by the tablespoon. Add the vanilla and nuts, mixing until blended. Pour into the pan.

Bake 30 minutes, or until a cake tester comes out clean. Cut into squares and cool.

## Almond Macaroons

4 egg whites
½ teaspoon vanilla extract

1 cup powdered sugar
2 cups (½ pound) ground almonds

Line 2 cookie sheets with brown paper. Preheat the oven to 250°.

Beat the egg whites until stiff but not dry. Add the vanilla. Combine the sugar and nuts. Fold the mixture into the egg whites thoroughly.

Drop by the teaspoon onto the paper, leaving 1″ between each macaroon.

Bake 15 minutes, or until delicately browned and dry. Cool slightly and remove carefully with spatula. Recipe makes about 36 macaroons.

## Hazel Nut Cookies

3 eggs
½ cup sugar
½ teaspoon vanilla extract
2 teaspoons cognac
2 cups (½ pound) ground hazel nuts
1 tablespoon bread crumbs
18 hazel nuts, cut in half

Preheat oven to 300°.

Beat the eggs, sugar, vanilla and cognac until thick and light. Fold in the nuts and bread crumbs.

Shape teaspoons of the mixture into balls. Place on a greased cookie sheet, 1″ apart. Press a half nut on each.

Bake 15 minutes, or until delicately browned. Makes about 36 cookies.

## Milanese

1 cup plus 2 tablespoons sifted cake flour
⅛ teaspoon salt
3 cups ground almonds
3 tablespoons sugar
4 tablespoons butter
2 tablespoons grated orange rind
1 egg, beaten
2 tablespoons heavy cream
Candied cherries

Combine the flour, salt, almonds and sugar. Work in the butter and rind with the hand until thoroughly blended. Add the egg, mixing until a ball of dough is formed.

Wrap in aluminum foil or waxed paper. Chill for 2 hours. Preheat oven to 425°.

Roll out on a lightly floured board as thin as possible. Cut into desired shapes with cookie cutters. Brush with the cream and place a cherry in the center of each. Place on a buttered cookie sheet. Bake 7 minutes, or until delicately browned. Makes about 24 3″ cookies.

## Anise Cookies

1¾ cups sifted cake flour
1 tablespoon baking powder
¼ teaspoon salt
1 tablespoon anise seed
¼ pound sweet butter
1 cup sugar
4 egg yolks
2 teaspoons cognac
3 tablespoons heavy cream

Sift together the flour, baking powder and salt. Add the anise. Preheat oven to 300°.

Cream the butter, gradually adding the sugar. Beat until light and fluffy. Add 1 egg yolk at a time, and then the cognac. Beat in the flour mixture.

Roll out ¼″ thick on a heavily floured surface. (If the dough is too soft, add a little more sifted flour.) Cut into desired shapes. Place on a cookie sheet, ½″ apart. Brush with the cream. Bake 15 minutes or until delicately browned. Makes 36 cookies.

## Langues-de-Chat

¼ pound butter
½ cup sugar
1 teaspoon vanilla
4 egg whites
⅔ cup sifted cake flour

Preheat oven to 450°.

Cream the butter, gradually adding the sugar. Beat until light and fluffy. Add the vanilla and 1 egg white at a time, beating after each addition. Sift the flour over the mixture and fold in thoroughly. Press through a pastry bag (plain tip) onto a buttered, floured cookie sheet. Make the cookies about 2″ long.

Bake about 3-5 minutes or until edges are lightly browned. Remove from pan immediately and cool. Makes about 4 dozen.

## Cheese Cookies

2¼ cups sifted cake flour
⅛ teaspoon salt
½ pound butter
¼ pound cottage cheese, drained
¼ pound cream cheese
1 egg yolk, beaten
1 egg white
¼ cup sugar

Sift the flour and salt into a bowl. Work in the butter, cottage cheese and cream cheese with the hand. Add the egg yolk, mixing until a ball of dough is formed. Chill 2 hours.

Preheat oven to 375°. Roll out the dough as thin as possible on a lightly floured surface. Cut into desired shapes. Brush with the egg white and sprinkle with the sugar. Place on an ungreased cookie sheet. Bake 12 minutes, or until browned and crisp. Makes about 4 dozen.

## Tonilles

4 ounces butter
¾ cup sugar
1¼ cups flour
3 ounces ground filberts or almonds (unblanched)
Honey
Confectioners' sugar

Cream the butter, add the sugar and beat until light and fluffy. Mix in the flour and work until it is well distributed. Add the ground nuts. Turn mixture out onto a pastry board and roll out a little less than ½″ thick. Cut in 1½″ rounds with a cookie cutter. Bake on a cookie sheet at 350° until a delicate brown, about 8-10 minutes.

Remove, cool, sandwich two rounds together with honey, dust each sandwich with confectioners' sugar. Makes 12.

## Viennese Vanilla Crescents

¾ cup (1½ sticks) sweet butter
4 tablespoons powdered sugar
2 cups sifted flour
½ cup ground almonds or hazelnuts, unblanched
Pinch of salt
Confectioners' sugar flavored with vanilla bean

Cream the butter, slowly add the powdered sugar and work in the flour, a little at a time. Add the ground nuts.

Chill mixture for 2 hours in the refrigerator. Roll out on a floured board and make a finger-thick roll. Cut into segments 3″ long and curve each to make a crescent shape. Bake in a 350° oven on a cookie sheet for 10-15 minutes. Remove at once, and very gently toss the crescents in flavored confectioners' sugar (to make this, put a vanilla bean into a container of sugar about 2 hours before making the cookies; put about ½ cup of this vanilla sugar in a bowl for cookie coating) until well covered. Makes 24 cookies.

## California Coffeecake

1 cake or package yeast
¼ cup lukewarm water
¼ cup warm buttermilk
⅓ cup sugar
½ teaspoon salt
1½ tablespoons vegetable shortening
1 egg, beaten
1½ cups sifted flour
2 tablespoons brown sugar
½ teaspoon cinnamon
2 tablespoons melted butter
3 tablespoons chopped walnuts or almonds

Prepare the cake the day before it is to be served.

Soften the yeast in the lukewarm water. Combine the buttermilk, 1½ tablespoons sugar, salt, shortening, egg, half of the flour, and the yeast mixture mixing steadily. Beat with a spoon until smooth. Add the remaining flour gradually, adding just enough to form a dough.

Knead on a lightly floured surface for 1 minute. Cover with a damp cloth for 5 minutes. Pat into a greased 8″ square pan.

Mix the remaining sugar, brown sugar, cinnamon, butter and nuts together. Sprinkle over the top of the cake. Cover with aluminum foil and chill overnight.

In the morning, remove foil and bake in 375° oven for 35 minutes. Serve warm.

## Swedish Coffee Bread

2 packets active dry yeast
2½ cups warm milk
1 cup melted butter
1 cup granulated sugar
½ teaspoon salt
20 crushed cardamom seeds
8 cups flour
½ cup blanched, chopped, browned
   almonds
Coarse sugar granules

Dissolve the yeast in ½ cup warm milk. Mix the butter with the remaining milk, sugar, salt, cardamom seeds and a small amount of the flour. Beat until quite smooth, add the yeast and, gradually, the rest of the flour, beating with a wooden spoon until smooth and firm. Sprinkle the dough with a little flour and cover it with a clean cloth. Allow to rise in a warm place until double its bulk (about 2 hours). Then turn out onto a lightly floured board and knead until smooth. To shape the bread, divide dough into 2 or 3 parts. Cut each part into 3 pieces of equal size; roll into long ropes with the hands and braid. Place on a buttered baking sheet, cover and allow to rise. Brush with beaten egg. Sprinkle the top with chopped almonds and the coarse sugar granules. Bake in a 375° oven for 35 minutes.

## Saffron Bread

2 cakes compressed yeast
2½ cups warm milk
1 teaspoon saffron
1 tablespoon brandy
1½ cups granulated sugar
¼ teaspoon salt
2 eggs
1 cup melted butter
8 cups flour
½ cup ground almonds
1 cup white seedless raisins
½ cup chopped citron peel
½ cup chopped orange peel
Grated rind of 1 lemon

Dissolve the yeast in ½ cup warm milk. Put the saffron and brandy in a mortar and pound with a pestle until smooth. Mix the remaining milk with the saffron, sugar, salt, eggs, half the butter and a small amount of the flour. Add the dissolved yeast and, gradually, the rest of the flour. Beat with a wooden spoon until smooth and firm. Sprinkle with a little flour and cover with a clean cloth. Allow to rise in a warm place until double its bulk (about 2 hours). Turn out dough onto a floured board and knead until smooth. Cover with a cloth and leave for ½ hour. Then roll out into a long sheet, brush with the remaining butter, sprinkle the top evenly with the almonds, raisins, citron and orange peels and grated lemon rind, pressing them down well with the back of a wooden spoon and sprinkle well with granulated sugar. Roll up like a jelly roll, very tightly. Chill well for 1 hour, then cut into ¾″ slices. Place on well buttered baking sheets and allow to rise in a warm place for ½ to ¾ hour. Brush with a mixture of milk and sugar and bake in a 375° oven for 15-20 minutes, or until lightly browned.

## French Bread

### THIS RECIPE MAKES 1 LOAF

The *pain ordinaire* of France and Italy is made without milk, sugar or fat. It gets its crustiness by being brushed with cold water at ten-minute intervals during the baking period. It is a relatively heavy dough and requires the maximum time for rising.

*1 cup lukewarm water*
*1½ teaspoons salt*
*1 cake compressed yeast*
*3½ to 3¾ cups sifted flour*

Pour the lukewarm water over the salt and crumbled yeast. Add 2 cups of the flour and beat well. Add enough flour to make a soft dough—until the dough begins to clean the sides of the bowl and can be easily handled. Turn onto a floured board and knead until smooth and elastic to the touch—10 to 12 minutes. Place in a greased bowl; cover and allow to rise in a warm place (80 to 85 degrees) until double in bulk—about 2 hours or until an impression remains when a finger is pressed deep in the side of the dough. Punch down dough; let rise until double in bulk—about 1 hour. Place on floured board; cover and let rest for 10 minutes. Roll into a 9″x18″ rectangle. Beginning from the wide side, form a tight roll jelly roll fashion. Pinch the edges together. Place on a baking sheet. Make ¼″ deep gashes in dough at 3″ intervals. Brush with cold water and place uncovered in a warm place for about 1½ hours. Bake in a preheated oven for 40 minutes at 400 degrees, brushing with cold water at 10-minute intervals.

### VARIATION

Add 1 tablespoon sugar and 1 tablespoon butter to the lukewarm water. Proceed as above. This makes a softer loaf.

## Swedish Limpa Bread

### THIS RECIPE MAKES 2 LOAVES

*1½ cups water*
*¼ cup molasses*
*⅓ cup sugar or corn syrup*
*1 tablespoon salt*
*1 teaspoon fennel seed*
*1 teaspoon anise seed*
*2 cakes compressed yeast*
*Finely grated rind of 1 orange*
*2 tablespoons soft butter*
*2½ to 3 cups sifted wheat flour*
*2½ cups sifted medium rye flour*

Boil together for 1 minute the water, molasses, sugar or corn syrup, salt, fennel and anise seeds. Let cool to lukewarm; add the crumbled yeast, grated orange rind, butter and wheat flour. Beat until smooth. Gradually add the rye flour and mix to a medium stiff dough. Turn out on a lightly floured board and knead until smooth and elastic to the touch—10 to 12 minutes. Put in a greased bowl; cover and let rise in a warm place (80 to 85 degrees) until double in bulk—about 2 hours or until an impression remains when a finger is pressed deep in the side of the dough. Punch dough down and allow to rise again for 1 hour. Turn onto a floured board; cover and let rest for 10 minutes. Divide and shape into 2 round loaves. Place on opposite corners of a lightly greased baking sheet. Let rise in a warm place for 1 hour. Bake in a 375 degree oven for 30 to 40 minutes.

## Brioche

*1 cake or package yeast*
*½ cup lukewarm water*
*4 cups sifted flour*
*1 teaspoon salt*
*1 tablespoon sugar*
*¾ lb. softened butter*
*6 eggs*

Soften the yeast in the water for 5 minutes. Stir in 1 cup flour, mixing until smooth. Cut a cross on the top. Cover and set aside until double in bulk, about 1 hour.

Combine the remaining flour with the salt, sugar and butter, mixing very well. Add 3 eggs and beat for a few minutes. Add remaining eggs, and then the yeast mixture. Cover and set aside to rise for 3 hours. Beat again and chill overnight.

Break off pieces of dough large enough to half fill muffin tins or fluted brioche molds. Roll into a ball, place in the buttered tins and make a crisscross on the top. Roll small pieces of dough and insert in the crisscross to make the crown of the brioche. Cover and set aside to rise in a warm place until double in bulk, about 1 hour. Preheat

oven to 425°. Brush the tops with beaten egg yolk. Bake 20 minutes, or until browned. Serve hot.

Note: The brioche may be baked the night before and reheated in the morning.

## Baking Powder Brioche

*2 cups sifted flour*
*½ teaspoon salt*
*½ cup sugar*
*1 tablespoon baking powder*
*4 eggs*
*¼ cup milk*
*1 tablespoon cognac*
*¾ cup soft butter*

Prepare the dough the night before it is to be used.

Sift the flour, salt, sugar and baking powder together. Beat the eggs in a bowl. Alternately add the flour mixture and the milk mixed with the cognac. Beat in the butter. Put in a cool place (not the refrigerator) overnight.

The dough may be baked in a buttered 12″ loaf pan or in buttered muffin tins. Bake in a 375° oven—loaf 30 minutes, or until browned, muffins 15 minutes or until browned. Serve hot with butter and strawberry jam.

## Croissants

*1 cup milk*
*1 tablespoon melted butter*
*1 tablespoon sugar*
*1 teaspoon salt*
*1 cake or package yeast*
*¼ cup lukewarm water*
*2½ cups sifted flour*
*½ lb. butter*
*1 egg yolk*
*2 tablespoons light cream*

Prepare the dough the night before it is to be used.

Scald the milk and combine with the melted butter, sugar and salt. Cool to luke-

315

warm. Soften the yeast in the water for 5 minutes and stir into the milk mixture. Add the flour and knead until the dough is smooth and elastic. (It may be necessary to add a little more flour.) Place the dough in a bowl and cut a cross on the top. Cover with a cloth and set in a warm place to rise until double in bulk (about 1½-2 hours). Chill in the refrigerator for 1 hour. Punch down the dough and roll out into an oblong ¼" thick. Shape the butter into an oblong and place in the center of the dough. Fold over first one side and then the other to form three layers. Press other sides together. Roll out into an oblong again and fold over as before. Repeat 3 more times. Chill in refrigerator overnight.

In the morning roll out ⅛" thick and cut into 3" squares, and then into triangles. Start at the long end of the triangle and roll up loosely. Turn ends in slightly to form a crescent. Let rise in a warm place for 30 minutes. Preheat oven to 400°. Brush with the egg yolk mixed with the cream.

Bake in a 400° oven for 5 minutes. Reduce heat to 350° and bake 15 minutes longer or until browned. Serve hot.

## Hot Cross Buns

THIS RECIPE MAKES 24 BUNS

*1 cup scalded milk*
*½ cup butter*
*½ cup sugar*
*1 teaspoon salt*
*1 cake compressed yeast*
*1 egg, well beaten*
*About 4 cups sifted flour*
*¾ teaspoon cinnamon*
*1 cup currants*
*1 egg*
*1 tablespoon water*
*Icing*

Pour the scalded milk over the butter, sugar and salt; cool to lukewarm. Add the crumbled yeast and let rest for 5 minutes. Add the egg, flour and cinnamon to make a soft dough. Fold in the currants. Let rise in a warm place (80 to 85 degrees) until double in bulk—about 2 hours. Shape into large buns and place an inch apart on a buttered baking sheet. Let rise in a warm place until double in bulk—about 1 hour. Brush tops of buns with 1 egg slightly beaten with 1 tablespoon of water. Bake in a preheated oven for 20 minutes at 400 degrees. When cold decorate top of each bun with a cross, using the following icing: Place ½ an egg white in a small mixing bowl. Using a wooden spoon, beat in as much powdered sugar as the egg white will absorb and add 1 teaspoon of lemon juice gradually as the mixture thickens. Spread at once as mixture hardens quickly.

## Scones

THIS RECIPE MAKES 12 SCONES

*2 cups sifted flour*
*4 teaspoons baking powder*
*½ teaspoon salt*
*2 teaspoons sugar*
*4 tablespoons butter*
*1 egg*
*1 egg yolk*
*⅓ cup cream*
*1 egg white*
*Sugar*

Sift the flour, baking powder, salt and 2 teaspoons sugar together. Cut in the butter as for pie crust. Beat the egg and egg yolk until thick and lemon-colored; add the cream; add to the flour mixture; stir lightly with a fork to blend. Turn onto a lightly floured board and knead for 30 seconds. Pat out to ½" thickness; cut with a diamond-shaped cutter; brush with egg white and sprinkle with sugar. Place on buttered baking sheet. Bake in a preheated oven for 15 to 20 minutes at 425 degrees. Serve hot with butter and marmalade or jam.

# Index

Acorn squash, baked, Martinique, 253
Almond:
  biscuit tortoni, 292
  butter sauce, 223
  chocolate torte, refrigerator, 291
  gateau favorite, 304
  macaroons, 310
  meringue torte, 308
Anchovy:
  and pepper antipasto, 26
  and vermicelli, 232
  butter sauce, 221
  butter with saddle of veal, 152
Antipasto, anchovy and pepper, 26
Appetizers (see Hors d'oeuvre)
Apples:
  baked, and noodle casserole, 284
  crème aux pommes, 284
  crêpes Normande, 288
  fritters, 288
  fromage, 294
  rice pudding, 285
  snow, 284
Apricot:
  cream, 293
  sauce, 225
  soufflé, 297
Arroz con pollo, 243
Artichoke:
  bigote, 25
  crab meat stuffed salad, 269
  hearts, with spaghetti, 236
  roses, 25
  salad, 272
  stuffed, barigoule, 249
Asparagus:
  cold, vinaigrette, 25
  hot appetizer, 25
  with Maltese sauce, 248
Aspic:
  boeuf à la mode (cold), 94
  chaud-froid of veal, 150
  chicken breasts in, 22
  cold salmon in jelly, 74
  duck, 170
  egg fantasies, 14
  eggs in fancy dress, 14
  fish loaf, gastronome, 76
  ham in cider, 136
  jellied pigs' feet, 131
  oeufs pochés à l'estragon, 57
  shrimp ondines, 78
  Strasbourg beef filet, 88
  stuffed shoulder of veal (cold), 149
  terrine of veal, 143
Avignon rolls, 20
Avocado mousse, 278
Bacon:
  and cheese noodles, 231
  and macaroni salad, 237
Baked Alaska pie, 291
Balkan goulubsky, 241
Banana bombe, 292
Barbecue, 192-203 (see under Beef, Chicken, Duck, Fish, Frankfurters, Ham, Hamburgers, Sausages, Lamb, Turkey)
Bass (see under Fish)
Bavarian cream, 293
Bavarian cream, chocolate, 293

Beans:
  dried:
    braised pork shoulder, 126
  French bean salad, 274
  green:
    Arabic salad, 274
    Parisienne, 251
    lima poulette, 251
Béarnaise sauce, 87, 222, 255
Béchamel sauce, 216
Beef, 84-100:
  à la Bourguignonne, 96
  à la mode, 94
  barbecued:
    beefsteak Jerome LePlat, 196
    beefsteak pizzaioula, 196
    chateaubriand marchand de vin, 196
    churrasco, 195
    cooking timetable, 195
    cuts, 194
    general suggestions, 195
    hamburger, plain, 199
    hamburger, savory, 199
    kebabs, 197
    saté with steak, 197
    sliced larded filet on French bread, 196
  braised brisket with sauerkraut, 98
  braised short ribs, 99
  braised with olives, 94
  broiled steak, 90
  cappelletti with, 239
  carbonnade Flamande, 97
  charcoal broiled steak, 90
  chateaubriand à la Jackson, 88
  Chinese beef rice, 93
  collops flambés, 89
  corned, 98
  corned, cold, 98
  corned, salad, 267
  cuts, standard, 86
  filet, 87
  filet with red wine, 88
  flank steak, 92
  kidney stew, 100
  liver julienne in cream, 100
  London broil, 92
  marinade, 266
  oxtail ragoût, 99
  pan broiled steak, 91
  pot roast Niçoise, 94
  prime rib, Burgundy, 87
  roast ribs, 86
  roulades, 93
  salad:
    boeuf marinade, 266
    corned beef, 267
  sauces for, 91, 92
  sauerbraten, 97
  sautéed steak, 91
  scallops with cognac, 89
  steak and kidney pie, 95
  steak au poivre, 92
  Strasbourg beef filet, 88
  Stroganoff, 90
  suggestions for serving steak, 91
  tenderloin:
    chateaubriand à la Jackson, 88
    Chinese beef rice, 93
  tongue, Alsatian, 99
  tournedos Bayard, 89

Beef (cont'd)
  tripe with red wine, 100
  two-rib roast, 87
Beets:
  borsch, clear, 39
  borsch, vegetable, 40
  hot, with tarragon, 262
Beignets, 288
  Dauphine, 289
  grandmère, 289
  Medicis, 289
  soufflés, 289
Bercy sauce, 52
Berry sauce, 225
Biscuit tortoni, 292
Black bottom pie, 290
Blanquette de veau, 148
Bombe:
  banana, 292
  tri-color, 292
Borsch:
  clear, 39
  vegetable, 40
Bouchées Grenelle, 19
Bread, 313-316
  baking powder brioche, 315
  brioche, 315
  coffee bread, Swedish, 313
  coffee cake, California, 313
  croissants, 315
  French, 314
  hot cross buns, 316
  limpa, Swedish, 314
  saffron, 313
  scones, 316
Brioche, 315
  baking powder, 315
Broccoli:
  soup, iced, 43
  with sauce Béarnaise, 255
Brown sauce, 54, 212
  simplified, 212
Brown stock, 212
Brussels sprouts and braised chestnuts, 256
Butter:
  almond sauce, 223
  anchovy, 152
  anchovy sauce, 221
  caper sauce, 221
  Colbert, 222
  maître d'hôtel, 221
  marchand de vin, 222
  meunière, 221
  olive, 91
  Polonaise, 221
Cabbage:
  and noodles (kraut fleckerl), 236
  Balkan goulubsky, 241
  braised pork shoulder, 126
  partridge with, 183
  soup, 40
Caesar salad, romaine, 270
Cake, 300-310 (also see Cookies):
  cheese:
    cheese cake, 295
    cheese torte, 307
    Sicilian cassato, 295
  large:
    chocolate flake, 305
    delicate spice, 303
    gâteau favorite, 304

Cake: large (cont'd)
    Genoise, 302
    kugelhoff, 306
    mocha melon, 303
    nougat, 304
    nut and honey, 303
    open fruit, 305
    orange mousseline, 305
    party, 306
  rolls:
    chocolate, 309
    ice cream, 295
    walnut, 308
  small:
    Dutch butter cakes, 310
    fudge squares, 310
    lady fingers, 309
    Madeleines, 309
  torten:
    cheese, 307
    chocolate, 307
    chocolate almond, refrigerator, 291
    Linzer, 307
    meringue almond, 308
    orange, 308
Cake fillings and frostings:
    butter cream, 302
    chocolate pastry cream, 304
    mocha cream, 308
    mocha frosting, 304
    ricotta, 295
Capon (also see Chicken):
    Nob Hill, 162
    on a spit (India), 162
    roast with rice stuffing, 163
Cappelletti with beef, 239
Caramel:
    cream, 294
    poires aux crème caramel, 286
    sauce, 225
Carbonnade Flamande, 97
Carrots:
    dill-spiced, 274
    Flamande, 256
    soup, cream of (potage Crécy), 33
    Vichy, 257
Cauliflower soup, cream of (crème DuBarry), 33
Caviar:
    and shrimp tartlets, 18
    toast, 19
Celery amandine, 249
Celery root salad, 274
Celery seed dressing for fruit salad, 280
Chateaubriand (see Beef)
Chaud-froid of veal, 150
Chaud-froid mayonnaise, 224
Chaud-froid sauce, 150
Cheese:
    and bacon noodles, 231
    cake, 295
    chicken soup, fromage, 35
    chilis rellenos con queso, 63
    coeur à la crème, 295
    cookies, 312
    cottage, salad, 276
    Elena's rice-chili casserole, 244
    farmer's salad, 276
    fondue, 64
    Helvetia soup, 42
    olive tart, 64
    patio salad, 276
    rice-chili casserole, 244
    ricotta filling for cake, 295

Cheese (cont'd)
    roquefort cream dressing, 279
    Sicilian cassato, 295
    soufflé, 60
    stuffed tomato salad, 276
    torte, 307
    Welsh rabbit, 64
Chestnut:
    and chocolate omelet, 60
    and rice dessert, Austrian, 287
    braised, with Brussels sprouts, 256
    Mont Blanc, 287
    quail with, 189
    soufflé, 296
    soup, cream of, 34
Chicken (also see Capon):
    arroz con pollo, 243
    barbecue and rotisserie:
        baby, on spit, 201
        Far East, 207
        garlicked, 200
        ginger, 200
        grilled hearts, 201
        roast, Pierre, 207
        saté ajam, 201
        spitted roast, 200
        tarragon, 200
    breasts château, 161
    breasts in aspic, 22
    breasts with tomato and wine sauce, 161
    curry, 159
    deviled, 158
    fricassee, brown, 161
    fried, 158
    jasmine (India), 159
    Kiev, 160
    liver:
        and ham omelet, 60
        and rice, 242
        and spaghetti, 233
        appetizers, 21
        Indonesian nasi goreng, 241
        risotto Parmigiana, 242
        salad, 267
        tartlets with port, 22
    oven fried, 159
    paprika, 162
    roast, 158
    salad baskets, 23
    soufflé, 61
    soup, fromage, 35
    southern fried, 159
    spaghetti casserole, 233
    stewed fowl, 161
    with mushrooms and pâté, 160
Chili:
    rice-cheese casserole, 244
    sauce, 232
Chilis rellenos con queso, 63
Chinese recipes:
    beef rice, 93
    broiled scallops, 81
    fried rice, 128
    Oriental lamb steaks, 198
    pork balls in noodle wrappers, 240
    roast duck, 168
    steamed pork and ham (Jing gee yuke beang), 134
    sweet and pungent pork, 127
    tenderloin, Orientale, 128
Chocolate:
    almond torte, refrigerator, 291
    and chestnut omelet, 60
    angel pie, 290
    banana bombe, 292

Chocolate (cont'd)
    Bavarian cream, 293
    flake cake, 305
    fudge squares, 310
    party cake, 306
    pastry cream, 304
    pots de crème, 294
    roll, 309
    sauce, hot, 298
    soufflé, 295
    torte, 307
Choron sauce, 222
Choucroute (also see Sauerkraut):
    froide (salad), 275
    garni, 133
Churrasco, 195
Clams, 79
    cherrystone on half shell, 17
    chowder, New England, 36
    sauce, white, 231
    Spanish fish bowl, 18
    tart, 79
Cod (see under Fish)
Coeur à la crème, 295
Coffee:
    cream, 293
    mocha frosting, 304
Colbert butter, 222
Consommé, 39
Cookies:
    almond macaroons, 310
    anise, 311
    cheese, 312
    hazel nut, 311
    langues-de-chat, 311
    Milanese, 311
    tonilles, 312
    Viennese vanilla crescents, 312
Coquilles St. Jacques, 15
Cornbread stuffing, 164
Corned beef, 98
    cold, 98
    salad, 267
Corn fritters, 250
Cottage cheese salad, 276
Coulibiac, 75
Crab, 78
    pilaff, 79
    salad, 268
    soufflé, 79
    Spanish fish bowl, 18
    stuffed artichoke salad, 269
Crayfish, Spanish fish bowl, 18
Cream, sour (see Sour cream)
Cream desserts (see under Desserts)
Crème:
    aux pommes, 284
    caramel, 294
    coeur à la, 295
    frite flambé, 289
    poires aux crème caramel, 286
    pots de, chocolat, 294
    pots de, vanille, 294
Crêpes and pancakes:
    Avignon rolls, 20
    crêpes, 287
    crêpes Normande, 288
    crêpes Suzette, 287
Croissants, 315
Cucumber:
    and mint soup, iced, 43
    Neapolitan, 251
    salad, French, 23
    sour cream, 275
Curry:
    and pea soup, iced

Curry *(cont'd)*
  (potage Singhalese), 44
  chicken, 159
  egg salad, 275
  Indian shrimp (Trinidad), 77
  lobster (Singapore), 80 ·
  shrimp soufflé, 62
Dessert, 282-298:
  beignets:
    dauphine, 289
    grandmère, 289
    Medicis, 289
    soufflés, 289
  cream:
    apple fromage, 294
    apricot cream, 293 ·
    Bavarian cream, 293
    Bavarian cream, chocolate, 293
    black bottom pie, 290
    cheese cake, 295
    chocolate angel pie, 290
    coeur à la crème, 295
    crème caramel, 294
    crème frite flambé, 289
    pots de crème (chocolat), 294
    pots de crème (vanille), 294
    ricotta filling, 295
    Sicilian cassato, 295
  crêpes, 287
    crêpes Normande, 288
    crêpes Suzette, 287
  frozen:
    biscuit tortoni, 292
    coffee cream, 293
    refrigerator chocolate almond
      torte, 291
    strawberry soufflé glacé, 297
    tri-color bombe, 292
  fruit:
    apple fritters, 288
    apple rice pudding, 285
    Austrian rice and chestnut
      dessert, 287
    baked apple and noodle
      casserole, 284
    crème aux pommes, 284
    Mont Blanc, 287
    peach pudding, 285
    pêches sabayon, 285
    pineapple rice Bavarian, 286
    poires aux crème caramel, 286
    riz à la compagne, 285
    snow apples, 284
    strawberries Romanoff, 286
    strawberry rice mold, 286
  ice cream:
    baked Alaska pie, 291
    baked melon glacé, 291
    banana bombe, 292
    ice cream rollup, 293
    omelette Norvégienne, 290
  sauce:
    apricot, 225
    berry, 225
    caramel, 225
    fruit, 298
    hot chocolate, 298
    jubilee, 226
    lemon, 298
    Parisienne, 225
    sabayon, 225
    vanilla, 225
  soufflé:
    apricot, 297
    Brazil nut, 296
    chestnut, 296

Dessert: soufflé *(cont'd)*
  chocolate, 295
  demoiselle, 296
  lemon, 297
  orange, 298
Dove:
  roast, 182
  sautéed, 182
Dressing, salad (see under Salad
    dressing)
Duck:
  aspic, 170
  broiled, 169
  casserole, 169
  roast, 166
  roast, Chinese style, 168
  roast, Spanish style, 168
  roast, with cherries, 167
  roast, with figs, 167
  roast, with orange, 167
  wild, 179
    charcoaled, 180
    Chaucer, 182
    oven roasted (rare), 180
    oven roasted (well done), 181
    pressed, 181
    with cognac, 181
Duckling (barbecue and rotisserie):
  broiled, 202
  Long Island, gourmet, 208
Duxelles (mushroom paste), 68
Egg, 48-63 (also see Soufflé):
  à la tripe, 52
  boiled, 50
    hard, 51
    soft (mollet), 50
  Câreme, 52
  durs boulangère, 53
  en cocotte, 55
    Lorraine, 55
    Sagan, 55
  Florentine, 56
  in aspic:
    fantasies, 14
    in fancy dress, 14
  in nests, 56
  mollet, 50
    brandade, 50
    en surprise, 50
  omelets, 59
    chestnut and chocolate, 60
    ham and chicken liver, 60
    mushroom, 59
    watercress and sour cream, 60
  poached, 57
    à l'estragon, 57
    Georgette, 57
    macédoine mayonnaise, 58
  salad:
    curried, 275
    mixed hard-boiled, 51
  scrambled, 53
    August, 53
    Française, 54
    turbigo, 54
  shirred, 55
    à la Grecque, 56
    bock, 56
    Bretonne, 55
    Sicilian, 14
  timbale:
    cardinal, 59
    molded in, 58
Eggplant:
  Bordelaise, 252
  moussaka (with lamb), 113

Eggplant *(cont'd)*
  with mushroom and cheese filling, 252
Endive, braised, with ham, 249
Fennel with mustard sauce, 250
Filet (see under Beef and Fish)
Fillings and Frostings (see Cake fill-
    ings and frostings)
Fines herbes sauce, 215, 220
Fish, 66-82:
  bowl, Spanish, 18
  broiled fillets, 70
  broiled:
    fish steaks, 72
    oysters with herbs, 81
    scallops Chinese, 81
    shrimp, special (India), 78
    whole, 71, 203 (barbecued)
  butterfish, sautéed whole, 73
  cod:
    broiled fillets, 70
    fillet en papillote, 68
  coulibiac, 75
  curry:
    Indian shrimp (Trinidad), 77
    lobsters (Singapore), 80
  dabs, sautéed whole, 73
  escabêche, 76
  flounder, broiled fillets, 70
  frozen fillets en papillote, 68
  grilled:
    mixed grill (barbecued), 203
    with herbs, 72
  haddock:
    broiled fillets, 70
    fillet en papillote, 68
  kipper, soufflé, 61
  loaf, gastronome, 76
  ocean perch:
    broiled fillets, 70
    fillet en papillote, 68
  oven fried, 73
  pike:
    poached, 74
    poached cold fish, 74
    whole stuffed, 72
  porgies, sautéed whole, 73
  red snapper:
    broiled fillets, 70
    poached cold, 74
  salad:
    artichoke stuffed with crab meat,
      269
    crab meat, 268
    herring, Hedwig's, 268
    lobster tails with dill, 269
    sardine, 268
    shrimp and potato Provençale,
      273
    tuna, 269
    tuna sardine, 19
  salmon:
    cold in jelly, 74
    coulibiac, 75
    loaf, gastronome, 76
    smoked, mousse, 76
  sardine:
    appetizers, 16
    salad, 268
    tuna salad, 19
  sautéed, whole, 73
  sea bass:
    broiled fillets, 70
    Niçoise, 73
    poached cold, 74
  sea trout, poached cold, 74
  shad fillets en papillote, 68

Fish *(cont'd)*
  shad roe en papillote, 70
  shell fish (see Shrimp, Lobster, Crab, Crayfish, Oysters, Clams, Mussels, Scallops)
  smelt, sautéed whole, 73
  sole:
    broiled fillet, 70
    broiled fillet with shrimp sauce, 71
    fillet en papillote, 68
    fillet Florentine, 71
  soup, Russian, 38
  stock, 36, 216
  striped bass:
    poached cold, 74
    stuffed en papillote, 69
  trout:
    en papillote, 68
    sautéed whole, 73
  tuna fish:
    salad, 269
    sardine salad, 19
    spicy sauce, 231
  white fish, gastronome, 76
Fleckerl, kraut (noodles and cabbage), 236
Fondue, Swiss cheese, 64
Frankfurters (barbecued), 199
Fritters (also see Beignets):
  apple, 288
  corn, 250
Frostings (see Cake fillings and frostings)
Fruit (see under Desserts)
Fruit cake, open, 305
Fruit salad:
  buffet, 277
  honeydew salad, 278
  with poppy seed dressing, 277
Fruit sauce, 298
Game (see under Dove, Duck, Goose, Grouse, Hare, Partridge, Pheasant, Quail, Rabbit, Snipe, Turkey, Venison)
Garlic soup, iced (tourain à l'ail), 45
Gâteau favorite, 304
Gazpacho (iced vegetable soup), 45
Génoise, 302
Gnocchi:
  green, 238
  potato, 238
Goose:
  Montmartre (rotisserie), 208
  roast stuffed, 170
  salmis, 170
  wild, au Madeira, 187
Goulubsky, Balkan, 241
Green beans:
  Arabic salad, 274
  Parisienne, 251
Green mayonnaise, 279
Green potage, 42
Grouse:
  broiled, 183
  roast, 183
Guinea fowl:
  Saxony, 172
  with sour cream sauce, 171
Haddock (see under Fish)
Ham (see under Pork)
Hamburgers (see under Beef)
Hare:
  à la royale, 179
  saddle, 179
  sautéed young, 178

Helvetia soup, 42
Herbs:
  fines herbes sauce, 215, 220
  tossed green salad with, 270
Herring salad, Hedwig's, 268
Hollandaise sauce, 221
Honey-cream dressing for fruit salad, 280
Honeydew salad plate, 278
Hors d'oeuvre, 12-28:
  anchovy and pepper antipasto, 26
  artichoke:
    bigote, 25
    roses, 25
  asparagus:
    cold vinaigrette, 25
    hot appetizer, 25
  Avignon rolls, 20
  bivalves on half shell, 17
  bouchées grenelle, 19
  caviar:
    and shrimp tartlets, 18
    toast, 19
  chicken:
    breasts in aspic, 22
    salad baskets, 23
  chicken liver:
    appetizers, 21
    tartlets with port, 22
  clams, cherrystone on half shell, 17
  coquilles St. Jacques, 15
  cucumber salad, French, 23
  egg:
    fantasies, 14
    in fancy dress, 14
    Sicilian, 14
  fish bowl, Spanish, 18
  ham croûtons, 20
  lobster gratinée, 16
  melon coupe, vodka, 28
  mushrooms:
    Cambon, 27
    caps, savory turkey, 26
    in sour cream, 26
  mussels on half shell, 17
  oyster:
    on half shell, 17
    Parisian patty shells, 17
    smoked, salad baskets, 18
  pâté, quick, 21
  Russian salad in scallop shells, 28
  sardine:
    appetizers, 16
    tuna salad, 19
  scallops, 15
  shrimp:
    and caviar tartlets, 18
    chafing dish, Normandy, 16
    ramekins, hot, 15
  sweetbreads (bouchées grenelle), 19
  tomato:
    cups, 24
    salad, French, 24
    tongue, hot appetizers, 20
    tuna sardine salad, 19
    vodka melon coupe, 28
Horse-radish sauce, 219
Hot cross buns, 316
Ice cream (see under Dessert)
Icing (see Cake fillings and frostings)
Indonesian nasi goreng, 241
Irish stew, 116
Italian sausages:
  grilled, 199

Italian sausages *(cont'd)*
  with spaghetti, 235
Jellied soup:
  minted boysenberry, 46
  tomato, 46
Jing gee yuke beang (steamed pork and ham), 134
Jubilee sauce, 226
Kebabs, 197
  Persian, 114
Kidney:
  beef:
    and steak pie, 95
    stew, 100
  lamb:
    and bacon en brochette, 118
    sauté, 118
    with scrambled eggs, turbigo, 54
  with veal, rotisserie, 205
Kipper soufflé, 61
Kraut fleckerl (noodles and cabbage), 236
Kugelhoff, 306
Lady fingers, 309
Lamb, 102-118:
  barbecue and rotisserie:
    breast, 112
    kebabs, 197
    kebabs, Persian, 114
    roast leg, 198
    roast leg, Hong Kong, 205
    shashlik, 115
    shish kebab (I), 112; (II), 114, 205
    shoulder, 198
    steak, 111, 198
    steak, Oriental, 198
  baron, roast, 108
  blanquette d'agneau, 115
  breast:
    diable, 112
    marinated, 112
    Oriental, 112
  chops:
    baby, 110
    broiled, 110
    English, 110
    French, 110
    herb stuffed, Helen Brown's, 110
    loin, 109
    pan broiled, 110
    rib, 110
    shoulder, 110
  crown roast, 107
  cuts, standard, 104
  Irish stew, 116
  kidneys:
    and bacon, en brochette, 118
    sauté, 118
    with scrambled eggs, turbigo, 54
  leg:
    cold, 107
    picnic gigot, 106
    roast, 105
      gigot bouquetière, 106
      gigot Bretonne, 105
      with a spoon, 106
  liver, julienne, 117
  moussaka (I), 113; (II), 113
  navarin, with spring vegetables, 115
  Oriental ragoût, 115
  rack, roast, 108
  saddle, roast, 107
  shanks, braised, with lentils, 111
  shoulder:
    à la crème, 108

Lamb: shoulder *(cont'd)*
  braised, 109
  braised bonne femme, 109
  braised Provençale, 108
  roast, 108
  rotisserie, 109
  steaks:
    broiled, 111
    Oriental, 111
  tongue:
    pickled, 117
    poulette, 117
    vinaigrette, 117
Lasagna, 234
  Bologna fashion, 233
  stuffed, Naples style, 234
  verde, with shrimp, 239
Lemon:
  sauce, 298
  soufflé, 297
  soup, Greek, 44
Lentil:
  soup, 41
  with braised lamb shanks, 111
Lettuce, braised, 255
Lima beans poulette, 251
Liver:
  and rice, 242
  beef, julienne in cream, 100
  calves', baked pâté à la Perigord, 154
  chicken:
    and ham omelet, 60
    and spaghetti, 233
    appetizers, 21
    Indonesian nasi goreng, 241
    risotto, Parmigiana, 242
    salad, 267
    tartlets with port, 22
  lamb, julienne, 117
  pork, pâté, 134
Lobster, 80
  and spaghetti Fra Diavolo, 232
  bisque, 35
  curry (Singapore), 80
  gratinée, 16
  oeufs en timbale cardinal, 59
  paella à la Valenciana, 243
  Rossini, 80
  Spanish fish bowl, 18
  tails, with dill, 269
London broil, 92, 195:
  chili-Oriental, 93
  Oriental, 92
Macaroni:
  and bacon salad, 237
  and shrimp in chili sauce, 232
  custard, Italian, 235
  luncheon salad, 237
Macaroons, almond, 310
Madeleines, 309
Maître d'hôtel butter, 221
Maltaise sauce, 221
Marchand de vin:
  butter, 222
  chateaubriand, 196
Marinade:
  basic, 278
  boeuf, 266
  lamb, 112
  venison, 176
Marinara sauce, 240
Marron (see Chestnut)
Mayonnaise, 58, 223
  chaud-froid, 224
  green, 279

Mayonnaise *(cont'd)*
  ravigote, 223
  sauce Niçoise, 223
Meat (also see under individual names):
  and vegetable salad, 266
  glaze, 212
  salade boulangère, 266
  sauce, 241
Melon:
  coupe, vodka, 28
  glacé, baked, 291
Meringue:
  almond torte, 308
  baked melon glacé, 291
  baked Alaska pie, 291
  omelette Norvegienne, 290
Meunière butter, 221
Mexican sauce, 63
Minestrone, 42
Mocha cream, 308
Mont Blanc, 287
Mornay sauce, 218, 254
Mousse:
  avocado, 278
  ham, 136
  smoked salmon, 76
Mousseline sauce, 221
Mushrooms:
  Cambon, 27
  caps, savory turkey, 26
  duxelles, 68
  in sour cream, 26
  omelet, 59
  sauce, Spanish, 234
  soufflé, 62
Mussels:
  on half shell, 17
  soup, 37
  Spanish fish bowl, 18
Mustard sauce:
  for fennel, 250
  for fish, 219
  for meat, 95
Mutton kebabs, 197
Nasi goreng, Indonesian, 241
Newburg sauce, 219
New England clam chowder, 36
Noodles:
  and cabbage (kraut fleckerl), 236
  casserole with baked apple, 284
  cheese and bacon, 231
  Chinese pork balls in wrappers, 240
  creamed ring, 230
  homemade, soft, 239
  pudding, with spinach, 236
  with Spanish mushroom sauce, 234
Olive:
  and cheese sauce, for spaghetti, 230
  butter, 91
  cheese tart, 64
  sauce, for wild duck, 181
Omelet (see under Egg)
Onion:
  amandine, 258
  and potato casserole, 259
  sauce, 146
  sauce soubise, 216
  soufflé, 62
  soup au gratin, 38
  stuffed, 257
Orange:
  mousseline cake, 305
  soufflé, 298
  torte, 308
Ossi bucchi, 148

Oxtail ragoût, 99
Oyster plant Italienne, 257
Oysters, 81
  and creamed turkey, 166
  broiled with herbs, 81
  minced (Cambodia), 82
  on half shell, 17
  Parisian patty shells, 17
  smoked, salad baskets, 18
  soufflé, 82
  stew, 37
Paella à la Valenciana, 243
Pancakes (Avignon rolls), 20
Parisienne sauce, 225
Partridge:
  broiled, 183
  cold stuffed, 184
  en brochette, 184
  roast, 183
  with cabbage, 183
  with orange, 184
Party cake, 306
Pasta, 228-240 (see under Cappelletti, Gnocchi, Lasagna, Macaroni, Noodles, Ravioli, Spaghetti, Vermicelli)
  sauces for, 240, 241
Pastry:
  cream puff paste (pâte à chou):
    for beignets, 289
    for chicken salad baskets, 23
    for gâteau favorite, 304
  gingersnap pie crust:
    for black bottom pie, 290
  puff paste (pâte feuilletée):
    for steak and kidney pie, 95
Pâté:
  à la Perigord, 154
  liver, 134
  quick, 21
Patio salad, 276
Paupiettes de veau, 144
  Ali Bab, 144
  Italian (I), 144; (II), 144
  paprika, 145
  with cream, 145
Pea, Peas:
  à la bonne femme, 248
  and curry soup, iced (potage Singhalese), 44
  and vermicelli soup, cream of (potage Longchamps), 34
  Scoville, 248
  soup, cream of (potage St. Germain), 34
Peach:
  pudding, 285
  sabayon, 285
Pears aux crème caramel, 286
Peppers:
  and anchovy antipasto, 26
  stuffed, 254
Perch (see under Fish)
Perigueux sauce, 215
Pheasant:
  braised with sauerkraut, 185
  Italian, braised, 186
  pioneer style, 185
  plain roast, 185
  Pompadour, 186
  Souvaroff, 186
  with Triple-Sec, 186
Pie:
  baked Alaska, 291
  black bottom, 290
  chocolate angel, 290

Pie *(cont'd)*
  steak and kidney, 95
Pike (see under Fish)
Pineapple rice Bavarian, 286
Piquant salad dressing, 279
Pizzaiola sauce, 240
Poivrade sauce, 177
Polonaise butter, 221
Poppy seed dressing for fruit salad,
  280
Pork, 120-136:
  and ham, steamed (Jing gee yuke
    beang), 134
  balls, Chinese, in noodle wrappers,
    240
  barbecue and rotisserie:
    kebabs, 197
    loin, California style, 206
    loin with sherry, 206
    shoulder Robert, 206
    spareribs, Island style, 206
    spareribs, German style, 206
    suckling pig, 207
    tenderloin, Orleans, 206
  chops:
    baked chilied, 129
    baked in milk or cream, 129
    charcutière, 129
    grilled, 129
    Milanaise, 129
    Niçoise, 129
    sautéed, 129
    stuffed, 130
    stuffed flambé, 130
    with sauerkraut and beer, 130
  choucroute garni, 133
  crown roast, 126
  cuts, standard, 122
  feet, jellied, 131
  ham:
    and chicken liver omelet, 60
    Avignon rolls, 20
    barbecued steak, 199
    croûtons, 20
    en croûte, 135
    glazed, 135
    in cider, 136
    mousse, 136
    stuffed peppers, 254
    with braised endives, 249
  ham, fresh, 123
  hocks, with sauerkraut, 132
  liver:
    roast, 123
    roast jardinière, 123
  liver pâté, 134
  loin:
    pot roasted, 125
    roast, 124
    roast, French, 125
    roast, Gascogne, 124
    roast, rosemary, 124
    roast, with prunes, 124
  sausages, grilled, 132
  shoulder:
    braised, with beans, 126
    braised, with cabbage, 126
    carbonnades, 127
    sweet and pungent, 127
  spareribs:
    favorite, 131
    roasted, 131
  sukiyaki, 125
  tenderloin:
    broiled, 128
    Orientale, 128

Pork: tenderloin *(cont'd)*
    sautéed with cream, 128
Pot-au-feu, 41
Pot roast, Niçoise, 94
Potage (see Soup)
Potato, Potatoes:
  and onion casserole, 259
  Anna, 258
  baked, with herbs, 260
  cake, Austrian, 259
  cakes, chef's, 259
  caramel, 261
  casserole Niçoise, 261
  Chantilly, 261
  country creamed, 261
  garlic-herb, fried, 260
  gnocchi, 238
  green, 260
  green gnocchi, 238
  herb, 260
  Italian, 259
  Lorraine, 259
  mousseline, 258
  orange, 258
  salad, 273
    and shrimp Provençale, 273
    German, 273
    with piquant dressing, 273
  savory scalloped, 261
  soups:
    and tomato, cream of, 32
    and watercress, 32
    green potage, 42
    Vichyssoise, 43
  sweet:
    sherried, 262
    soufflé, 262
Pots de crème:
  chocolat, 294
  vanille, 294
Poulette sauce, 165
Poultry (see under Capon, Chicken,
    Duck, Goose, Guinea fowl,
    Rock Cornish game fowl,
    Squab, Trussing, Turkey)
Pudding:
  apple rice, 285
  peach, 285
  spinach noodle, 236
Quail:
  broiled, 188
  d'Octobre par Alain, 189
  roast, 190
  with chestnuts (aux marrons), 189
  with cognac, 190
Rabbit:
  sautéed, 178
  tarragon, 178
  with carrots, 178
  with mushrooms, 178
Rabbit, Welsh, 64
Ragoût:
  lamb, Oriental, 115
  oxtail, 99
  venison, 177
Ravigote sauce, hot, 222
Ravioli with cheese, 238
Rice:
  à la compagne, 285
  and chestnut dessert, Austrian, 287
  and liver, 242
  apple pudding, 285
  arroz con pollo, 243
  Balkan goulubsky, 241
  Elena's cheese-chili casserole, 244
  fried, 128

Rice *(cont'd)*
  Indonesian nasi goreng, 241
  paella à la Valenciana, 243
  pineapple Bavarian, 286
  risotto, French Piemontaise gour-
    met, 243
  risotto, Milanese, 242
  risotto, Parmigiana, 242
  squash bombe, 254
  strawberry mold, 286
  stuffed peppers, 254
  wild rice stuffing, 164
Ricotta filling, 295
Rock Cornish game fowl:
  broiled, 172
  roast, 172
  St. Loraine, 172
Roquefort cream dressing, 279
Rotisserie, 204-208 (see under Chick-
    en, Duckling, Goose, Lamb,
    Pork, Veal):
  seasoning, 204
  spit roasting, 204
  timing, 204
  trussing, 204
Roulades:
  beef, 93
  veal, 153
Russian fish soup, 38
Russian salad in scallop shells, 28
Sabayon sauce, 225
Sage and onion stuffing, 170
Salad, 264-280:
  artichoke, 272
  avocado mousse, 278
  Belgian tomatoes, 271
  boeuf marinade, 266
  Bohème, 272
  boulangère, 266
  Caesar, 270
  celery root, 274
  cheese-stuffed tomato, 276
  chicken baskets, 23
  chicken liver, 267
  choucroute froide, 275
  corned beef, 267
  cottage cheese, 276
  crab meat, 268
  crab meat stuffed artichoke, 269
  cucumber with sour cream, 275
  curried egg, 275
  dill-spiced carrots, 274
  farmer's, 276
  French bean, 274
  French cucumber, 23
  French tomato, 24
  fruit buffet, 277
  fruit with poppy seed dressing, 277
  green bean, Arabic, 274
  hard-boiled egg, mixed, 51
  herring, Hedwig's, 268
  honeydew, 278
  lobster tails with dill, 269
  luncheon, with Italian style saus-
    ages, 237
  macaroni and bacon, 237
  meat and vegetable, 266
  patio, 276
  potato, 273
  potato, German, 273
  potato, with piquant dressing, 273
  potato and shrimp, Provençale, 273
  Russian, in scallop shells, 28
  sardine, 268
  sauerkraut (choucroute froide),
    275

Salad *(cont'd)*
surprise, 271
sweetbread, 267
tossed green, with herbs, 270
tuna fish, 269
tuna sardine, 19
zucchini, 272
Salad dressing, 278-280:
celery seed for fruit salad, 280
French, 278
green mayonnaise, 279
honey-cream for fruit salad, 280
marinade, basic, 278
mayonnaise, 223
piquant, 279
poppy seed for fruit salad, 280
Roquefort cream, 279
spiced, 278
Salmis, goose, 170
Salmon (see under Fish)
Sardine (see under Fish and Hors
d'oeuvre)
Saté ajam chicken on spit (Indo-
.nesia), 201
Saté with steak, 197
Sauces, 210-226:
aïoli, 224
Albert, 220
Allemande, 219
almond butter, 223
anchovy butter, 221
apricot, 225
aurore, 217
Béarnaise, 87, 222, 255
béchamel, 216
Bercy, 52
berry, 225
bigarade, 214
Bordelaise, 213
Bordelaise, quick, 88
brown, 54, 212
brown, simplified, 212
caper butter, 221
caramel, 225
chasseur, 213
chaud-froid, 150
cheese and olive, for spaghetti, 230
chivry, 218
chocolate, hot, 298
choron, 222
Colbert butter, 222
diable, 216
dill, 203
epicurean, 202
Espagnole, 212
fines herbes, 215, 220
fruit, 298
glace de viande, 212
Hollandaise, 221
horse-radish, 219
jubilee, 226
lemon, 298
Lyonnaise, 214
Madère, 215
Maître d'hôtel, butter, 221
Maltaise, 221
marchand de vin, butter, 222
marinara, for pasta, 240
mayonnaise, 223
mayonnaise, chaud-froid, 224
mayonnaise, Niçoise, 223
mayonnaise, ravigote, 223
meat, for pasta, 241
meat glaze, 212
meunière, butter, 221
Mexican, 63

Sauces *(cont'd)*
mornay, 218, 254
mousseline, 221
mushroom, 220
mushroom, Spanish, 234
mustard, for fennel, 250
mustard, for fish, 219
mustard, for meat; 95
nantua, 217
Newburg, 219
olive, 181
onion, 146
Parisienne, 225
Perigueux, 215
pizzaiola, for pasta, fish, steak, 240
poivrade, 214
poivrade, quick, 177
Polonaise, butter, 221
porto vino, 219
Portugaise, 215
ravigote, hot, 222
Robert, 215
Romaine, 214
Rouennaise, 215
sabayon, 225
shrimp, 71
smitane, 217
soubise, 216
sour cream, 171
spicy tuna, for spaghetti, 231
stock, brown, 212
stock, fish, 36, 216
stock, white, 216
suprême, 218
tomato, for pasta, 241
vanilla, 225
velouté, 218
venaison, 214
verte, 224
vinaigrette, 225
vin blanc, 220
Sauerbraten, 97
Sauerkraut:
and beer, with pork chops, 130
garni, 133
salad (choucroute froide), 275
with braised brisket, 98
with braised pheasant, 185
with pork hocks, 132
Sausage:
grilled, 132
grilled, Italian, 132, 199
Italian, with spaghetti, 235
luncheon salad, 237
Scallops, 81
broiled, Chinese, 81
coquilles St. Jacques, 15
Scallops, veal (see under Veal)
Scones, 316
Sea bass (see under Fish)
Shad (see under Fish)
Shad roe (see under Fish)
Shashlik, lamb, 115
Shellfish, 77-82 (see individual
names)
Shish kebab, 114, 205
Shrimp:
and caviar tartlets, 18
and macaroni in chili sauce, 232
and potato salad Provençale, 273
bisque, 36
broiled (India), 78
chafing dish, Normandy, 16
curried, Indian (Trinidad), 77
curried, soufflé, 62
en papillote, Floridian, 77

Shrimp *(cont'd)*
fish loaf, gastronome, 76
lasagna verde with, 239
ondines, 78
ramekins, hot, 15
sauce, 71
Spanish fish bowl, 18
Sicilian cassato, 295
Snipe:
broiled, 187
roast, 187
spitted, 187
Sole (see under Fish)
Sorrel soup, cream of, 46
Soufflé (also see under Dessert):
cheese, 60
chicken, 61
crab, 79
kipper, 61
mushroom, 62
onion, 62
oyster, 82
shrimp, curried, 62
sweet potato, 262
Soup, 30-46:
bisque:
lobster, 35
shrimp, 36
borsch:
clear, 39
vegetable, 40
cabbage, 40
clam chowder, New England, 36
consommé, 39
cream:
carrot, 33
cauliflower, 33
chestnut, 34
chicken soup, fromage, 35
pea, 34
pea and vermicelli, 34
potage gentilhomme, 32
potato and watercress, 32
tomato and potato, 32
fish, Russian, 38
green potage, 42
Helvetia, 42
iced:
broccoli, 43
cream of sorrel, 46
cucumber and mint, 43
garlic, 45
gazpacho, 45
Greek lemon, 44
pea and curry, 44
tomato and mint, 44
Vichyssoise, 43
jellied:
minted boysenberry, 46
tomato, 46
lentil, 41
minestrone, 42
mussel, 37
onion, au gratin, 38
oyster stew, 37
pot-au-feu, 41
Sour cream:
and watercress omelet, 60
cucumbers, 275
mushrooms in, 26
sauce, 171
Spaghetti:
al burro, 230
alla papalina, 231
al pesto, 230
and chicken livers, 233

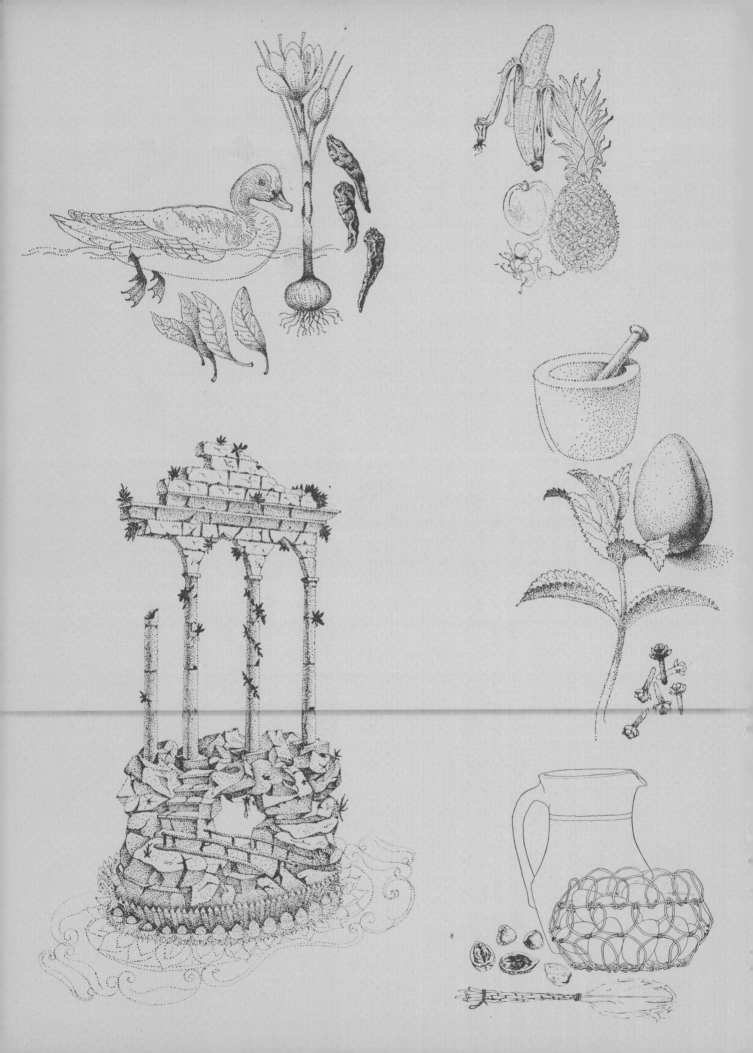